DON'T STAND IN LINE: A Memoir

DON'T STAND IN LINE: A Memoir

GERDA BARKER

Cover design by urzulka

Back Cover Photograph ©1993 Paul Elledge

ISBN 979-8-9851964-0-5

eBook ISBN 979-8-9851964-1-2

Library of Congress Control Number: 2021925152

gerdabarker.com

To my darling children

ACKNOWLEDGMENTS

My deepest gratitude to Afra Ahmad, Cynthia Albritton, Georgette Bienvenu, Michael Brokaw, Rick Buscher, Dave Collins, Larry Crandus, Leila Eminson, Maria Ferrero, Doug Freel, Sarah Hadley, Katherine Houston, Patrick Houston, Ellen Hunt, Patty Jourgensen, Sean Joyce, Steve Lafreniere, Amanda Macias, Ruth Mainey, Jane McIntyre, Steve Miglio, Franke Nardiello, Lee Popa, Marnie Warren, Rey Washam, and Greg Werckman. Special thanks to the late Bill Rieflin who always knew.

INTRO

I don't like being told what to do. But I'm amenable to expert advice. For instance, someone told me I needed a few lines at the beginning of this story to let the reader know what it's all about. Fair enough. Here's what it's about:

A slew of little stories magically colliding to make up a life. The word "slew" is defined as a large number. The word "slew" is also the past tense of "slay." My story is about how I shook hands with a slew of famous types and discovered I could slay a few dragons along the way. My parents would be very pleased by that last bit. You see, my parents came to the United States in 1956 on a Flying Tiger. This story is for them.

i.

My name is Gerda. It's "Getta," as in get a life. G-e-r-d-a. Five letters strung together sow such confusion in the mind of the reader. Teachers never got it right—the first time or any other.

I am the first American-born member of my clan. As the middle child of five to Polish immigrants, I'm good at deflecting the bad stuff. In the middle, you learn early on you will never run away from home, because everyone else already has. You will never complain about wearing your sister's hand-me-down shirts and jeans, because there is no money for new ones. But you also daydream. You buy Italian Vogue for nine dollars at Walgreens, because you know the world out there is immense.

In my parents' home there were no guidelines for the future except work hard in school and get a good job or a good husband. No discussions about college or what you may want to do with your life. My parents bought the five flat building we lived in in the Humboldt Park neighborhood of Chicago, and that to them was success.

At the age of three, I experienced my first city trauma wandering away from my family at Montrose Beach. I was curious about small stones and shells and seeing the great expanse of Lake Michigan. It was an hour or so before anyone noticed I was gone and longer still before I was found and delivered to the official beach house by two very nice, elderly black women. As my mother explained to me years later, after this experience I didn't speak for an entire year. I shadowed my mother's steps to the point where she started calling me her "ghost." I was quietly watching everyone else.

ii.

To the bewilderment of my parents, after my year of silence passed, I finally spoke up, and my first words were, "I want to go to school." At four years old, although I was too young for the public school system, my parents convinced the local Catholic school to take me. My older siblings were already enrolled at Maternity BVM (of the Blessed Virgin Mary), and so my education began. I wore a dark blue-and-green tartan uniform jumper with a white short-sleeve blouse underneath and walked to school every morning with my brother and sister.

As students, we went to mass, what seemed like, every day. In chapel my focus wandered from the priest's incantations in Latin rising and getting louder in a kind of song. My focus instead was on what was protected in the side dressing room to the right of the altar, the room from which the priest would suddenly emerge with his colored robes and vestments already in place. Fabrics in sumptuous colors filled the frame of the open doorway for a brief moment before the priest himself emerged with two altar boys. On holidays, his robes were suddenly deep purple or red or green. I wanted to be an altar boy and have a peek at the treasures behind that door. I was told I couldn't be an altar boy, because I was a girl.

Hearing the mass in Latin, that strange otherworldly language was all the song I needed to assure my five-, six-, and seven-year-old feelings that God was indeed watching over me. I did not wish to disappoint him. We attended confession once a week, where I made up petty crimes I'd committed against my family. It was a contrived, quickly assembled checklist in order to have something to say to the silhouette on the opposite side of the mesh-patterned screen in the confessional. I understood the sound of silence intimately the first time I stepped into that dark, soundproof box. I was too embarrassed to say I had nothing to admit other than I was a shy and curious child. I wanted to know why the morning glories only bloomed on the chain-link fence of one house I passed on the walk home from Maternity BVM ("BVM" for short) and didn't bloom anywhere else. What was the magic behind this? I had so many concerns to clarify. But the one thing I struggled with more than any other, was the notion that Jesus was born on December 25th and died a few months later as a thirty-three-year-old man. How was that possible? Was this a miracle?

The teachers at BVM were all nuns, except one. My third grade teacher was a civilian and Chinese. Mrs. Wong's shoulder-length black hair and smooth, white skin were a softer color scheme than the nuns who taught in long, black robes and black habits with white brims and collars pulling their faces back like napkin rings. In the final month of third grade, Mrs. Wong assigned us an art project. Draw something in nature. Using vividly colored crayons as an undercoating, we would then cover it all in black. We were each given an implement to use to scratch a drawing into the black and reveal the colors underneath. Our goal was to be chosen for an exhibit in Washington, DC, an exhibit of third-grade art. I scratched out a boxy outline of a flower pot. One single bell-shaped flower, similar to the lily of the valley, hung from the singular stem in the pot.

When our pictures were finished and graded, we topped them with wax paper loosely taped on the back to take home. Mine stayed. Mrs. Wong handed me a note to bring home to my parents asking their permission to send my drawing to DC for consideration. My mother was thrilled to sign off. My father had no opinion on this "kid stuff," and for the first time I felt I had a special talent. I was an artist. Before this, I imagined I would be a writer, painting visual pictures with words. Words had movement, and they kept moving across the page until you arrived at the end of a sentence. But now, I had to make a choice. What was I? I wanted to be a writer. I wanted to see more words, not make drawings. I wanted to see more flowers in real life. The lilies of the valley and the violets were my secret companions waiting for me at home in the gangway between our house and the one next door, in the dirt patches where slivers of sunlight would cut past the red brick facades and feed the occasional flower stems growing there in the dark.

The school year ended with the expectation I would go on with catechism, confirmation, and back to being taught by the nuns. When my parents discovered they could not afford private tuition for four and then five children, they visited the parish rectory and met with the priests and the head of the school to work something out. The school officials were not interested in a payment plan for our family of seven, despite that we attended church every Sunday and tithed at every mass. My immigrant parents assumed the church would take care of us as the church had always taken care of families where they came from in Europe. My parents were mistaken.

Dismayed by what they viewed as the church's greed, my mother and father removed their three school age kids from Catholic school, and Chicago's D. R. Cameron Public School accepted us into its institutional fold. Because I was always the youngest in class, having started so early, I rarely made friends. Kids in the neighborhood attached to my siblings, who were their ages, but not to me. I read books instead and spent many hours at the public library on Pulaski and North Avenue. When I discovered Charlotte's Web and was able to read it through, I reread it over and over and finally had the nerve to ask a librarian if there were more books like this one. I checked out and returned so many books so quickly it didn't take long before I'd gone through the age appropriate volumes and started in on the young adult books. The librarians gave me a pass, since their books were returned on time without any harm to the pages. I worked hard in school, believing my parents' vague notion this would equal my success and happiness. Every year I would be at the top of my class. I was going to be exceptional.

iii.

In the public elementary school, I rarely spoke to anyone. The girls who did speak to me had other friends on their own streets to socialize with after school. In class, there was the Puerto Rican girls' clique. Milagros, their most vocal mouthpiece, would interrupt anything I said with, "Be quiet, Pollacko Girdle," a tribute to my heritage and the odd sound to my name.

I had something to say but couldn't form the words out loud at the moments when I needed them. I had something to say, whatever it was. I felt I was called to a higher purpose; I just hadn't found it yet. I felt a connection to the seasonal wild flowers, violets and lilies of the valley, struggling to find glimpses of sun between the building next door and ours. A flower would grow in one small patch of dirt, another three feet away heading into shadows. I would carry a cup outside to these random sprouting stems and give each a bit of water. I would do my part to help them stay healthy and beautiful and looking up to the sky, out of the darkness of the buildings trying to mask them. I obsessed over my sister Uli's cologne—Muguet by Coty. It had the scent of lilies of the valley. I wanted Muguet to be my cologne when I grew up, too.

My first period came when I was just nine. I stood up from the toilet yelling for my mother that I was bleeding. She pushed open the bathroom door with my brother Raimund behind her—he was laughing. I started to say something, and everything went black. I fainted for a few seconds as they both carried me to a chair in the kitchen, and I could feel my panties turn wet in an uncontrollable fashion as if I sat down on a rain-soaked bench. My mother's explanation: "Girls just get this," she said in German, looking embarrassed and now realizing I was not even ten and could get pregnant. "Girls just get this." Get what?

Get what? I learned what *binden* were—pads—and I'd have to place one in the crotch of my underwear to catch the blood trickling out of my body. Before it happened, I tried to piece together why my sister Uli sometimes left soaked reddish-brown pads in the bathroom garbage bin. I seemed to think this new "blood" would one day come out of the side of my hip, judging from the few illustrations I saw in books and on the box of pads Uli kept hidden away under her bed. When the real thing happened, I was distressingly unprepared. I thought I was dying. My ascension into womanhood continued at a frighteningly early pace as my breasts slowly grew outward from my chest a year later. I would listen to the other girls gossip about making out with boys and wonder if I should go back one grade to catch up with my peers.

The only social interactions I had were at school and on the one occasion when I was invited to Natalia Medina's birthday party at her parents' house. Her family were Mexican and lived in their own free-standing bungalow and not an apartment like most other kids I knew. Natalia's father had strung a piñata in the basement for all of us to whack, as we hoped anxiously we would be the "winner" and popular for a solid minute of party time. There was a record player spinning the Jackson Five, kids were dancing, and it was fun. My father had a sour expression when he arrived to pick me up. He questioned why I needed to hang around with "buncha Mexicans." "Natalia is my friend," I told him.

My father didn't see any value in having friends. "Friends don't give you nothing," he would say in that peculiar, crude English he picked up at work. His first job in Chicago was as a journeyman in refrigeration at the stockyards before they closed for good. From there he moved on to work for big hotels and finally a large south side hospital as its chief engineer. My father tried to show the world he was a self-made man. He didn't need friends.

I excelled in school and was gaining a reputation as being often the smartest student in class. Between the fourth and fifth grades, my parents were twice asked their permission to "double promote" me, allowing me to skip an entire grade level. By my math, I briefly fantasized entering high school at age eleven. My parents said no both times. I had no voice in the matter.

It was during the fifth grade that I, along with a handful of other students, were chosen to learn math by computer. It was 1967. Cameron School was suddenly the recipient of giant computer towers collected into a room twice the size of the custodian's closet, where a visiting technician explained how to submit answers to the machines. I found it a relief to get out and away from my classmates, and I took pleasure in getting immediate feedback from this faceless "teacher." My absence from class only served to alienate me more from the rest of my class. I wandered around the schoolyard at recess and one large, dirty-blonde new girl came up behind me and locked her arm around my neck. She was routinely bullied—"Hey, bulldog!"—and now she had an opportunity to put the smart kid in her place. I told no one.

In the sixth grade, the first black family moved into our school district with their four children. Marilyn Boyland was tall and shy looking as she stood before my class and was introduced and welcomed by our teacher. I thought maybe I would try to be friends with Marilyn these first few days. She was so odd and dark and alone, and that resonated with me in my own awkward placement amongst these other kids. After a week or so, Marilyn was comfortably friendly with the Puerto Rican girls, and I again was the lone oddball.

Approaching the summer of 1969, my parents pooled together enough money to send their four girls to Germany and Poland to meet with our grandmothers, aunts, uncles, and cousins. My father had taken my brother the summer before. It was the first overseas trip for me. It was my first time on a plane—a Lufthansa 747 jumbo jet. I was eleven. I could hardly wait to see Europe. Finally, an adventure out of the neighborhood.

Two nights before the trip, I woke up from a fitful sleep. An image in a dream startled me awake. I saw a disembodied head, a floating, depleted mask of a gaunt, gray-haired old man who opened his mouth as if to speak. Instead of words, a procession of individual teeth fell from the opening and into the dark void around his face. In the morning, my mother told all of us she looked forward to seeing her uncle Peter in Germany after thirteen years of cards and the rare letter.

"We won't see him," I said. The words seemed to leave me without any volition of my own. My mother stopped short of raising her voice and gave me a quizzical look. "What do you mean?! He's your great uncle. Of course we'll see him." I recounted my dream for her, and she gasped. "That's not good. *Zähne* (teeth) mean death." My mother crossed herself and stared at me. She said she had a "*Sechsten Sinn*," a sixth sense, and I must have it, too.

On our flight to Frankfurt, my mother and I relished the cold salad platters Lufthansa staff served us, while my siblings ignored theirs. The food was familiar to my mother and new to the rest of us. I daydreamed about what other new adventures lay ahead. I imagined visiting museums and parks and taking train rides and seeing windmills and cathedrals. What I imagined was of course nowhere close to the reality of being a child in a foreign country reliant upon the only adult in the group—my mother—whose itinerary stopped at my Oma's front stoop. "Steigerstr. 11. Hamborn, Duisburg." Cobblestones and row houses built for coal miners in the century before.

I loved writing "Steigerstr. 11" on the envelope to my Oma twice a year and hearing my mother remind me to, "*Mach ein Strich*,"—put a dash, a little hook over each of the "1s." That was how it was done in Europe. A European "1" looked like the crochet needle my mother used to make scarves. She would tell me stories of my Grandfather Maximillian, who she said was the one person I took after the most. "Opa Max" had been involved with the Polish Underground. He was one of those who paid for the state sanctioned newspaper at a stand, and there would be something else inside. He had more than one nervous breakdown during the war, routinely running from authorities, from the Nazis, and for his life. It was he who insisted my parents move away from Europe and head for the United States in 1956. He was an intellectual, who as a young man had chosen to leave his bourgeois family in Poland to become a coal miner in Germany. Although I never met him, my Opa Max became my talisman. I wanted to forge a life of my own like my grandfather, whether through resistance or sheer will to be my own person.

According to my mother, my Opa Max believed words and language were as essential as eating three meals a day. "My father told us, 'You can kill an enemy with words. You don't need bullets,'" she would say.

Opa Max encouraged my parents to go to the United States where class and nationality didn't matter. They would have a better life for themselves and their children in a place that was politically diverse, stable—safe. He made a point of telling them there was one downside to their new country. They would have to save as much money as possible as soon as they found steady work. In America, there was no guaranteed health care nor guaranteed pension in old age. As a bon voyage gift, my grandparents gave my parents the family silver service in a velvet-lined wooden storage box. It would be their insurance policy to sell if things didn't work out in America and they wanted to come home.

I thought about my grandfather as I walked into the apartment where my mother was born, and where she had lived with her parents before marrying my father. My Oma still lived in this apartment, across the street from worker housing for Turkish *Gastarbeiter* (guest workers) currently employed at the mines. My Oma was waiting at her open window for our cab to arrive from the airport. The first thing she said to my mother was, "*Peter ist gestorben.* (Peter died)." Uncle Peter passed two nights before our arrival. I knew. There were no men of his generation left in the family.

My mother and I and my sisters spent two weeks in Hamborn, before taking the overnight train from West Germany into East, through Berlin, on our way to Poland. The train had an extended stopover in Berlin as uniformed, armed German soldiers put flashlights to our faces, studied our passports, and moved from one train car to the next for passkontrolle. Their comrades outside the train ran mirrors and dogs underneath it to ensure there were no extra passengers or defectors hiding in the underbelly of all that iron and steel. It was nighttime when we stopped in Berlin. There was no chance of seeing how the Berlin Wall cut through buildings and neighborhoods in a seeming random filleting of the German psyche on either side. After a long delay, the train finally pulled from the station bound for Poland, where my father's mother and his two brothers lived.

The previous summer when my father made this same trip with my brother, it had been over twenty-five years since he had seen anyone in his family. My father was taken from his church choir in Poznan in 1941 by the Nazis to become a slave laborer for the Germans for the duration of the war. He was forced to work, was starved and beaten, and told every day by the last farmer he finally ran from, that that day would be his last. He was rescued by American soldiers toward the end of the war. They offered him a few options for a new life: go back to Poland, be sent to Argentina or France, or finally, join the Polish division of the American Army in Germany. My father chose to become a soldier. It was on the military base in Germany where he met my mother. His experience as a prisoner shaped a lifelong rage in his temperament, something bitter and noisy and violent that would occasionally reveal itself in outbursts through the course of my childhood.

My three sisters and I trailed behind my mother those first two days in Poznan, walking around the old city center, dumbstruck by stone and concrete walls of apartment buildings still bearing gaping holes caused by bomb blasts from WWII. My Uncle Jurek lived with his wife and kids in one of those buildings. Several other extended family members joined us there for dinner on our first night, and every one of our relatives fell silent when the "family communist" arrived unannounced. She was in her twenties. She had a privileged job and was indeed a member of the Party.

The second day in my father's birth city, my mother tired of my complaints and decided we would go bra shopping. My womanly features were becoming too obvious. My Polish aunt directed us to one area with shops, and we walked into a bland provisions store on a main street. I hoped to find something in my size, whatever that size currently was shaping up to be. I wanted something not too plain, something with a soft color or lace. But there was nothing hanging on display in the women's lingerie section. A single six- or seven-foot-long "dump table" with four-inch-high sides to prevent items from slipping to the floor held piles of knotted together bras in varying sizes. My mother held a few white items up against my body, and we quickly paid a girl in a smock and left the shop.

There was no way for any of us to know before we arrived in Poland on this trip, that my mother and I and my sisters would be camped out two days later with our Uncle Raimund and his family in their farmhouse in Krosno, Poland, a farmhouse they shared with another family in this communist state, and that so many of us would be pressed shoulder to shoulder, some sitting cross-legged on the floor, staring at a ten by twelve black-and-white television picture of Neil Armstrong as he stepped onto the surface of the moon. We were in Poland, in a farmhouse with family, watching America's and the world's first moon landing.

We stayed in Poland for another week and then were back on a train to Germany, passing once again from east to west. I thought about how our Polish family had their lives rationed out for them in dozens of eggs they were able to keep from the chickens they raised. The rest, they were forced to give up to the state. They lived very simply. I watched my uncle Raimund raise an axe to one of his chickens. It became supper for the night.

Back in the comfort of my "German" Polish grandmother's apartment on Steigerstrasse, I waited for her with shopping nets in hand. We walked together to the open market to buy cherries and stuffed pickled herring. I had my first Italian gelato at a cafe. It was blackberry. I had the sense I was now a citizen of the world.

Returning to the United States, back to Chicago, seemed a letdown. The kids we met in Germany were friendlier than the kids in our own neighborhood. It didn't occur to me at that age that the German kids thought we Americans were the cooler kids.

We spent the rest of the summer in Pell Lake, Wisconsin, a small town just over the Illinois border. My parents were tipped off by a Polish friend that land there was cheap. Impressed by the rural quiet and clean country air, my parents bought an acre and a half of property to build a house on, a house we all helped to construct in small ways. There was a lake close by for swimming and fishing. That summer, the foundation of the house was finished. I was handed a staple gun and told to staple fiberglass insulation that looked like pink cotton candy to two-by-fours framed out for the house walls. After a while I told my mother I was tired and sweaty and wanted to go to the lake. I changed into my bathing suit and shorts, grabbed a towel and some change for an ice cream, and joined my siblings for the walk to the beach three blocks away.

I finally had a new two-piece bathing suit I liked that didn't have me spilling out of the sides on top. It was white cotton with boy shorts and a thin strip of black piping around the leg openings and all the way around the bathing suit top.

I spent months finagling money from my mother to buy Vogue and 16 Magazine. I knew the trends. My new suit was stylish. I was chic and couldn't wait to stand on the beach or sit on the pier and have everyone admire my good fashion sense. It *was* 1969.

I was still learning to swim on my own without lessons or help. I left my glasses onshore and stayed close to the pier in shallow water to have something to grasp if I chose to float on my back like the teenage girls diving from the metal raft further out anchored in deeper water.

I was alone, ducking under the water to wet my hair and coming up to squint and look back to the shore for anyone new, or anyone in a stylish, new bathing suit like my own who might be dropping their towel on the sand and heading in for a swim. Weekends were crowded, but during the week there were less than twenty people at the beach in this small unincorporated town with no lifeguard or budget to hire one.

I crept along the side of the pier, slowly making my way to the end where the water was less than four feet deep. I could hear someone yell, "Cannonball!", then a splash as another body plummeted into the deep water by the raft. I stayed still where I was, holding my head just above the water line, contemplating whether to lift myself up onto the end of the pier to rest in the sun and dangle my feet over the water.

I looked at the end of the pier and saw a baby crawling in my direction, wavering and pausing to sit back on its bottom, then attempting to stand up on its feet. This pattern went on for another minute while I watched. I guessed the baby was a girl. There was no one with her. On the opposite end of the pier close to shore, two women sat side by side talking with their heads down.

I watched the baby try once more to stand and sit down, when her foot suddenly missed the pier's edge, and her leg continued its gravitational journey down into the water pulling the baby's body along with it. I watched her head go under a few feet away from me. I pulled my legs through the water to the spot where she went in, looked down and saw her floating body rotating underwater slowly like a soda bottle, ending in an upward facing position.

The baby's eyes were open wide and staring at me. She had a dreamy expression as if waiting for me to make the next move. My hands reached out and under her arms. I pulled her from the water and placed her back on the pier. We stared at each other for a second, and I pushed away from the pier, watching the drenched infant cough and start to wail. There was sudden movement from the other end of the pier as the two women rushed over to their charge, and I turned my head away.

My legs were heavy as I pulled away and further out into the water. All else in the lake was calm again. The teenagers by the raft played their game, and small bluegills brushed my shins when I finally stopped moving. I lowered my head into the darkening water and held my breath for as long as I could stand it. It didn't register in my thoughts that I had just saved someone else's life. It was something automatic—and necessary. At that moment, I was that baby. I was saving myself.

iv.

In the spring of eighth grade my English teacher, Mr. Jarus, clapped his hands and announced that two girls from Cameron were being invited into the fall Lane Tech freshman class. I was one of the two. The other girl was Natalia Medina. This was big news for everyone . . . everyone else. Lane Tech was a college prep, boys only, magnet high school on Chicago's northside and had been that way since 1908. The all-male public school attracted a full spectrum of personality types from the northside—boys growing up in high rises along Lake Shore Drive, westside blue collar sons destined for factory work or the police academy, and some less fortunate sons raised in the projects like Cabrini Green. Other than gender, they all had one thing in common—they were above average in their test scores. Historically, girls were barred from attending Lane or even being asked. Some tried in earlier years to end this exclusivity. It was, after all, a publicly funded school. Then in 1971, after lawsuits were threatened again, Lane Tech allowed 368 girls into its five-thousand-plus student body. I was one of them. My parents were relieved I wouldn't "need" to attend an all-girl Catholic high school.

I had no desire to go to Lane, no desire to ride two city buses to a place that didn't really want me there to begin with. But the alternative was Orr High School in my neighborhood, a place where race riots routinely shut down the campus just a few years before. For me, Lane Tech it was. I was not only going to again be one of the youngest students, but all of the girls admitted had to be academically at least one year ahead of the boys. Our test scores had to be higher. We were guinea pigs testing out the coed waters, but not generic test subjects—we were super girls. I had to convince myself being so exceptional would feel like stardom. I was thirteen and ready.

v.

On the first day of high school, someone put two fingers under my skirt and groped me from behind while I stood crushed into a pack of faceless students making their way into the factory sized, red brick building on Addison Avenue and Western. I couldn't move or turn to see who it was. I tried to visualize the north branch of the Chicago River flowing just beyond the football stadium and auto shop on the ground floor. Focus. I thought of Wrigley Field situated a mile or so down the street.

In machine shop, my instructor clearly did not like having female students around. A middle-aged former drill sergeant, he entertained our class with a story about how he beat his dog for misbehaving in *his* house. I began sobbing. The instructor sent me with a note to the guidance counselor to see if I needed to be transferred to a different class. I stayed. He reminded me of my father, I told him. After this event, he never again spoke of mistreating animals or anyone else in class. In Drafting I, the only girl who successfully garnered the teacher's attention happened to be my table partner, a tomboy who would go on to wear a Chicago Blackhawks jersey to school every day, except picture day. Go Hawks.

I stepped onto the Addison bus at the end of that first day of class, took a window seat and watched the line outside the bus grow shorter as seats filled and the aisle bulged with gym bags and bodies standing up side by side. The cacophony of boys shouting, raucous laughter, and the bell dinging at every stop was almost soothing in drowning out my anxiety. The bus moved along at a lulling pace. I watched the storefronts and small factory buildings flash by. I wondered how I would ever make friends in such a large population of personalities from all over the north side—most of them, boys. My thoughts were abruptly interrupted by something brushing my knee. I looked down at the pinky finger of the dark-haired student sitting next to me. He immediately withdrew his hand. He had a five o'clock shadow and appeared older. An upperclassman. I looked out the window and tried to flatten myself against it as best I could. After a moment, the touch of a fingernail was back against my knee.

There was nowhere for me to go. On that bus I wasn't exceptional. I wasn't one of the few hundred new Lane Tech girls. I was just another girl. If I yelled, I'd have enemies on all sides. I pulled the cord for the next stop, stood up, kicked my way out of my seat, and glared at the face sitting on the aisle. He stared straight ahead as if nothing had happened. I got off the bus and began walking home. It was five miles.

After a few weeks, things seemed to calm down with the native population at Lane having adjusted to the invasive species of the female kind. As was my habit, I mostly kept to myself but gravitated toward the art and music students at lunch, on the wide lawns outside and at the Jack in the Box across the street. I began to see that being exceptional in elementary school didn't matter in a high school where everyone was exceptional to some degree. My grades were average. I listened to T. Rex and Led Zeppelin with the art crowd outside during breaks. At home, I played my brother's records: Al Green, Janice Joplin, Cat Stevens, the Rolling Stones, Jefferson Airplane, and The Isley Brothers. One of my few friends at Lane routinely dressed for class in Alice Cooper drag. "Eddie" sometimes fell off his platform shoes, sometimes did too much acid, and once had to be carted away in an ambulance while telling anyone who'd listen that he was in fact "a duck." It was 1972, and who didn't fall down at least once in those shoes? I quietly disputed rumors that Eddie was gay. You couldn't come out as gay in high school in 1972, not unless you craved a physical bashing or bewildered stares.

"Stop it. His dad is a diplomat. So what, he has money for clothes. What's wrong with looking good?" I would say. Eddie had a Japanese girlfriend with whom he was close, and he would spend hours after school at her place. I imagined they had sex every day. I loved Eddie's daring to be different and stylish. He was exceptional.

A few years later, while in New York visiting the Whitney Museum for the first time, I approached the admissions counter and recognized a familiar face. There was Ed, all grown up and still obviously attending to those stylish details that set him apart from the rest.

"Gerda—oh my God! It's so good to see you. Hold on . . . I want you to meet my boyfriend, he's over here." I could barely focus on the rest of his words. I found myself half listening and thinking about how we allow ourselves to perceive what we need to perceive. Now, with Ed, I finally had the whole picture, editing frame for frame, in real time, in my head. It was as distracting as wandering around the galleries in The Whitney and being confronted by a real live Willem DeKooning painting challenging me from its place of distinction on a wall. Seeing a photo of the same painting in a book was different from seeing it in the flesh. I liked DeKooning, and I felt happy for Ed, and I left feeling tricked at the same time by both.

In high school, I spent a summer going on diets to look less like the voluptuous fourteen-year-old my mother regarded with great praise, and more like an artist, like the models in Vogue. In my house, we spoke three languages— German, Polish, and English. My mother would tell me in German slang that I was lucky to have *atom Busen* (atomic bosom). I cringed at the thought of my chest being my calling card, my focal point, one third of the way down from my brain and my thoughts. I made an appointment at the Pivot Point hair school in Evanston, following the advice of Eddie (he was the most stylish friend I had) who told me fashionable cuts performed by students at the school came cheap. My thick, curly, long locks were transformed into a short, "stack permed," pyramid-shaped wedge which was striking with my thinner, less curvy new body. I looked even more alien than ever in my Humboldt Park neighborhood, where girls squinted through shag hairdos or sported long, straight hair cut by someone at home. The attention was now undeniably back on my head. I borrowed a copy of Our Bodies Ourselves upon the recommendation of my classmate Julie, the first person I knew in high school who got pregnant and had a legal abortion.

Returning to campus after summer break sporting my new hairdo and new body, I was introduced to the student lead of the hall guards at Lane. Someone told me he had a crush on me. The hall guards made sure people got to class, dinged the ones who were late, and pretended to keep order amongst the swelling rushes of students racing across campus and the halls within their few minutes of "passing" time. My new hall guard friend invited me out on the only formal date I had in high school. He made reservations for us at Nick's Fishmarket in the First National Plaza downtown.

I was thrilled to go. The First National Bank and plaza were built on the former site of the grand Morrison Hotel. My father worked at the Morrison briefly as a heating and air technician and had certain privileges because of his job. I recalled taking the elevator as a little girl and going up to the carousel restaurant, a place with a view of downtown that slowly revolved as we sat and ate ice cream sundaes. The hotel was long gone, but the carousel ride left an indelible picture of glamorous dining possibilities in the center of downtown Chicago. My family didn't otherwise venture out to restaurants—only at Christmas. My mother took all the kids on the North Avenue bus to the Damen el train, and we'd head downtown to see the windows at Marshall Fields. Afterwards, a walk to Tad's Steakhouse on State Street next to the Chicago Theater, where we'd have the special $1.49 steak dinner with baked potato. Our booth could barely contain the six of us, including my mother.

My high school date night arrived, and my new friend came by in his own car to take us downtown. He handed his keys to a valet as we walked onto First National Plaza, where I discovered that to get to Nick's Fish Market you took an elevator down below the bank plaza to the dining room. It was all so clandestine. There we were, downtown in the Loop, disappearing into some private sphere of personal service. I couldn't believe people had money for these things. My date was smartly dressed in a shirt, tie, and jacket. I wore some dress no doubt borrowed from my older sister Uli. Fortunately, I had read about expensive restaurants in magazines. I was feeling very sophisticated and very much at ease while waiters hovered nearby poised to comb crumbs from our tablecloth. "Is that damask," I wondered to myself, touching the linen on the table to verify the quality of my surroundings for my mother, who in her younger years had apprenticed with a tailor.

My date seemed impressed with my ability to eat properly with a knife and fork—the European way, as my parents had taught us early on. His own father was somehow "connected" he hinted. After dinner, my date thought it would be fun to circle overhead around the Loop on one of the trains. My strappy heels tapped up a flight of ornamental iron steps to the el platform. We boarded a Ravenswood train and headed north. I felt like a tourist with this new ability to look inside office windows two stories up from the street, then ride level with sidewalks through neighborhoods on the north end. This was all new to me—a real date I had dressed for, like going to a prom.

After our date, I didn't see my friend again. Life intervened. My sister Uli, my twenty-one-year-old role model, took a road trip to Six Flags in Missouri and on the way was in a car wreck with her live-in boyfriend. She did not survive. Neither did her boyfriend. They died instantly. I was sixteen and miserable.

I was excused from driver's ed and began cutting some of my other classes. I hated being in that institutionalized setting while my thoughts were focused on the meaning of life itself. My sister Uli had taken me to my first concert when I was eleven and she was sixteen. We had tickets to see Engelbert Humperdinck, one of her favorite singers. He performed at the Auditorium Theater downtown, a room with near perfect acoustics. Engelbert's voice resonated in that hall and in my eleven-year-old soul sitting in the balcony. Overwhelmed that one human voice could convey such passion, I didn't want to leave my seat when the concert was over. "Let's stay up here," I said to my sister.

Uli and I were five years apart, but she was a role model for my own ambitions to get out from under the limited schooling and interests of our immigrant parents. Without Uli to look up to, I had no other female role model. I loved my mother, but being a housewife was not an ambition I shared. My mother listened to WJJD country radio at home, teaching herself English while she smoked Salems and managed the bills. By the time I reached puberty, I knew the lyrics to most of country music's song catalogue and the backstory of some of the biggest country stars based on the content of the songs they sang. On most nights, my parents would watch the news, a further nightly English language tutorial that was free. My mother read as much as she could of the mundane materials lying around at home: the newspaper, when someone would buy it, the strange sales pitches coming in the mail, Woman's Day magazine we'd buy at the grocery checkout line. My mother and father both were learning about American life at the same time their children were.

After Uli died, my parents walked around like zombies. Had I suddenly taken to dressing like a call girl or openly shooting drugs at home, I honestly believed no one would notice. I was completely directionless. I rode buses to school and once there, avoided going to class. Instead, I would leave campus to catch the Addison bus, then take the el to the Art Institute downtown, where I'd wander around not really knowing too much about art history but deciding on my own what I liked (modern art) and what I didn't (Impressionism).

My English teacher during this time, Helen Klinger, insisted we write weekly essays addressing a prompt—some topical news bit or big life question aimed at getting us out of ourselves and onto a page. At the end of the week, she would have the best one read in class by its author. My essays kept popping up for performance time. Not in the mood for this kind of spotlight, I began cutting her class, too, as soon as I turned in my paper. Ms. Klinger was a tiny, dark-haired New Yorker who enjoyed playing up her accent. She would pass me in the hall as I hid in a throng of students after missing her class again and would yell across the hallway, "You COULD grace us with your presence now and then, Ms. Serba."

I told someone at school I was afraid I wouldn't pass the academic year because of all of my absences, to which they responded "Well, you know_____, don't you?" (my one-night date) "He'll take care of that." Whether he did or not, my extended absences never became an issue to anyone again. I passed all of my subjects by the end of the academic year. I wasn't really accustomed to getting special treatment from a guy, if in fact he had doctored my attendance records. I wasn't too consumed with guys at all. I was becoming more and more ghostlike, as my mother had said. I was becoming more exceptional. I read Yukio

Mishima's Confessions of a Mask, while my classmates read Carlos Castaneda books. I read Gertrude Stein's How To Write and Sylvia Plath's Ariel for the pure palpable power of words. As much as I disliked being put on the spot to read my own writing out loud to my classmates, I found solace in my ability to create pictures with words.

My brother Raimund and I were closest in age amongst the siblings. At one point he stood in the kitchen of our family's apartment, looking perplexed about his own identity, whether he would go to college or work as a waiter for a while and figure it out.

"I'm at the end of my rope," he whined.

I thought he must be going through what I was—interrogating the stillness of life.

"So, buy some more rope," I said.

We both doubled over laughing. I suspected at that point that what my brother was going through was a much bigger issue. I also suspected he was gay and didn't know how to tell anyone, let alone me. It would be a few years before we had that conversation:

"So, your obsession with Claudia Linnear and Tina Turner was just a ruse?" I asked.

"Oh no. I LOVE Claudia and Tina," he said, punctuating that thought like a course correction, a straightening of the wheel.

While my parents lived in their own world of grief, I decided to press ahead out of my depression or whatever it was I was experiencing with my sister's death. I decided to work after school jobs to afford my own clothes. My art student friends all had jobs at LaSalle Photo, a lab not far from Lane Tech. I was hired by Mr. Yamamoto after giving him my assurances that I, like all of his other Lane Tech student employees, would study hard and work hard—the Japanese way, the immigrant way.

With my new income, I bought a violet-colored Mickey Mouse T-shirt and pastel colored 50/50 jeans. I began visiting thrift stores and trying on men's shoes and shirts. I saved enough to finally go to Tops & Bottoms on North Avenue and buy the gray, collarless, zip-up rabbit-fur jacket I knew would allow me more freedom to wear whatever I wanted underneath. I could spend a little more on black T-shirts and tight, knit glitter shirts I'd tried on. I was satisfied that I didn't look like a neighborhood girl.

I bought a neon green Legnano Italian bicycle with sew-up tires and rode with my bike mechanic friend Brian to the lakefront and back. It didn't matter that the tires often blew out while gliding over booby traps hidden in the concrete along North Avenue, riding past Humboldt Park and the great National Guard Armory building anchoring the park on its west end.

I imagined I gave the impression of a budding writer. I began writing poetry while I sat in my senior Lit class and admired Marvin Garcia, another of the star pupils in the class. Marvin and I became friends long enough for me to invite him to meet me at my parents' building with his bike, and we would go from there. That first time, Marvin arrived to see my mother's face redden as he wheeled up onto the sidewalk and stood straddling his bike wearing a violet-colored top tied up above his waist midriff-style. His skin was dark. He was a Puerto Rican boy who wrote poetry. Marvin led the way over to his older sister's apartment in the Ravenswood neighborhood. Our bicycles covered miles of side streets, old trolley tracks, and railroad crossings until we arrived at our destination.

Marvin's sister had hung colored beads in every doorway to compliment the flocked red walls and couches in her living room. There, Marvin introduced me to the music of the Fania All Stars. He taught me the basics of salsa dancing. I had ridden my bicycle so many miles that morning, I couldn't help but stumble over the step patterns. He mentioned the Puerto Rican independence movement. From the glances his sister gave me, I determined I was very fortunate to be receiving salsa lessons from such a fine, agile dancer. I didn't wonder at all if I was welcome here with my Northern European white skin or my awkward name. I was welcome, because Marvin made it so. At home I spoke German, Polish, and English. Here, Marvin and his sister spoke Spanish. It didn't matter. As I left the apartment for the ride back home, I hoped I could experience other people's lives every day, as I had just experienced the lasting red "dance floor" of Marvin's sister's home. There was a wholeness to the memory of that encounter.

I was building a belief in truth in friends and truth in art. I would stand in front of a canvas and gauge my first impression—did I like it or not?—and when not, where did it fit in, in history or modern standards. Truth. If you don't have it and appreciate it, then what do you have?

***

I looked around the walls of my parents' apartment, at the family paintings done by my great uncles Franz and Johann in the 1930s and '40s in Germany. They were pictures not of turmoil but of flowers in a vase, a mountain rising up behind a stream. On the opposite wall were pictures of two wood ducks separately painted on pieces of wood block, carved into horizontal oval shapes the size of a man's shoe. These paintings didn't tell you the artists actually worked in the coal mines. These paintings told you to hope.

I was desperate to tell stories, to write something, anything that made sense of why I was living where I was, and stories that would get me where I should go. I was desperate to make it out of that apartment building, away from the sameness of the parked cars belonging to neighbors who could afford them, and away from the sensibility that this way of living was good enough. I was desperate to make it out of there with my ability to write decent wayward sentences that could maybe lift me above the rest and out of the ordinary. I didn't want to have a funny name or to long for some faceless man to marry me away and off of this street. I was seventeen years old and finished with high school.

I knew if I didn't do something soon, I'd never get out of there and never read the important books I was supposed to be on track to read, and I'd never have people over to my salon like Gertrude Stein—tragic, especially since we shared the same initials, GS, and I took it as a sign I was destined for greatness. I called up another high school poet friend, Robin Washington, and invited him to my eighteenth birthday party at my parents' apartment building and told him he could read some of his poems to the guests I had not yet otherwise invited, nor did I know who they'd be. All I knew was I needed to leave here and go far away, or at least closer to the lakefront. I was on my way.

Before my birthday, Robin invited me to his mother's place in Old Town near Wells and North Avenue. The two-story house was tucked into a side street adjacent to old horse stables now crowned with the el tracks making a curve overhead before heading north in the city. The street had an aura of mystery to it and the scent of long-gone carriage horses. I knew Robin's mother was white and Jewish, his absent father was black and had a '60s radical intellect, from what I gathered. I didn't see any doorbell on the ground floor of the old wooden carriage house as I approached and knocked a few times. No one answered. It looked like a hallway door. I tried the knob and it opened. I stepped into the cramped bottom of the stairwell and looked up the flight of stairs ahead of me and saw a spotted gray cat. The cat slowly made its way down to where I stood, stared up at me for a few seconds, then continued down to my feet. It wrapped its tail around my leg and seemed to be showing me the way to the top of the stairs. I followed, and as I reached the landing, an anxious Robin Washington looked shocked that I was there.

"How did you do that?!"

"How did I do what?" I replied.

"My cat never lets anyone come up here alone."

I looked at the cat again and something seemed off. The cat was the wrong size for a house pet, slightly longer and lower to the ground, perhaps. I was looking at an ocelot. Robin had neglected to tell me his "cat" wasn't like all others. Apparently, I wasn't either—to the cat. It was not long before Robin agreed to come to my party and debut some of his new work.

On the night of my eighteenth birthday party, the guests arrived: a few of my brother's friends, my brother Raimund himself, and Robin Washington, ready to start things off with a birthday poetry reading. Before he began, we heard a quiet knock at the front window. Odd. No one used the front entrance to the apartments, except to shoo away salesmen and Jehovah's Witnesses. Everyone, including the mailman, used the side stairs and hallway where the mailboxes hung. I opened the front door and there stood two couples who said they happened to be walking by the house when they'd overheard one of my guests mention a birthday, and they liked the music they could hear from the street. We were listening to The Isley Brothers. The four people standing in front of me were roughly the same age as my brother. One of them had tattoos on his neck. They all looked Puerto Rican. These two couples decided to crash the "neighbor's" party. Hm. Their expressions were friendly, and I was feeling adventurous. My parents were out of town for the weekend. I opened the door and invited them in saying they were just in time for a poetry reading.

The four strangers accepted beers from my brother and took their seats on a sofa. I imagined I had just let the Latin Kings into my parents' house. I didn't care. Robin read his poems, wished me a happiest of happy eighteens and everyone applauded. This is what it's all about, I thought. Let's keep going.

1

In 1976 I was well into my freshman year of college. The decision to attend
Northeastern Illinois University was easy. My poet friend Robin recommended
Northeastern, which to his mind had an excellent creative writing program. I
trusted Robin's judgment. He'd been writing poems and submitting them to little
magazines for awhile. He already knew what "chapbooks" were. I didn't know
anything. It had been a bit of a struggle to step foot onto a college campus at all.
My parents were willing to pitch in limited funds for tuition while I continued
working part-time, but they were opposed to applying for loans to fund the rest
of my college expenses. My parents were instinctively wary of the government,
and in this case, especially wary of what they saw as governmental intrusion
into their personal finances. I made do. Almost no one in the neighborhood even
thought about going to college, especially not the girls. All I thought about was
getting out of there as quickly as humanly possible.

Northeastern embodied a small, lush campus tucked into a quiet residential
pocket of civility near the city's border with Lincolnwood. On the north end of
campus, Bryn Mawr Avenue was the walking path for studious young men in

black hats that covered their heads and allowed corkscrew tendrils of hair to fall down like vines framing their faces. A nearby rabbinical school told you where these men spent their days. On the same two block stretch of Bryn Mawr was a Jewish deli where you could buy authentic fresh bagels so far removed from the frozen hockey pucks available at the local Jewel stores. With my notebooks and bookbag I anxiously crossed campus each day with the expectation of feeling welcomed into this new society of higher learning. Nothing else mattered.

That year I had the very good fortune to be in a writing workshop at Northeastern with Ted Berrigan, a poet whose conversations in class inevitably turned to Frank O'Hara and the New York School of poets. Ted was a charter member of the second wave of New York School writers. He was related to the Berrigan Brothers, priests who'd become household names in the Vietnam War era of anti-war protests and civil disobedience. Ted wasn't one to pamper his students. If he thought your writing was crap, he said so. Our small class gathered at the writing center, a tiny storefront a few blocks from campus. Afterwards, Ted liked to go for shots at the bar next door. I had just turned eighteen.

Visiting poets came to Northeastern for readings. I went to every event I could get to, imagining the sheer number of readings would contain something solid and unique to my ears. At one house party the guest was a touring writer in his seventies who lived in Montana and kept horses. The graduate students and near graduates in the room were anxious to talk shop with the poet who appeared receptive but bored. I was too young, too green as a writer to add any cogent thoughts to the discussion, and it all seemed so dull and technical anyway, but I had the need to make human contact with a living breathing potential mentor. I walked over, took a seat next to the poet, and asked him if he had a favorite horse, and what was that like?

"Probably similar to having children, I suppose," he said, eyeing my young face, then his own hands. He appeared to be caught off guard. His polite tone gave way to a personality no longer "on" for the cameras. He asked me about my name. He wanted to know where my family was from. The poet of the hour then recommended some newer writers he liked. It was my first lesson in how the famous can be, and often are, just like the rest of us mortals. I began to appreciate how life events offstage often shape the aesthetic and allow artists the room to create their art.

From Ted Berrigan I learned I could write about anything. Common objects and phrases came to life. An early example: "*Su credito es bueno*," a sign in a store window on Chicago Avenue held my attention with its internal rhythm. My first poem for the workshop was a meditation upon the North Avenue bus and the Hamm's Beer sign dangling over the front door of the neighborhood tavern on the corner of Springfield and North where I had stepped onto the bus each day of high school. Ted liked my poem and countered with a lesson on "The Songs of Bob Dylan as Poetry." I liked Ted as a teacher and devoted fan of the great Frank O'Hara. O'Hara understood the American cadence in his voice just as a musician can hear sounds between notes.

I needed to find my own apartment. My parents gave up city living and sold their apartment building, and I couldn't have been happier to get out on my own. For months we heard gunshots in the early evenings. It was enough. In the last few weeks of living in my childhood apartment, I found a job waiting tables part-time at Sylvester's, a sometimes comedy club on Lincoln avenue. I would take the bus home late after work, stop at the tavern on the corner, and buy a single bottle of Pepsi to carry as I walked in the dark, down the center of the street, for one block to where I lived, thinking the bottle was my defense if some guy tried to hassle me. The streetlights could illuminate the street, but not the sidewalks meant for pedestrians and women heading home. It was eerie at night. Silent. The deaf and mute couple who lived a quarter of the way down the block were the only people left with whom I was familiar, and they would be useless if I started screaming for help. My nightly walks from the bus stop became easier as moving day drew closer.

I moved to an apartment in Uptown near the lake, fulfilling one of my dreams for adulthood. I worked, studied, and made new friends. I enjoyed being alone, writing about whatever touched my senses enough to leave an impression. That impression was only there for a second, absorbed and used or brushed away by my hand on a bus window wiping away the fog on a winter's day in Chicago. I wondered if I would ever live anywhere outside of Chicago. Why would I?

2

I met Franke "Fun" Nardiello in 1978 in Chicago, probably at La Mere Vipere, one of the first punk rock clubs in America. La Mere was around for about a year. Franke was a regular. He was funny, would pronounce my name slowly, "Gehhhhda" and tilt his head sideways while he made some fashion discovery of the day. "My pants are too tight. Oh . . . well . . ." his voice would taper off and come back into a resounding laugh realizing he was so alluring to whichever sex was interested.

I went to La Mere a few times with my friend Steve Miglio, a fabulous painter. Steve and I waited tables together during the day. Afterwards, we would walk around the neighborhood—New Town, as it was called then—stop for cigarettes and coffee and admire each other's style of smoking. On some nights, we'd head to La Mere.

Noe, the bartender and owner of La Mere, would hand over beer mugs full of Amaretto, since Steve didn't really drink, and I wasn't really legal. We would dance for a couple of hours and catch a cab home. The first time Steve and I danced next to each other at La Mere he said, "Getta Girl, you dance like a little black girl." Not that that mattered. La Mere was a divey place where anything was fashionable, as long as you had a dedicated spirit. You could dance alone, talk to yourself, dance with someone else. No one cared. No one bothered with Mod Todd and his albino, buzzed blonde hair when he plopped down on the side of the dance floor with his own record player to spin something only he wanted to hear.

My friend Steve wore a starched tuxedo shirt to work, collar turned straight up, cinched with a perfectly tied black bow to frame his black sculpted beard. He was small, elastic, and, to me, looked like Toulouse-Lautrec. Steve wore turquoise-painted cowboy boots and sang in a band called BBSpin. Unlike the jerking movements of the punk rockers on the floor at La Mere, Steve's style of dancing was more dervish-like, going around and around. When he wasn't waiting tables, Steve worked on his art, making paintings and drawing.

That year, I saw my first Ramones show with Steve at the Aragon Ballroom, an enormous 1920s era venue with terrifically bad acoustics and a crowd capacity of five thousand. We hurried into the cavernous lobby and were nearly side swiped by the reporter Geraldo Rivera strutting through the crowd with a film crew. He was there gathering footage for a documentary on punk rock in America. Geraldo was taller than I expected. Steve was a sucker for celebrity and yelled, "Hey, Geraldo!" Geraldo didn't say a word or acknowledge us at all, despite being five feet away and practically staring right at Steve. Standing in his pressed blue jeans he apparently didn't feel the need for small talk with actual fans of the music. Geraldo and his crew were partially blocking the way into the venue. Steve looked at me and said out loud what both of us were thinking. "Wow. What a jerk that guy is."

In 1978 Steve and I were each other's dates for a handful of rock shows, which our spectacle hungry souls couldn't live without. In May, Lou Reed was on tour and performing at "B'Ginnings," a club in Schaumburg, just outside of Chicago. Steve's friend Tommy Tedesco—or "Tommy T"— gave us a ride to the show. Tommy's normal manner of speaking was like an auctioneer's, heavy with alliteration and rhyme. I believed at the time he was a male escort. When we first met, Tommy T dubbed me "GettaGargoyleGirl." My name seemed to provide endless amusement for new friends.

Steve had to be front and center in the audience to get the best view of Lou Reed. Being slightly claustrophobic, I didn't fancy being crushed against the edge of the stage, but we were just a few feet away from one of our icons. Lou Reed smoked during the entire set, tossing butts to the floor. After each cigarette, and risking ejection from the club, Steve hoisted himself half onto the stage and pocketed the discarded remnants. It was an intimate performance. After the show, Steve handed me one of his souvenirs. He was overjoyed. This had more meaning than any hand scribbled autograph could ever have.

Steve safely archived his charred little mementos, years later giving up one to a fundraiser for AIDS patients in New York. I was a little heart broken when Steve finally decided to move to New York to paint. I'd get postcards from him with the simplest message: "When ya movin' to New York, Getta Girl?"

*

It was my habit to walk everywhere in Chicago. I loved the street-level perspective of the city. Being able to stand in the shadow of a high-rise building and stare at the enormity of its frame was much more satisfying than passing it on the bus. When I walked along the lakefront, I would meditate and count: 1 . . . 2 . . . 3 . . . 4 . . . 5 . . . 6 . . . 7 . . . 8, over and over again in my head, keeping pace like a metronome. It established my rhythm, my gait. Sometimes I thought I must be bonkers doing this. Why did I prefer the rhythm of walking to all else? It was a meditation, a calming of the senses, a chance to clear my mind and explore details around me at an unhurried pace.

On a Friday morning in April of 1979, I walked down Lincoln Avenue toward the Apollo Theater where the Italian clothing maker Fiorucci was holding "auditions" for staff for its store opening at Water Tower Place on Michigan Avenue. Hundreds of alarm clocks had shrilled into the ears of the crowd now filtering into the theater to showcase their talents. The city's mechanics and theatrics meshed for this one-time event. A girl in leather bondage gear was taxied to the Apollo on a fire engine the size of the theater. Lives seemed to hang in the balance as the auditions got underway.

My friend Franke Fun (Nardiello) was auditioning for a spot with the Italian cool gear shop. I came as a spectator and sat through the auditions wondering, what's going on here, why is a store doing this? I knew Fiorucci's was a great fad hag hangout and one place in New York where you could find groovy new accessories no one else had. But this was new, this talent search, and it was all about style—could you pull it off. Many of the characters auditioning that day were untrained in the style points Fiorucci was after. But Franke, oh Franke. When his name was called, Franke and his demi pompadour hydroplaned across the stage like a speed boat on a rescue mission. A triumphant Franke was not overlooked in the crowd of hopefuls.

Fiorucci's opening party on May 4th was an art event not to be missed, if you could get in. Naturally, all of the club kids oozed their way in. Local art dealers were falling over themselves for this 1970s style "happening." Andy Warhol flew in from New York. I went as a member of the press with a cigarette-pack-sized laminated headshot of the model Twiggy hanging from my neck as proof of my bona fides, my pedigree. Signor Fiorucci, the founder of the business, walked over and absently stared at my laminate. His only words: "It's living art, man."

My press credentials weren't backed by any steady reporting I was doing for a local news source—not exactly. Months prior to the Fiorucci party, Steve Miglio introduced me to a couple of graphic artist friends who were launching PRAXIS, a glossy magazine covering art openings, the club scene, and music in Chicago. Franke Fun contributed his talents, hanging out at Jackson Grey Graphics where the magazine was produced and putting in his design ideas. Everyone knew I ventured out to poetry events around town, and I could write. I was asked to be the magazine's literary editor.

I regularly showed up to poetry readings popping up around the city, to listen, yell at, and applaud the good ones. There were always a handful of regulars stepping up to the mics. One of the standouts was Jerome Sala, who, if there were such a thing, could be the leader of a church for Latter Day Beatniks. I could listen to him for hours and smoke a few cigarettes in the meantime. Jerome Sala's poem, "I beat up Willem DeKooning" was a crowd favorite. I was happy as a clam to extricate that poem from smoky backroom readings and onto the pages of PRAXIS. That was my role as literary editor: decide who got in and acknowledged.

The poets, painters, musicians, and fashion plates on the scene showed up regularly to the same events. First Friday gallery opening nights were especially popular for free wine and generous spreads of party food, pu pu platters, and cheese boards, and you got to see not only what everyone was doing, but more keenly, what everyone was wearing.

"Do you love this? I got it at Amvets. Yeah, I found it before 'Horses' did," came the hungover inside scoop. "Horses" was the avant garde theater group who lived above the thrift store on Halsted. Horses' actors had the privilege of proximity that allowed them to scour the racks at Amvets before anyone else could.

PRAXIS magazine arrived on that scene with its glossy oversized format filling a void in the local print media scene of free papers like Chicago Reader and hand stapled fanzines, Coolest Retard and Gabba Gabba Gazette. PRAXIS was splashier than anything else out there. People noticed. I was getting noticed as a staff member. I felt lucky to be a part of it, even though none of us had a clear idea of what "it" was or where it was going. The whole point was to have fun and document that time period in the city's art scene. We certainly weren't getting paid. We showed up, threw story ideas around, and mulled over submissions coming in. There was a looser, run-with-what-ya-got feel to the work ethic.

Franke Fun sometimes slept at the offices overnight, avoiding the cleaning crew who came in after hours. The office had a tucked away attic-like space to crawl into for a nap. I didn't know if Franke was in between apartments, or if he just liked the vibe of the place after hours being in the south Loop—a desolate place in that time frame following the exodus of downtown office workers and parking attendants. I could picture Franke sleeping in that framed out small space with his leather jacket thrown over him for warmth and the quick getaway. I wanted to stay in that office at least one night just to feel what it was like with no one else around. Quiet. I managed it once, convincing the magazine's publisher that I was working on a piece and it would be easier to finish if I just stayed there overnight. Having a private office downtown to sit and write stories in was a dream I held onto. It was a safe place to be.

PRAXIS magazine stayed alive for six issues. Brian Shanley shot most of the photos—raw glamor shots of punk rockers at O'Banion's and bands performing at Mother's, Tut's, and impromptu rooms that would have them. Brian went to the same art parties and openings I did. He was a Cynthia Plaster Caster fan and reveled in the chance to photograph her in her Chicago apartment reflecting on her career as a groupie superstar. I met Cynthia at PRAXIS. She was very shy, almost awkward, and private about where she lived, but she got along spectacularly with everyone at the magazine. To look at Cynthia you would never guess she could coax musicians into letting her make plaster casts of their penises for posterity. But that was her groupie "in," a way to meet the bands, and she had ten years' experience already practicing her pitch. She could always tell a good story, too. Cynthia made me laugh.

I became friends with Steve Lafreniere, who did music reviews and band interviews for PRAXIS. He was convinced of his own excellent taste in music. He was also a fantastic, funny writer. Steve and I both admired Julie Burchill and Paul Morley who wrote for the New Musical Express (NME) in England, and Lester Bangs writing in the US. Steve had a tendency to color his conversation with French phrases culled from a diet of art magazines, underground films, rock journalism, and living in Louisiana. He was also part French. I had a hard time following his train of thought at times, wondering what exactly he was getting at.

"Sooo, Getta Girl . . . look at this photo (a Brian Shanley shot of a male torso from the waist down). I know those jeans . . . that belt . . . Franke Fun . . . looking good . . . n'est-ce pas?"

Steve's knowledge of pop culture trivia was comforting to me as a person who had been shut away from much of contemporary culture as a child of immigrants. But Steve and I were both obsessed with Chicago architecture, as anyone with a brain and interest in art history would be. In one of our discussions on favorite walks in Chicago's neighborhoods, I told Steve I had found the quietest little spot in the city along LaSalle Street close to North Avenue.

"Oh c'mon, where?!"

"It's just a window in a basement facing the street. A little coffee shop maybe? 'The Rainbo,' I think that's what the neon sign says in the window," I said.

I was being very earnest. I knew what feeling it evoked in me when I walked by—like the allure of a Fibonacci curve. A bent, faintly glowing thin arc of neon that was the only color on the apartment building attached to it. Ten square feet of resonating basement window.

Steve didn't believe me. He eventually went over and took a look for himself.

"You know, I hate to say it, but I think you're right."

Steve then went on to tell me he had once lived in the town where Tabasco sauce was manufactured, and everywhere you went in this town, the smell of the sauce was so prevalent it could even sting your throat.

Steve interviewed Robert Fripp for the June 1979 issue of PRAXIS. Fripp was experimenting with what he called "Frippertronics," his method of making and recording tape loops. Steve convinced Fripp to release a red flexi disc of himself performing "Silent Night" à la Frippertronics, as a bonus insert for the upcoming Christmas issue of PRAXIS.

Fripp's performance was recorded and sent over to us to preview. Steve Lafreniere and I put our heads together to listen to the mastered "Silent Night" before it went off to Evatone in Florida for pressing. The engineer put the tape on, and we thought to ourselves, well . . . ok, this vaguely sounds like Fripp. After a few more plays, and just for laughs, I asked the engineer to play the tape backwards. Slowly, as the volume went up, we could hear distorted strains of the Christmas classic. This "save" for the magazine was a revelation. I was learning to trust my gut, learning to question everything. Lean in and look from a different angle.

I was the youngest staff member at PRAXIS. Everyone else seemed so much older, hipper. Although PRAXIS was unpaid work, the magazine budgeted enough cash for me to fly to New York and interview my friend Lynda Kahn and her twin sister Ellen. Lynda had been living in Chicago for a while and had just moved back home to Manhattan.

Ellen and Lynda were visual artists. Together they created their own design house "Twin Art" as a way to make accessories affordable to the street crowd. They fashioned jewelry from lifeless phone cords, resistors, and chips bought on Canal Street around the corner from their apartments. They made and wore their own rubber belts and constructed party dresses from plastic sheeting—garbage bags, essentially. The twins were their own walking billboards. They had also just orchestrated a window of their designs for the New York Fiorucci's. I was thrilled to know Lynda, the first woman artist I met who could actually make a living doing her art. She was a trained sculptor but wasn't interested in making pieces to be seen by a privileged few in a museum. She made pieces meant for a larger audience of fashion hungry club kids getting on with their busy routines. From Lynda I was learning to appreciate there were diverse paths to exploring the function of art, especially if you were doing what you loved to do.

Lynda and her twin had a new project they were excited about—their own band. They called it Taste Test. Already obsessed with using readymade objects to create fashion pieces, they now had some song ideas. The first song: "Instant This, Instant That." I was flown to New York to interview them, sit in on the recording of the single, and do a write up for PRAXIS.

It was my second trip ever to Manhattan. I packed a light bag with clothes for three days, looking forward to staying with Lynda at her place on Broome Street and getting a tour of Soho. When I arrived at LaGuardia I waited for my bag and watched everyone else on the flight leave with theirs in hand. My luggage disappeared. I didn't yet know the cardinal rule of air travel—pack a day's outfit separately in your carry on for emergencies. With my luggage touring the airport, I survived in a borrowed shirt from Lynda, hoping a taxi would eventually show up with my things. It arrived two days later. In the meantime, I tagged along with my friend to Canal Street where we burrowed through her regular indoor and outdoor vendors, searching for art pieces and jewelry parts for her, cheap notebooks and Chinese slippers for me.

On the second day in the city, I cabbed it over to Radio City Music Hall where the band booked studio time. Inside the building, I lingered over the lobby wondering what kept places like this going, and when could I have a chance to visit the automat I espied on the way over. I headed to the elevator, where the real live elevator operator informed me I needed to go "seven floors up and two flights of stairs," to get to Plaza Sound Studios. Why the circuitous route, my architecture-attuned brain wished to know. Is this place a secret?

I'd never been inside a recording studio. Walking in, I had the sense of being in a private club while Debbie Harry's face stared down from the interior walls of the place. Her band Blondie had recorded in this room. The Taste Test band were huddled around their microphones. There was one additional singer, a bass player, and someone playing a synthesizer. More instruments were laid out on a side table: a blender, coffee grinder, a toaster, and unopened cans of soda. Lynda blurted out her simple lyrics ("Instant this—Instant that!") and made two fists under the microphone like a skier's grip as she prepares to race downhill. It was new wave performed as the maids of the house might do it—everyday noise using everyday objects.

After the session, Lynda and I went to Fiorucci's, where I bought a dangerously tight pair of windowpane patterned black-and-blue cotton summer pants. I was thrilled to be in New York.

The interview and photo spread for TWIN ART appeared in the second issue of PRAXIS, along with a flexi disc of their single. But I was too busy to really keep in touch with Lynda now that she was staying in New York. This was pre-internet, a time when friends still mailed one another found art and poems. We wrote postcards back and forth a few times. I later heard she and Ellen moved to LA and were producers on Pee Wee's Playhouse. From what I was told by other friends, they were responsible for the "Connect the Dots" segments of the show. It all made sense.

At PRAXIS magazine music was constantly on everyone's radar by word of mouth, reviews in the NME, local fanzines popping up everywhere, or listening to the college radio DJs breaking-in alternative bands on their shows. We could listen to bands from different parts of the country and the rest of the world—not the same rock icons lamenting the one who got away or their lives growing up working class. Who wouldn't rather hear the Buzzcocks "What Do I Get?" over Tom Petty's "Refugee"? When Bruce Springsteen appeared on the cover of Time,

I gave up one college friendship arguing over his relevance. To me, Springsteen songs were overblown beer anthems. Period.

My love of soul music and funk was alive and well, and I kept up with what was new there. On a Saturday morning towards the end of 1979, I prepped for my morning ritual, turning on the lunchbox-sized TV in my apartment. After a minute of low voltage, mellifluous, Don Cornelius sleepy intros, I jumped up to call my photographer friend, Brian Shanley.

"TURN ON SOUL TRAIN NOW!" "Funkytown" was making its debut. A perfect dance song, and Brian and I liked to dance. Brian was an equal opportunity dancer in the clubs, shuffling around to "Hammerlock" by the Cramps just as soon as "Harlem Shuffle" by Bob and Earl. Since high school, I couldn't get enough of Soul Train's weekly line dance and shout outs. Every Saturday, we all marveled at Don Cornelius's introductions, his catatonic delivery. I once saw him repeat the exact same three lines twice while interviewing a band, as if he had hypnotized even himself with his own voice. The singer interviewed was unfazed, and being a true professional, answered the question again. Every week, Brian and I waited for Don Cornelius to flub his lines while barely moving his head and sporting what appeared to be an invisible neck brace.

Brian and I were compadres at PRAXIS and remained friends years later when we both found actual paid work. The collaborative air at PRAXIS was full of possibilities, real and fantastic. When the rest of the staff at the magazine learned Brian's parents lived in Geneva, Illinois near the Fermilab, we were determined to do a piece for the magazine on current levels of nuclear research in our fair state. Yeah.

Fermilab was built in 1967 and housed the most powerful particle accelerator in the world. We got it into our heads that we could pay a visit to the lab and shoot some pictures, since the place looked like a Bond movie set and our friend's parents lived in the neighborhood. Simple enough. Thrilling conceptually. But for obvious security reasons, our plan was not meant to be. We settled instead for mixing highballs at Brian's parents' wet bar, staring at the flat suburban prairie outside beyond the backyard. The afternoon wasn't entirely wasted. The Shanleys had a snazzy bar set up, and the cocktails were free.

Having eyes too big to match the contents of my wallet, I spent as much time as possible looking at art hanging in public and private spaces and imagined how I would cover my own walls, if I ever had the money. Brian Shanley's black-and-white portraits were beautiful, timely images, and I managed to snag a gorgeous eight by ten of Rick Buscher, the singer for the St. Louis band Raymilland, for a nominal fee. Raymilland performed at Tut's in 1980 and were the band slated to open for Joy Division for their US tour, which sadly was cancelled when Ian Curtis died. PRAXIS magazine collaborated with Raymilland to include their seven inch single "Talk/Distant View" as a bonus insert with issue number five. Rick Buscher and I became good friends around that time.

PRAXIS magazine had a lifespan of only a couple of years, but it allowed me to meet a lot of artists, solicit literary contributions from local writers, and collect work from notable writers across the country. Their contributions inspired me to write more and imagine other possibilities for myself. I couldn't believe how easy it was to get famous people interested in submitting work to a glossy art magazine with a distribution limited to four thousand. Everyone, it seemed, wanted in. Maybe it was the time. There was an abundance of restless energy in Chicago. No one really needed to see another glossy art rag, and yet, they kept coming up with submissions. Inevitably, at times the work just didn't fit in. Gerard Malanga, Andy Warhol's former assistant and a published poet, was one memorably awkward contributor. An accomplished poet yes, but I wasn't honestly moved by what he had to say. And if there were a choice, I wanted local writers in the magazine. And I wanted to be moved.

Just prior to the magazine folding, Steve Lafreniere thought it would be a good idea for me to meet his friend Marnie, a painter from Cleveland who coincidentally lived on the opposite side of my block on Belle Plaine Avenue. Belle Plaine, "Avenue of the Coquettes," I would say with mock formality if someone asked where I lived. In my mind, wherever I lived was a fabulous set piece for a story unfolding.

Marnie Warren painted six-foot-tall portraits in dayglo-colored oil paints. The completed figures were pulled together from bits and pieces of hundreds of photographs she took of her subjects. When I entered her studio for the first time, I felt the presence of other people in the room. But she was alone, standing in front of her portrait of Stiv Bators. Marnie became friendly with Stiv, the singer of the Dead Boys in Cleveland, and he wandered into her studio one day for a session. In preparation for the photo shoot, Marnie asked Stiv to find something personal to bring with him, an object symbolizing who he was, something that "looked like him." Stiv chose a garter that once belonged to Nancy Spungen, Sid Vicious's girlfriend. When Sid died, his mother mailed a box of his personal effects to his pal Stiv Bators. Nancy's garter was in the box. Hanging from the side of the garter was a tiny charm-bracelet-sized gun. "A Sex Pistol," Marnie said.

In Marnie's painting, Stiv stands defiant, loosely gripping a Carlton beer bottle which may or may not have been later thrown at the photographer. Nancy Spungen's garter is pinned to the wall behind him. I had never seen anyone so vividly colored and yet so untouchable, so angry.

While I let my eyes wander over Marnie's studio, she began a monologue, speaking nonstop as if she hadn't seen another live human in weeks. She moved around her studio like a rockstar, all the while exuding a 1940s' glamor in her black-cherry-colored bangs and bob, scorching red lips on a smile full of teeth— more a sneer than a grin. She reminded me of Elaine DeKooning in a silk shirt and black '40s style dress pants.

Marnie continued her tale, her hands gesticulating toward memories, gushing stories about the time when the polluted Cuyahoga River in Cleveland caught fire, about her family's Hough Bakery empire, and her summers decorating cakes. And did I know David Thomas from the band Pere Ubu was a Jehovah's Witness (I did). I was exhausted keeping pace with her narrative. "Can she not tolerate silence?" I thought. Marnie seemed to be thinking out loud with quick shifts in topics all having to do with Cleveland, her hometown. She punctuated each story with a "*mais oui*," while I stood there patiently, mentally cancelling out her French: "Good lord, speak English, *please*."

I loved Marnie's paintings, but I told Steve afterwards, "She talks too much." Many years later, I bought the painting of Stiv to go along with two other Marnie paintings I already had.

In November, Steve Lafreniere and his friend Michael Thompson conspired to host an "End of the '70s" party at Michael's storefront on North Avenue. Even this tentative decade was ripe for a celebration, a final blowout for all of us and for so many interesting characters Steve and Michael collectively knew. All of the guests were asked to arrive in costume. Marnie Warren was voted best costume: she painted a smoke-belching skyline of Cleveland on her eyelid. The rest of her body was fully encased in a German flag. The portrait of industrial waste was complete. That vision of Marnie, for me, was the beginning point of an industrial art landscape.

At the party, I was standing in a corner of the kitchen wearing my emerald-green, velvet harlequin skinny pants bought at a Salvation Army thrift store purely for the tiny rhinestones dotting the front like a self-contained night sky. I imagined my legs sparkled as I stood there talking to someone about writing poetry. A small group of painters stood off in an opposite corner. I started to mention the "beingness" of Frank O'Hara's poems when all of a sudden one of the painters came racing over. "You're absolutely right!" I laughed, thinking it felt good to be alive in the company of creative people whose art (and opinions) I was getting a glimpse of. Everyone at the party was familiar to some degree, people I'd seen at La Mere or working with PRAXIS magazine or drifting through the galleries and clubs looking for something new. Not missing an opportunity for self-promotion, my new painter friend, Anthony Bruck, invited me to his apartment to have a look at his work. Of course, it was my journalistic duty (at the very least) to go.

When I later visited Anthony, I didn't know what to expect from his art. He was a fan of Barnett Newman. I discovered Anthony's own paintings were dark, monochromatic abstract images, small canvases not much larger than album covers. Everything about Anthony was pared down to the essentials. Spartan. At a time when others revamped their look daily, his uniform never varied: dark suit jacket, black jeans, white button-down shirt, and a black tie. There was no food in the apartment that I could see.

Anthony asked if I wanted something to drink. The refrigerator was empty save for a chilled bottle of vodka. We had cocktails and admired the view of Lincoln Avenue from the apartment window. Directly across the street was a McDonald's. Anthony said he drew inspiration from the "gorgeous teenagers" hovering in the parking lot, especially the boys. That was a surprise.

After our visit, I saw Anthony often at shows, and he contributed a piece of art criticism for PRAXIS number six, the essay "Abstraction Tensed and Tempered (On the Visible in Painting)." I felt a kinship with Anthony, who generally struck me as asexual. He may have similarly wondered why he never saw me with a steady boyfriend. Theoretically, we were too busy being students of the spontaneous, evolving art and music scene in Chicago to have any serious relationships diverting our thoughts. I loved the fact that Anthony once lived in an apartment in Chicago that had a Murphy bed. It fell from the wall like an ironing board. Anthony was not the first, nor the last artist I'd met who felt compelled to riff on my name. He called me "Gregor Samsa," a play on Gerda Serba, my birth name. Was I like Franz Kafka's Gregor, who wakes up one day to discover he's been transformed into a giant hard-shelled bug? Yes, I could identify. I didn't feel feminine, masculine, young or old, just armored and interested in what was coming next.

I was happy to feel somewhat part of a scene, far removed from the landscape of the northwest side of Chicago where I'd grown up, with its Brach candy and Schwinn bicycle factories. In my childhood neighborhood there were few people who ventured very far from the neighborhood or the nine to five ethic of happiness. Everyone had a relative who was a cop or city worker. I had the desire for more options in my life. I was excited to be writing, going to art events, and attending college on the north side of the city, a bus ride away from my apartment. I felt alive.

It was the end of my teenage years, my life was moving at a fun pace for reflection, for parties, for learning. Things were going swell. I had more friends who were artists than those who were not. I was compiling a collection of poems to submit to the university literary journal. I couldn't have been happier with myself and with life.

3

On a rare day off from classes and waiting tables, my phone rang. I recognized the voice; although, it seemed distant. It was one of the neighborhood boys I had grown up with, an old friend of my brother's. I rarely thought about the other people in that neighborhood. I had grown up without a best friend or really any friends at all. I was more of a happy émigré, relieved to have missed the days of sniffing Carbona from paper bags with other kids in the alley or smoking pot with older siblings and chasing the local drug dealer for twenty-five cent Quaaludes scooped from a black garbage bag behind the driver's seat of some guy's car. Like my brother before me, hanging out "on the corner," any corner, claiming some sort of allegiance to the working-class goals of our neighbors was a foreign concept. Life was so much bigger than the northwest side of Chicago.

I had managed to get out of the neighborhood with my bigger ambitions intact. Raymond Ianotti, the person calling on the phone, had never left. He still lived in the same house across the street from my parents' old apartment building. He still lived with his parents. Ray was my brother's age, and they'd bonded with the rest of the neighborhood boys until high school. Ray was calling to ask how to get in touch with my brother, and where did he live?

I wasn't sure my brother Raimund wanted to maintain old connections to his own childhood. I told Ray my brother's exact whereabouts were fluid now, moving around a lot with roommates, which was partially true.

"You really don't know where he lives?" he persisted.

I suddenly felt as though I was being interrogated. I wasn't close with my brother at the time, having my own social life and friends. We occasionally met to go dancing at The Bistro or The Broadway, a gay bar off of Belmont. I told Ray I'd be happy to pass on a number to call. During our phone call, Ray never offered his number in exchange. He managed to find mine along with my address by calling "Information." I was listed. I hung up the phone and thought it odd he would call me, instead of asking neighborhood people who maybe kept in touch.

The following day I was alone in my apartment when the buzzer rang. It was Ray. I didn't think twice about letting him into the building. We lived across the street from one another for over ten years. I knew him. He had been in my parents' house countless times. What I didn't know was in the interim years, after all of his friends had left the neighborhood, Ray had become unhinged in a fundamental way. His mind and moods were unpredictable.

Ray walked across the threshold into my apartment and stared at my bookshelves filling up with philosophy, novels, criticism, and art. "I'll bet you've read every one of those, haven't you?" he asked with his back to me. I paused, and in that brief second felt an adrenaline rush, a vague panic. I closed the apartment door and now had my back to him. I tried to turn around.

In that fraction of time, I suddenly felt hands pressing my throat and pushing me onto the floor. The hands tightened around my neck. I could hear my own faint voice whispering, coughing out "Raaaay . . ." I closed my eyes thinking, this is crazy . . . I should pretend I'm passing out if he's going to kill me anyway. My mind juggled scattered images. Lights flickered on, then off. I chastised myself for thinking I had left the violence of the neighborhood behind when I left. I flashed on the time I sat with legs dangling from my sister Uli's bicycle handlebars while she rode us around our block and onto the next street. I was six years old. We were suddenly stopped by an older boy who jumped in front of us on the sidewalk. He was a stranger, not from the neighborhood. "Get off the bike, or I'll stab your little sister (me)."

Ray's fingers held my neck, and I had a vision of walking through a small town somewhere, lit up like a Hollywood set, not familiar at all, with steep hills and narrow streets propping up tiny storefronts. I had never been to Mexico, but felt I was wandering in a mining town there with shiny objects on display in the windows. There was no sound, but a bedeviling tempo hung in the air. I was floating, like in a pot-infused dream, the same sensation I had had during one of the only times I smoked a joint in high school. It was at the apartment of a friend's friend who wore a black cape to Lane Tech every day and told everyone he was a sorcerer in the making, a character from a Castaneda novel.

I don't know how much time passed. It could have been minutes. When I woke from these visions, I was beating my own head against the floor unable to move my arms. The apartment door was open. I was alone. It took what seemed like hours to push myself to the phone on the table by the door and call the police. My body, I guessed, had gone into shock. I was wet with my own bodily fluids escaping onto the carpet beneath me. The next waking image I had, I could see police officers moving around slowly in my apartment taking notes, me looking at them, and my brain seeing a clashing of visual perspectives. My eyes tried to focus, but the images emerging were refracted, split, like looking through shattered glass.

My attacker beat someone else with a thick length of chain later that same day and hours later was eventually picked up by the police. Perhaps not so coincidentally, Ray's brother was a Chicago police officer. I was told Ray left my apartment, returned to our old neighborhood, and had a conversation with "Big Mike," a brooding hulk whose nickname didn't leave you guessing, someone who had had a crush on me growing up. Ray told Big Mike he thought he had killed someone.

The next time I saw Ray was in a courtroom. There was no trial. There was a plea agreement, and Ray was sentenced to five years probation with medical supervision—this, for almost, not quite, completely choking the life out of me. I wondered what the sentence would have been had I died on the floor of my apartment. In court, the judge flinched when he saw the pattern of broken blood vessels around and in my eyes, and the red ringed pattern circling my neck like a tattoo. Probation. This couldn't be right. In that moment, my ability to trust anyone—especially anyone in the court system—vanished.

Strangled in my apartment. I would reference the event over and over with those exact words. Site specific words. The experience would have felt completely different in another setting—on the street, in a hallway. The intimacy of invasion. A piece of my self was ripped away. I was numb. I didn't want to leave my apartment, but I didn't want to stay there, either.

The detective assigned to my case kept in touch for months afterwards, affixing his card to my mailbox when he couldn't reach me. Perhaps deep down and actually looking around my world he knew what I didn't—criminals tend to return to the scene of the crime? I finally accepted his offer to go for a ride in his unmarked car through my Uptown neighborhood. It was a simple exercise to get me out of the apartment. I was quiet as we drove up and down Broadway, where he would point out city attractions like a tour operator.

"See that glory hole right here—you go to the bars? That gay bar you don't wanna go in." We drove south past the loading docks on North Avenue at the Chicago River, where "the hookers are waving at ya at all hours." I guessed he was trying to make me feel I would be safe if I didn't shut down, if I only kept my eyes open.

I lived alone for a while longer, fighting the notion that my life was now going to be a series of panic attacks. I would get off the Broadway bus at my street, slowly scan the way home looking for anything out of place, and sometimes head into the corner convenience store where I became friendly with the Middle Eastern family who owned the business. A few weeks after the attack, I walked back to my apartment building and as I pushed open the outside hallway door, I could see the interior was dark. The hallway light was out. Keeping my hand on the doorknob, I stepped backwards, staring through the glass with each footstep. I turned and ran back to the convenience store. Shaking, I mumbled to the owner that I needed a big favor. He looked at my eyes, said a few words to his brother, and held onto my keys as we walked back to the apartment building. It was as if a ghost had been there as we went into the hallway and up the stairs to my apartment. Nothing awry. I thanked the man for his kindness, and he went back to work.

I didn't catch even a hint of my attacker again. I dropped out of college, thinking I would return when the time was right. I promised myself I would trust my instincts if something ever felt off in a public situation, then get out fast without apologies to anyone. Self-preservation. It was a toss-up. Hide in my bed or get back into the rhythm of life. Or both. I had things to do. How do you become a fist when you're always in shadow?

***

My attack erased the one thing which kept me moving, going away from where I grew up and into the world of possibilities—fearlessness. My attack foisted an anchor of fear into my consciousness that I didn't even know was possible. A weight, a pinch in my throat when I thought of directions I wanted to take, and there it was. Anxiety. Something telling me I wasn't good enough or interesting enough to anyone else to be worth my efforts. What did I want out of doing anything?

I thought of Franke Fun's audition for Fiorucci's at the Apollo Theater. What did Franke want from that? I hailed a cab and asked the driver to let me off by the Apollo. On the way over, the taxi passed the bar where I had worked my first waitressing job after high school. Sylvester's sometimes had comedy acts perform. I was hired to work a few hours on those nights. It was my first waitressing gig, and I had no clue how to take an order, how to act. The dynamics seemed so seamless for other people, but the reality was much more random and chaotic for me. Syl the owner was Polish and gave me the opportunity to learn the basics by shadowing his sister for a shift. Business was slow, but I learned how to chat with strangers in a dark club to get better tips. Many of the customers were regulars and locals from the neighborhood. The acts were forgettable as comedy nights can be, except for one newcomer named Shelly Long. She dressed like someone who had a day job doing admin work downtown. She walked in, ordered food at the bar, and when I brought her the plate, she barely acknowledged me and kept talking to someone else at the bar. She was one of my very first customers. I didn't realize she was the talent for the evening. Aloof, with an air about her as if she were too good for this place. Maybe she was. Maybe her dreams were set on somewhere else—LA or New York. The big time. But she was here at Sylvester's to practice her act. A short while later I picked up her empty dinner plate. She had already left for the night. She did not leave a tip.

My taxi pulled up in front of the Apollo Theater and I got out. I stood there staring at the sidewalk and paced around the front of the building. I didn't know what I was looking for—inspiration of some kind, I guessed. I tried to light a cigarette and changed my mind. I needed a walk to clear my thoughts. I didn't like walking and smoking any more than walking and eating and decided finally to head south on Lincoln Avenue. Steve Lafreniere, Steve Miglio, and my other painter friends practically begged me to go check out that record store on Lincoln where everyone went in their spare time: painters, writers, party boys, punks. It was on the way. I needed some inspiration. I was going to pay a visit to Jim and Dannie at Wax Trax Records. I was looking for a new job and Wax Trax was the magnetic north for most of the people I knew. This was the place to go for new releases from English bands and independent US bands. Collectors came looking for out of print records, bootlegs, limited releases, '50s, '60s and '70s rock that mattered, oddball celebrity one-offs, soundtracks, reggae, and punk. Steve Lafreniere had helped transplant the two owners (along with their record store idea) from Denver to Chicago. They were old friends. Steve's extensive pop-music education seemed to track with Jim and Dannie's. The three of them had stood side by side at punk rock shows and glammed up together to see Bowie in concert. What I learned from my association with Steve at PRAXIS came in large part from his frenzied appetite for what was new and ultracool. Jim and Dannie were similarly afflicted and they had a record store to help them indulge their tastes. I could go for that.

I was finished with waiting tables. I hated the hours, the customers, the black clip on bow tie, and the smells of food lingering in the threads of every article of clothing I wore. I needed to collect my thoughts and find something to do to make money and still be around creative people with new ideas to shake up the world.

When I neared the front of the record store, I noticed tiny white tiles on the building's façade, which gave it a bathhouse feel, like the Russian bathhouses scattered on the north side of the city. Before Wax Trax, this storefront housed a funeral parlor. A few doors south on Lincoln I could see the marquee of the Biograph Theater, the site of the infamous John Dillinger shootout. I walked into Wax Trax not knowing anyone there, but they knew every smart and creative person I knew.

Jim Nash and Dannie Flesher moved from Denver to Chicago to open a record store for music fans like themselves. It was a place to hear and buy a lot of music that wasn't mainstream. Wax Trax had imports nearly impossible to find anywhere else, unless you had a connection overseas, or you traveled a lot. Walking inside, the place looked like a work in progress with hand lettered signs telling you here's Ultravox, over here Television, and here the Buzzcocks. A poster of Julie London in one corner next to the Sex Pistols Bollocks dayglo screed. I'm not sure why I was hired. Someone said I looked like Jim's ex-wife Jeanie. More likely, I was hired because I hung out with the art crowd, the poetry crowd in Chicago, and Jim wanted some affiliation with that scene. Music wasn't his only interest.

Jim and Dannie knew Franke Fun and everyone else I knew. After I was hired, and for the duration of my five-plus years tenure at Wax Trax, Jim Nash never let up with his catty digs about my "artiste" friends and why didn't I "just become an art dealer and get it over with." Of course, most of my friends were also his friends. My response was always the same. "Look around you, Jim. You're the BIGGEST art dealer I know." He'd cackle to himself and rush off to the back room of the store where the resident pot smokers were pricing records and doing the ordering. Jim always seemed to be running. That was his pace.

4

My first few days at Wax Trax didn't feel like work at all. I was surprised I could smoke and drink on the job. If there was an impromptu beer run or other recreational substance delivery, bills were counted out from the store register. I watched with dismay as one of the other employees slipped a handful of bills to someone looking like their personal drug courier. I didn't want to lose this job or watch someone else skim funds from my new bosses. I pulled Jim aside later and told him what I'd seen.

"Oh. Yeaaahh. That was for me, silly," he said.

I felt a bit like a rat, but Jim assured me he was grateful he'd hired someone with a backbone. No one really kept track of these entertainment expenses, as far as I could tell. And it was none of my business beyond that. I was happy to retire the waiter's uniform and be surrounded by what was a storehouse of music history and the cutting edge, along with the local scene. My path to higher education was on pause indefinitely. It didn't matter. I was absorbing valuable cultural history right here. There was so much happening in local music and art, both good and bad. But while the rest of the world outside was falling down trying to find itself, working at Wax Trax was like being invited into someone's tree house—a safe place to hang out.

I began playing records from the collection of vinyl behind the counter to get a bigger sense of where I was and what music I liked. A lot of the music I knew up to that point was from word of mouth recommendations. I soon realized most of those insights had come from this place. When the store wasn't busy, I could explore genres I didn't even know existed.

A familiar song I'd heard at La Mere or at someone's apartment or at a gallery opening suddenly had a band name attached to it: X-Ray Spex, "Oh Bondage Up Yours!" The New York Dolls. The Velvet Underground. Pere Ubu. Wire. It was eye opening. I was learning a new language. I was accustomed to combining words and reviving forgotten idioms— "swell"—words that needed to stay animated and out there. I was a walking language historian. I felt at home at Wax Trax. These were my brothers and weird uncles surrounded by deco ashtrays and curvy vintage tables that never screamed kitschy or gay. The furniture and interiors changed so often, like a slow motion drag show, constantly stripping away layers. Dannie was building new shelves, a new magazine rack or fitting an accordion door on the back dressing room, while I sold some Krazy Kolor to teenage girls and guys thrilled to wipe out their identities.

I didn't own a record player or have a stereo at home. It didn't matter when I could listen intentionally to music for hours every day at work. There was always something new to hear. Album cover art became a cheap source of visual therapy for me. I discovered The Last Poets at Wax Trax, drawn in by the nerve of a group of black men standing next to trash cans on the street in 1970s New York City claiming the word "poets" for themselves. The Last Poets were the original rappers, whose influence inspired Grandmaster Flash and a cavalcade of rap and hip hop artists to follow. The more I explored the record racks, the more it became clear to me I was working somewhere special. Jim and Dannie were always in the background curating, "renovating" the store on pace with the latest music trends. The walls in front were lacquered black. In the back boutique, suddenly hot pink. The two of them hammered, painted, and paused only to talk to customers, offer them a beer, or try and suggest a new band to someone who was in for the first time.

No longer feeling comfortable living alone in Uptown, I had to find a new apartment. Jim Nash's brother Mike needed another roommate. Mike and his business partner Bill had just moved from Denver to Chicago. Bill liked to tell people I stole his job—the one he was supposed to get at Wax Trax when instead Jim hired me.

Mike, Bill, and I moved into a place a few blocks from my old apartment. The new place had an enclosed back porch, which my roommates soon put to use silk-screening T-shirts for Wax Trax. Their company Interzone became the primary supplier of band shirts to the store, eventually securing licensing rights from the actual artists. Box fans on the back porch kept our apartment from being consumed by toxic fumes. When they were on a roll silk screening, Bill would pop his head into my room with the offer, "Anything you want printed?" And just like that, I acquired an exclusive set of bath towels. No longer "basic white, by Fieldcrest," but now black on white Unknown Pleasures by Joy Division.

That year Mike Nash had the brilliant idea to host a fondue party at our apartment and invite all the Wax Trax people and friends for a cheese meltdown. He liked entertaining at home. Mike was all smiles standing watch over an enormous stock pot of molten cheese in the kitchen, with Roxy Music blaring on the stereo, and everyone drinking cocktails or half-assed dancing in the living room. Rooming with Mike and Bill and being around Jim and Dannie, I was listening to a lot of Bryan Ferry, Roxy Music, David Bowie, and Brian Eno. My future co-worker Ruth Pellicore arrived for the fondue party in ruby-red, spangled hot pants with lipstick to match and go-go danced in the living room to Roxy's "Let's Stick Together."

At one point in the evening, we noticed Franke Fun under the dining table below the punch bowl. The tablecloth hid most of his body from view. Why he was hiding was anyone's guess. Parties we went to occasionally produced human landmines by the end of the night—someone falling asleep drunk, in their coat, under a pile of coats on a bed at Jim and Dannie's. In the winter, it was a practical alternative to getting up and stumbling back to your own apartment. Usually, the same people needed to be put in a cab and sent home. It was not always Franke. Besides, Franke had the best two second delay with one liners. I imagined him peeking out from under the table, his head turning in the direction of the kitchen and fondue apparatus there, and interrogating the lyrics to a familiar nursery rhyme: "And the cheese stands ALONE?!"

***

Snagging a job at Wax Trax seemed a good alternative to writing pro bono for PRAXIS and waiting tables to survive. I was accepting the direction of my life had to change after the attack in my apartment. I needed a break to breathe and figure things out. And it wasn't as if I was a complete music novice. There had been the nights at La Mere, listening to Patti Smith records at friends' apartments, and going to shows when I could afford it. Growing up in Chicago and being a product of public school, I also had an early perspective of how heavily music would make or break a good day. In elementary school, on a field trip to the Morton Arboretum to learn all about the local flora, my classmate Juan Montez broke the boredom of the bus ride with a vote. "Listen up people. Once and for all time, who IS Soul Brother #1—James Brown or Michael Jackson?" If you lived in the suburbs, the answer might have been the poppy Jacksons. Not on this bus. The crowd pledged allegiance to The Boss.

In the summers, there were summer songs on repeat in my head as I rode my bicycle to Foster Beach. "Golden Lady" by Stevie Wonder. "Be Thankful" by William DeVaughn. My ride followed the path along the beaches down to Fullerton Avenue. There, just inside the street entrance to the water and sitting on the rocks were the Puerto Rican boys and men playing congas, jamming. It was a summer ritual, a kind of summer song all its own that opened up possibilities for an adventurous day. With inner city soul as my backdrop, Wax Trax became my new soundtrack.

***

Jim and Dannie were very democratic in staffing at the store. Mark Clifton, Nic Leuthauser, and Greg "the Wicked" Pickett ordered new releases and bought vintage vinyl from sellers. Carol Blank and Hope Peck did the buying for the boutique. But everyone occasionally worked the front counter, with its tiny center island holding the store phone and the glowing neon that read "Joy Division," a final tribute to the band and late singer Ian Curtis.

Greg was the wonder boy with a photographic memory. Having seen the price once in a trade magazine he could instantly recall the current value of used records that came in. Greg also had a side business venture of producing some David Bowie bootlegs. Almost everyone at the store deejayed in the clubs when they could to make extra money and have a social life. Lucky Number (later, 950 and Club 950) and Neo's welcomed the Wax Trax crew to spin the week's new releases and surprises nabbed from personal record stashes. At the store or at the club turntables, everyone was busy pushing open the cultural window, playing new sounds, new bands, and creating their own devoted Monday night, Saturday night, or Thursday night following.

I wasn't interested in deejaying, although there were plenty of opportunities around. I did agree to one guest spot on one night at Lucky Number, so long as I could tag team with Larry Crandus. I only knew what songs I wanted to hear in what sequence according to how I thought someone on the club floor would respond. The mechanics of back and forth between turntables, setting up, and all that smooth transitioning was frankly too distracting. I wanted to listen more than learn how it's done. That was fine with Larry, whose reputation wouldn't be tarnished by an amateur like me.

I was adjusting to my boss Jim's B-movie sarcasm and trailer trash sense of humor, a synthesis of his own coming to terms with being gay, having once been married to a woman, and having kids to raise from afar. He also had an ego to rival any rockstar whose music we championed. Jim would pester me endlessly about why I didn't have a boyfriend: "There are so many cool guys coming in here every day, girl. Don't you wanna jump on any of 'em? Gedda, are you a lez-be-in? Is THAT it? C'mon, you can't be liking muff. I know you like men— C'mon over here and give your daddy a blowjob." And it went on. If that line of inquiry wasn't picking up any traction, Jim tried another more personal tact. My maiden name is Serba, a very old, Polish surname: "You some kinda Serbian-

Croatian terrorist or somethin'? That why you don't have a guy? I'll help you not be a lesbian, Gedda. Oh c'mon— get WITH it, girl!"

On the other hand, if I made a point of saying someone was good looking, Jim's inevitable follow up was, "Oh HE'S gay. I can tell." Despite being a gay man himself, I couldn't believe Jim knew more than I did just by looking at someone. I said, "Jim, you think anyone with clean, trimmed nails is gay." He looked at me in disbelief. "Well, they probably ARE."

I didn't mind that I had no boyfriend for long stretches. I liked spending time alone. At Neo's one night, a guy friend said to me, "Everyone's afraid of you. You work at Wax Trax for God sakes. You're too cool to make small talk." Such lack of courage! Why would I want to talk "small" with a visual and sonic circus parading past me (and all of these timid bachelors, if they paid attention). I didn't mind, as I spent afternoons filling my head with music and the English rags — NME, The Face, and I-D. As a books, magazines, jewelry, and clothes buyer for the boutique, I enthusiastically promoted limited-run editions of Little Caesar (a literary journal) and hand-stapled books of Raymond Pettibone art, and the early print-only issues of Sub Pop. The record racks were a never-ending loaves and fishes for the young and barely employed, like me. Had I not been busy soaking up music history at Wax Trax, I would never have discovered Bikini Atoll was a nuclear test site in the Marshall Islands, as well as a short-lived post-punk English band. I would have had a slim chance of regularly listening to Amon Duul or Kraftwerk in German and comparing the English versions in my head to see if they were true to the band's native tongue. Instead, I would become an expert on John Waters' and Russ Meyers' films, Tom of Finland art, and accept the possibility that my boss Jim may have also hired me because I resembled his ex-wife, as some had said.

As provocative as Jim was, his partner Dannie was quiet in getting things done. If I buzzed Dannie from the back counter to let him know some kid was trying to stuff LPs under his coat, Dannie would muscle through the crowd, hoist the offender by the collar, and haul him out the front door—all the while managing to hang onto the cigarette dangling from the corner of his mouth. Whatever happened outside I didn't ask. I felt protected around Dannie. He was one of the few people who made me feel safe. I didn't like surprises or even the slimmest chance of someone going off on me in the store. Loud music, crowds of leather jackets, and steel toed boots, a skinhead bunch here, someone tripping on acid over there. "Wow . . . did you KNOW these walls are painted black?!"

"Baby . . . you wanna beer?" Danny's way of saying hello.

He was usually in good spirits, with the perpetual cigarette balancing act. Typically, a Saturday shift at Wax Trax meant an early beer run to the liquor store across from the Biograph Theater. An early cigarette to start my store clerk's day, and a quick round of calls to see who was doing what after. Beer tops were flipped early, as the steady crowd of characters made its way through the front door, past the photo booth, the new arrivals bin with its promises of a good time and the turntable cranked up for loud listening pleasure. Wax Trax was like a free-form networking hub. People met, became friends, formed bands and attitudes and political alliances at the store. The self-professed communist who played his drum kit on State Street downtown for lunch hour tips, walked into Wax Trax with the same desire to hear and buy something new as everyone else. On one Saturday morning, a skinhead girl crossed someone's "line" and was knifed a few doors away. No one was shocked. Some people we knew thought she had it coming.

Growing up with three languages I had a natural patience and ability to decode accents—regional and foreign. It was all about rhythm and patterns. I thought everyone knew that. One of my regular customers was an English woman named Lorna. Lorna had a heavy Birmingham accent and the softest sounding voice. It drove Jim Nash crazy, and not in a good way. The first time Lorna came in the store wearing a basic metal chick uniform of leather and black and hauling a large black artist's portfolio almost equal in size to her muscular small frame, Jim greeted her with a big smile. His expression soon changed to consternation as he put his arm around me and whispered, "I can't understand what she's goin' on about Gedda, but could you figure out what the hell she wants?"

Lorna's muffled voice and accent seemed to swallow her words, while she finished with one thought and segued into another. Everyone else at the store seemed to avoid engaging her in conversation and had difficulty dissecting meaning from her verbal patterns. But she bought a lot of records. She hauled her drawing portfolio at her side, propping it against the counter as she stood before me in black jeans, well-worn black leather jacket, and steel-toe lace up boots and wanted to know what I thought of the new CRASS record. I had lived with three languages constantly intersecting in my head, and I could naturally translate "Lorna-isms." Jim would jog by and say, "Your friend's here," roll his eyes, and entrust this peculiar bit of "customer care" to my skills. Jim thought by simply speaking louder to her, she would respond in kind in a more audibly understandable way. Jim raised the volume of his voice often when speaking to customers. I wondered if he was losing his hearing from years of seeing live shows or if turning up the volume of everything was his personal mantra to get him through the day.

Lorna was an Ozzy Osbourne fan. "Muh hometown boy." I didn't always make out 100 percent of what she said. But I was comfortable enough to ask what she was working on that she could show me from her drawings. That was the connective tissue that kept the conversation going in clipped images and fragments of words. Maybe she was a brilliant talent and just not a talker. That was okay with me. A few years later, during my last weeks of working at Wax Trax, Lorna appeared one day and said she had something for me. It was an intricately rendered eight by ten ink drawing of a ghost ship and crew; there was nothing commercial or "metal" about the image. It was simply beautiful, mounted in its thin black frame. More original art for my collection.

At Wax Trax whoever had a spot at the front counter could play to their own mood, unless Jim was around campaigning for the new vinyl releases we'd stocked up on for the weekend. Sometimes I felt the need to shake up the serenity of the sea of black leather bent intently over the record bins in the store. It was crowded. I had had enough of Heaven 17's single "Let Me Go." As much as I adored it as a pop song, I didn't adore anything five times within an hour. I would pull from the wall behind me the Joy Division Warsaw picture disc. We sometimes had a copy of this collector's gem, and the rawness of the songs suited Saturday morning's post-date night crowd congregating in the aisles. The needle touched the vinyl. Customers looked up from their searches and started walking to the counter. "What is that?" Jim came bursting through the back, through the boutique's swinging door, raced to the front counter, and yelled, "What are you doing?! We don't have copies of that for sale!" I answered, "Well. We have this one. I'm educating the public. AND I wanted to hear it." The going price for the disc was somewhere between 100 and 150 dollars. Jim was pissed. I didn't care.

At other times, I would put on Implog's "Holland Tunnel Dive." The track begins with a fairly benign, steady, reggae rhythm. After a minute, a muffled voice comes in, droning, "Leaving for the other side . . . going to take the Holland Tunnel dive." Then creeping in slowly, comes the sound of a vacuum cleaner edging closer. It's actually a jet engine. The noise becomes louder and louder over the course of twenty seconds, reaching its crescendo in an ear-splitting peak. Not a dance number. Definitely a great song to play on a Friday night near closing time to give those customers left in the store that extra nudge to let us lock it up.

There was a definite flavor to what got played inside the walls of Wax Trax. That was by design. It was impossible to play everything for everyone, even the stuff that would quietly sell itself. There were ample slots in the racks for every imaginable Police album or Kate Bush single, for example. Some regular customers bought all of them, even Japanese pressings for $10.99, seven-inch pieces of vinyl that would never be heard in any version at the store. It was too much. Kate Bush's look, her taste in clothes couldn't pique my interest to give a listen. It wasn't until decades later when I accidentally heard the band Placebo do a version of "Running Up That Hill," that I had to consider Kate Bush as a serious songwriter. I had always imagined her songs must be some kind of operatic fluff akin to Nina Hagen or Lene Lovich or any number of other women over-dressed in carpeted layers of folksy fabrics of questionable ethnic affiliation. Jim just said, "Oh, Gawd," when her name came up. That was an adequate enough review of Kate Bush for me. But Placebo's cover resonated emotionally with me at the time I heard it. It worked. Funny how a different voice and interpretation can do that. Like Nina Simone's version of "Here Comes The

Sun"—a soul wrenching lullaby to be played again and again, compared to the flea market flavor of George Harrison's original hit. I never cared for the original.

***

After a year of rooming with Jim's brother Mike and his partner Bill, I was ready for a change. By chance, my coworker Carol and her twin Christine were looking for a place too, as was Wax Trax's newest employee, Larry Crandus. Was there anything preventing the four of us (one guy, three girls) from getting a place together—other than the harem-like appearance of our lot? Not really. We rented a multi-bedroom apartment with enough space for an entire family and equipped with its own washer and dryer, a rare luxury for apartment living at the time. Our massively cozy new place was in the Edgewater neighborhood, a few blocks from the lake. It was close enough to the Thorndale el stop and far enough away from Lincoln Park and the clubs to give some respite from the party circuit. We all could use the break.

In the past, I rarely had friends over to my own place. Living with three other people, I could loosen up a bit. I sought guidance from my groupie friend (and ultra-party goer) Cynthia Plaster Caster about throwing a birthday party for two other twins we knew, Gabrielle and Giulietta Karras. While I was at PRAXIS magazine, we'd done a feature on the Karras twins who were style mavens, teenaged, and wildly entertaining to talk to. The Karras twins were turning eighteen. Why I was motivated to throw a party for friends who were so much younger than myself instead of assuming the twins already had plans for their big day was obvious. They needed help. The Karras darlings were raised as Jehovah's Witnesses. They didn't have parties.

I met Gabrielle and Giulietta for the first time at PRAXIS when they were fifteen and fabulous, living in Oak Park with their parents, antique dealers. The twins speed dialed their way to art parties and gallery openings, hanging out with creative types and novice fashion designers in the city. But as Jehovah's Witnesses, the twins were not allowed to celebrate birthdays with presents and parties. It was baffling to me that they were surrounded by celebrations of beauty—art objects at home and at their parents' shop, and fashion changes seen through their own eyes —and yet they were pulled away from celebrating themselves. They typically dressed in oversized thrift-store men's jeans, shoes, and tweed blazers in a style suggesting they were fans of Fran Liebowitz, the equally fabulous resident culture stalker at Interview magazine. The nod to Liebowitz was genuine. The Karras twins were culturally literate far beyond many people their own age. I thought of my own cultural debut for my eighteenth birthday, complete with live poetry reading and guest appearances from the (suspected) neighborhood Latin Kings. I proposed a twins' birthday bash to my new roommates Carol and Christine who agreed—yes. House party. It was the beginning of June, and invites were selectively doled out at Wax Trax with location and time scribbled on the back of store business cards.

I had just bought a large drawing from my painter friend Marnie Warren of her beau Paul Taylor. "Paul Sits at Home" was tacked to the wall in my new bedroom as a final touch of my personal taste. I couldn't afford a Marnie painting, but her drawings were equally arresting. My roommates and I had painted our rooms each to their own liking, and my liking was a Sherwin Williams deep mauve which eclipsed the spectrum of "raspberry sherbet." The room needed that extra something. It was the largest bedroom and was situated at the front of the apartment. The drawing of Paul Taylor was a moody meditation to offset the slightly feminine tone of the four walls around it.

My roommates crafted together a pu pu platter and were willing to handle deejay duties. I had no idea how many people would show up, but everyone loved Gabrielle and Giulietta, and the art and music crowd began trickling in. The twins arrived and appeared dumbstruck by all the attention directed at celebrating them. Marnie Warren arrived with some of her painter posse and friends who were distracted away from a Son of Svengoolie viewing party at Marnie's place that day. Marnie held regular Svengoolie watch parties in her studio, always confined to seven participants unfamiliar to one another. Her parties were small to avoid any mishaps around the ongoing canvasses in the studio. Svengoolie's B horror movies were background ambient noise to be absorbed under the skin, along with the martinis Marnie whipped together for her audience. She knew how to throw a party.

Marnie greeted the birthday twins looking as Elaine DeKooning-esque as ever in black stretch pants and red lipstick, and she seemed to purr as she waltzed in. She wanted to see my room. Marnie had told everyone I bought the drawing of Paul Taylor, and this was the official unveiling. I was secretly thrilled I had painted the walls that lovely shade of sherbet. I adored the color. Marnie did too. It was very new wave and appealed to her current penchant for bright, pastel peony shades of oil paint. Satisfied I had expertly hung her drawing in a prominent position on my wall, Marnie stood in the room with her head thrown back and her hands on her hips and asked, "Where are the cocktails, *mon Cheri*?" *Mais oui*. Her posse stood staring in awe behind her. Men proposed marriage to Marnie more times than anyone I had ever met. One potential suitor could not get a single date with her but kept up his pursuit. He often intercepted her at her part-time art store job downtown and would tell her her reasons for refusing him were useless. So what, she didn't find him attractive. So what, she had someone else in mind. All he asked for was dinner. He was finally rebuffed for the last time when Marnie told him, "I'm sorry, I can't have dinner with you Wednesday, my father just died, and I have to fly to Cleveland." Her suitor gave up. Ironically, what Marnie told him every time was true, even the last time.

I ushered the party guests into the main room of the house where our large fireplace stood next to a turntable set up for spinning records. I found the birthday girls looking a little less shy about all the attention they were getting for just being themselves. I marveled over their sense of style, their sometimes odd ensembles—army fatigues with army boots and tutus pulled over the pants—but they were more subdued for their birthday, avoiding the tulle and costume effects. I felt a cycle had been completed as I looked over the dozens of people sharing gossip over drinks and welcoming the Karras twins into adulthood, officially. The girls looked happy to accept my gift of recognizing them as smart, curious, and creative women. I decided then they would be my new talismans. Taliswomen?

That winter of 1981 into '82 in Chicago was brutal. On a January day the temperature dropped to negative sixty degrees Fahrenheit with the wind. The el tracks froze. News stations blared warnings telling Chicagoans to stay home from school and their jobs. I didn't think anyone in our house was fully prepared to stay inside and skip work. Unfortunately, we didn't have enough food at home for the next few days in the event the weather got worse. Being the only true city kid in our house and having been inconvenienced by hometown winters before, I brilliantly suggested we go to the Jewish deli under the Thorndale el and pick up food supplies before they ran out too. We could play some records, light fake wood in the fireplace, eat some marbled Halvah, and throw on the Psychedelic Furs to inspire a few dance shuffles and warm up our legs. The Furs had played Tut's in the fall and would be back in the summer. They were a favorite in our house for a while, as were Factory Records's bands and new romantics, Visage and Spandau Ballet.

Agreeing to brave the cold, the girls in the house layered on two coats apiece, embarrassing double layers of everything else, and we mapped the route from our back porch to the storefront as the shortest path. Carol, Christine, and I linked arms vowing to hang onto one another for balance. We feared going down on the ice alone and freezing there. Being in a pack closed those odds. Carol was too glamorous for that scenario to play out anyway. And one day out of our lives we could face the public swaddled like babies, padded like punching bags, and moisturized like seals against the wind. Were we action figures, we would be the Closet Dump Barbies. From the moment our boots landed outside on icy pavement, my contact lenses began shriveling behind my Jackie O. shades.

There was no one on the street. Onward we shuffled in our boots and long johns, two blocks there and two blocks back. The shelves in the deli were almost empty. We managed to pick up an odd assortment of cheese, crackers, and canned soup for the next few days if needed. We made it back home frozen, but now ready for anything, and spent the rest of the day listening to music and eating in front of a blazing fireplace, like refugees yanked from their normal lives by a natural disaster. The forced air heat in the house never turned off, creating a constant background drone against our interior dance party.

Many mornings, Carol and I walked to the Thorndale el—an actual elevated stop—to catch the train down to Wax Trax. Other days, she would ride with Christine in her car on her way to her own job. As twins, they couldn't have been more different in attitude and demeanor. Christine had a straight job and seemed perfectly satisfied to be heading toward a business or management degree. Carol craved the limelight. Carol with her doll-like face masking a smoldering glamor as she stood on the el platform with her pale Shiseido face powder, black eyeliner tipping upwards, red-and-white eyeshadow, glossed lips, and long, black wool coat grazing the tops of her short, black buckle boots. Next to Carol, I was her bookish, pale cousin, unadorned except for lipstick. I'd had sensitive skin since childhood. Eczema breakouts prevented me from wearing anything but lipstick on my "delicate countenance." Carol's platinum razor cut hair and black roots earned her the name "Punky" and to some (in a not so nice way) "Skunky." To me, she was just Carol. We both liked books and looking at art. She sometimes sewed her own party dresses inspired by something seen in one of the English rags or in a painting. She and Christine were slightly older than my twenty-three years. They were more trend conscious, more complicated in looks; where I preferred red, black, and white basics and the occasional cool tartan. When Carol needed something to wear—a long formal dress for a New Romantic party she was deejaying—out came her sewing machine, and she sewed the dress herself with Christine's help. Yards and yards of satin, a metallic satin, stitched tight below the bust to exaggerate the natural décolletage. It was a dress to break hearts. Carol broke hearts across continents. There was a boyfriend in England who wrote letters she waited days to open. I didn't get how she could stand the wait.

It was no surprise Carol was attracted to musicians. Musicians were like fashion. She loved fashion and Vivienne Westwood-style shock value. Carol was attracted to the volatile waves of clothing design overall. When we first met in 1979, she loved all things mod. And because she loved all things mod, she also loved the English band The Jam. I didn't think too much about relationships with men, because most to me were clueless or just not that interesting to share my thoughts with on a romantic level. Musicians seemed further removed from my thoughts, their schizophrenic lives committed to infrequent opportunities to perform or too much competition and too much time on the road. Indifferent to romance as I appeared at the time, most of my friends were men. Many of them were gay. I generally didn't pay attention to men otherwise. I wanted to see the world on my own, not necessarily holding hands with anyone on the way. I intuitively knew I could never be a groupie. Not for anyone. In the same way I could never be a secretary, working for someone else's peace of mind and success. I refused to take a typing class in high school to erase that possibility. And I absolutely couldn't stomach the idea of being in the service of a rock star for a night. It wasn't in my DNA.

There were a few girls, regulars at the store and on the club scene, who made sport of chasing up-and-coming rock stars, as well as the established ones. That loose tribe of groupie hopefuls were abuzz when any English band was in town for a show. I was friends with Cynthia Plaster Caster, and that was all the groupie fun I could handle with a straight face. It was hilarious and sad to me that a girl would put herself out there before and after a show with the expectation of meeting someone famous. But that was their deal. I was a lousy fangirl but happy to be in a place where I could hear new music and see the accompanying circus, watching from the sidelines.

As Wax Trax's reputation grew, the store became a mecca for touring bands and musicians. If someone good was playing in town, they stopped by. The really big names often came looking for their own bootlegs. To some it was simply a matter of wanting to hear just how excruciatingly bad those recordings were. Phil Collins was particularly gracious as he wandered through the store one day pausing to say hello to anyone approaching him. I was happy to sell his girlfriend a jumper we had in the boutique from an emerging solo designer in New York whose work had coincidently appeared in Vogue that month. I couldn't have cared less about any of Collins's music, but he was a friendly guy the few minutes I spoke with him and his friend. Johnny Ramone would stop into Wax Trax whenever he was in town just to catch up with Jim and Dannie who knew him from their early days at the first Wax Trax in Denver. Johnny would sit on a stool behind the front counter with Jim while jaws fell open on every face coming through the front door.

Another Denver alum, Jello Biafra of the Dead Kennedys, would spend all afternoon rummaging through dusty boxes of castoff 45 singles in the backroom of the store, presumably finding the occasional oddball rarity for his pleasure. He leaned towards the obscure in name and sound.

On one of his stopovers, Biafra needed a ride to O'Banion's, a local punk club, and Larry offered to take him in his car. I tagged along. As we drove to the club, I wondered what, if any, social commentary Biafra might share about the black-and-white houndstooth check of the car seats and the University of Chicago window sticker in the back—a suburban cliché in the city, and not really what Larry was all about. Larry's parents were alumni and had given him the sticker. But Biafra said little in the car. I assumed he was just grateful for the ride or preoccupied with his mission, or he was just too cheap to get a cab. I had no clue what enabled musicians like Biafra to tour and move around so freely, other than the kindness of their fans.

I was fascinated with Biafra's fashion sense. He consciously chose to be anti-fashion. He wore off-the-thrift-store-rack clothes that didn't appear to fit all too well. He said he didn't want a look for anyone to copy. "Let the fans think for themselves" was his credo, and one I thought fairly radical for a pop star.

During that spring, walking up to work one morning, I came upon a black stretch limo double parked in front of the store. It wasn't an unusual sight. I stopped into Vie de France, the French café and bakery next door, to get some coffee. Usually, if Jim saw me with a Vie de France carryout, he'd feel pressed to comment: "Did you get a 'hwah hwah' with that coffee?" Jim's butchering of the word "croissant" would not rest, but he too couldn't allow a good French joke to get away from him. Jim was as unimpressed with the current surge of Francophile love in the city as I was. You could now find a decent croissant easier than a decent bagel.

I walked out of the café with my coffee and headed next door to the record store. As I reached for the front doorknob, I came face to face with Robert Plant.

My first thought was, "Oh cool. Robert Plant's in town. I better head in back and let the boys know he's here." Once again, I was not thinking this sighting was any more unusual than any other celebrity moment. I just didn't care. That didn't mean everyone else was on the same page. I walked to the back room and casually informed the troops we had a visitor.

"Robert Plant just walked in," I announced to the room.

Jim and Mark and Larry and Nic didn't move—it was as though I was suddenly transported into a stop-action game, a game of "freeze tag."

"Hellooo?" I searched for life behind those blank stares.

You would have thought I had announced the arrival of the popemobile to an audience of the devoted. Hands and arms were suddenly flying everywhere, grabbing up any Zeppelin anything we had for Senor Plant to sign. I headed upstairs to the newly relocated boutique (more Jim and Dannie remodeling mania). My good friend Cynthia Plaster Caster was upstairs paging through the latest edition of the NME, and I of course mentioned to her the latest celebrity sighting. I knew Cynthia had her own thrilling personal history as a famous groupie with Led Zeppelin. I couldn't gauge if she was thrilled by my newsflash or horrified that Plant was in the store. Knowing Cynthia, she was speechless first, wondering if she looked alright second, and about to throw up in the excitement of the moment. Before I could say anything else, Plant was upstairs snooping around. He approached the counter and asked if he could see something in one of the jewelry cases. I reached down to retrieve the desired item, and then I heard this:

"Well. You don't have to be nervous already."

Well. Wow. Really. Was he talking to me? I thought about this. Wow.

Here I was. I had somehow managed to traverse the mean streets of the west side of Chicago, had somehow survived integrating a former all boys college prep high school suffocating from its own male domination, landed back on my feet after being nearly choked to death by a madman in my first apartment as a single woman living alone, and this guy in front of me wants to calm my nerves.

Well, I'm nothing if not a wiseass. I paused a second, straightened up, laid the thing he'd asked to see on the counter, looked squarely at Comandante Zeppelin, and replied, "And you WILL get over yourself." I went back about my business.

I suspect at that point Cynthia had taken a dive into the clothing racks against the wall. I didn't see her anywhere. I saw the NME on the floor. In my mind I could also see the invisible arm of every gay waiter I had ever worked with making an arc in the air and then the "snap!" of the fingers. Mr. Plant quietly headed back downstairs.

I'd never been shy about my opinions, musical or otherwise. I was discovering that working at Wax Trax placed me at a constant risk of exposure to all sorts of ego-maniacal nonsense streaming from the mouths (and the outfits) of the famous and the wannabe famous.

"Oh brother, there goes Julian Cope in that ridiculous shearling mountain-man vest. Can't wait to hear Jim's take on the 'outdoor look,'" I would say, as the singer for the English band The Teardrop Explodes rushed past to meet Jim and Dannie in the back room of the store one day. Cope wrote terrific songs, but his fashion sense currently left him looking bored by his own handsome face. I was shameless in my off-the-cuff critiques. It was a skill I picked up with relish from my mentor/boss, Jim Nash himself. I appreciated a good drag outfit as much as anyone. I'd been to The Baton with Jim and Dannie to see the inimitable Miss Chili Pepper and the other girls work their stuff on the catwalk at the club. Missteps in daytime fashion, however, were intolerable in my view.

Although they were arbiters of taste in music and thus were in their own positions of power, all the local DJs who regularly came into Wax Trax were genuinely nice people. Curious souls who made their pilgrimage to their favorite record store, from Bobby Skafish at WXRT to Steve Albini spinning out of Northwestern, and Terri Hemmert and club DJs from Neo and Lucky number, all seemed just happy to nurse their craving for the new and share opinions with Jim Nash on what was relevant and cool at the moment. I came to appreciate that the music business was no different from any other. Big egos were for the stage, and the dance floor. I had no patience for arrogance in the afternoon masking as cool. No patience for guys in spandex who would come in on the weekends, lean on the boutique counter, and ask if they could have a discount because they were in a band. Hm. "No."

Wax Trax wasn't a place for mainstream consumers. One of the store regulars was a guy we called Blondie Bob. He was Jim and Dannie's age. Unlike Jim and Dannie's uniform—501's, cotton T-shirts, baseball-style jackets, or black leather—Bob wore polyester "slacks" with short-sleeved polyester knit golf shirts tucked in and belted just so. His look was not a campy shtick, either. It was just Bob. He could easily have been a leading man or an extra in a Russ Meyer's movie in another life. He looked completely out of context next to the black leather crowd in the store on a given day. But Blondie Bob was a rock star at Wax Trax. His Clark Kent façade, the dark framed glasses, and borderline greaser trimmed hair were all a disguise to keep his mother happy (we surmised). His appetite for all things Blondie or Debbie Harry kept him coming back for more whenever his bachelor's schedule (foreman, we guessed) would allow. He was genuine and enthusiastic about Debbie Harry. He probably had a shrine for her back at his bachelor digs. We held stuff for Bob behind the counter like porn shop merchants. He was genuine. He was an icon. Bob was a cool guy.

There were other customers who were equally "square" by current fashion and age barometers. Jim was particularly fond of another man also around his age whose honest to God name was Sander Dee. Sander Dee was a career waiter at The Berghoff downtown in the Loop and would come in sometimes on a Friday after his lunch shift after getting paid. He was of eastern European descent and close in age with the Hollywood actress Sandra Dee, who starred in the teen flick Gidget and was popular in the 1950s and '60s when she married teen heartthrob Bobby Darin. The name similarities aside, Sander Dee had no teen heartthrob looks or even a good wardrobe. He dressed like someone's uncle when he wasn't still sporting the waiter's white shirt and dark trouser outfit of his profession. And at The Berghoff, waiters were professionals staying on for decades making a decent living. Sander Dee's look didn't matter to Jim who usually sold him on the latest Brian Eno or German band or prog rock score.

There were stock traders who were friends with the painters I knew in town and who became store semi-regulars. I was particularly chummy with the brokers. They could afford to take some of the old money fees they collected from gambling numbers all day and spend the money on brand new canvases some of my better-known artist friends were producing. And they spent money— lots of it—on records. That made Jim happy and kept me working.

On occasion, local celebrities would appear in Wax Trax looking out of their element. Bill Kurtis, the longtime Chicago newscaster, gave us his blessing as he wandered around the racks with someone who appeared to be his college-age daughter. It was not so unusual to see a celebrity of his generation tagging along with someone younger and in the know. Kurtis smiled in that way that assured me he was just there as a guest, not there "on assignment." My DJ coworkers were undoubtedly mulling the possibilities of secretly sampling the newscaster's voice, so recognizable to anyone who'd heard him deliver a story in the last twenty years.

The most uncomfortable celebrity dash through happened late on a weekday night while we were aching to get the doors closed and gates up outside. Almost everyone was out of the store, except one small group. I hadn't noticed them coming in. Suddenly, standing in the middle of all of the record bins, in a near empty shop next to the couple he was with for the evening, was a very loud John Belushi yelling out "THIS IS MY FAVORITE RECORD STORE IN THE WHOLE WORLD!" Who exactly was he talking to? He looked so small. He was short in stature. I just wanted to go home. I wanted to say, "Blues Brother, take it outside, OK?" But Jim Nash and I stood there with stiff smiles as we would on any other slow night with any other last customer to leave. Who knew this customer would die of a drug overdose in LA soon after his visit to Wax Trax. Who knew?

Flashes of celebrity tone and color in the end were less interesting than the familiar faces I would see every day. Jim and Dannie, always hammering away at something or installing a new window display, something to change slightly the interior of the place. Dannie with his beer and cigarette, and Jim telling him what to do next. They were a two-man crew and self-sufficient, going their own way professionally and personally as a couple. It came then as a complete surprise, when I found out Jim's mother Betsy was coming up from Topeka for a visit. I couldn't picture Jim, first of all, having ever been married to a woman and secondly, having ever had parents who raised him.

Betsy Nash arrived at the store a petite, opinionated, slim granny in her dress and matching handbag ensemble, holding a lit cigarette before her like a divining rod. She struck me as someone blithely moving through time and space. Dannie paused what he was doing to follow her around the shop with an ashtray. She couldn't seem to square the hand-eye coordination of smoking with the fact that something was burning between her fingers and falling to the rug. And there was Dannie steering her clear of the record racks. Betsy was proud of Jim's entrepreneurial spirit, she said. But Betsy gave the impression she'd just wandered in off the street to ask where she could get a cup of coffee. She was on the go with that handbag.

5

Jim and Dannie would occasionally send two buyers from the store to New York for the boutique shows. Carol and I went together a few times, staying in Times Square hotels not far from the convention hall. In September of 1981 we were in New York for one of the shows. During the day, we visited the usual handful of vendors like Trash & Vaudeville to order their black 50/50 jeans. We stopped to see our friend Sunny Chapman to order her latest jewelry line and then filtered through the rest of the eighty percent junk and fake punk rock gear on display. Trade shows were thrilling for a few minutes, then the sameness of equally opportunistic fad merchants made the eyes wander and hope for a surprising new artist with fabulous one-off samples they were willing to sell you personally at cost, all with the vague agreement you'd order more merchandise later.

Our friend Sunny Chapman had a beautifully caustic wit, having by now been in the fashion business for many years. Some of her current designs were brilliant chunky statement earrings and necklaces, well crafted, hitting the right notes with Chinese and Ethiopian symbols. Sunny mined art history in a thoughtful and polished rendering of cool, a subtle contrast to the leather wristbands, skull rings, Ray Bans, and local handmade earrings we otherwise sold. Sunny's line went to little shops and bigger high-end stores like Bergdorf's. Other designers copied or attempted to copy her. Her line had already appeared a few times in Vogue. I walked into her booth to place my order at the show. Sunny kept eye contact with me as she slid over to a young man standing nearby unabashedly ticking off lines and curves in his sketchbook. Sunny smiled and said loudly to his face, "Get outta my booth, motherfucker," glided back over to me and continued the conversation. "Where were we?"

On this buying trip, after a full day of aesthetic eye torture, Carol and I made loose plans to go to a club or scout out a new band. We were in New York for a few short days. It was the end of September, and we decided to head out to a club we'd never been to, to see a band whose music we knew but had not seen live. The band was performing their first US shows and with not much else happening, we took a cab to the club in Union Square. There were possibly ten other people in the audience when we arrived, standing in front of the stage of a disco-era dance floor. We thought we'd made a mistake. The space was small. It seemed an oddly neighborhood-bar-like setting for a rock show.

When the band finally walked out and started their set, all of the bluster of the day's boutique show sales pitches and "trends" was wiped from memory, and I focused on this spectacle a few feet away. Working at Wax Trax, we had the luxury of seeing a lot of bands, virtually every week, for free. I, for one, felt fairly blasé about live shows as a result of overkill.

This was different. The singer held the stage as if he were facing a stadium of a hundred thousand people and not a handful of some neighborhood drunks and two out of town girls looking like they were in the wrong club. The band was The Birthday Party, and the "show" became one of my top ten live performances ever. I don't even recall what they played, just that it seemed so loud and focused on us. The cheesy lighting in the bar we could ignore—for THIS.

I read later that Nick Cave split his pants onstage. I couldn't say. Carol and I ran outside to find a phone. This was still the era of phone booths everywhere in Manhattan. We were on a mission to jump Superman style into a public phone booth and save the world from mediocrity. We called Jim and Dannie and shouted into the phone they HAD to book this band. It was already in the works. On

October 10th, Wax Trax sponsored The Birthday Party at C.O.D.'s in Chicago.

When we were back from our trip, I couldn't hype Nick Cave's performance enough. The Birthday Party was one band no one tired of. It was a time when at any given moment someone working at the counter would break into "Nick The Stripper," and the chorus, "Hideous to the eye . . ." The Birthday Party was the perfect foil to all the pretty boy bands, like Duran Duran, popping up that year.

Wax Trax was already sponsoring shows and having in-store appearances. With The Birthday Party due to arrive in town, Jim Nash went into art director mode. It was the band's first tour in the States, and they were to be given the customary personal treatment bands received when Wax Trax promoted their shows: in-house designed tickets and full-frontal visual assault window displays, usually designed by Jim himself. Forget cardboard cutouts or flat displays. Maybe there was a mannequin involved. Sometimes not. It was loud and dayglo or dark and a train wreck, and if Jim could have had live go-go dancers in the window, he would have pulled that off too.

With each new band Wax Trax sponsored to play in town, Jim and Dannie would have a meet and greet, a little pre-show party. By this time, they were living in a penthouse apartment on Surf Street. The place had high ceilings in the main room and space enough for a band to play, were that a realistic option in their relatively quiet building. The private parties they held to meet the bands were casual affairs, with unassuming finger foods and drinks, and a chance to relax with the Wax Trax staff—and maybe a few friends. When I arrived at Jim and Dannie's for The Birthday Party soiree, Nick Cave was lounging alone on a sofa in the middle of that cavernous space. I walked behind him and privately marveled at the enormity of his cranium. His head was bigger than mine—a wonder of nature, considering my hat size was seven and five eighths and difficult to fit. But I said nothing, keeping with the unspoken protocol. Jim and Dannie were ultimate fans. They wined and dined huge talents and tried to make everyone feel at home in their home, talking about things that they were obsessed with. There was no industry chatter, no sucking up. Just eat, drink, and talk about drag shows with real live drag queens or anything else other than life on the road.

The English band A Certain Ratio was booked to play in Chicago around the same time. Jim and Dannie made plans for their new guests' arrival, while Larry Crandus and I devised a scheme of our own. Larry was A Certain Ratio's "biggest fan." Larry had a knack for reaching a historian's level of obsession with performers he liked. He introduced me to the "vocal stylizations" of Ken Nordine and the "genius" of Jerry Lewis as a comedian. Larry and I had lively discussions about the lack of any (in our minds) funky vocal "huhs" in A Certain Ratio's catalogue of songs. Being devoted students of soul and funk, we made it our mission to somehow alert the band to the value of the down and dirty soulful grunt—at least try to—in the short evening hours they'd be a captive audience at Jim and Dannie's. We shared our music lesson plan with our coworker, Gary Jacobson. Gary was a big ACR fan, too. Gary was also the only black employee at Wax Trax (and Larry's pot smoking pal) and was hilariously quick to lay on his "ghetto" when an occasion called for it—never mind he was raised by parents who lived in one of the glass towers across from North Avenue Beach facing the lake. Gary agreed with us—A Certain Ratio's vocal stylizations needed some help. They needed to up the funk.

On the evening of the party, three newly minted, self-proclaimed musicologists—me, Gary, and Larry—had the brilliant idea to take advantage of the high-ceilinged acoustics at Jim and Dannie's and do some over the top throat clearing between hors d'oeuvre bites and cocktails, while we stole past band members hugging their drinks and probably wondering whether the three of us were sharing the same cold:

"Lookit here...UH!"

It was silly and a goof on the notion that mingling with pop stars was serious stuff. Had I smoked pot like everyone else that day, I might have made a complete ass of myself. I just needed a laugh, without the haze. Larry and Gary went back to their usual discussion of Betamax versus VHS tapes, and I wondered if the ACR boys were gay or straight.

Sponsoring touring bands had its perks. Free tickets, private meet and greets, moving through the club doors early, before the crowd. To see a private world beyond the stage was a gift: watching David Thomas of Pere Ubu play pinball in the public area of the club getting ready for their show at Tut's or assisting

Lux Interior and Poison Ivy from the Cramps as they quietly flipped through the used record bins in an empty store. Lux and Ivy were sweethearts with us, and I admired their calm regard for one another. This was their down time before later seeing them vamping, getting ready for a rumble onstage at Mother's. All of these things were a reminder again that the famous were human beings.

Wax Trax would not sponsor larger shows with more established acts, but depending upon the venue, we were able to block book tickets for ourselves for those events. Bigger shows allowed me to go out with Jim and Dannie and the rest of the Wax Trax brood and relax, without the responsibility of promoting anything. When Kraftwerk came to Chicago for the Computer World tour in 1981, everyone we knew was going. If you weren't at the show, you were either overseas, dead, or in jail.

We were out of our seats doing the audience scan at Park West, wondering collectively if Kraftwerk would actually play or would there be robots performing their parts. It was a fashion event in the audience as much as a musical miracle on the stage. The Chicago artist we knew as Dog Lady appeared, sauntering her way to her seat balancing her Raymond Hudd custom-designed hat on her short black coif. Hudd designed for Hollywood stars and celebrities and had a shop on Clark Street. Dog Lady's hat bore two extended helicopter-like blades projecting out on the sides. Their combined wingspan was somewhere near six feet. I honestly believed those blades would start spinning to lift her from the audience and onto the stage to meet the band. When the live fashion show and circus out in the crowd died down, the members of Kraftwerk emerged onstage in their own skin. It was almost anticlimactic. Almost. I was ecstatic like everyone else with every note, waiting to hear lyrics sung in German or in English. For me, one way would be an entirely different performance from the other.

Prior to the Park West show or sometime later that night, the band members of Kraftwerk made a stop at one of our hangouts—Neo's. We saw them collectively get into a cab in front of the club, bow their heads in unison, bend their knees in unison, and in one smooth choreographed collective slide they were all in the cab. It was a visual miracle.

There were other nights when it seemed everyone at Wax Trax came together for a group date—or group therapy session, unwinding from eight hour pop music overkill. Once or twice we headed over to Moon Palace in Chinatown where Jim and Dannie picked up most of the bill. They were such connoisseurs, you had to wonder how they were able to suss out the best ethnic restaurants when you yourself had lived in Chicago your whole life and hadn't figured these things out. Other times, we'd go see a show. Occasionally, it was a drag show at The Baton. Of the three times I saw James Brown perform live, the most memorable was again at Park West. Who cared how old he was as a performer? I sat with Jim and Dannie who were wearing their biggest smiles dancing next to me in our group seats. When James stumbled to his knees we gasped, waiting for his "rescue," pressing our hands together in mock prayer as Mr. Brown was miraculously revived.

It was a year for big shows. When the Jacksons played the Chicago Stadium during their Triumph tour, I sat a few rows from the stage with my old friends, Steve Miglio and Steve Lafreniere. Michael Jackson was just launching his solo career. As Michael rose from beneath the stage in a cloud of fog, a tiny black girl in a skirt, sweater, and heels, clutching her little handbag jumped between Steve Miglio and me with a brief smile and apology—she couldn't have been older than fifteen. "Oh, excuse me! I just want to see Michael."

Not much about working at Wax Trax seemed serious, except listening to a new band and fitting their sound into my memory bank of music. For me it was relatively easy to decide whether or not I cared about a song or a band by listening once or twice. I could sing along with Mark E. Smith to The Fall's "Totally Wired" any time of day. "T-t-t-totally wired!" I adopted the stance that when it comes to any art, analyzing it is a distraction. You either like it, or you don't. If you don't, there is always a way to clear your head, especially true when it came to music that was just plain annoying or bad.

At Wax Trax, despite the anticipation around weekly UPS drop offs of new video compilations, there were inevitably lots of duds. To relieve that aural pain, it wouldn't take long before the overhead TV screens in the store went blank and you could look up at the monitors to watch Faster Pussycat Kill Kill or SCTV tapes of Tex and Edna Boil's Curio Emporium or Count Floyd's Monster Chiller Horror Theater. All things funny could definitely clear your mind. At other times, when the mood in the store was slightly more contemplative, the screens would silently play Triumph of the Will, Leni Riefenstahl's Nazi propaganda film from the 1930s. Jim loved the footage. It was mesmerizing.

Before I actually knew it was happening, I became a part of this generous freak family of pop culture addicts. That was my new normal. Art and life were functioning side by side. David Byrne in the Talking Heads "Once In A Lifetime" video danced identically to my co-worker and friend Mark Clifton, jerking backwards on the dance floor, seemingly getting shoved in the chest by an imaginary bully. Anticipated record releases were celebrated with mini parades in the store. When the English band Pigbag released the single "Papa's Got a Brand New Pig Bag," Mark danced the length of the store to the back room and shouted, "The Pig has arrived!" This anthem of crazed horns became a club hit. Mark made it happen.

For all the Wax Trax nuttiness, there were some sobering mornings. The stretch of Lincoln Avenue where Wax Trax held camp notoriously had no basements. Underground vermin—rats—pushed their way into every business on the strip. When the temperature outside dropped below freezing, it was routine to arrive at work, go into the toilet under the stairs to the boutique, lift the toilet lid, and find a frozen rat floating. Dannie would have vermin removal duty that day.

After an intense night of partying at the gay bars—usually, I guessed, The Gold Coast—Jim or Dannie and sometimes both would walk through the front door sporting their collateral damage. Sometimes, a brand new black eye. Their relationship was all consuming with work, living their passion, and sometimes rough pickups. It wasn't a secret. They were game for adventure in every aspect of their lives, whether it was music, art, drugs, or sex. At one point I intimated to Dannie that someday I'd write a book. "Fabulous. Girl, say what you want. As long as you don't mention shooting up with _____, upstairs in the apartment." Agreed.

When the band Bauhaus were brought over from England for their first tour, they did a good deal of recreational partying upstairs with Jim and Dannie. They were also happy to do an in-store appearance. I knew Peter Murphy, their singer, read widely, and I decided to give him a copy of a Frank O'Hara book of poems, just in case he needed an American giant of breezy modern verse to round out the dark edges of his library. It was the closest I ever came to saying thank you personally to a band or member thereof. Thus, my contribution to fandom was a poke in the ribs, à la Frank O'Hara.

When I had worked on PRAXIS magazine, Steve Lafreniere would wait for my reaction to a piece of writing or visual art and then, having formed his own opposite opinion, would say, "Getta Girl, you only like art that's funny." That wasn't true. I gauged my pleasure in art by its ability to surprise—through a gesture, a line, a sound which instantly alerted my brain to follow that thing. If it happened to be funny, all the better. Working at Wax Trax I laughed more than I had ever done in my life at EVERYTHING. Whatever anxieties I had about living and finding a direction for myself were temporarily on ice, and that was a good thing. I still thought about writing but rarely spent time actually doing it for pleasure.

***

There were plenty of decent local bands coming in to drop off their cassettes and play something new for Jim and Dannie. During 1980 and 1981 in Chicago it seemed everyone with any artistic bent—musical, visual, or written—was in a band, starting a band, or looking for a band to join. Doug Taylor, one of our regulars, came in the store and placed a cassette on the counter in front of me. I was friendly with Doug and his brother Paul. I owned Marnie Warren's drawing of Paul that hung in my room at home. Doug had a proposition for me.

"You write. Can you write lyrics?" The cassette held a handful of songs. I hated the band name: The Vaguelys. "I'll try. I'll see what I can do." I thought it might be fun and was flattered to be asked. I had never written lyrics before. I wrote mostly poetry and some prose.

I listened to the Vaguelys' tape several times at home trying to find something interesting about the music. It just wasn't happening for me. I returned the tape and told Doug maybe writing lyrics wasn't my thing. The Vaguelys found someone else. The band submitted some of their songs to the still relatively new Sub Pop label. Their song "Sofa or a Chair" appeared on the Sub Pop 5 compilation. I suppose the label found something in that song that I couldn't see, not being a musician myself.

It was inevitable that Wax Trax would become a record label. Jim talked about it constantly, and his philosophy for doing business wasn't going to change. If Jim were a politician running for office, his campaign slogan would be a line I heard so many times: "I'm in the business of chaos." It was true. Wax Trax was an exercise in how to thumb your nose at business models. Jim and Dannie didn't seem overly concerned about bookkeeping and seemed determined to run the record label with gentlemen's agreements—nothing in writing. Details were left open. There was nothing to bind them to the bands they liked and vice versa. They just enjoyed the momentum of starting a label, releasing new stuff they personally liked, and hoping it would sell. The first release on the "official" Wax Trax label was a punk rock record from the Chicago band Strike Under, a group of guys who frequented the store as much as anyone else. It wasn't a great record, but it was a record Jim and Dannie could get behind and that was a first step.

Jim and Dannie's laissez-faire attitude created some trouble with the label's second release, Divine's single, "Born to Be Cheap/The Name Game." Jim was either unaware or uninterested at the time of the Divine release that "Name Game" was a copyrighted song. The original songwriters needed to be paid royalties for Divine's cover version. Talk of a lawsuit was floating around. Live and learn. They eventually settled with the songwriters, but the experience was an early example of Jim and Dannie's devotion to their label artists blinding them to the responsibilities of maintaining the label as a business. They adored Divine and his career and releasing a drag queen's cover of the '60's classic shout out to an imaginary posse was the ultimate. John Waters movies played on the video screens at Wax Trax as often as band videos. We couldn't help but memorize the lines from Female Trouble, where Divine discovers her mother bought her the "wrong" shoes for Christmas.

Jim would often improvise. "Where are my CHA-CHA HEELS?!" That line echoed in the store about as often as, "Has UPS come yet?" I met Divine when he came to visit after Born To Be Cheap was released. He was soft-spoken with a bald head as smooth as a honey dew melon—hardly the bewigged brute of his character who levels the family Christmas tree. Perhaps releasing a record with a couple of pop culture obsessed hillbillies was a natural progression for Divine.

The Wax Trax record label was becoming more important to Jim than paying attention to the record store. Bands came in with demos to play for possible promotion, knowing there was a built-in audience in-house for new music that didn't reflect mainstream tastes. Jim and Dannie were into everything. The label started with a punk record, moved onto a campy cover, and for the next release they chose to work with a relatively unknown talent, Al Jourgensen, for his new project, which didn't quite have a name yet. Sometime early in 1981 Carol and I were working the back counter when Jim raced out of the back room and announced he and Al needed to come up with possible band names. Jim played us a tape. I didn't like the music much. Jim asked what we thought of variations on the name "Ministry." Ministry of something. Defense. Partying. It didn't matter what he came up with. I said, "Name's too long."

I barely knew Al, but he and Franke Fun had performed together in the band Special Effect, and I loved Franke. I saw Al in the store occasionally, racing by with whichever current cocaine-fueled girlfriend he had, heading to the back room. Al wasn't any more appealing than any other guy wanting to make music and pitch ideas to Jim. He just had prettier, more exotic looking girlfriends. I viewed Al as just another hustler, who occasionally wore eyeliner and painted his nails. Perhaps I was so disinterested in Al's world because he looked a little bit like my first serious boyfriend, who was half Spanish, half Japanese, and also dabbled in drugs.

My ex had eventually decided to go back to his previous girlfriend, a Joni Mitchell lookalike more than a foot taller than he was. Perhaps she kept him more visually engaged than I did when he craned his neck upward to look at her. My ex's record collection consisted of jazz standards, David Bowie, and yes(!) Joni Mitchell records. He was obsessed with his stereo "system." The old boyfriend liked to think of himself as a drummer and eventually wandered into Wax Trax a few years after we had split up. No longer dating Joni Mitchell's American twin, he came in with someone equally as petite as himself. I stood there in my outfit for the day—a deep-red, long-sleeved fine rib corduroy button-down shirt and black pants, looking very Kraftwerk Mensch Maschine. As he approached the front counter, I handed him a copy of Joy Division's Closer and suggested that's all he needed to buy today. This was a guy who insisted Castilian Spanish was the only pure form of the language. He also insisted his towels needed to be refolded a certain way (hotel style) in the bathroom of his apartment, saying it was a very "Japanese thing." It bewildered me to think of why I was attracted to him in the first place, but he had a lot of style. He wore stacks of silver bracelets, multiple rings, and smoked cigarettes like a champ. He also took me to see Al Green at the Arie Crown Theater at the point in Al Green's career when he was still handing individual rose stems to the "ladies" in the audience lined up for that bit of audience participation during the show. Or maybe I was attracted to the ex because of his job. He worked at a Porsche dealership and could freely take a car out for a test drive. Yes, please.

As I ruminated on my indifference to Al Jourgensen's current music, Jim Nash was growing agitated and wanted a little more positive encouragement from me and Carol about the potential choices for a band name. Carol said nothing, which was unusual considering she often would side with Jim over his opinions on what was cool. Her DJ sets were also heavily dance oriented. What we were listening to seemed right in line with Carol's tastes.

I didn't care for what I'd heard so far. My own taste in current music could sooner align with the Pop Group's "The Forces of Oppression" than anything Al Jourgensen "Wanted to Tell Her." Al's music was a little too light for me. It reminded me of too many other bands: Orchestral Maneuvers in the Dark (OMD), Depeche Mode. I preferred darker sounds: Cabaret Voltaire, Joy Division, The Fall. "Name's too long," I said again.

"UGH . . .Girls." Jim threw his hands up.

"Well, you asked our opinion!" I said. Jim stomped off, disappearing into the back room. I felt honored that he wanted feedback, but if I didn't like the music, why would I care what the project name would be?

Al eventually settled on the name Ministry, and life went on without any inkling of just how intertwined my life and Al's would become a half dozen years later.

***

Carol and I were booked for another New York boutique show, and it happened that Joe Shanahan (local party boy, club DJ, and friend of the store) and his partner in exploits, John Sulak, were also going to New York for a visit. Joe would eventually go on to open the very successful club, Cabaret Metro, in Chicago, but on this day in New York, Joe and John were slumming. When Carol and I met up with them, we were staying in midtown at the Milford Plaza. Joe and John were staying in Chelsea at the YMCA. None of us had high paying jobs, but Wax Trax footed our bill as an expense.

I don't know exactly why those two guys were in New York, except to check out the club scene. Carol and I picked them up, and we all cabbed it down to the Mudd Club. The line, as always, was busy, with the doorman hand picking who went in. He pointed to Carol and me, and we moved ahead to the front. Just as we stepped up to pass into the club, Shanahan and Sulak were at our sides linking their arms in ours and slipping their way in. The two of them at the time were thinner than the two of us, and they moved through the doors like bracelets on our arms.

A Certain Ratio was also in town and at the Mudd Club when we arrived. The band members stood together in the dark on the side of the dance floor in identical white dress shirts and matching trousers, looking like Mormon interns eagerly clutching "literature." I liked the band very much, but we didn't dare approach them in this awkwardly loud setting. I wished Carol and I had had more time to get out to the museums or wander around St. Mark's Place, but celebrity sightings and street art was about all we were going to get on this trip. That, and an egg cream, was just fine with me.

Some of my coworkers at Wax Trax were as interested in visual art as I was. Carol, of course, was one. Kevin Lovell made art. He and I would dish on whatever was hot in the galleries around town. Marco Pezzati worked at the store for a time. Marco and his brother Jeff were in the band Naked Raygun. Marco moved on from making music to creating "performance art" with his girlfriend Leslie. Those two words always struck me as redundant. Performance art. Blech. I once said to Marco, "Help me out here Marco, isn't all art a performance?" He gave me a look. "Oh Gerda, such a purist, such a gadfly," while he lazily rolled his eyes and changed the subject to his favorite topic—Jim Thirwell and all things "Foetus." When Marco said, "performance art," I thought of vaudeville, burlesque, beat poetry, Frank O'Hara, and David Bowie. I generally hated labels, whether it was new romantic, new white soul, noise, or the vomit inducing "performance art."

I was on a roll with my Marco needling when on an afternoon shift, I walked up into the boutique and saw Marco standing on a ladder changing a light bulb in a ceiling lamp. He was tall, a Roman column, wearing his signature black dress pants and white dress shirt. His nails were painted black. He looked prepared to go onstage. I couldn't believe my good fortune. I rushed up and whispered, "Marco, shouldn't I be documenting this for you?"

Even if I wasn't making music in a band or stepping up at a poetry open mic or exploring the qualities of acrylic versus oil paint (and from which year's stock?) I understood the commitment of artists. I also understood the truism of not taking yourself too seriously. If you knew this was the real deal, this something you made was so uncomfortable and not ready for accepting audiences, run with it. Maybe it was not even considered good. There was a reason why Joy Division's sound felt so genuine. We got to hear Ian Curtis's effortless take on Gogol's novel Dead Souls. The best cover of Velvet Underground's "Sister Ray." It was different. It was all performance art.

My aesthetics were constantly shifting, but some things were so ingrained in my identity they were a reflex, a comfort. The only makeup I wore was red Chanel lipstick. I refused to pierce my ears. I would get annoyed working at Wax Trax on Saturday nights when The Rocky Horror Picture Show was playing at the Biograph Theater down the street. Rocky Horror had a residency at the Biograph that seemed to go on for years, much to my chagrin. There was always a crowd of a hundred or so people squirming in line to get in. The line stretched to the black iron security gates outside of Wax Trax. The line of preconceived, costumed characters clutching rolls of toilet paper to throw during their life-absorbing movie made no sense to me. Everyone at Wax Trax loathed them and hated their dull stares through the front window. The Rocky Horror fans were not cool and not funny at the end of the work day. No imagination. You revisit a fairy tale. Where is the challenge in that?

By this point, our joint lease was up for me and my three roommates. Larry and I decided to move in together, while Carol and Christine went off to find their own new place. Larry and I found an apartment on Halsted Street, directly across from Uncle Frank's, a Chicago hot dog institution. From our apartment window, we could eternally see a two stories high, glowing neon fork spearing an enormous "dog" in the sky. Twenty-four hours a day. Cynthia Plaster Caster lived around the corner. Wax Trax was a few blocks away. Life was theater, or so it seemed. The Illinois Lottery had begun selling tickets for a new game, and I played multiples of seven. My ticket won. So did the tickets of so many hundreds, thousands of others. So many won, the final haul for each was somewhere around twenty-four bucks. I went back to work.

One of the perks of being in a front-facing public job at Wax Trax was getting to know the public and accepting freebies from loyal customers. One of those loyal regulars left a ticket for me to see the Steppenwolf Theater group's current play. The group performed in a temporary space near our apartment on Halsted. Although seeing live theater wasn't high on my list of continuing art education, seeing a live show other than a rock show was tempting. Variety inspires. Guerilla theater was something I was interested in learning more about. I didn't know much about Steppenwolf, just that they were a newer company, but with a free ticket, why not?

I wasn't up on contemporary playwrights, either. In this case, the playwright was Sam Shepherd who had cowritten a previous work, Cowboy Mouth, with Patty Smith. I didn't like it, but I did like Patty Smith's writing and was willing to see what else Shepherd had to say. The Steppenwolf production was Sam Shepherd's True West with Gary Sinise and John Malkovich in the lead roles.

The theater space was small enough where if the actors were so inclined, they could flick a cigarette at an audience member with pinpoint accuracy. I sat on a folding chair together with the other fifty or so people in attendance. I wondered if the intimacy of the space would draw my attention more discreetly to what was happening between the characters. I wondered if I would care. The character dialogue was definitely in its own world, something I felt sucked into in such close proximity to the actors. The character of Lee appeared, confronting his own demons and laying waste to the domesticity of the apartment and his own brother. The performances were raw, believable snapshots of two brothers ready to kill each other over coffee. There was nothing ambiguous about their emotions. It was breathtaking, a kick to my persistent hunt for the memorable live show. This became one of them. Like seeing a punk band, where you felt as though anything could happen.

***

I wasn't wired to be a joiner. Cliques and sororities made me nervous with their self-conscious agreement to be "one for all, all for one," or something like that. Gangs were gangs under any label. I dropped out of college in the late '70s in part as a snub to the writing program at Northeastern Illinois. My mentors offered to write recommendations for me for the Iowa Writers Workshop after my first year. But I could intuitively sniff out the Iowa graduates when the latest American Poetry Review came through the mail slot at my apartment. They all sounded alike. I wasn't interested in being in that club. I wasn't leaving Chicago just yet. I would explore my own voice without outside pressure or the cachet of having gone to Iowa.

I made one exception to my disdain for private fraternities. In 1982, Factory Records announced it was opening a members only dance club—the Hacienda in Manchester. A few of my favorite bands were on the label. Love for all things Factory was nearly a job requirement at Wax Trax. From the Peter Saville designed record covers to Martin Hannett producing, what wasn't there to love? How cool would it be to go to Manchester on a reconnaissance mission for the store and be the first to do it? Larry and I signed up to become Hacienda members, had our membership cards mailed to us, and made a plan to fly to England. On our record store salaries, overseas trips seemed impossible. Fortunately, Larry's parents owned a travel agency in downtown Chicago, and they worked their own system of celebrity discounting to fund our trip. We were soon on our way, thanks to Herald Travel. The name of the agency was a spin on Larry's dad's name—Harold—and Herald Travel became the unofficial agency for Wax Trax business and pleasure trips.

I couldn't wait to get out of town. Flying anywhere, whether it was New York or overseas, meant opportunities for more stories to fill my journal, more experiences to step headlong into and figure out where my life was going. Thrills awaited—or at least new restaurants, languages, voices. I had the bug. It had been two years since I'd taken a trip overseas, back to Germany and Poland with my father and my youngest sister. On that trip, I encouraged my father to take the train with us to Warsaw. He had never seen it. Having been born and raised in Poznan until his teenage captivity by the Nazis, my father was eager to discover the other big cities of his homeland. It was the summer of 1980, a month before the Solidarity movement happened. The coming political uprising was palpable. Not a single smiling face on the streets in Warsaw. We stayed for two days in a fancy hotel where the dining room in the evening served French food and was practically empty but for three Americans and a table or two of elegantly appointed communist party sympathizers. We attended the annual Chopin concert in an orchestra hall filled to capacity with (again) members of the party: bejeweled and perfectly coiffed young blonde women on the arms of significantly older men in bespoke elegant suits and gold watches. Russian gold. Pink.

It had been almost two years since that trip. Traveling with my (now) boyfriend was a novel experience. We could go wherever we wanted to, indulge the chance encounters, and not be beholden to foreign relatives waiting to cook us supper. Having the week off from the record store and full of adrenaline after our long flight, Larry and I arrived at Heathrow in London.

It was an overcast day in September 1982. It was my first time in England. Stepping off the plane and walking into the terminal, my mind was open to seeing whatever peculiarly English billboards were in the airport, whatever public art. I wanted to see it all. But the reality of what awaited us wasn't provincial in the least. It was somber, urgent, and extraordinary in its own display of international solidarity.

Cautionary poster boards awaited us at the gate. They were everywhere and unavoidable: Tylenol. Dangerous. If you have pills with you, bring to airport security—that sort of thing. While the two of us were sleeping on a plane ready for adventure, the world was in a poisoning panic. People were dying from ingesting extra strength Tylenol pills, and no one knew how widespread this thing was. And we—being obsessed with all things Factory Records—didn't really care.

When we arrived at the hotel and entered our room, I was surprised to see a tidy welcome basket on the desk. Quaint.

"How old do your parents think I am?" (I was three years older than Larry.) He shot me a look as if I'd insulted his family's reputation. The basket, I was told, was de rigueur for all the corporate clients.

Franke Fun was staying in London at the time, working on music. We all thought Franke convinced a friend to marry him so he could stay in the country and just be Franke and fabulous. It was a highlight of any day when I could see Franke, and this trip to England was no different. Larry and I met Franke for lunch and drinks at a neighborhood pub and listened to him complain about what a "queen" Marc Almond was and how overexposed. "God . . . he's everywhere!" Soft Cell's "Tainted Love" had long ago faded from the clubs but was still hugely ingrained in our psyches. It was almost as rotten as having to hear U2's "I Will Follow" ever again, having endured far too many spins of the anthem-like pleadings of Bono, who you just knew was convinced of his own place in pop music history. U2 made good songs, but nothing was good repeated on an endless loop. On an endless loop, it was Muzak.

We finished lunch, and I gave a hug and a kiss to Franke, and we were off to engage in my favorite pedestrian meditation—city walking. It was my first time in London, and I was trying my best to look left instead of right at crosswalks. I was getting better at it. As I focused on the corner coming up, there came into view what looked like a dance troupe in V formation heading toward us on the walkway. The group appeared camera ready for some sort of video shoot, with coordinated makeup and hair. I was convinced now that London was so glamorous. We drew closer to the group, and I recognized the lead strutter. It was Marc Almond, of course.

We kept walking. I wanted to see Trafalgar Square and possibly catch some midday political rant or poetry reading. We had only one non-negotiable destination planned for London. Lewis Leathers. We were looking for boots. In Chicago, we pined after motorbike boots with double straps and back zips that were all the rage in ID and The Face. Along with just about everyone else we knew back home and at Wax Trax, Larry and I were fanatical about industrial design and having the right boots. Were there an army of industrial culture soldiers out in the world somewhere, they'd be wearing those boots. After scoring our own, I wandered the racks eyeing leather motorcycle jackets in crazy colors I had never seen in Chicago. A peacock blue leather hanging all alone on a circular color wheel caught my eye. It was marked down to fifty pounds. That was the equivalent of sixty-four dollars at the time, and that I could afford in a pinch. Blue leather. Pool colored. I was liking the image of wearing something out of the ordinary, something leather that wasn't black.

Loaded with new gear and wondering if we'd have to wear it all on the plane home, we headed back to the hotel to pore over club listings looking for the night's entertainment. I anticipated London nightlife would be infinitely more exciting than the clubs in Chicago—wouldn't it? Where did I ever go? Lucky Number, Neo's, Limelight—maybe. Okay. There WAS that one time exiting Neo's early, bored with the crowd that night and walking down the alleyway to the street, and who should I almost run smack into because I was in a rush? Who, walking shoulder to shoulder like criminal conspirators—rather short in stature, but not in nerve—who, but David Bowie and Iggy Pop? The two of them stopped for a moment, stared at me, and walked on by. I knew Bowie was in town doing the stage version of The Elephant Man. I later learned Bowie and Iggy were at Neo's to score cocaine. Alas, how ordinary.

No, London couldn't possibly be ordinary. It was full of bands whose music saturated our daily lives at Wax Trax. Larry and I might have the chance to see a new band before anyone else. That was a real possibility. I thought of how Steve Lafreniere's friend Michael Thompson happened to be in England in 1978 or '79 and had the rare pleasure of seeing Joy Division live in a club. His account of Ian Curtis dancing himself into an epileptic frenzy was the Pulitzer winner of all live show reviews. If only we could see something original like that, something surprising.

I left navigating and getting around to Larry. He'd been to London a few times before with his family. We didn't seem to have an obvious choice of where to go this evening, but somewhere along the way, we ended up at a performance by William Burroughs.

I'd never been a fan of Burroughs, and his old man, droning delivery of lines out loud through a microphone was too much for my ears. Yeah. I got it. Cut ups and combinations. Bloody reality. Poets did it all the time. Jazz musicians did it all the time. Wasn't that part of the struggle in being an artist? Make something new out of nothing? Maybe I just didn't care about the secret life of junkies. Maybe I was partial to the exacting melancholy of ordinary life. After a few more minutes, I still didn't care about Burroughs—blasphemy, to some in the club, no doubt.

We didn't stay long. Looking over the crowd, it was clear Burroughs's writing was appealing to yet another generation of the hip, high, and disaffected, and who was I to judge other people's tastes. Larry spotted "Sleazy" from the band Coil and had a chat with him. The most fun I was having was in matching real-life faces we encountered in London with the photos we'd seen in the music rags in Chicago. Living in London must be a little bit like living in Hollywood or New York, I thought.

The following day, we boarded a train to Manchester. It seemed the perfect mode of transport in our love affair with all things industrial. I knew Manchester had been a hub for textile manufacturing during the Industrial Revolution. It drew workers to its mills, even children. Wages were high, but dismemberments and death happened. I thought of some of the bands I liked who I associated with Manchester: Magazine, Joy Division, The Fall, A Certain Ratio, and oddly enough, The Smiths, whose singer Morrissey was not even my brand of romantic crooner.

Staring out at the overall patterns of criss crossing railway tracks, billboards, and housing blocks swooshing past with increasing speed as we left London behind, I daydreamed about Manchester and all things "Mancunian"—a beguiling moniker identifying people from Manchester and their accents. Northern English. They dropped their "hs." "Really 'appy to see you." London accents were charming, but dropping consonants and vowel sounds was much more mysterious—blank spaces to color in. "Mancunian" evoked otherworldliness: Martian; Lilliputian; Mancunian—not an ad campaign a travel agency would ever pay me to create. I thought of Howard Devoto, the singer from Magazine, and how he looked like a bare lightbulb from the shoulders up. He was Mancunian, Martian-like.

Ian Curtis of Joy Division committed suicide two years before our trip to Manchester. Was his act a desperate escape from the mundane around him? I imagined a sense of loss, lost dreams, those dead appendages on factory floors. I imagined Ian Curtis with his shy expression. It seemed to me a mix of worry and crumbling identity. I had escaped the mundane environment of my own childhood, barely getting out alive. But I never lost hope. I trusted there was a rich world out there. Something better. I had only to find my place in it. I had things to do.

My impression of Manchester from the train was close to my image of my mother's birthplace, Duisburg, Germany. There, everyone worked the coal mines. My Oma still lived in the apartment she was born in, with a communal toilet down the hall, and her sister still lived in the apartment upstairs from hers. Behind their building was a communal garden space, where the neighborhood kaffeeklatsch would carry on about politics, children, and their deceased spouses. I imagined the same scenarios in the backyards here in Manchester.

When we arrived in the city, Larry and I were anxious to have a look at the Hacienda as soon as possible. Soon being, during the day. The club had opened four months earlier. We had traveled a long way from Chicago to exercise our membership privileges in the flesh, and we managed to coax a hapless employee into giving a daytime tour of the club. Not much to look at, aside from silver scaffolding framing out the dance floor. I wasn't sure what we were expecting to be different from other clubs.

We returned at night to a nearly empty room. It was a perfect opportunity to quiz my world-traveled traveling companion, Larry.

"Where are the Mancunians?! Where's the all-night party, the one that goes on and on and on (according to A Certain Ratio)?" I wanted to know. It certainly wasn't here at the Hacienda.

Maybe it wasn't in a club anywhere. It would be two years before I finally recognized that energy I longed for. I would see it at The Funhouse in New York, in the movements of the break dancers there, face down, flat on the floor one minute, flipped upright in a flash, then back down, one leg sweeping the floor under the other like a wiper blade gone mad. Nothing like that to see here in Manchester. Ho hum.

We sat on a banquette on the main floor of the Hacienda, a blue light washing over the dance floor. Was this all there was? Nightclubs here or in Chicago or New York or London just had different cliques, from what I could see. They were as suspicious and curious about us as we would be about them. What mattered at the end of the day was we'd made it to Manchester. We came and searched for a bit of ourselves in the industrial backdrops, where Anton Corbijn might have taken his iconic shots of Joy Division, in that peculiar light creeping around the commercial buildings of the city. This was our Mecca, for the moment.

We headed back to the train and back to London. Larry insisted we go to Harrods Food Hall and Selfridges and have the national breakfast fare: beans on toast. Not wasting any more time with clubs and intentional scene making, the last bit of cultural treasure hunting was appropriately saved for another national icon—Fred Perry. Polo shirts, specifically: Larry's was black. Mine, white. Very mod.

I said farewell to the driver of our black taxi as it pulled away from the terminal at the airport. We sat and waited for our flight in a lounge area at Heathrow surrounded by tourists, Krishna devotees, and that inevitable shifting rhythm of fresh faces passing by with baggage trailing behind. I wore my new leather jacket, in part to avoid the headache of declaring it at customs, but also to break it in and have a lighter bag to take home.

Absorbed in note taking and eavesdropping on the chatter of passing flight crews, I looked up briefly to check the flight updates. There, directly in my line of vision, a group of uniformed soldiers were passing in slow motion and in formation. There were five or six of them, moving forward inches at a time, then stopping in unison. The soldiers made no sound, said no words between themselves. They turned their heads ninety degrees and back, scanning the immediate area around them, just a few feet. They stepped a few more paces, repeating this exercise, holding military grade weapons against their bodies, alert to anything out of the ordinary. Their guns were the same color as their uniforms, blending in, making it difficult to see where one ended and the other began. I had never experienced this level of security in an airport. I guessed Heathrow was a constant target for the IRA. The soldiers' choreographed movements were beautiful but ultimately so sad. Larry didn't seem to notice. He had been in this airport before. I wondered what living in London was really like. And I wondered if Franke would ever come back to Chicago as I walked with Larry onto our plane for the flight home.

I thought about the moment I was first attracted to Larry. He was wearing a Fred Perry shirt and jeans, leaning against the kitchen counter in the house we shared with Carol and Christine. He was tall, a recovering Mod, a far cry from his upbringing in a conservative Jewish home in one of Chicago's north shore suburbs. He had the cultural chops to effortlessly coin my favorite dance floor comeback to anyone impinging upon my physical space:

"Groove elsewhere."

Larry made me laugh and not take things too seriously. He also liked to say, "Funny's a crutch, you know."

6

It was the fall of 1982. Cynthia Plaster Caster and I were becoming better friends the longer I stayed at Wax Trax. She came in at least once a week to say hello and take advantage of her celebrity discount. She made me laugh out loud with her matter of fact accounts of rock stars' "dicks" as they were plunged into her prepared container of dental alginates for their castings. I came to appreciate her reverence for Frank Zappa and her stories of living in LA and being supported and housed by Zappa, who treated her plaster casting work as she did. It was her art. I wanted to know why she hadn't written a book by now. I wanted to know what kept her motivated to keep pursuing her craft. Her answer: "It's all in the diaries, Gerda!"

I was fascinated by Cynthia's bold move to break from the groupie pack and establish herself as a desirable commodity for something else besides sex—well, sort of. On the whole I felt pity for other groupies. There wasn't anything life affirming in chasing sex with a bass player in the stall of a men's john backstage at a club. To me, that was death. To someone else, it was their ticket into the boys' club. No thanks.

Cynthia fancied herself a modern day Samuel Pepys, the greatest diarist of all time. Pepys was English, a member of Parliament, and kept a detailed diary of daily life in Britain during the years 1659–1660. It was fitting for Cynthia to be a fan, considering Pepys wrote candidly about his affairs with theater actresses, his distress over crowded city life, and living through such fun events as The Great Plague and The Great Fire of London. Yes, Cynthia versus Samuel Pepys. One writing about penises, the other about the plague. Close enough. Cynthia emulated Pepys's firsthand, blow by blow approach to getting the facts. I could barely contain myself when she started in on "dick" sizes—nary a penis in sight—widths, lengths in inches, textural nuances, and colors. Yes, it was everyday stuff in the life of a Plaster Caster.

During daytime hours, Cynthia worked a straight job as a typesetter, setting other people's words into place for printing, and she had not found the time or concentration to have a go at her own story. Unbelievable, to me. The way I saw it, she could quit typesetting and not have to worry about carpal tunnel syndrome in her hands ever again. After much discussion, and probably many drinks at Lucky Number, we decided I would transcribe her groupie diaries, and we would make an attempt at compiling her life's history. She had been trying for years to put a narrative together on her own.

Cynthia and I recorded seven hours of interview tapes. I tried to be as casual as she was matter of fact with my follow up questions. I wasn't one to giggle. On the tapes, I giggled a lot. My measured tone was broken up with awkward stifled laughs, while Cynthia soldiered onward. I felt like a teenager, learning sex ed for the first time:

"Gerda! His dick was so magnificent, I felt like crying!" Cynthia took great pleasure in using such elegiac words when it came down to describing her "babies."

I felt blessed to be tasked with creating an accurate historical record for the pop culture historians who would undoubtedly be tripping over one another writing academic papers on Cynthia Albritton, aka Cynthia Plaster Caster, when our project was finished. There was only one caveat: they would have to wait for "The Warden" (Cynthia's mother) to leave this mortal coil.

It was convenient for us to collaborate. Cynthia's apartment was near mine and a few blocks from Wax Trax. It was December, two months after the trip to England with Larry. Cynthia came into Wax Trax one night to pick up her records and talk about the week. A Certain Ratio was playing in town, and we planned on going to the show. We moved into the mail order room behind the boutique to talk about our book project in private.

During the conversation, Carol Blank walked in. She was a little peeved with her sometimes boyfriend and seemed as though she wanted to vent her disgust or disappointment. Mindful of all our "dick talk," Cynthia and I sympathized. It seemed odd Carol would confide in us. She was a fairly private person and had been so even when we were roommates. She had other friends now. Carol honed her reputation as a star DJ within a whole circle of people I didn't really know well. We didn't socialize together much at all when she and Christine moved into their own place and Larry and I were in ours. But we worked together all the time.

Cynthia tried to lighten the mood and tell Carol about our progress with the book. Carol was focused on something else entirely, almost rudely, and seemed distracted. She started to head back into the boutique. She turned to look at us and said something to the effect that "Yeah, well maybe everything will be different tomorrow." It seemed just an off handed comment underlining her frustration. It seemed obvious to us she needed a different boyfriend.

I came to work the next day and was busy setting up the back counter, when I got a call from Christine, Carol's twin. The customer at the counter asked me if I was alright, but by then Dannie Flesher was running by. You could count on seeing Dannie's cheery self, first thing any day of the week. Not this time. He looked stricken. "It's Carol," he said, as his features flashed by on the way to the backroom to deliver the news. Carol—our Carol—had taken her own life in the apartment she shared with her sister. Christine found her. Carol had hung herself.

How was this possible? My thoughts in that moment veered from sadness to anger.

I was furious with myself, as if I could have somehow prevented this, desperately running through imagined clues as to why she did it. And yet, I couldn't help wondering why Carol had lost hope, had stopped believing in herself. Sometimes nerve and believing in myself was all I had to keep me going. I couldn't begin to comprehend the numbing pain she must have had inside of her. I couldn't imagine Christine now having to live without her, to have that lasting image etched into her consciousness. As twins, the two of them could share secrets and painful thoughts, but not everything. No one can know another person that well.

Everyone in the store was utterly wrecked by the news. Longtime customers were coming up looking as devastated as we were. Everyone was crying. Carol was our friend. She was someone who always seemed so forward thinking, so ahead of the curve. She was a girl DJ with a coterie of fans in the clubs—an uncommon distinction in 1982. Carol was full of ideas and style. She was a trendsetter. She didn't seem any moodier or angst-ridden than the rest of us knuckleheads. And now, she was gone.

I embraced my memories of Larry, Carol, Christine, and I living together in that house for a year and enduring one of the coldest winters on record in Chicago. I thought of our buying trips to New York and going to clubs when Carol was spinning records. We worked together in an environment that promoted excess, but neither Carol nor I drank much or did drugs. We had dreams—other things to think about. We were above the kind of anxiety so many of our peers struggled with and tried to drown out—or so I thought.

I reached out to my mother, still attempting to put some order to something so illogical, so non-creative coming from such a creative person in my life. My Catholic mother was quiet on the phone for the longest time. Then I heard something human and plain, something I needed to hear: "It's not a sin for the really young and the very old. They don't know what they're doing." Here was a way out of this bewildering new feeling. She didn't consciously know what she was doing.

I never seriously considered attending Carol's funeral. I pulled myself together enough to go to the wake to try and offer emotional support to Christine. I avoided funerals. My last attendance at a funeral had been when I was sixteen, when my sister Uli died in a gruesome car crash on the way to Six Flags in Missouri. An eighteen-wheeler transporting coffins crossed the highway median and struck her car head-on. No funerals for me.

Unlike myself, Larry volunteered to be a pallbearer at Carol's service. When the day arrived, he stood in the kitchen of our apartment in a black trench coat, wearing the motorcycle boots we'd bought on our trip to England. "Carol would be smiling," I said, approving his choice of uniform for the service.

The mood in the apartment was deeply sad. None of this made sense. And now, it was officially time to say goodbye to Carol. What did that even mean? I had already explained to Christine that I wasn't going to be at the service. How then, would I say goodbye?

Larry was ready to leave and heading for the door, when something very odd happened: a tiny black-and-white bird suddenly appeared out of nowhere and flew past us. A songbird. Life seemed to be suspended all around us, except for the flitting singular bird. We followed the bird's flight path from room to room. Somehow it had managed to get into the apartment. We watched it bumping into walls and knocking little objects to the floor. It occurred to me it must have flown down the chimney of our fireplace, and now it had nowhere to go. It was December. It was desperately cold outside. I had the sense there was something awkwardly familiar in this two-toned body invading the otherwise gray day. The tiny thing flew around a bit more. I started crying. Larry and I looked at one another, opened a window, and let it go.

Carol Blank talked about being a singer. When she deejayed she was a force, setting the mood and pace of everyone else's escape into their own trance, on their own safe spot, on whatever dance floor was there. I remembered her smile, pure mischief on her face when she looked up from the turntables at a club. She had it—whatever "it" was. She had friends all over the music community in Chicago. Many private conversations in bars and between friends later, I was thankful she was very publicly honored by Ministry and Al Jourgensen, who dedicated their record With Sympathy to her memory. A chapter was ending, and the familiar urge to see something new was reappearing, overtaking my thoughts. I smoked more cigarettes. I switched to Dunhills for a while. I was looking for the language I needed to connect my thoughts and dreams again.

7

It was a new year—1983. After three years working full time at Wax Trax, it was time for a change. I was ready to go back to school. A larger university environment would guarantee new friends, wider discussions, and possible collaborations while I finished my degree in English. I transferred to the University of Illinois-Chicago and felt happy to move around the tiered walkways connecting its 1960s Brutalist-style buildings. I could step off the el and be right there on campus, just west of the Loop. It was time to break from the security of the Wax Trax home base.

Each time I met a new artist, I felt a longing to challenge myself creatively and make a life on my own. Being in that bubble at Wax Trax, going to shows for free, going to the bars, and getting comped drinks because all the club people knew I worked at Wax Trax—none of it mattered. Jim Nash encouraged me to move on. "You don't wanna be working for a record store the rest of your life—like me." Of course not. I wasn't a musician or a DJ. I had other aims in my life. I didn't think Jim was surprised, and I felt relieved I could work around my class schedule. I knew there had to be a way to make a living in the arts, writing or helping artists understand how to secure ownership of their intellectual property and maybe survive by making money through their work. Going back into a university environment was a way to complete something I had begun at a younger age in a healthier frame of mind, before being literally thrown to the floor and so narrowly averting death. I knew there was a reason I survived. I just had to keep moving, become leaner in thoughts and with the company I kept.

After Carol's suicide, I made a conscious effort to spend more time with the few women friends I had. I sat for high tea with Ruth at the Drake Hotel, slipping in a martini or two for a more modern feel. My photographer friend Sue Bowman and I would get together after classes at UIC or at her apartment. Sue was always late in getting out the door. I imagined her Jamaican travels and Jamaican boyfriend had shifted her pace to a slower rhythm. Mine was accelerating. My circle of "girl" friends was for the first time spreading outward. Larry and I split up. He was back in school, too, studying art history at the University of Chicago, and I was thrilled for him. I moved out and was on my own again in a tiny studio apartment far north on Damen Avenue.

I didn't understand why my new place was so inexpensive, until the lights were off that first night and the room slowly came alive with cockroaches. My closet soon doubled as part bedroom, part sanitized bunker, and I routinely swatted the kitchen counter to disburse the loitering residents. The building had one thing going for it—an elevator. I lived on one of the higher floors.

The Wax Trax record label occupied more and more of Jim and Dannie's time and money. Al Jourgensen had found some success with Ministry's first record, and moved to Boston for a time, where he met his future wife, Patty Marsh. Al returned to Chicago with Patty, and they moved into an apartment a few doors up from Wax Trax. Jim and Dannie were eager to work with Al again and keep the Wax Trax label forging ahead. Al's new wife Patty became pregnant with their daughter Adrienne, and after Adrienne was born, my coworker Ruth would often babysit. Ruth, Patty, and I decided to have a girls' night out at Ruth's place, where she and Patty came to the conclusion that I needed to finally pierce my ears. Patty had a piercing gun. I didn't know Patty well at all, but Ruth trusted she could do the job without any slips. It would be quick and painless.

I felt it was a dare to get me to look more glamorous, more feminine. I liked my style of lipstick and not much else just fine. Why was everyone so concerned with making me their project? Jim Nash perpetually played matchmaker (in his own head) and directed my attention to the day's in-store "catch." Manning a counter filled with leather and other cosmetic touches, who was I to stand there with no flair of my own, I suppose. It was time to quit kidding myself with clip on earrings, Patty said. Clip ons were uncomfortable and limited to heavy globs of costume-y fare. Ruth convinced me it was time to frame my face with "jewels." I looked in the mirror and wanted to see streams of light and color and geometric outlines against my cheekbones. I had a beautiful neck. I would start with earrings, then work my way into vintage Vera scarves or I could scuttle the jewelry updates altogether and try a new brand of cigarettes instead! What the hell were they thinking? For the moment, Ruth and Patty were not letting me out of arm's reach.

A quart of cheap vodka later, Patty brushed my earlobes with a vodka-soaked Q-tip, grabbed her piercing gun, and fired away. This must be what it's like in a women's prison, I mused—without the liquor, of course—or maybe? I felt slightly violated. My party mates for the evening looked victorious. I was a real woman now. I could wander in and out of airports in the simplest T-shirt and jeans and have a "finished" look to go along with my future travels. I was waking up to the reality that my passion for art and writing needed focus. Piercing my ears was the first step in a sustained pattern of physical and intellectual fitness, I thought. I didn't understand why, but I felt like a grownup. Onward.

I spent the next two years roaming the campus at U of I, taking German classes along the way, finally learning the formal rules I could only guess at when I was a child. I studied art history, labor history, geology, and English literature, finishing as an honors student in English. I reveled in researching Chicago's literary history. Poetry magazine was founded in the city. James Joyce's Ulysses was first published in The Little Review before being yanked by the censors for obscenity. I felt a thrill sitting in the dark in front of a screen and clicking layers upon layers of microfiche in the library to read ancient issues of the Chicago newspapers to follow the money of philanthropists who made fortunes in railroads and meat packing, and who often had no idea what constituted great art, but were willing to fund it to bring themselves up the social ladder and finally embossed in a plaque on a landmark building downtown.

I had the notion in my head now that I wished to be surrounded by original art, and the only way to do that was to buy it or swap writing work with an artist friend. I bought my first painting from my longtime friend Marnie Warren with money I'd managed to save from extra hours at Wax Trax. It would eventually take two years to pay it off. Marnie came by the apartment with my painting, accompanied by another friend of hers who bought art. He saw the drawing of Paul Taylor I had and asked if he could buy it. I told him to give half the sale price to me and half to Marnie and it would be his. My apartment couldn't accommodate two big pieces of art at once. It was a deal, and the exchange felt like kismet.

I didn't have a clear plan for supporting myself with the talents I had. I was too smart for a lot of careers, and too disinterested in having a business of my own. At the start of my last year of college, my honors mentor asked if I'd ever thought about taking the LSAT and going to law school. I hadn't. Growing up in the city the way I did, it was a huge accomplishment to get a bachelor's degree let alone go beyond that.

The practice of law was still a boys club. Another clique. In the mid-1980s there were few women lawyers; although, I had to admit Jim and Dannie had a female lawyer for Wax Trax matters, Linda Mensch. She was an entertainment lawyer. If I really wanted to do meaningful work connected to the arts, becoming an advocate for artists seemed the apex of involvement. In my spare time, I could write and do whatever I wanted. Making an actual living as a poet seemed more and more a remote possibility and teaching didn't interest me at all. There were no lawyers in my family history that I knew of, only the lone intellectual voice of a grandfather I never had the chance to meet, whose curiosity and sense of social justice I'd apparently inherited. I liked the idea of studying the law, and no one in the world ever successfully told me, "No, you can't do that." If I wanted it, I could do anything.

If I committed to law school it would be impossible to work during the academic year. There would be no time to have a social or work life, no time for anything but studying and going to class. Something in that concentration, that stoicism appealed to me. Oddly enough, I was tired of listening to music. Working in that environment all day wasn't satisfying on an intellectual level any more nor pleasurable as a way to pass time while I decided what to do with my own nonmusical talents. I bought a tape of Gregorian chants at Rizzoli's bookstore in Water Tower Place and immersed myself in human voices untreated, not synthesized, or mixed with instrumentation of any kind. Pure human generated sound. At home, I still played my copy of From Brussels With Love, a gorgeous compilation of twenty-one tracks—music by Harold Budd, Durutti Column, John Foxx, The Names, and other Factory bands. There were interviews with Brian Eno and the iconic French actress Jeanne Moreau. The Brussels tape I kept as a sentimental reminder of my time at Wax Trax.

Without the help of any prep courses, I took the LSAT and achieved an average score good enough for middle range law schools, but not the top. I applied to a handful of schools, all in Illinois except one—George Washington University in DC. I was waitlisted for DC and accepted at DePaul University's College of Law in June of 1985. The acceptance letter made it official—I had a new plan for my life. Wax Trax was my cultural safe haven for over five years, and I wanted more of everything outside of that world. More travel. More art. More knowledge and with luck, more money to see the world.

There was a sense of freedom, relief from uncertainty, in becoming a full-time law student with some part-time Wax Trax affiliation in the summer. I could keep up with store events and visit when I wanted to, but I was ready for a change. Leaving the record store clerk's life was necessary. I had that distinct feeling like visiting a foreign country on vacation and it's the last day. You want to remember this as it is right now. Your flight's in a few hours. You have to leave for the airport soon. You have to go.

I once lost all confidence in the legal system, but now I could learn how it worked, use it, and carve out a niche for myself being useful to others, especially artists, who in my view often needed all the help they could get. From my own dealings with many friends, I discovered artists are often bad at talking about what they do, as if they want to explain so you get it. But, as the great Frank

O'Hara once said about making art, "How can you really care if anybody gets it, or gets what it means? . . . Why hurry them along?" As a lawyer, I could at least bring some clarity and direction to the commerce end of things. That was my grand theory, anyway. My priorities were changing but heading into the unknown this time was again the right thing to do. Change is good for the soul, I convinced myself.

**

I was twenty-seven years old and currently involved with someone who was a skateboarder, a DJ, my coworker at Wax Trax, an all-around great guy, and eight years younger than me—Sean Joyce. That liaison was the perfect segue from the rolling party at Wax Trax, with its growing reputation as an influential independent record label, into the quieter world of contracts, copyrights, and constitutional law. Sean and his drinking buddy Joe Haggerty, two compact Irish boys looking for trouble, came to a party my old roommate Christine was having with her drinking buddy Jim Short. Sean and Joe walked in, commandeered the turntable in the apartment, and put on Madonna's "Into The Groove." Sean reached for Joe's fingertips like a ballroom dancer connecting with a partner. The two of them rose up and over to the middle of the room and with their free hands lifted their T-shirts to expose their navels, closed their eyes, and performed a belly dance to the music like good fanboys. So sweet. Let's have some fun.

During our brief time together, Sean explored his passion for graffiti. At night he roamed the subway tunnels, only to bomb the first underground station he knew I'd see in the morning as I made my way to classes at UIC. When the train rolled to a stop, there on a side wall would be some hasty message screaming my name and a sweet line drawing framing Sean's tag.

Practically no one I knew was surprised I was heading to law school. Once again, I had no guidance from my immigrant parents. They were stunned I was really doing this—becoming a lawyer—and offered to pay my rent for two years preempting any later speculation within their small circle that their oddly brilliant daughter had to dig ditches to pay for law school. My mother said Opa Max would be speechless in heaven. I was rekindling and carrying his intellectual torch.

As only my mother could say, *"Bei Frauen und Pferden, kuckt man auf die Zähne"* (With women and horses, look at the teeth). I had the spine and stamina of a racehorse. I thought of my grandfather, and his belief that words could be more effective than bullets to topple an enemy. Language could save your life, or it could take you down. Whose side was I on now?

8

Where Wax Trax and the music community had been so accommodating and accepting, law school was a completely different animal and an unfriendly place. Women were in the minority in class and in the profession. I didn't take it personally. I was there with as much desire to make use of my intellect as every man (and woman) in the class. Every individual there was in competition with every other. That was the nature of the practice—be an advocate, for something or someone at the expense of your opponent regardless of who they were. My classmates who were hyper-driven to be the best in class were obsessed with making law review. Earning a spot on DePaul's scholarly legal journal wasn't something I cared about. It was another exclusive club debating (in print) the pros and cons of cutting edge legal issues. I'd rather be in the trenches where the issues were unfolding. That was more my style.

I was comfortable being forced to rely upon my wits and learn to argue both sides of a case. I spent my adolescent and teenage years perfecting an identity to project to the world, and I felt comfortable now despite having no clear idea where I was going, with my thoughts focused only on studying the law and thinking about writing and art.

Constitutional Law saved my sanity the first year of law school, focusing a torrent of thoughts on bias and discrimination against women and minorities. It touched a nerve. After class, I would occasionally see my instructor Professor Blackman walking in Lincoln Park near the zoo. He lived close by, he told me, during one of these brief encounters as I walked through the park on my way home. Blackman was hard to miss, reed thin and tall, slightly leaning over as if he were readying himself to sit down in a chair or leaning in to make a point to a jury. Seeing him outside of a lecture hall he looked as vulnerable to life's mishaps as anyone else. In class I once raised my hand and asked, "What prompted the Anti-Defamation League to file amicus briefs in all of these civil rights cases?" As soon as the words stumbled from my mouth I knew why, and I felt like an idiot. Professor Blackman humored me, thankfully.

As a law student you realize the law is a living, evolving cultural force as much as music and art. As a law student you breathe the law, dream about the law, decode life around the law. You suddenly look at traffic accidents and natural disasters and purse snatchings in an entirely new way. There were nonobvious reasons why skyscrapers in the Loop took so long to go up: just stand at the clerk's office and zoning and permits counters where mechanics' liens are filed, and you finally know what they are, and why one person in that collection of contractors gets paid for installing windows that will look out across the south Loop and the Board of Trade building, with its statue of Ceres, goddess of agriculture, on its peak peering down, and pedestrians below on the street can safely go about their business. Every aspect of modern life is regulated or touched by laws around us. We can live with them, or we don't think of them at all. There were policy underpinnings to most laws, grift and payback supporting the rest. But when the stalls in the restrooms below the Walgreens downtown suddenly lose their coin slots because someone went to court and made a big enough stink over lack of access for the poor to use the facilities, there are no more dimes to collect for the chance to pee.

The law is a rich world of history and drama and people doing foolish things that get them arrested or land them in jail for crimes or for exercising their freedom of speech. I was so eager to figure it all out, to give in to this escapade of living an almost monastic life as a law student. It was a life of self-isolation. Self-examination. At times I wondered if I would ever find love in my life as a lawyer, and what would that look like, as I searched the faces of fellow law students and lawyers I brushed against in the halls of the Daley Center downtown where I'd go to study and do research in the law library. It was a place where I could get away from classes, from my apartment with its own monastic still life details. I found a collective peace in the faces hitting the books at the Cook County law library, some young faces, some old. I thought about that peace and the precise language in those books. They were all signposts telling me I was on the right path, where I should be in my life at the moment. I was twenty-seven years old, a "late bloomer." I was careful not to think about my zodiac sign's traits or the tarot card reading back in high school where it was determined I would be a late bloomer. Late for what? Why was I late—because I was a Capricorn?

In-class discussions at times tested my patience. The inflated ego of a classmate could easily strangle a discussion on criminal law. Some bloviating ass, usually a political science major, puffing up their chest and entertaining us with the history of the Magna Carta. I wanted to rise up out of my chair and yell, "Oh yeah? I once told Robert Plant to get over himself—what else ya got?" After a few months, I managed to connect with five other women to form a study group. Without the group, I don't think I would have survived.

As a law student there are basic principles to memorize and internalize. That internalization process became easier when I looked for the stories behind the cases we read. Who knew the bandleader Glenn Miller had tax problems unique to his fame. I learned the First Amendment was big enough to accommodate George Carlin's "Seven Dirty Words" only at certain hours of the day in certain forums.

In law school, it is impossible to memorize everything you're taught, and so you are trained how to think like a lawyer. That skill never goes away. As a lawyer you approach a single set of facts and throw analytical darts in multi-colors to see which hit the target and explode into the most colorful argument to gain the most points. Raised in an immigrant household, I was open to diverse opinions from people with diverse backgrounds. Studying law forced me to analyze the "why" to what motivated those people to say or do anything important affecting their lives.

I was beginning to make sense of where I didn't want to go in the legal community. I didn't want to have anything to do with corporate law, doing government work, or insurance defense, all fields my classmates were hoping to pursue. What I wanted was to represent and advise artists in how to protect their work and what to expect from galleries and record labels. I studied copyrights, trademarks, and patents. The required classes for all students included Constitutional Law and Contracts, necessary groundwork for representing artists.

The law school was in the Loop on Jackson. On days when I needed to reconcile my interest in a rather staid profession with my love for the arts, I could walk up Michigan Avenue, past the sculpted lions guarding the entrance to the Art Institute and a sliver of sidewalk where for years the artist Lee Godie would stake her claim for outdoor exhibition space. Lee Godie was self-taught, in her seventies, and a prolific Chicago legend. By appearance alone she could easily be mistaken for a bag lady—homeless. She would stand to the side of the front entrance to the museum, opening her oversized coat to flash a drawing for sale to passersby—but only those people she thought worthy. Collectors stalked her designated sidewalk gallery waiting for a glimpse of her new art. They were more often ignored than offered a canvas to buy. Lee Godie had a place in my heart reserved for outsider art. She did her own thing. And I imagined her ghost waving as I passed along the stone fence and headed north on Michigan Avenue for the long walk home.

The walk was five miles north along a winding lakefront path to Montrose Beach and back to my new apartment. I had moved again, away from the cockroaches, closer to the lake. If I ever moved to another city, it would have to be somewhere close to a large body of water. The water was freedom. It leveled my thoughts, skipping like stones above the waves.

My parents now lived one block north of my building in a high-rise condo with a panoramic view of Lake Michigan and the beach. They bought the apartment with proceeds from the legal settlement paid from my sister Uli's car crash. My parents and other surviving families of the victims in the crash filed suit against the truck driver, the tire company, and others for wrongful death. My parents lost their eldest child senselessly, and now they could move forward, out of their grief with the steady landscape of tide changes at Montrose Beach and Lake Michigan, as seen from every window in their apartment.

I visited my parents when I had time. They had simple needs, having survived the Nazis and the Depression. My father and I were never close, but he took advantage of the fact that I was now in law school. He was an inventor and assumed I could and would help him explore patent possibilities for himself. When I reminded him I was really busy with law studies, he'd look away annoyed and say, "So you think you're so tough . . ." It was an odd choice of words coming from someone who left post-war Germany with his wife, an infant, and my three-year-old sister Uli to emigrate to the United States. He was tough. As a fourteen-year-old in Poland he was wrenched from his church choir by the Nazis and spent the duration of the war in forced labor. Self-reliant and controlling, my father was unable to compliment anyone else's successes after the war, especially his own children's. "So, you think you're so tough." In the back of my mind, I felt guilty sometimes for not making time to help him with his patents, but I had no time. I steered him in the right direction with earlier ideas he'd worked on and gave him the name of a patent lawyer to pursue the rest.

My friend Ross reminded me I alone had gotten myself to law school, and I needed to let the guilt about my father go. He thought my father's comment was a curiously juvenile spin on pursuing higher education. I told Ross my father had no vocabulary for what I was doing because he had always worked with his hands.

Ross and I met while I was working at Wax Trax, and we stayed in touch as I transitioned into law school. While still a student at the University of Iowa, he would show up some weekends at Wax Trax with a posse of Iranian expats, students who were into hardcore. Ross later moved to Chicago to finish his degree at UIC, my alma mater.

Ross played drums in bands and worked as a librarian at UIC part-time. I knew he was solidly a member of my society when he walked into Wax Trax one afternoon and started singing "White Horse" before even saying hello. "White Horse," crafted by a Danish duo as an anti-drug ditty, had had the opposite appeal. It was danceable and mildly dumb, an ideological cross between "White Lines" and "Jungle Boogie." It was the B-side of an otherwise forgettable single, which we were both slightly embarrassed to admit we liked—a lot.

Early in our friendship I would meet Ross at the Red Lion, an "English-style" pub across from Wax Trax. Over fruit and cheese platters and Weissbier (decidedly non-English fare) we discussed Foucault's philosophy, the ordinariness of living in Iowa, and music.

Ross and his girlfriend invited me to my very first Indian dinner at Moti Mahal on Belmont down the street from Tut's, where we'd all seen scores of bands play. I arrived early and was nauseated by the smell of curry and put off by the prison-issue metal plates segmented to keep everything about your dinner separated from everything else. But I was curious enough about Indian cuisine to overlook new nauseating food smells. I found the yogurt sauce visually benign enough to encourage my senses to go back a second time. I was slow to see what everyone else raved about, trying different vegetarian dishes, and taking home samosas that were cheap, crunchy, and simply delicious. Moti Mahal grew on me. Its attached grocery store was where I eventually found henna for my hair, disguised in cardboard packaging with decades old graphics and instructions in Hindi.

Back in college, Ross and I were both English majors and broke, like everyone else we knew. Grants and scholarships kept me in class, while my record store hours paid the rent. At one point the English department was holding its annual awards presentation with special recognition going to select honors students. I was awarded a small scholarship of $1,500. Ross came by for the ceremony as a show of friendship and to rub shoulders with the department heads and graduate students. I excused myself to the ladies' room before my name was announced, returned, and somehow managed to collect a tiny strip of toilet tissue now poking out from the heel of my summer sandal. Ross noticed it. The student sitting next to him noticed too and pointed to the floor. This was the stuff of a story I'd read somewhere: ingénue, not quite sophisticated and polished as she would have the world believe, unwittingly exposes herself. I was embarrassed but couldn't exactly in an elegant way reach down and dislodge the tiny traveler stuck to my shoe. I kicked myself for not wearing different shoes—as if that mattered.

Thankfully, my mind was doing its usual post-lunch daydreaming, and I suddenly remembered a story about an American author, possibly Gore Vidal. The author, bored with being interviewed in yet another pricey Manhattan restaurant, had the idea to test the integrity of his fame. When his salad course arrived, he began picking at the greens and popping them in his mouth with his fingers. No fork. No one noticed, not the interviewer nor any other diners. Taking my Gore Vidal cue, I kept eye contact with the awards presenter as I made my way up to the lectern to accept my award and imagined everyone else in the room was sporting confetti strips of toilet tissue on the heels of their own shoes. I deserved this award. I shook my professor's hand with a quick thank you, smiled and stared straight ahead. It felt so easy to distract with nothing more than sheer confidence.

Ross was now pondering going to law school himself. We saw each other occasionally on a friendly basis while he applied to schools and I was beginning my first year. He and his Iowa girlfriend had by then split up. I met with him a few times to talk about law school life. In Constitutional Law we were focusing on racial discrimination and the Brown vs. Board of Education case. I was happy to argue social policy with a non-law school friend, who was interested in these things too. I gave Ross a copy of the Brown opinion to read for himself how the case had played out. It was history. Discrimination mattered. As a woman, I knew that intimately. I had been scrutinized twice over, despite having stellar grades and extraordinary test scores, hand-picked for the privilege of joining the boys at Lane Tech High School, with their own very average academic records.

My friend Ross had all the attributes of a perfect partner in crime. He was smart, tall, handsome, and someone I could talk to easily about art. He worked at the university library, and for all I knew would have a degree in library sciences when he finished. A librarian in the making—theoretically, he was a man after my heart. He laughed at my piss-on-everything attitude and admired my hennaed hair. Ross understood me better than most and was not very forthcoming about his personal life, which I didn't really mind. Our conversations were stretching later into the evenings.

I woke up one morning at his apartment. It was the weekend. I could afford this tiny pocket of social engagement, I thought. It was a Sunday in October 1985—the day of the Chicago Marathon. Ross lived in a building along the race route. I stood in the coffee room of the apartment, staring out the window, watching the fastest female runner alive straddled by a motorcade in a steady trot down Waveland Avenue. Joan Benoit was doing the impossible. She was running for her life to be the best. I wondered what that meant. Best by whose standards? I had placed myself on this path of discovering what else I was capable of in my own life. I was moving forward. Forward was good. It was what I had, for now. And, for the first time in my twenty-seven years, I soon discovered something else. I was pregnant.

It never occurred to me that I could become pregnant using birth control. It never occurred to me to choose to continue a pregnancy as a full-time law student—unattached, unemployed, and not ready for motherhood. I was shocked when I found out, staring as the color changed on the home testing stick I bought at a drugstore downtown after class. In 1985, having an abortion was as logistically uncomplicated as ever. I knew where the Planned Parenthood clinic was closest to where I lived. I knew from experience with friends the procedure was safe, relatively quick, and I needed to have a friend with me to take me home afterwards. A regular handful of protestors picketed out front, but I knew my legal rights, too. It was my decision alone if I wanted to have a baby or not, and no one else's business. There was one overriding reason why I used birth control: I had no desire currently to have children. Period. I became pregnant a block and a half from where I was born, on Racine and Clark, and I was very unhappy.

For all of the swell insights we shared, I couldn't stand telling Ross I was pregnant and had very little money for an abortion. I was a first-year law student. I couldn't foresee having a child with Ross. I told him when I found out. He knew, as I did, there would be no baby. I didn't know he was still seeing his ex. In the next week, he simply left a small sum of money on the table in my apartment. It was what he could afford. A friend from Wax Trax kindly escorted me to the clinic. Afterwards, I was relieved and a bit overwhelmed, to be thrust into such an emotional predicament I couldn't ignore.

There was little friendship with Ross after that. The geometry of friendship, our friendship, dissolved quietly. I buried my head in my books, wondering how I was going to make this matter—all of it. Law school. Pregnancy. Directions in life. Sometimes I had doubts. Studying law was like entering the priesthood, a training for some higher purpose. The routine of classes all day, coming home to my apartment, and dropping legal pads and books on the back stoop to sit, review, and read for a few more hours. The door across from mine would open occasionally, and the black guy who lived there would stop for a minute and tell me about his day. I needed that. He was training for the FBI. We shared a life trajectory of sorts: both kids from the inner city, training our bodies and intellects to be weapons or shields in someone else's battle.

I mentioned that to him once. He disappeared into his apartment and was soon back on the landing with a six pack of some brand of imported beer. "I got this as a gift. I don't drink." He held it out for me.

"I don't either, really. I'll put it in my fridge in case someone comes over," I said. I was once again actively abstaining from the trappings of a social life, so the odds of company were slim. I took the beer and stashed it away for that unforeseeable rainy day. But for now, I was leaving behind virtually everything of my life up to this point to focus on the law once again.

I watched as one girlfriend after another got engaged or married or pregnant with their first child. Ruth at Wax Trax was marrying Bill from Wax Trax. Bill was one of my old roommates. Two law school friends were expecting. Did I have a desire for any of that? No. That life didn't look like fun at all. What did look fulfilling, then? Wearing tailored suits and Italian leather heels, crossing the federal plaza downtown to stop at Berghoff's for cocktails with my girlfriends— that sounded like a lot of fun. Give me that, instead. Drinks at the Berghoff were especially gratifying when we discovered women were denied access to its bar prior to 1969. Outrageous. Cheers, ladies! One law school friend had her nose fixed over the summer; another began a course of Accutane to rid her face of acne. I was content with my looks and frankly didn't understand how such intelligent women could agonize over law books and their own vanity at the same time—too much work.

Law school was becoming less and less engaging and more soul draining. My Contracts professor, a native of Barbados, gleefully employed the Socratic method—which I loved—but not much else stimulated my need for the new. Professor Leacock was in fact a barrister and would present himself in full white wig and barrister robes for special events, a dramatic contrast to his natural black Afro sculpted high atop his head. He habitually wore slightly outdated suits (flared pants) with the confidence of a fashion icon. I admired his intellect and graceful attack mode when standing in front of our class and indirectly making a student look and feel like an idiot if they didn't directly address his query: "Feel free to formulate your own hypothetical on your own time Ms. Lamb, but your answer in the here and now is incorrect!" He taught us to really listen to our opponents and our clients.

Some of my fellow students wore button-down shirts and business casual wear to class. I indulged my own fashion sense, appearing one December day in gray wool men's trousers, a mauve and gray sweater, heather-gray wool cropped jacket, and black patent leather men's oxfords that were the last clothing purchase I'd made at Wax Trax the previous summer. The shoes were the only non-thrift store item I had on. My study group ally Leslie, who was from New York and shared a broader view with me of how professional women should dress, ran over and whispered, "Oh my god . . . you're a symphony in gray."

I had my detractors and critics. A baby-faced male classmate sporting a typical preppy look and a paunch, who had a common Chicago South Side Irish surname, approached me in the hall after class.

"Nice cop shoes," he snidely remarked.

"Only you would know," I answered. He came from a family of police officers, with a judge on the bench. I brushed off the critique. What possesses some people? I asked myself. Two years later, universal karma would exact its own critique of Mr. South Side Irish. When the hour arrived for us all to sit for the summer bar exam, my critical colleague was caught blatantly attempting to copy another candidate's exam. The jig was up, as they say in some legal circles. The bar examiners hauled him out of the room, and one fat Irishman was forever barred from the practice of law.

The lack of camaraderie, the intense competition, and sometimes outright nastiness in law school didn't align with my ideas about art and generally raising social consciousness. This law thing had to serve a higher purpose, I thought. What were my options as a student? I looked over the job boards outside of DePaul's career office, scanning for part-time internships. One attracted my attention. I applied for an internship with the Chicago office of the ACLU.

Working for the ACLU was neither a fashionable nor desirable option at the time for many of my classmates, who were consumed with making friends in large, corporate law firms. My classmates were inspired by the glamour of LA Law on television every week, while I happened to be engrossed in my own thoughts and ideas about constitutional law. I was thrilled when the ACLU called me for an interview. During the interview, I stressed my interest in civil liberties was borne out of daily life with parents who'd both lived through Nazi occupation as teenagers in Germany. I didn't need the primer on basic human rights. I heard about it every day growing up. I was hired.

I was where I wanted to be. The ACLU and I were going to get along just fine, at a time when my classmates were groveling for mentors in the business and government sectors of Chicago. Law for me was never strictly about making money or climbing the social or political ladder. Whose company would I be keeping when I'd theoretically reach the top rung? Recognition in dollar amounts seemed so pedestrian. I had loftier aims, to champion ideas, images, radical new music—something—and keep my down-to-earth friends and my sanity.

The internship with the ACLU meant working alongside some of the best attorneys practicing in the city. Their job was to protect individual rights and liberties. I wanted to breathe that air. I wanted to be on that cutting edge. These lawyers could all be working in the private sector for double or triple their salaries, but the work and opportunities for notoriety were more enticing at the ACLU. Within the office one attorney was lead on First Amendment cases, one did prisoner and institutionalized persons' rights, and another handled the reproductive rights cases. When there was a protest rally downtown, I would see Jane Whicher, the First Amendment expert, heading out the door. She had to make sure "her people" were safe.

The most comprehensive project I was assigned at the ACLU was to research AIDS legislation coming down the pike in each of the fifty states. It was the mid-1980s. Patients' identities, their privacy, and access to care, all of these considerations were unfolding with the growing masses of primarily gay men who were afflicted or being tested and treated. It was heartbreaking each time I'd see a pale face dotted with lesions on a frail, young body seated in the handicapped section of the Sheridan #151 bus while I made my way downtown to class.

There was a great sense of calm urgency in the offices of the ACLU. I loved being there. Like being at Wax Trax, I felt invited into someone's treehouse, privy to the cutting edge of ideas, and safely harbored away from dramas outside.

Reporters occasionally arrived at the ACLU offices looking to snag a soundbite from Harvey Grossman, our legal director. Mary Ann Childers from the local ABC station showed up very early one morning sporting a leopard-print top and stilettos with her camera crew in tow making a grand entrance. "Harvey . . . Harvey! Can we get your thoughts on . . ." as she hurried into a conference room already prearranged for the visit, upsetting the usual calm of the place. Our office was nothing fancy. She looked overdressed, but she was doing her job, I guessed. Breaking news.

Harvey crisscrossed yellow police tape over his office door when work took him out of town; it was a curious way to keep cleaning crews and nosey others out. What surprised me most about the small group of lawyers working so closely together on important constitutional issues was the reality that they had their differences of opinion about the law relevant to other causes in the office. They were not all in agreement on every issue. Some weren't as devoted to prisoners' rights as their colleague Ben was. Abortion rights weren't necessarily foremost in the minds of others, as they were with Colleen. I was surprised to learn one of the attorneys had great success in filing for attorneys' fees after cases ended in the courts. To think these lawyers thought about money at all! There was a real sense of being in the moment at the ACLU. I loved it and extended my internship until they had to let me go to allow some other law student the opportunity to do grunt work.

My "plan" after law school was evolving—practice entertainment law, in whatever way that was possible. I didn't realistically expect there would be money in this specialty, having known a solid cross section of the arts community in Chicago by the time I stepped foot in a law library. I expected to have to build a practice with a fair degree of bartering back and forth—a good way to start an art collection, I thought. I debated theories about justice with one crowd and theories about art with another. Both were equally perplexing.

To counterbalance the philosophical with the practical in a legal context, I signed on for a year at DePaul's legal clinic to help people with limited finances navigate routine legal matters. The clinic was full of women; the only man employed there was the director. The other attorneys and support staff were all women. I was mentored and welcomed. As a student attorney, I couldn't sign my name to any documents, but I could research and draft the briefs. My paperwork had to be signed by a staff attorney after review. I did often go to court, escorting husbands and wives through the court system for simple no-fault divorces and social security questions. These were lawyers' bread and butter cases, routine and repetitive but good for flexing muscle memory.

I'd always believed that serendipity was a myth. I'd always believed we find what we seek, even if we do it unconsciously. And true to my theory, as if the universe wanted to bring me right back to the immediacy of the ACLU, a novel healthcare case appeared in the legal clinic, and I was on it. Literally, it was a matter of life or death for one little girl. Her parents came into the clinic with what they thought was a straightforward claim against their health insurance company. Their three-year-old daughter had cerebral palsy. The insurance reps began denying physical therapy treatments for their little girl, telling the parents the treatments weren't covered under their policy and (because of her condition) their daughter was going to die anyway. The family's income put them squarely in the middle class and normally would have disqualified them from the clinic's low-cost services. But these desperate people were selling everything they had and draining their savings to pay for their child's treatments to continue.

By this time, I knew enough contract law to focus on particulars of their policy and away from the obvious "ick factor" and sheer mean-spirited responses to their pleas for mercy. I felt there must be some policy reasons to argue in front of a court. The insurance company had already paid for some treatments, why not continue? I delved into the case law and called the attorneys on the other side to set up a meeting. The law was clear: exclusions to treatment had to be specifically named in a policy, any policy. Some examples were no "experimental" treatments, or more common at the time, no birth control. The couple's child wasn't receiving experimental therapies—the hospital staff had a standard protocol for these kinds of cases. The insurer simply didn't want to pay.

The day arrived for my appointment with the insurance company's lawyer. I walked over to one of the nondescript, modern glass towers on Michigan Avenue, a few doors south of the river. My finger hit the floor button in the elevator, and I decided to treat this meeting like an investigative reporter. Insurance companies had excellent litigators, trained to make plaintiffs go away with a feeling that they were the ones engaging in bad behavior, and by the way, "We can hold our breath for as long as it takes and still keep our costs down." They could afford the high rent glass towers, which to my disappointment were not even Mies Van Der Rohe designed. They'll take me about as seriously as the guy who shines their shoes in the subway tunnel below the Daley Center, I thought. Aside from the money, I couldn't fathom why anyone would choose to do insurance defense. Political decisions level moral considerations, I guessed, as I waited in the glass and stainless steel reception area for my appointment with the other side.

When she appeared promptly on the hour, I vowed to reserve judgment against the young, black woman before me, who was my age. But I couldn't, I simply couldn't get past her standard fit dark suit, standard size diamond engagement ring, and possible lunch-break makeover executed by trained hands at one of Marshall Field's endless makeup counters, impassable to any woman walking by wearing professional clothes. Fields was only a five-minute walk away. The woman greeting me possessed a demeanor so formal and stiff, as if this were the one manicured, scripted performance of her day. Sit through many training videos? I wondered. Big law firms invested big dollars into their freshman attorneys, and they expected results.

Picking up cues from the attorney's accent, I guessed she was from Chicago. Being a woman, of a minority, in a profession which was at best civil to women lawyers, I hoped she didn't harbor some feelings of entitlement or superiority being on staff at a big-name firm. I thought I'd keep things simple.

"The law's clear. Physical therapy treatments are covered under my clients' policy. There are no exclusions preventing coverage," I told her.

I hoped she would offer some hint of settlement for my clients, who were by appearance alone very sympathetic plaintiffs. Their child embedded in a wheelchair when out in public would be a major distraction for potential jurors to linger over. (Why am I even here?)

"I disagree. The case law is not so black and white," she said. "We're not prepared to make such blanket concessions at this time."

Sonofabitch, I thought. They want to explore their options, let the clock run on this kid's life. So, my meeting was for show, billable hours, see what the low-rent plaintiff's attorney looks like and has to say. I couldn't wait for the elevator doors to close, to shut out the corporate number crunching, actuarial tables, and corporate bonding exercises the lawyers in that office undoubtedly embraced in pursuit of money and their own egos. They had a formula for my client's life in place already, following their quick cost/benefit analysis. The stalling was like politics—a game. It was a dirty way to make a living, denying medical care to people who really needed it, to pad their client's bottom line.

The case dragged on, with the insurer no doubt betting the parents would either run out of money or simply give up when their child died. By the end of my final year of law school, the insurance company was still fighting. When I called the clinic again two years later, the staff told me the company finally settled, and a sick little girl had some peace of mind. It was gratifying to have helped one family negotiate with a battalion of attorneys hired for the specific purpose of denying payment for vital care. My long hours of studying, zero social life, and mental exhaustion became the currency for these remote tangible victories.

9

In the summer of 1986, after my first full year of law school, I worked for a few hours at Wax Trax when Jim Nash was feeling generous, and I really needed the money. I was working upstairs when Judy Pokonosky stopped in to say hello. Judy took over my job at Wax Trax when I left for law school. At the moment she was on break from working at the store and was hired to go on tour with the band Ministry as their merchandise person. When she came upstairs to the boutique, Judy insisted that I really needed to meet this "great guy." Whenever anyone told me I needed to meet someone, I considered that advice on par with someone recommending a great new restaurant. Tastes are all different. My great is not necessarily your great.

Judy told me this great guy was a musician. He played bass with Ministry. He spoke German and was really smart. I played along. My body language was always the same when one of my friends told me I needed to meet someone or I'd really like someone. I listened attentively, maintaining eye contact and what appeared to be an open mind. I always indulged my friends their fantasies and concerns about my love life. Especially Wax Trax friends. Especially Jim Nash. I would nod, give a look of having suddenly remembered my purpose in life, then say, "I gotta go," and off I'd flee in the opposite direction. Unfortunately, when Judy brought this great guy up the stairs that day, I was cornered. I was picking through a UPS box.

"Gerda, this is Ion," she said.

Oh brother. Great—someone so full of himself he changes his name to accommodate the excess. Who was this guy already? I was fairly uninterested in the current Ministry hype and was happy to let Jim Nash be their cheerleader. I frankly had no time to keep up with music much at all now. I listened to Gregorian chants at home when I studied. That brought me peace. And Ministry hadn't ever done much for me anyway so, "Hi there."

My first impression of Paul (Ion) Barker: He was wearing a beret. Okay, he had some style. Why was Judy so convinced he was right for me? On the other hand, I wasn't sure anyone was right for me at this point in my life.

My second impression: He was too tall and thin, possibly bald—he was wearing a beret and had shaved his sideburns to the top of his ears, similar to how I'd done mine before law school. His manner of leaning over and trying to talk to me on the other side of the counter was almost comical because of his height (6'4") and frame (170lbs). He appeared like a scientist observing a specimen in a cage. I was someone he wanted to study, I thought. It made me uncomfortable. He seemed very European. I couldn't get past the beret. Was he French or something? (He was, in part.) We chatted about Ministry's show coming up soon at the Riviera Theater. Was I coming to the show? Probably not. Classes would be in session again. Maybe I could stop by the label party Jim and Dannie were having this weekend? Yeah, maybe. I was already going to Ruth's bridal shower, but maybe after. (Again—why did Judy think this guy was so special?)

The following day, not having anywhere else to be after Ruth's shower and still dressed in my long, knit tube-skirt and ballet flats, I took a cab over to the record label. My co-worker Kevin Lovell was in the kitchen, and it was a relief to see someone who was always interested in talking about art shows coming up, whose work was good, and whose put us to sleep. Kevin and I wisecracked for a while, standing in the kitchen as a dozen people passed through to the back porch or to the front of the apartment to mingle. We turned our attention to a pile of absurdly ugly painted canvases someone had left on the outside deck. I noticed Ion sitting at a makeshift table with Dannie Flesher, Franke Fun, and Franke's boyfriend Dave. At one point I looked over again, and Ion flashed a smile and went into the office to talk to Jim Nash.

I entertained myself studying faces of people arriving, trying to come up with witty things to say in response to the inevitable, "How's the law treatin' ya?" I was already mentally preparing myself to go back. My second year of law school was coming up and would be no less taxing than the first. I wanted to stay physically in shape over the summer, doing my usual five-mile walks every day, and I had a schedule. I needed to go home.

I asked Kevin if I could share a cab ride home with him. I said, "Wiedersehen" to someone in the kitchen. Ion creeped into the room and said, "Well now. You look like you're getting ready to go." What is up with this guy, I thought to myself. "I think you should come into the front room for a while," he said. At that moment, despite my mental exhaustion, I felt a completely unfounded faith that this conversation would be fun. Why not? Something in his voice attracted me. Here was someone new who was obviously very interested in me, and he had a rather kind demeanor. And I finally took a long look at his face. He was dead handsome. We carried on a little bit in German, a little bit in code.

Ion and I talked for an hour about language and art, living in Germany, and Jim and Dannie. He told me he learned to speak German while in the army. He was stationed there for a couple of years. It didn't register in my mind at the time that he might have been at the same base where my parents met. Ion spoke German without an accent, from what I could tell. Impressive.

My attention span was beginning to fade with the late hour, and I really needed to go. I told Ion we might see each other again if he was going to Ruth and Bill's wedding. I bid farewell to Mr. Ion and took myself home in a cab.

Ruth and Bill's wedding took place on October 6th. Lou D'Angelo, another Wax Trax alum, was still cutting my hair at the time and was my date for the evening. After the reception at the Belmont Hotel, Franke Fun, his partner Dave and some other people were going for coffee at the Wagon Wheel on Clark Street. I liked hanging out with those guys, so I tagged along. Ion was there too.

We again chatted exclusively, and he told me he was leaving for London with Al Jourgensen "soon." They were working on a new Ministry record. They would be living there for six months. The more we spoke, the more I felt a connection to him. Ion had a lot of opinions and shifted easily from talking about music to wanting to know what it felt like to study law. "Let me have your address. I'd like to write to you when we're settled," he told me.

I left the restaurant, and as I stood there hailing a cab on the corner at Diversey and Clark, I was surprised I felt as though I already missed him—someone I barely knew. I wanted to know this person more, and he was leaving the country. Terrific. For such a "great guy" he had really bad timing.

I spoke to Jim Nash a few days later and told him, "I think I finally met someone I really like." It only took twenty-eight years. Jim was very interested and always vigilant about my sex life. I told him it was Ion. "Oh, GREAAAT, GIRL!" And in typical Jim fashion, "He's got a big one, you know. I've seen it."

A few weeks later, reaching into my mailbox I pulled out a letter with English postage stamps across the top, addressed in the hand of someone practiced in letter writing—or at the very least, someone practicing their own stylized vocabulary. Curious. What was the significance of this man writing to me now? I was busy but amused by the intimate details of Ion's daily life. He tried to simplify in layman's terms what a Fairlight did, and why he was so excited to play with it in the studio. It felt good to have a long-distance pen pal. On some raspberry-colored stationery I had sitting in a drawer I wrote back with some witticism about being "LIVE . . . and DIRECT," as if I were some dub superstar. I was relieved to have this common music connection, a shared history, even if it was a fiction for the time being.

I constantly ruminated over language and clichés and reviving pet phrases from earlier eras. Ion found that amusing. I would say things like, "Solid, Jackson," at the most inappropriate times. I didn't care. I didn't have to go anywhere but my mailbox to be connected in this small way to the music community I was not really much a part of anymore. Ion wanted to know more about me, what I liked. I told him Frank O'Hara was one of my heroes in the literary world. He told me about dreams he'd had the night before. There was no mention of a definite return to the States. We exchanged a few letters, mine vanishing into the mailbox in a mauve-colored twist of the wrist.

I spent my waking hours studying or preparing to study the law. My schedule had no room for socializing, other than the occasional late lunch and drinks at The Berghoff with the women in my study group. I had faith in momentum alone. It was my mantra: "Keep moving."

***

The new year came and went without much fanfare. My classwork consumed my intentions, leaving little room for idle thoughts about my pen pal overseas. I longed for spring when I could resume my walks at the lakefront.

Early in March, my phone rang at home. There were no cell phones yet, so anyone calling either heard you live when you picked up or had the pleasure of hearing your voice on the answering machine. I happened to be home. I was not expecting to hear Ion's voice. I suppose I never expected him to keep tabs on me.

"Where are you?" I asked, mentally trying to calculate the time difference in my head, when he said, "I'm at Wax Trax." I tried to adjust my thoughts to my schedule for the day. "Let's have dinner."

I made reservations for dinner at Cornelia's, an intimate restaurant down the street from Chicago Trax recording studio. I knew the chef at Cornelia's, Rich Ladd. Maybe we'd get a good table. "I'll wait for you on Halsted. I'm wearing my blue leather jacket," I told Ion. And there, a little more than six months after our first meeting, we met again.

During dinner, Ion was so animated trying to describe what he and Al Jourgensen were working on, he reached over the table and tipped his full martini glass in front of me. Maybe there was more to this guy. I still couldn't believe he was sitting right there. I kept looking away, feeling as though I was losing myself in the darkness of the restaurant. I hadn't had a proper date in months. The last time, I had dinner with a law school classmate and was shocked he knew so little about art. It was exasperating. But here, staring me in the face was a lot of what I wanted. I was probably smiling way too much.

He asked me how much longer before I became a lawyer. Another year and a half of classes, then the bar, I said. I then told him I was exactly where I needed to be.

"You're ambitious. I love that. Not many women I meet are." He looked at me again, as if he were examining a rare archaeological find.

"Well, what's the point in standing still, settling? Settling for what?" I asked. "Besides, no one's ever told me, 'No, you can't do that.' If they had, I wouldn't have listened anyway."

Our conversation picked up from where we left it six months before, dissecting theories on language and making art. I said, "I think we're all walking collections of words. Words of mine, attract words of yours. Tone of voice is an element, like heat."

He looked at me, then said the most peculiar thing: "I love women." Just like that. Like another person would say, "I love chocolate." It was so innocent—or arrogant—but such a tell. He needed women in his inner circle? Was this something rehearsed, some Marcello Mastroianni moment, what? Was he unconsciously letting me know he'd occasionally lose his mind over someone in a crowd? Was he looking at women as simple objects of beauty to admire? That comment drove me crazy. I couldn't fathom saying, "I love men," to anyone. Certainly not to my potential new boyfriend. I needed to stop over thinking everything. For god sakes he's a really nice, talented guy, and here he is excited to tell me about the Indian curry he'd had in London. And about Lee "Scratch" Perry. Something about his limbs—knocking over his drink, crossing and recrossing his long legs, and checking under the table to be sure he wasn't stepping on my shoes. It was so charming. That's it . . . he had a body like Veruschka. Oh no. His sense of humor was effortlessly syncing up with mine.

I collected my thoughts, lit another cigarette, and noticed a piece of bread crumb attached to the freshly shaved stubble on his upper lip. He's even handsome with food on his face. He kept talking about the mix he and Al were working on. He wanted to know what my plans were after dinner. I looked directly at him, lifted my index finger to my own face, and proceeded to mock brush something from my lip to indicate he should do the same.

"What. I have something there?" he asked, lifting his napkin, and wiping the crumbs away.

He sat back in his chair staring at me for a second, then said, "You know, that's the kindest thing anyone's ever done for me." I believed him. "Some people can be really tacky," I said. "Or tack-LESS," he noted.

After dinner, I planned to check on my parents' apartment nearby, off of Lake Shore Drive. They were on a trip. "I'll go with you. I could use a walk." The two of us walked a mile up Broadway and over toward the lake. We entered the building, I waved at the doorman, and we rode the elevator up. I had doubts and questions running through my head. Is he really this interesting? I wonder if this will go anywhere.

The apartment was on the fifteenth floor of the building at Clarendon and Montrose. It faced the lake. We walked in, past the functional, windowless, neatly ordered, and "German clean" kitchen and went into the main living room. We stood there facing the picture windows staring out at Lake Michigan and Montrose Beach where, as a toddler, I had wandered away from my family and lost my ability to speak for a year. Looking down at the lake, I felt at that moment I was really home. I felt something was coming together with my life. I was going to be a lawyer and a writer. I felt safe with this "Ion" standing next to me here at this moment—this guy who loved women. There was something extraordinary about the excitement in his stories—it made sense. Here was an artist whose life was interesting to me, not only his work. We stood there for a few long, silent moments. He reached for my hand, and we walked into my parents' bedroom. I have my period, I said. He didn't care—exactly what I wanted to hear. Finally, a man who didn't expect me to be a polished princess, perpetually spinning a slow striptease on demand for his entertainment. What did it all mean?

***

My currently organized, analytical mind went all over the place after that first evening with Ion. Becoming a lawyer was all-consuming, serious stuff, leaving precious little time for fun and games. But I was a human being, with a rich emotional life forever animated by new art and listening to new music. Someone to share dinner with and music tastes was the release I needed to level the anxiety of my last year of law school. I wanted to know more about what moved someone—a particular someone—to devote all of their time to making music and playing. Tremendous talent and luck was part of it but not everything. In an ironic twist, my love life was intensifying at the same time it was enhancing one of my professional goals: to represent artists. I was getting the backstory, gritty details, behind the scenes practical considerations affecting creative work. I could handle this brand of fun. As a bonus, after several more rendezvous I realized I was in love.

10

When the Ministry sessions had wound down and their work visas expired, Ion and Al left England and returned to Chicago. Ion was staying at Julia Nash's apartment. I had known Julia for several years already from working at Wax Trax, when Julia was just a kid from Topeka visiting her dad Jim on holidays and vacations. Julia was an adult now, living in Chicago on Damen Avenue down the street from Franke Fun. I didn't have a driver's license, let alone a car, but Ion was able to borrow Julia's Karmann Ghia, and he and I went sightseeing through the neighborhood and north towards my place. My new companion was so excited to be back in Chicago, driving a fun little car, that he drove too fast under a viaduct with a near hairpin curve. We spun out doing a 360 in traffic. It was dangerous . . . and fun.

Julia happened to be home on one of my visits to the apartment. When Ion was out of the room, she leaned over with a look of feigned indignation and said, "I always know when you're with him in his room. You guys play the music SO loud!" Lee "Scratch" Perry and Mark Stewart were on heavy rotation at the time.

Ion had a thing for car racing and motorcycles. Growing up in Seattle, he built model cars from kits when it rained and had cultivated a connoisseur's eye for certain vintage models. He didn't have one of his own. Not yet. He drove an ancient turquoise-blue van he and everyone else called, "Icky." What is it with men naming their cars anyway? I asked. He told me it had something to do with an ex-girlfriend. I didn't want to know the details.

Ion also had an Italian motorcycle, a Moto Morini, and would ride over to my apartment where I would slip onto the back for rides along the lake in our down time. He and Al were often locked down for twenty-four-hour time slots at Chicago Trax, the recording studio where they booked time to work on new songs. The studio was a ten-minute ride from where I lived. Ion kept riding over to my place and spending the night. My building manager finally asked him not to park on the sidewalk in front of the building. It wasn't legal. He suggested parking the bike under the stairs next to the back stoop. I was amused by Ion's constant attention. I finally decided this was ok. This somehow worked, and he kept coming over. He was like no one else I had ever met. He was so interested in learning about the Chicago that I knew, and I needed the distraction after eight hours of law classes, study groups, research papers, and nagging feelings about how I would find my place as a lawyer and still be a human being involved in the arts. We had so many of the same friends in common. My life at Wax Trax was over, but this new relationship kept me connected to my network of friends still there.

After another night at my apartment, Ion woke up and saw me standing on one leg in the kitchen with the heel of my left foot resting and balancing against my right knee.

"Hey, what are you doing?" His eyes opened wide, and he looked amused.

"What do you mean, what am I doing?"

"That thing, that thing with your leg . . . like a stork."

"I always do this. It's relaxing. It's what I do."

"NO, that's what I do!"

I congratulated him on his fine choice for meditative exercises and asked him if he wanted a cup of coffee. Never had I been so scrutinized over the simplest mannerisms, but it made me pause for a second to reorganize my thoughts, and that was a good thing. Healthy. Studying the particulars of the moment, that's what I did, too. We did have quite a few quirks in common.

A few months went by. In July of 1987, I was again free from my classes. I applied for and was hired again part-time for a summer clerking gig at the ACLU to make a very little bit of money. Ion was busy in the studio with Al Jourgensen. This was becoming routine. Our time together revolved around his writing and recording schedule. I came to know everyone who worked at the studio, Chicago Trax, and often sat in the "A" room while Ion, Al, and their studio engineers plastered their mixing board with torn pieces of masking tape, ticked off in black Sharpie notations on every piece—some vital reference for the engineers in capturing the sound they were fleshing out at the moment. I would walk into the A room during playback of a song, and the repetition of discreet sounds playing at maximum volume over and over again sounded like gunfire. It was exhilarating to see music making in action. They were creating a wall of brutal sound like nothing else, as distinct and identifiable as their own personalities.

I loved the loose, clublike vibe at Chicago Trax. The receptionist at the front would wave me in, I would wait on a couch, peek into the A room, or wait until Ion came out to take a break. It felt familiar being allowed into this ad hoc boys' club. I was often the only woman there. The only other time I'd been in a recording studio was my stop in at Radio City Music Hall in New York to interview my TWIN ART friends for PRAXIS magazine. Watching Ion working in the control room, I came to appreciate how time-consuming studio work could be.

An unexpected highlight of the summer came when he called me at home to say he and Al were going to the movies, and did I want to come? I couldn't exactly envision a group field trip, but summer was the time to catch up on art and pop culture, and I agreed to go. The two of us spent time alone together contingent upon his studio schedule as it was, so the idea of a movie date with Al tagging along was probably something I should have expected. We were on our way to see Robocop.

The film had just opened and was playing at Water Tower Theaters on Michigan Avenue in a tonier part of town. A song Ion and Al had worked on with Ogre, from the band Skinny Puppy, had prominent placement in the film.

Because of contractual limits with Ministry's current record label, their song had to be credited under a different band name. The new name PTP was an acronym for Programming The Psychodrill. This will be interesting, I thought. What was even more interesting was the fact that Ion had decided he'd outgrown his alias and wanted to be called by his given name now, Paul.

Paul, Al, their engineer from Chicago Trax, and I were in our seats at the theater surrounded by a full house of strangers. I wondered if their music in the film would be obvious to me. I wondered if my brief visits to Trax, hearing snatches of songs spliced together in a studio environment at maximum volume would have predisposed me to being able to identify a Paul and Al mix. I wondered where the sequence would emerge, where it was synced in with the film. It was the first time any of their music was used in a big budget movie. As I sat next to Paul, I felt the familiar joy of being in the moment, not examining history, and in the company of people performing at a level so few others in their profession ever reached.

During a chase scene in the film, Robocop pursues his target into a disco, and this is precisely where the PTP track comes in. It's the music playing, enervating bodies on a dance floor, while the world outside of the club is a dystopian crime scene. The music hits the audience's ears as loudly as music in a club once inside the front door. The impact is immediate to make the audience feel they are in the club, too.

The storyline, wardrobe, virtually everything about the film was enthralling. The four of us sat through to the end, my movie dates squirming in their seats, tightly wound bundles of impatient adrenaline. It was a great movie; it had a great story. What an honor to be an integral part of that story. I was really happy for my seatmates and proud of them. We watched the credits roll. Finally, there was no one left in the theater but us, waiting for it—the song credit—acknowledgment of their time and talents.

At the very last credit line, the screen displayed these words: "Show Me Your Spine, performed by PTP." There it was. We were all out of our seats finally, yelling "YES!", high fiving, Paul and Al locking hands and hugging one another, Paul giving me a big hug. It was worth the wait to see the expressions on their faces and share the moment. It was a giant turn-on for these two self-professed "studio rats"; this moment of recognition on the big screen before it abruptly faded to black. If I had had any doubts about Paul working with Al, about the value of any of the music, those doubts were dwindling. Al's musical output to this point had never interested me much. This new stuff with Paul, this was serious, professional level, and cool.

Over the course of the next year, Paul and I spent every spare minute together, while things in his and Al's creative collaborations moved at a chaotic pace, like a surgical team in a warzone. So much editing, finetuning, and so many side projects overlapping, catching the castoff song ideas from the Ministry sessions. Wax Trax Records' ever expanding record label, along with Sire Records, were funding their studio time with seeming abandon. Jim Nash had funded Al's first record and trusted Al could deliver more that would sell. Jim would gladly take and promote the hell out of any and all side projects Ministry had to unload on the Wax Trax label. Al took great advantage of Jim's generosity and laissez-faire business practices.

One side project consuming their studio time was the Revolting Cocks. A Cocks tour was coming together on the heels of insane studio hours, writing, recording, and negotiating song splits. Paul had control of his own music publishing and was his own publisher under the name Spurburn Music. Al and the other songwriters agreed Spurburn Music would be the main publisher on all of the joint projects, whether it was Ministry, Revolting Cocks, or one-offs like PTP. It was a more efficient way to deal with licensing and royalties if potential licensees had one contact to negotiate with in the band. With the Robocop credit to their names, the odds of similar offers to come were looking inevitable.

I felt privileged to see actual copyright and record royalty issues playing out in front of me. This is what I wanted to complete the cycle of reading and theorizing all day in a classroom—transferring those ideas into practice. Much later I learned the clearance departments for TV and film productions would periodically call with requests that had to be approved within twenty-four to seventy-two hours. Those licenses may not have happened if every writer working with Paul and Al at the time had been their own publisher.

Paul told me it was never his intention to become rich as a music publisher. He was more interested in having fun making "ugly music" with people he liked. But he wasn't stupid. He knew talented people don't always know or care about the business end of the music business. He had already been in another band, The Blackouts, where the notion of equality amongst the members was the credo, and it worked. As a publisher his priority was to make sure everyone contributing to a project received the proper writer's credit and got paid—clean and simple, without third parties making money off of the band. Originally, Spurburn Music took an administration fee of 1 percent to cover bank fees, paper costs for royalty statements, postage, and time for registrations with BMI (the performing rights society Paul was affiliated with) and the Copyright office. It took time to establish songwriting splits, current home addresses, and social security numbers. Some of the writers were Canadian or from another country. With that basic information, it took time to record and calculate actual royalties collected, with sometimes five writers on one song on an album with nine or ten tracks. Excel spreadsheets did not exist yet. What Spurburn Music did was mirror what the labels Alternative Tentacles and Wax Trax were doing—oftentimes, those statements were handwritten. There were multiple collaborators on Ministry songs and on future side projects like Pailhead or LARD. Eventually, Spurburn Music's fee was upped to 10 percent and no one complained. Spurburn made no profit for its efforts in the beginning and maintained the 10 percent rule when Ministry's reputation became global.

11

In 1987, I was in my second year of law school. I lived in a studio apartment in a building directly next door to Governor Jim Thompson's Chicago residence, and a mile and a half due north from Chicago Trax studio. After a full day of water rights, patents, and administrative law, I studied for one or two hours at home. My energy level exhausted, I would leave my apartment for a walk down Broadway, then Halsted, passing Town Hall (the neighborhood cop shop), and down to Chicago Trax to almost drag Paul out after some marathon session in the studio. At the time, they were doing final production and mixes for Ministry's The Land of Rape and Honey album. I would arrive to find he couldn't recall when he had last eaten real food, washed, or seen natural light during relentless studio hours. I wanted to share a meal and get Paul away from studio mode. He apologized for not changing his clothes and complained about the pointless shower at "Trax" being used for everything but showering. This chaos seemed normal now to him. It was not normal to me.

We were becoming regulars at Las Mananitas, a Mexican place within walking distance from Trax. I was starting to understand that I brought a sense of grounding to our relationship, something he with his dreams of being a pop star so desperately desired. Paul watched with great fascination as I pulled a familiar tiny blue tin of Nivea from my bag and headed to the ladies' room to wipe chili oil from my lipstick after our Mexican dinners. We both smoked Camel straights, and the time it took to smoke an after-dinner cigarette was calming in itself.

Las Mananitas was popular with everyone at Trax and a reference point for visiting musician friends. The restaurant was owned and nightly hosted by a local Mexican TV celebrity who was a not-so-secret flaming queen. We ordered green enchiladas and fish en papillote with perfect margaritas to sip and calm us down. Paul ordered the fish in paper not only because it was delicious, but also there was a ceremony to eating it—cutting the parchment, pinching it open, and watching the steam escape. He loved the ritual. Our usual waiters, Manuel and Guillermo, were huge Ministry and Revolting Cocks fans—the Revolting Cocks being Paul's other current studio project. Our waiter friends had friends in Mexico who couldn't wait for news about the Ministry world of recording (and partying).

In early fall of 1987, I played the Illinois lottery and won nearly five thousand dollars. I could buy a briefcase and a suit for the coming spring of interviewing and job hunting. With some money left over, and a little time off, Paul suggested we take a road trip. Under the pretext of loosely shadowing the Tackhead tour of the east coast, we invited Franke Fun and his partner Dave Collins to come along for the drive. The break from classes and the money I won allowed us to hit the road without the usual money anxieties. Paul seemed to be living on studio air but had money for gas and smokes. Franke and Dave and Paul and I piled into Icky and headed east. We swapped nap times in the back of the van with driving up front.

When we arrived in Boston, we met up with Marston Daley. Marston and Franke were getting music together for their own Wax Trax label band, My Life With The Thrill Kill Kult, and Marston was in the process of moving to Chicago. Having survived our long drive, we ventured over to the venue for the Tackhead show. Did we even need a reason for this road trip? I had so much fun listening to how everyone else was strategizing new projects, songs, and business models in making music, that the outside shifting landscape went down like dessert.

After the show, Paul spoke with Adrian Sherwood, who was along for the tour and was catching some air outside of the club. Paul knew Sherwood from the Ministry sessions at Southern Studios in England months before where Paul and Al recorded some of what would become the album The Land of Rape and Honey. Sherwood was a legendary dub producer in his own right. I was impressed Paul had such a network of connections and musician friends, a support system of high performing people who needed him as much as he needed them. I was beginning to understand the concept of the "mutual appreciation society" in the music world my companion inhabited and functioned in so seamlessly.

The hours on the road allowed me time to reflect on where I was professionally, emotionally, and as a human being. I was in a serious relationship with the most interesting man I had ever met. I was privy to hearing iterations of songs that would later become MTV hits and standard bearers in the canons of alternative and industrial rock music. Video shoots and photography shoots were open to me with the privilege of seeing some of the best artists and technicians do what they loved best. I felt as though the universe wanted me to be present in and personally connected once again to the music scene, my "family" for so many years. I sensed the looks from Paul's old acquaintances in Boston wondering what the hell was he doing with a future lawyer, and what was I doing with a musician, but it didn't matter. Paul and I understood one another's ambitions. He wanted to be a pop star. He had written it down many times in his journals. I knew that. I wanted to combine my talent for writing, my knowledge of the arts, and my desire to be useful as an advocate somehow. My parents had given me very little in the way of material things, but as immigrants their capacity for change and growth was endless. My father with his tinkering and patent applications. My mother, who left her birth country to start from scratch and learn a new language and culture and raise a family. I'd never held myself back from experiencing the new, whether that meant taking a van road trip or cold calling big name entertainment lawyers in Chicago for a job. I made decisions over time because no one told me I couldn't. No one said, "No."

As much as I liked Tackhead, for me the big highlight of our shadow tour came as the four of us were driving into Montreal. Heavy traffic in the city center suddenly stopped altogether. I had never seen gridlock like this before, not even in New York. Nothing was moving, as if the city's entire power grid had suddenly been switched to off. Car horns were beginning their own symphony in the street as if that would change anything. We opened the doors to the van to see what was holding things up. Dave was getting restless, went off to relieve himself in an alley, and got stuck behind a wall of men in kilts playing bagpipes. So much fanfare. Did we stumble into a national holiday parade or victory celebration for the Montreal Canadiens hockey team? What was the occasion?

Looking across multiple lanes of traffic heading in the opposite direction, we could see a stopped motorcade. If the other drivers in their cars weren't as bleary eyed as the four of us, they would have clearly detected a diminutive pastel figure emerging from her limousine. With a gloved hand, she offered a pivoting wave to her subjects. There was Elizabeth, the Queen Mum herself. It seemed like a good omen for the future for all of us—a royal blessing.

"Oh look at herrrrr . . ." Franke seemed annoyed (but wasn't really).

"Oh, you're just jealous," I said.

"Well . . . YEAAAH."

We finally pulled away from the traffic snarl, and were so starved we wandered around looking for any restaurant at all that wasn't thoroughly packed with tourists. For the intrepid traveler there comes a point where spontaneity has stretched its limits and any place with seating looks acceptable. The four of us had reached our limits. We ambled into a bread bar or bar "au Pain"—a café where the specialty was toast.

I thought it was a gag. All these smiling professionals on their lunch breaks working at their individual toasting "stations." And there we were, three guys and one girl, more appropriately outfitted for an authentic greasy taco truck than a sit-down restaurant with a theme. We dubbed the place the "Bar of Pain" as we endeavored to mimic the locals preparing their own bread masterpieces tableside. The four of us had more fun with the name of the establishment, burned a few pieces of bread, and decided dining out should be a little more satisfying than just playing with your food. Common food. Canadian food culture, it seemed, left a lot to be desired.

The journey to the east coast and back really was more about taking a break away from Chicago and our daily routines, the demands on our time. We were all in similar places professionally—learning the tricks of the trade, so to speak. Spontaneity was good for the soul. Cheap road trips were wholly American and necessary for people like us, whose sanity depended upon junk and pop culture for laughs and context. I thought about Jim and Dannie at Wax Trax. They had given all these guys money and their time because they believed in the talent pool staring back at them. I was grateful for being right where I was, sitting in the front seat of a baby-blue, old van, eyes on the highway ahead.

It wasn't until the end of the year that I actually saw Paul sing live onstage for the first time. The Revolting Cocks/Ministry were booked to play Medusa's on New Year's Eve. A few of my law school acquaintances knew I was seeing Paul, and themselves being fans of Ministry and the Revolting Cocks, they were excited for me. Some of them were going to the rock show.

Chicago on New Year's Eve was characteristically frigid. The temperature on this New Year's felt like thirty below zero with the wind. Revolting Cocks devotees outside the club were huddling together waiting for the doors to open. Paul and I arrived, walked past everyone and into the warmth of Medusa's. I spotted my law school classmates and waved, thinking, "This is really nice, no wait time, just slip in—suckers." I guessed some of law school's competitiveness had rubbed off on me.

It may have been my first time at Medusa's. As with other venues, I was uncomfortable being close to a stage, but there was nowhere else to stand. When it was show time, a backing tape started, bodies on the dance floor pushed forward toward me, and the New Year's vibe was underway. I had by now seen hundreds of bands play, but this time what was happening onstage was more personal. Paul walked on wearing a black dinner jacket with no shirt underneath. From what I was told, Al injured his voice and needed a break from singing. Paul looked completely at ease. He held the microphone effortlessly and seemed to know exactly when to lean into, then away from the crowd. I realized at that moment performing live was one of the most intense pleasures for him.

A few songs in and their equipment failed, never to recover. Much audience commotion and grumbling later, Paul and I quietly slipped out of the club and into the new year.

A few days later, Paul, Al, and the Revolting Cocks were on the road, slated to do shows on the west coast and in Texas. On January 8th, my apartment phone rang around midnight. It was an emergency call. Paul and the Cocks were playing a show that night at Numbers in Houston. But in the meantime, he felt compelled to call me and be the first to wish me a happy birthday—it was my thirtieth, a much celebrated landmark in any person's life. I was thrilled to hear from him and thrilled to be heading into my last semester of law school.

Something I was not thrilled about was the notion I would be celebrating my thirtieth birthday alone in my apartment. Yearning for a touch of glamour to commemorate this milestone year, I called my painter friend Marnie Warren to ask if she had any interest in accompanying me to the Green Mill Lounge not far from my apartment and her own. A former speakeasy made infamous by Al Capone, The Green Mill was these days home to the weekly Uptown Poetry Slam. I felt it my cultural duty to keep up with the literary fringes in the city. At the least it would be fun to take in one slam before things got too busy in my life to care. Marnie and I cabbed it down together.

The best part of the evening wasn't the two martini minimum or the gorgeous, swirling green neon outside. The drinks were passable. But when the performers began delivering their lines in the same measured slopes up and down, the same elevated volume with little behind the noise but self-aggrandizing attention to footsteps walking away, broken hearts, and the importance of house pets as companions, I'd heard enough. I leaned over and told Marnie "Anybody can write a rap song." Sitting upright again, I opened my mouth, and projecting loudly to the poet reading, I said, "Tell us something we don't know already!" The end of my twenties was now complete.

Mark Smith, the curator for the slams, made a mock apology for the bad poetry onstage this evening, and the performers carried on. I told Marnie this "slam" was pretty tepid stuff compared to the raucous events we'd been to ten years earlier in less glamorous settings, with potent illegal drinks, and a crowd prepared for a real fight. This current crop of poets had no spark in them. C'est la vie, as Marnie in her pitch-perfect French would say.

***

The year had turned over. It was 1988, and I smoked a pack of Camel straights every day, as did my constant companion Paul. We smoked in restaurants, at the studio, at my apartment in bed. What were we all about anyway? Smoking was enjoyable, stylish, and still civilized. It was tactile, a ritual. Paul smoked the very occasional cigar, if offered one. We were both martini drinkers, having one or two with dinner. Neither one of us did drugs or closed down bars. We were busy absorbing the mundane details of life and ecstatic to be in each other's company—oftentimes, while riding on a motorcycle. His world of making music and touring, against my world of legal theories, writing, and thinking about where it was all heading, could all be shut off for a few hours to eat, have a conversation, hop in bed and enjoy every second of it.

Paul was so different from other men I'd been with, more outwardly affectionate. Sometimes he seemed overwhelmed with emotion, like a critical care patient coming home from a long hospital stay to recuperate. After ruinous hours in the studio, he would return to my apartment, put his arms around me, and plant multiple kisses on either side of my face like a child. His reputation as a badass pop music rule breaker was something for the critics and listening public to marvel at. He loved that attention and needed it. They were his public family. But what he seemed to need more than anything was a private, demonstrative, loving family to stroke him and cheer him on. I was more than willing to fulfill that role.

My law school life was isolating. I had learned to be alone and not feel culpable for what happened outside of my four walls. Having Paul in my life changed that. Learning someone else's habits was a revisiting of social mores and how it was that we didn't all go around killing each other. Paul was a bass player, a massively talented musician, and whatever anyone else thought about the so-called rock-n-roll lifestyle was a myth in my world, which now included him. Take soft boiled eggs.

I couldn't tolerate extraneous kitchen gadgets cluttering my space, and I considered egg holders WASP-ish and quaint, until I watched Paul deftly hack the top off a soft boiled egg (still in the shell) with his butter knife (a clean break) and balance it on his plate at breakfast. I liked them soft, too. I did not, however, possess the skill for balancing a runny egg with such panache, and eventually we found some interesting egg holders (Danish design) and then had to fret about hand washing the petite pedestals.

Having begun in fall of 1987 and into 1988, Paul and Al were in the studio at Chicago Trax producing Ministry's The Land of Rape and Honey album, Paul's Lead into Gold Idiot EP, Pailhead tracks, and the Revolting Cocks' You Goddamned Son of a Bitch album. Whatever didn't make the final cut for a Ministry track would suddenly be massaged into a Revolting Cocks track or stored away for some other side project. Chicago Trax was a business on the outside, but like a lot of studios, a revolving door for opportunists looking for a party, for drinks and drugs, and for musicians of every caliber. And curiously, we came to be familiar with Jerry the Cop.

Jerry worked out of the Town Hall precinct, three blocks north on Halsted. I had the impression that Jerry was a neighborhood beat cop. He had the uniform. He would show up unannounced at Trax for an update on the recording sessions and occasionally partake in the partying going on. He may well have been a really great cop, but the sometimes non-stop bacchanalia at the studio was hard to ignore. At Chicago Trax, his stature was elevated like everyone else's. He became Jerry the Cop. Everyone was renamed and became part of Chicago Trax mythology—Jeff "Critter" Newell, engineer. Jeff "Abner" Ward, drummer for LARD. Keith "Fluffy" Auerbach, engineer, with his cascading shoulder length curls. Reid "L'chaim!" Hyams, the studio owner who appeared to have fallen asleep at the end of the 1970s and kept the same look going. Chris "Pinky"Connelly. Paul "Ion" Barker (and "Frenchy"). Al "Alien" Jourgensen. Other friends weren't spared: Joe "Shagnasty" Shanahan, owner of Cabaret

Metro.

"Mistuh Crittair," Al announced to no one in particular when he saw Critter, their engineer, dragging his way into the studio. Critter was hardly obsessed with his public image. He was as big as an offensive tackle on a football team. He wore work boots perpetually unlaced with one pant leg half tucked into the boot and half out, as if he'd just returned from the men's room and hiked up his jeans too high on one side. His hair was a thin mess, pushed behind glasses balancing asymmetrically on his face to compliment the pants. Critter's appearance seemed lazy and indifferent, but I knew he was valuable in the studio simply because he was there.

For me, dropping into the studio was like barging in on someone else's fire, someone else's creative process. I was invisible. I once walked into the A room, and Chris Connelly was pacing in front of a sofa with notebook paper in his hand, muttering words out loud and notating the page with a pen while some few seconds of music were playing over and over again. Paul and the engineer rolled back and forth in their chairs before the console full of knobs, switches, levers that moved up and down, and the ever present bits of masking tape with black Sharpie-drawn letters and numbers. Chris was composing Revolting Cocks lyrics, from what I could tell. I didn't want to interrupt. I just watched and thought he must be a genius to be able to attach words automatically to sequences of musical notes on the fly. Paul labored over lyrics after the fact.

During one of my drop-ins at Trax, Paul introduced me to Ian MacKaye, who became the singer and one of the cowriters on the Pailhead songs. Paul and I met with Ian at the Chicago Diner, a vegetarian place a couple of doors north of Trax on Halsted. Ian MacKaye, like so many artists I had come to know, shunned the mainstream. He was the singer for Minor Threat and founder of the hardcore label Dischord Records in DC. Paul and I were discussing how, when a label suddenly discovered they're sitting on a band that could sell a lot of records, the label would inevitably expect the band to do a ballad.

"We're not doing any fucking ballads," Paul informed me.

Good. Was that even a thing? (Apparently, it was.)

Ian sat across from us. He was dressed and spoke like a young political canvasser knocking on doors to collect signatures for a clean water initiative or something else geared towards saving the planet. He was polite and barely cracked a smile. He seemed so normal and intensely interested in the idea that I was studying law. I wondered what someone so straight edged had to offer this Pailhead project, but he had that drive in his voice and in his thoughtful manner of speaking to the point.

Later, when I would write checks for Pailhead royalties and mail them out once or twice a year, each time we would get a thank you postcard from Ian MacKaye. The picture on the card was a random image of Americana—the crown logo on the rear quarter panel of an old Chrysler Imperial was one. The return address on the card was hand stamped "Ian c/o Dischord" in DC or "Fugazi c/o Dischord." The card carried a succinct message, "Dear both, thanks for the check. Glad the Pailhead stuff is still generating cash for everybody" (made some TV money, etc.). Usually the note included a hello to Al, "if you should run into him."

The Pailhead songs were popular with skaters and often licensed for use in skateboard videos and for in store play in the shops. The TV royalties Ian alluded to were for one of the songs being used in the opening sequence in the season premiere of the show Cold Case. The episode opens with some kids preparing to shoot up a mall.

The appeal of Pailhead songs carried into several years of sync licenses. Ministry as a band would "fucking never" write a ballad, as Paul predicted. Pailhead as a short-lived project wouldn't touch that formula either. Instead, or in lieu of the formula, the Pailhead members composed one song in their repertoire sardonically entitled, "Ballad."

Toward the end of May of 1988, I was finished with law school. Paul was off tour, and we could ride around on his Morini during the day. The bike needed some essential vintage parts and only one dealer in the US had them, a one-man warehouse/garage in Port Clinton, Pennsylvania. The owner of the business was a man named "Hermy." Paul was eager to fix the bike and thought a drive east would be beautiful in the summer. Besides, we could investigate Pennsylvania Dutch country (whatever that was anymore) while we were there. He was game for exploring, and I needed a break before sitting for the bar exam.

On our way out of town, we picked up coffee at the Belden, a neighborhood restaurant in Lincoln Park. Some kids there eyeballed us, concluding we were competent enough to steer them towards the nearest punk rock club, and they asked us for directions to "Exit." I forgot to bring a journal for the road trip. Curiously, I did have a small packet of three by five index cards in my bag, leftovers from a research paper writing spree, no doubt. With minimal supplies, we left Chicago at 10:30 p.m. Paul drove Icky to the Ohio border. I took over for a mere three minutes and discovered I may have night blindness. We decided to stop in Ohio for a few hours' sleep.

It never occurred to me when he finally said, "Let's stop for the night," after driving six or seven hours straight, what Paul meant was, let's look for a rest stop to park the van and go to sleep. I didn't have disposable income for hotel rooms. I didn't even have a job yet. But for some reason, I assumed Paul had brought money to pay for a room. He had money for Morini parts waiting for him at Hermy's shop. I only had a little bit of cash and a new, unused credit card.

"Okay, let's stop," I said, wondering how I would wash my face in a rest-stop sink. There was a note of such self-assurance in Paul's voice that told me this was an acceptable way to travel across the breadth of the Midwest. I soon discovered he'd outfitted the van with extra blankets in case the nights in Ohio or Pennsylvania were cooler than I was accustomed to. What a thoughtful, innocent soul I've found here to spend time with, I thought. Who cares if he doesn't have money for hotels?

We napped in the van until the sunrise roused us back to consciousness. I took over the wheel. I was perpetually driving "on a permit" and highway driving was still new to me. The freeway became two lanes in each direction, while we focused on decoding road signs to fit them into our growing, shared vocabulary: "Runaway truck ramp." I had to ask Paul the purpose of the sign. Only one of us had done van tours with their band, and that one was not me. "Curva Peligrosa" was easy—dangerous curves. Paul decided that was an apt description of his current road companion—me. Seamlessly adapting my body to this new landscape seemed like a fair fantasy tradeoff. I loved that Paul was a curious student of everything around him. He told me he sometimes wished he had gone back to school after studying German in the army. His facility with language probably had much to do with being a musician and playing music. He had the ear for sounds in language as I did. His interpretations were different.

I had a penchant for reviving discarded words. I collected dictionaries of slang and books with tantalizing titles such as, Diseased English. There was plenty of material to work with. We were both fans of the American Heritage Dictionary with its photographs and illustrations accompanying a hodgepodge of selected words, as if someone's grandmother had scrapbooked the whole collection together and decided which ones needed visual aids: "dervish" was one. Paul paged through the American Heritage while I kept my eyes on the road. We passed one more distant farmhouse and flat fields that went on for a few more miles, when abruptly the van lost speed. The engine died.

I pulled over to the side of the road. We were still somewhere in Ohio. I stepped out of the van while Paul slid into the driver's seat to try and restart the engine. He was good with engines, a skill he'd picked up working in the motor pool in the army. He quit after barely turning the key. "Oh."

What?

"We're out of gas."

I hadn't paid attention to the gas gauge. I didn't know to do that automatically. Here was Paul—a precisely tuned man who would set the trip meter on the dash to record actual miles traveled on a long trip and who would log mileage and stops for gas on a running tally in his wallet—and me, the girl running the gas tank dry. As we sat there considering our dilemma, a pickup truck stopped behind us, and a young man walked over. Paul told him we were out of gas. There was a station not far back down the frontage road, he told us, smiling at me like he wanted to pat "the little lady" on the head for being so distracted on the open road. He offered to give Paul a lift to fill up a gas can. Paul left with our new friend, returning about twenty minutes later. There was now a case of beer in the truck and two on the dash. Our new friend offered me one. He and Paul already had theirs in hand. One for the road.

The van was back in operation, Paul driving this time. Our relationship was still so new there was rarely a moment of silence between us. We had been together just over a year, taking time when we could to talk about big life desires and little things, such as what soap to use in the shower on tour (Doc Bronner's peppermint). Being in the van for hours on end, playing with the radio to find something other than country and classic rock stations, it was refreshing not having to be on anyone else's schedule for a change.

When we arrived in Port Clinton, we headed straight for Hermy's motorcycle shop. It was a cinch to find in a town of about three hundred people and one restaurant attached to a bar with two hotel rooms above it. Mr. Hermy recommended the restaurant, the bar, and the hotel, seeing as they were all on the main strip. The room was eighteen dollars for the night. I could afford that. There was an open transom above the room's door that wouldn't shut, so privacy was "at your own risk." For eighteen dollars, it was better than sleeping in the van again. We were both so tired from driving, we didn't really care if anyone could hear what we were up to in our eighteen-dollar-a-night room, anyway.

Back at the motorcycle shop, Paul was engrossed in studying the quirky collection of Morinis in stock. His own bike had a beautiful long frame, and I loved riding on the back, but tutorials on the mood swings of vintage Italian parts made my brain freeze. In the shop were two red "three and a halfs", a brown three and a half, and a mixed bag of "Italian red" and black bikes crammed into too little space to accommodate much more. With the shop talk finally over, we went back to the hotel, had a lousy dinner and decent drinks at the bar, and went to bed.

In the morning, Paul set off for Hermy's alone to pick up what he'd ordered and to haggle over some extraneous gems he couldn't live without. A mirror. A collection of moto stickers. Vital stuff to admire. We were soon back on the road, cruising the countryside in search of authentic Pennsylvania Dutch hexes—pagan symbols adopted by "fancy" Dutch settlers who'd made this part of the state their home. The simpler Amish, by contrast, didn't believe in symbol worship. I discovered this fun fact while chatting with the hotel bartender the night before.

Hexes. They stood out like colored wreaths on the sides of buildings and houses we passed. Geometrical shapes inside circles like secret codes, signposts to passersby. A childhood memory crossed into my daydreams as we drove along this hex-dotted landscape: there was my mother leaning over me when I was a little girl, after I hatched an ingenious plan to go with our neighbor's son Bobby on the way home from school and collect Christmas card envelopes left in hallways and on doorsteps by the mailman, whose bag was overloaded, and the mail slots were already full. Bobby and I were five years old. We wanted "presents" to take home to our moms for Christmas. Bobby and I were unwittingly committing a federal crime. My mother was not appreciative when we dropped our stash on the kitchen table. "*Kleine Hexe*!" she said. German, for "little witch."

We drove on, past a sparse landscape of farmhouses branded with the ubiquitous hexes, eventually catching sight of a bookstore/diner on the side of the road. The place carried a small collection of hand stapled Pennsylvania Dutch cookbooks and histories of common hexes. We bought a few souvenirs. I still had a little bit of money left to splurge on dessert and coffee before the long drive home. Paul and I sat on diner stools and ordered shoofly pie, one of the regional specialties, and after tasting that first bite in unison vowed to never, ever order shoofly pie again. Ever. It had all the appeal of chewing wet paper.

***

We were back in Chicago, and in short order Paul was on the road with the Revolting Cocks for their You Goddamned Son of a Bitch tour. I was finished with law school. Because of road commitments, Paul missed my graduation. In the interim weeks before summer began, I was invited to a law school graduation dinner at the 95th in The Hancock building. My law school friend Mary Von Mandel was hosting with her husband Mike. Our entire class was invited. Paul was missing that dinner, too. Another milestone in a string of milestones missed or nearly missed because of tour commitments, but nothing I could realistically get upset over.

Paul or no Paul, there was no way I was going solo to Mary's graduation party. It was The Hancock for god sakes, a modern icon. Paul and I had often discussed our dream apartments, and the only place in Chicago we had in common was The Hancock building. I and my crowd of under-employed musicians and artists had only ever had enough cash to go for expensive drinks at the 96th-floor bar in the building and usually only for one drink. This was dinner at The Hancock. I needed a date. I called my dear friend Rick Buscher in St. Louis, who almost died when I asked him. I had known Rick since 1980, around the time I started working at Wax Trax and was coming off of my gig with PRAXIS magazine. Rick's band Raymilland recorded a single that appeared in PRAXIS for issue number five as a bonus insert. Rick was reliably stylish, tall, and movie star handsome with straight, black hair usually falling over one eye. I could see him mouthing the words, "OH MY GOD" when I asked if he would be my date. He was happy to drive up to Chicago, dress up, and be glamorous for one evening at The Hancock with a fabulous view as backdrop. He may have had additional plans while in the city, but those were of no concern to me at the moment.

In the early 1980s Rick and his band occasionally came to Chicago to do their own shows and to open for other bands like Adrian Belew and Tuxedo Moon. Most notably, his band was slated to open for Joy Division's ill-fated American tour. Although he was now in his late twenties, Rick's speaking voice still reminded me of a thirteen-year- old boy's. But Rick's singing voice was unbelievably deeper and darker, a cocktail blend of Bryan Ferry and Peter Murphy of Bauhaus. I once heard him do a cover of David Bowie's "She's Got Medals" at Tut's, after being goaded by my roommate at the time, Mike Nash, who was screaming like a groupie from the audience. You would swear Bowie himself was in the house.

Like me, Rick was a thrift store junkie whose hunter's instinct seemed to rise to DEFCON 1 status with every new discovery of yet another St. Louis warehouse filled with new/old menswear stock. The area around St. Louis was ripe for archaeological excavation by even some vintage store owners we knew in Chicago. Rick had a knack for spotting the rare vintage designer sample, as I did myself. Even with all his style acumen, he still killed me with the occasional cornball jaw-dropper: "Gosh, I don't know!" and "Gee whiz, let's go for a drink."

He was also friends with Jim Nash and Dannie and Cynthia Plaster Caster—we knew a lot of the same people on the circuit in Chicago.

I pleaded with my mother to accompany me in finding a dress for the party, knowing she would be thrilled to pick through luxurious fabrics. She relished any opportunity to study the craftsmanship of a well-made garment. I spent all the money I had and bought an off-the-shoulder dress from the designer sale rack at Marshall Field's. Black on top, silver satin flouncy skirt below, cinched with a three-inch black fabric belt. I could sit at a table and smoke cigarettes in this little number, I thought.

Studying himself in front of my mirror before the party, Rick Buscher wore a vintage silk tie and jacket, and in a second his black hair fell down and covered an eye. Perfect. We made a beautiful couple. Being well-versed as a performer onstage with Raymilland, Rick the civilian was ready to hold his own in a dining room full of future lawyers and a lot of hot air. We were off to dinner at The Hancock for the first time ever for either of us.

When we were safely seated at our table, Rick played the role of glamor boy to my glamor girl as friends came over to ask who my new beau was. We had fun watching everyone else get loose, dance badly at cocktail time, and I winced overhearing discussions of private versus public law salaries and studying for the upcoming bar. It had taken three years to reach this level of comfort around some of the people here, but I realized it was possible I'd run into many of them out there in the real world of courtrooms and conferences. Be nice. Most of these people are decent and trying to make sense of their own lives, I told myself; although, Rick and I couldn't resist the occasional discreet eye roll to the right or left when someone obnoxious walked by.

I excused myself at one point to find a ladies' room. I walked past the husband of another of my law school friends. He got up from his table and followed me to the elevator. I barely knew him. I turned to face the front. The elevator began moving between floors. I felt a pinch through my dress. We were the only two people there. I was . . . shocked. My little reverie to myself on the decency of the crowd was over.

My classmate hinted once or twice that her spouse wasn't faithful to their wedding vows, but this move was brazen. I felt the urge to turn around and punch him in the face but didn't want to make a scene at someone else's party. I didn't want to soil or rip my dress, either. Maybe he was drunk. It had been years since someone had grabbed me in public. But wasn't that how these guys operated—assured they won't get caught, and who cares if they do? I glared at him and stepped off at the next floor. I debated telling my friend her husband was an asshole. But she knew that already. I let it go. The rest of the evening Rick and I exchanged knowing smirks and savored our splendid dinner—the spoils from hard work and the guilty pleasure in feeling massively lucky to be at our window seats swooning over the view below.

With Paul still on tour I alternated between art shows and studying for the bar. Cynthia Plaster Caster called and alerted me everyone was getting tickets for David Johansen's new incarnation, Buster Poindexter, performing at George's, a supper club near the Merchandise Mart. David Johansen had been the vocalist in the New York Dolls, one of the seminal bands to perform in the early days of the New York punk rock scene. I was too young to have ever seen the New York Dolls in concert or have much familiarity with their music, other than the song "Personality Crisis" that had regular rotation on the turntable at Wax Trax. I was however aware of a rare New York Dolls Live in Dallas bootleg with cover art depicting a recreation of the Kennedy assassination. In the center frame sits David Johansen dressed as Jackie Kennedy in her pink suit. Jim and Dannie referred to that cover persona as "Jackie Jo." I was fond of the record sleeve for the contaminating, shameless quality of appropriation, but also because it was designed by my good friend Steve Lafreniere. I decided I liked the idea of seeing someone with a big voice like David Johansen's in a supper club setting, decidedly very anti-punk rock. Buster Poindexter currently had a hit with the song, "Hot Hot Hot," a saccharine conga line number I could live without seeing live, but the entertainment options for the weekend were otherwise tepid. I bought my ticket and headed to George's.

The show was underway, and I was reminded of why I enjoyed seeing pro drag queens onstage. Camp was great fun in doses, and we all needed to support the old guard trying to flex their chops, still around just trying to make a living performing live on a stage. After the set, I left my table to touch up in the powder room. I soon found myself crowded into a small alcove waiting in line with three other people: David Johansen with his shirt collar loosened up, flanked on either side by two considerably taller female backup singers. I believe they were female. I couldn't believe David Johansen was my height. Another diminutive rockstar.

"What's up, Jackie Jo?" I said, innocently recalling his demur likeness in that devastating pink suit. He lost the smile and stared at me closely, as if trying to recall where we'd met before. His Herman Munster like facial features and denture-perfect wide mouth were a counterpoint to the cover girls at his side. I ducked into the Ladies not waiting for a response. "Hot Hot Hot!"

The Revolting Cocks tour was over at the end of the month. I opted to leisurely spend what little time I had left with Paul before sitting for the July bar. Many of my classmates already had jobs or were mulling over offers for the fall. I hadn't begun seriously searching for a job yet. I was comfortable waiting until after the bar exam to get on with my career path. I wasn't even sure I had one yet.

Fourth of July holiday was the last grace period before taking the bar and exhausting my intellectual gears and muscles one last time to satisfy the board of examiners that I was worthy of the title Counselor, Attorney at Law, or Esquire. "Abogada," anyone? In my own mind, I longed for some colorful distraction to remind me of the frailty of life, the fragile daily moving landscape pushing out of our grasp ever so quickly, not waiting for us to engage it and fill it with laws and regulations. I told Paul I wanted to see the fireworks at the lake.

Fourth of July fireworks would be loud, a spectacle, perhaps even fun, and for once, we could say we went, if anyone asked. From Michigan Avenue in front of the Art Institute and crossing over to Grant Park would be the best places to view the lightshow. Paul and I ventured into a crazy traffic night, with individual cops standing at intersections waving cars away from already full lots and spaces. We were riding the Morini, snaking through the cars, watching the fireworks each time we stopped, until the next cop and the next whistled at us to "move it along." I reminded Paul constantly that in Chicago you stayed in your lane on a motorcycle. You couldn't weave through cars as you could on the west coast, not without getting a ticket. There were traffic cops all over downtown now, but they had the bigger picture to keep them busy on this night. Paul ignored my advice, and we edged closer to the explosions going on over the lake. I let all thoughts of taking the bar slip away for another night.

Two weeks later, like all candidates sitting for the July bar exam, I was photographed and fingerprinted. The sober reality of that physical act, offering my hand to be inked, underscored the responsibilities I would be entrusted to carry out as a practicing lawyer. I felt confident going into the room, confident that I was my best rehearsed and prepped self. I promised myself I would go somewhere with Paul when it was all over, and we could forget about serious matters like job hunting and "studio rat" time.

Closing the exam book at the very end, I hoped my classmate Dan survived sitting for two days with a bad case of shingles. He was a nice guy, and that was a rarity in law school. With the exam over and results not available for three months, I was mentally spent. I had no appetite for food. There was a nagging hunger to get back on the road and engage in mindless exploration of Americana I'd missed in all my years of studying while friends split town for Mardi Gras and trips to both coasts. When I saw Paul again, we debated driving to Graceland. It wasn't much of a debate. Neither of us had ever made the pilgrimage to Elvis's monument to himself. "Let's go." Memphis was midway to New Orleans. I'd never been there either. The rest of the summer off was a good excuse to take in as many cheesy cultural clichés we could possibly stomach.

On our drive down to Memphis, Paul and I agreed to be surprised no matter what lay waiting—along with Elvis's body—at the family estate. As a child growing up in Chicago, I remembered driving north along Sheridan Road, gateway to some of the richest suburbs in America. Beyond Northwestern's campus in Evanston was Glencoe, the idyllic backdrop to the fabulous Bahai Temple. On through Highland Park, Winnetka, and the rest, we would marvel at the sheer mass of homes growing more spectacular the further north you went. Modern glass houses, grand English-style country homes, Tudor wonders, and mock Tyrolean castles—they were all there, and you could guess who was old money and who was new. It was a panoply of architectural styles, some custom designed, others executed in a cut and paste builder's notion of what would please a buyer. How would Elvis's mansion stand up against some of those places? I wondered.

We followed the road signs into Memphis, loud teasers for the tourists: "Graceland—almost there!" navigating our way to an official ticket office/ souvenir and tchotchke emporium, where we determined our chances were excellent for taking the official tour of Graceland that day. We pulled into a strip mall parking lot and waited for the shuttle bus to rescue us from the common folk and begin our journey to "The King's" palace.

Waiting in line, the two of us may have appeared stylishly subdued in our walking shorts and muscle-tee shirts combatting the summer heatwave, next to the pompadoured, gelled aging rockers escorting their scented, nail-biting dates: fellow passengers clutching cameras and programs, taking their own quiet moments to reflect before landing at the front door to the mothership. I wondered what these people did for a living, beyond emulating their hero Elvis. During a lull in our tour guide's prefatory remarks welcoming us to Elvis's inner sanctum, my companion Paul decided to squander his usual good manners. It had been a long drive.

"I heard 'The King' was spotted at a 7-11 in Florida last week," Paul said, waiting for some reaction to this bit of inside skinny on the King's current location. My gut tightened a bit.

"I heard that, too!" someone chimed in, captivated by a new enthusiasm.

I leaned over and whispered to Paul, "This is it?" as we turned into a moderately graded driveway, and the shuttle bus puttered to a stop. We muffled our enthusiasm looking out the bus window at what appeared to be a modestly embellished two-story mini-mansion sitting quietly like a realtor's model Home of the Week. Paul, still highly amused by his own contribution to current Elvis lore, leaned over and kissed my cheek then hopped off the bus to line up and listen to southern-style etiquette: "Keep the line moving, and please respect the family's wishes that you not touch anything."

I was by no means a huge Elvis fan, but Elvis and I shared the same birthday, along with David Bowie. I refrained from revealing that propitious bit of information to the small crowd surrounding us, lest my good fortune detract attention away from the marvels that lay within the confines of Graceland. We went inside. While we were escorted from one splendidly painted, banana-yellow room housing a collection of (yes!) carved monkey statuettes, and on to sacred, gold records in plexi-glassed aspic, it was clear the interior decorating was nothing short of studied rags to riches. Where's the free popcorn, I wanted to ask.

We toured Elvis's yard, where his headstone curiously displayed a misspelled (or not) version of his middle name, "Aaron." Graceland, in the end, was just as spectacularly pop suburban as we could have envisioned on our own. I was underwhelmed; so was Paul. We couldn't wait to hustle onto the shuttle and back to the tchotchke emporium, where Paul was compelled to purchase a copy of Elvis, His Most Intimate Secrets, for ninety-nine cents; a glossy revelation no bigger than a pack of smokes. I nabbed a prayer-book-sized, condensed guide to my zodiac sign: Capricorn. That's right, me and Elvis at the head of the pack—in the horoscopes, anyway. On to New Orleans.

When we returned to Chicago and Paul was back into the studio grind, Al and Patty Jourgensen figured they needed a shopping break before Ministry's Land of Rape and Honey tour. Patty needed a leather jacket. Paul asked if I wanted to come along for the ride. I was happy to spend time with him any chance I could get, and I was game to do just about anything not involving another trip to Chicago Trax. I could go look at new leathers.

We picked up Patty and Al and some studio hands and headed out to a Harley shop in the suburbs. Patty's slight frame opened up the possibilities for new leathers, leaving only essential design details to consider: belt or no belt, side grommets, quilted shoulders, regular or tab collar, and price. She settled on a classic black jacket, but realized she and Al had no credit cards between them, and they'd neglected to bring enough cash. I had in my possession a new American Express card burning a hole in my wallet, thanks to an outpouring of unbelievably "generous offers" I'd received in the mail after graduation. I told Patty I could buy the jacket if they could pay me back immediately. I wondered if she would balk at the offer. A mutual friend had told me Patty thought I was a snob.

Patty agreed to let me break in my new card. I then wondered if she still thought I was a snob. It was an awkward moment, but I knew Al probably had no credit. He'd once filed for bankruptcy, a little known footnote to the saga of Al trying to disentangle himself from a record deal gone sour. I handed my credit card to the clerk. Patty slipped her arms into the jacket, and we walked out of the shop.

When Paul and his workmates needed a diversion from twiddling knobs in the studio, I would get a call. Dinner—Siam Noodles and Rice; Las Mananitas; drinks someplace new, grown up fun, away from the mental gymnastics of the studio for him and the law books for me. Time to be waited on, impressed by someone else's efforts. What an ordinary pleasure. So, I was surprised when Paul asked on one of their breaks if I wouldn't mind going with everyone to Six Flags out in the suburbs. A trip to an amusement park. I frankly didn't understand the pedestrian appeal for such sophisticated denizens of music's "cutting edge." Amusement parks didn't sound very amusing to me. My eldest sister perished on her way to visit one. There couldn't possibly be anything fun about manufactured fun. But there was a ride Paul and Patty were all excited about, one they'd been on at another park. Since I rarely had time for art shows anymore, and couldn't imagine Al and Patty being interested in that kind of entertainment anyway, my sense of adventure won out, and I tagged along.

When we arrived at Six Flags, I discovered the ride Paul hyped so enthusiastically entailed bracing yourself while standing still and being potentially slammed with a wall of water. There was something oddly thrilling in that physical vulnerability, but I declined the offer, cognizant as I was of the possibility of losing an eye (one of my contact lenses). My prescription was on the high end. Without the function of both eyes, I might be partially blind and unable to walk a straight line. I watched everyone else get on with it, while I studied the hordes of fun seekers milling around the park, mostly families with kids. Some couples. Some teenagers. I had the feeling people at the park were looking at us like we were an attraction no one told them about—like a herd of elk in a Home Depot parking lot. I sensed these kinds of stares a lot when Al was around.

Paul went back into the studio. Always on the hunt for new restaurants, we went for the first time to the Star Top Café for dinner. It was a musician friend's recommendation that brought us there. The chef and the co-owner hosted late night entertainment industry movers and shakers, theater actors, and the occasional young financial wizard from the Board of Trade. We rode the Morini to the restaurant on Lincoln Avenue, a few blocks north from Wax Trax. Sitting behind Paul, the warmth of his thighs pressed against mine, the heat of the bike under us, my fingers locked around his waist—we were in the open air. I was a free agent coming to the final scenes of my law school career, but I could indulge this small bit of dependency, mixed with the illusion of freedom.

The restaurant was small with seating for about thirty people. Perched in the storefront window was a console "hi-fi system" with a turntable. Across from it was a small sofa and stacks of vinyl records. Michael Short, the chef, would blast music he wanted to hear while cooking during the dinner service: The Doors, The Commodores, Parliament Funkadelic. As we walked through the front door that first time, Michael was leaning over the turntable and "Give Up the Funk" was setting the mood. This should be fun, I thought as I looked over and smiled at Paul, who was doing the same. Michael came over and immediately asked if the Morini outside was ours. He had an Italian Laverda. Brotherly love was imminent for Paul and our new acquaintance.

Michael cooked with the abandon of an artist. He drank with a nose divining toward the exotic: a shot of grappa here, twelve-year-old scotch over there. He pleased his own tastes in food, and that passion translated well in attracting a steady clientele. The menu had some unlikely marriages of odd spicy sauces with exotic main courses. Skate wing dressed with wasabi crème sauce became one of our favorites. We drank happily concocted drinks from the restaurant's makeshift bar, (more take-out window than toastmaster's workstation) and Michael or his business partner Bill Ammons would emerge from the kitchen to have a drink with us. Michael's girlfriend Ellen Fairey waited tables at Star Top, and the four of us became friends. Paul and I forged a camaraderie with the two of them over our shared love for a wide range of music, books, art, and of course, Italian motorcycles.

Michael and Paul planned rides together, "Ellie" and I on the back of the bikes, flipping each other hand signals at stop lights. We would inevitably end up at a bar where all the chefs went after their shifts. Michael knew the in spots of that crowd. Once or twice we ventured over to the Palmer House hotel downtown, a seemingly unlikely late-night drinks hotspot, but old school perfection for a connoisseur like Michael Short.

Ellie had started reading Martin Amis's book Money. I picked up a copy for myself, and before long Paul started reading it, as did Michael. Amis's world, of a publishing whore in perpetual hangover mode, wasn't any different from the rigors of the working musician's and working chef's lives we were all so familiar with. Always chasing the next hit, in whatever shape it came. I had the distinct feeling I was the designated "straight man" of the crew. I was a new kind of oddball, without even noticing the transformation in my own life. But I was going into a straight profession now. Did that mean I needed to get even MORE serious? For some on the outside of our circle of friends, yes. But I didn't see the badge of my profession as the end all to life's questions. There was so much yet to learn every day from new friends, from Paul, from my law school friends, and all the lives I connected with. Having a law license wasn't going to prevent me from having fun or forgetting what motivated me and saved my ass during the first thirty years of living on this earth.

We visited the Star Top once a week or so, when things were winding down at Chicago Trax. Al and Patty would come by Star Top occasionally. It became a favorite destination for other musicians we knew. Occasionally, a customer would ask Michael or Bill Ammons if they wouldn't mind turning down the music just a hair. Michael in all earnestness would say, "I DO mind. We don't like people telling us what to do." He'd walk away from their table and head back into the kitchen. Michael's philosophy of food was to feed only people who wanted to be in the moment of the day, wanting to experience delicious food and loud music as a package deal. He and Bill had once turned away an entire television crew—actors and all—on the premise that Michael thought their show was utter "shit."

It was the end of summer, 1988. My apartment lease was coming up for renewal in the fall. I mentioned to Paul I needed to move and find a bigger place, possibly closer to downtown. I knew he would help me move. We were both living on tentative incomes. I was looking forward to finding a job and being able to leave studio-apartment living behind me. I also knew what else was coming.

"Let's find a place together," he said, calmly. "I love you. Let's get a place together. I want to be with you."

I was uncommonly happy in our relationship and happy to have Paul stay with me, whenever that worked. I loved him tremendously. There was no doubt about that. There were so many moments when it didn't matter what we were doing together, looking at a restaurant menu, studying a piece of art, combing through junk in a thrift store—our concentration on that thing was absolute. The rest of the world didn't matter. But I was not happy with the idea of making joint decisions about where I should live. I liked living alone again. It had taken years for me to get past my discomfort with going home to an empty apartment. I had already spent plenty of years of my life living with roommates. Mike Nash and Bill Mainey. Carol, Christine, and Larry—all of us in that big house in Edgewater. Then a couple of years of living only with Larry. I told Paul, "I've already lived with one man. If I'm going to live with a man again, he's going to be my husband." Paul thought for a moment. He said, "Okay. Then let's get married."

Wait a minute. What just happened. What was this? I was thirty years old, Paul was a year younger.

Wow, I thought. Did that just happen? Is this how it goes when two people love each other and decide they can't live without each other? I didn't want to live without him in my life. Paul was someone I could walk through fire with, game for anything. He was someone to whom I could say, "You're too tall," and he'd get the joke. We had an effortless rhythm of coming and going away and always having so much to say to one another, thrilled to explore new things, perpetually questioning old paradigms in general, and the music business as a discrete subset. Is this how it goes, no, "Will you marry me?"

I had worked so hard to get here, to become a lawyer, to learn about things that interested me, so why should I get married? Was that another thing to discover? How to become bigger than just yourself? I supposed I wanted something like that. I wanted "more." Paul was telling me in his own indirect way he wanted something like that, too.

"I want to spend my life with you," he said finally.

"Okay. Let's get married." I couldn't believe I was actually having this conversation. We looked at each other and started laughing. I wanted to cry, I was so happy.

"Alright then. Uh . . . do we tell anyone? And how do we tell Patty and Al?"

I never thought I would get married. I never thought I would meet someone I could spend the rest of my life with. I was much too focused on how societies functioned, how art mattered, and how I was going to fulfill my childhood dream of having an office in one of the buildings downtown, a place where I could write stories about other people's lives. So many questions now. How was he going to tour if we were getting married? Ceremony or no ceremony?

"Let's go to Las Vegas."

"Yes! We can see Nudes On Ice while we're there! We'll get a car and drive down. Something with a rag top. We'll play blackjack. We'll have to do it on the longest day of the year—June 21st."

Perfect. The longest day of the year slapping us annually with the "agony of defeat," the reminder that marriage was interminable. Like hell. Brilliant. This was my kind of drama.

Paul phoned Al and suggested we all go for drinks at the Hancock building; it was a special occasion. They had just finished one tour and record, and another tour was coming up, so we could all celebrate at least that much. He didn't tell Al our news.

Paul was still driving his baby blue van "Icky." We picked up Patty and Al, and the four of us walked into the lobby at the Hancock building and waited with a few other adults for an elevator up to the cocktail lounge. I was by now more comfortable with being stared at in public when Al was around. He was his usual showman self, speaking louder than everyone else, and directing the conversation where he wanted it to go.

We found seats at the bar and craned our necks to see past the bartender to admire the aerial view of Chicago's westside, the only way it could be admired really—lit up below and stretching out for ten, fifteen miles on a clear night. It was clear. The bartender placed two martinis in front of us. Paul cleared his throat with an exaggerated "Ahem," and prepared to make a toast. He turned to our companions.

"Al, Patty? Gerda and I have decided to get married." He lifted his glass.

I waited. Al had finally stopped talking. Patty's expression froze. The two of them appeared stricken by some existential threat to their being. Paul had veered away from the carnival to explore a silent canoe floating by on the river.

"Well . . . great, congratulations!" They both raised their glasses. "What's going on? When did this happen?"

"I was bamboozled! She gave me an ultimatum," Paul said, throwing up his hands like a card player folding.

Well, no. I never gave him an ultimatum. I didn't say, "Marry me or we're done." I had no intention of breaking up with him. I wasn't splitting hairs, either. What I said was, I didn't want to live with anyone again, unless that someone was my husband. I didn't say our relationship was finished if I didn't get my way. There was a difference. But I also didn't mind letting Patty and Al believe I had the upper hand in the matter.

Patty wanted details. She stood up from her barstool, walked over to me and whispered, "You're not pregnant . . . are you?" I sensed she and Al were less than overjoyed by the news. Maybe they still thought I was a snob, as I'd heard from other sources. A snob. Was it because I gave up the record store life for law school? Because I didn't fawn over Al like so many women and fans of the band? Was it because I never did coke with him? Did I pose a threat to Ministry's big plan for world domination? What was it? Whatever was cramping their style for the night, the pair of them must have realized not even our wedding plans mattered in the greater scheme of Ministry affairs. The conversation went right back to business.

Later when we were alone again, I said to Paul, "I have a nagging feeling Al doesn't like me." He sighed. "He thinks you're okay. He respects you."

Pondering their limp response to our news, I considered the fact that Patty was managing a lot of the band's affairs. I could see why she—they—would be thrown off by a wedding. Still, it would have been good for Paul's ego to get a word of approval from Al instead of a half-assed grin.

"This might be awkward," I said to him as we discussed telling our families and our other friends.

"Who gives a shit?" he said. "This is what we want to do. It's our lives, not theirs."

12

We now had a plan for our future together. Paul focused on Ministry's tour preparations, and I broadened my job search. I wanted more than anything to work for a law firm with a sense of mission, a cause. I thought about Paul's focus on making music, making a living at it, and being convinced he would be successful doing what he loved. What did I want? What interested me? I had researched AIDS legislation for the ACLU as a student intern. Working for the ACLU in Chicago was an honor. I had put in my year at the DePaul Legal Clinic that started the process of suing the biggest health insurer in Illinois for breach of contract. I wanted work that had a sense of urgency to it. I was hooked by the intellectual push and pull of individual rights and constitutional law. Where to have fun with this? I convinced myself I would look for a job doing almost anything but criminal law.

I had no connections in the legal community and turned to my law school's alumni services office for help. A few sterile interviews later, I wasn't getting anywhere with companies and firms who were steeped in their own culture. Their clients seemed lower on the priority list than the quest for a new BMW or Mercedes for some of these professionals. My law school friends were finding jobs with the State's Attorney's office under Richie Daley, and some accepted job offers at big firms, where they could look forward to working eighty hours a week reading documents. It seemed everyone got loaded after work at the local bars, wondering if this is what they really wanted to be doing. I told a career counselor at DePaul I was looking for some type of civil rights related work, anything but criminal law, as I still pondered counseling entertainment clients. "That's a tough one," she said.

I was getting married. My future husband's music career was accelerating with no pause in sight, while my professional aims were still coming into focus. Make a move already. Keep going, I thought, determined to find something solid to build up for myself.

I stepped outside the alumni career office, stopped to take a deep breath, and tried to recall why I went to law school to begin with. I needed to support myself. I was smart, a creative thinker. I loved walking around downtown Chicago, surrounded by the most spectacular blocks and blocks of historical buildings—landmarks—and thinking about the history of this city. I wanted to move every day through this landscape and make something, make a point, write a brief, save someone's life (maybe even my own) in the process. As I stood in the hall wondering if I would ever fit in with my new chosen profession, I looked over at the job board again. I wanted to be distracted from these questions in my head. I began looking at the names and fonts used in some of the postings on the board. The fonts . . . oh for cryin' out loud. What was I doing? Looking for visual cues from the universe? "Think. Open your mind. You have options here. You've never been afraid of challenges." When I finished the motivational speech to myself, I went back to the board. "Mitchell D. Kreiter & Associates— Criminal Defense." What's the "D" stand for? Who were these people? I had a brief moment of clarity when I suddenly realized I could apply my passion for constitutional law on a daily basis to criminal cases. Criminal cases. They were all about constitutional law. The Fourth and Fifth amendments? I had been dead set against practicing criminal law, but what did I have to lose? I couldn't stomach working for the government locking other people away from society. I could flip that narrative and defend the rights of the accused. Now that was a sexy alternative. It had possibilities. "Swingin'."

I submitted my resume and was called for an interview. I took my mother, the trained tailor, to Joseph A. Banks & Co. in downtown Chicago, across from Marshall Field's, and picked out the thinnest, gray-wool, cropped single-breasted suit jacket I could find, with a matching long skirt of tiny accordion pleats. It was the most flattering conservative suit in the place; something I could wear with a straight face at a time when in many courtrooms in the city, women lawyers were sneered at for wearing pants. Unbelievably, in 1988 a tiny handful of women still wore those awful little thin bows, tied around their shirt collars like cheap fabric bolo ties.

Tom Gibbons, the hiring partner at the firm, had graduated from my alma mater DePaul and was a former prosecutor. He liked my resume, the Legal Clinic experience, the ACLU hours. I felt confident I was in. Yes, this is where I needed to be. Everything happens for a reason, I told myself. The one area of law I definitely wanted no part of became my home. The lawyers who practiced criminal defense law in Chicago were a small club—nothing new to my ears. The best firms were known by the people who needed them through word of mouth. Mitchell Kreiter and Tom Gibbons were well known in the Hispanic community for their passion. I was happy for the association. I got the job.

***

My first day of work, I rode the el downtown, got off near City Hall, and walked north over the Chicago River, half wishing the firm were in the Loop, not three blocks away at Hubbard and Clark. I paced myself, lazily walking up Clark Street considering where there might be some landmarks in this neighborhood. I couldn't recall ever walking in the area, although the mix of older storefronts on three-story brick buildings seemed familiar. Was O'Banion's around here? I felt slightly disoriented because of the daylight. I might have passed this way at night going to a club or a gallery show.

As I came up on Hubbard Street, I could feel the sides of my mouth reflexively turning upward with amusement. I realized I was having a "gay" moment. I kept on walking, past the building where my new office was and marvelled at a building across the street. There, discreetly tucked in with the rest of the 1930s era storefronts was "The Baton," one of the oldest drag bars in Chicago. I had been a few times with Jim and Dannie and my Wax Trax friends. It was a place of high "classy" drama. It was where Bryan Ferry was spotted after a Roxy Music show in town. As I walked into my new employer's building I thought, what am I getting into?

Beggars can't be choosers, as they say. I had whittled my options down to a life of crime and punishment, so to speak. At the very least, I might espy an occasional "performer" in daylight on my rounds back and forth to court—fat chance. Drag queens saved their good looks for the night.

I walked into my new office and was told by the receptionist to have a seat in the conference room. Walking into that room, I saw a silver-haired, middle-aged man sitting at the head of the table, smoking. Was he a client? This guy was wearing oversized rectangular wire-rimmed glasses and a silk hand tailored suit, from what I could tell. Smoking. I looked at the suit, again. From my mother I had learned how to touch fabric, really feel it between your fingertips and look at the seams for sewing imperfections. She taught me to study movement in the fabric, the drape. I quietly admired this gentleman's suit. I knew this guy had a guy.

"How you doin'," he asked me, more as a statement that he didn't really care, than a question. "Where you from?" I was caught a little off guard. I wasn't expecting a post hire interview. "North Avenue and Pulaski," I said.

"Oh . . . Ok."

I kept looking at his gold rings, his watch, and that suit. He was mum after that. He studied some court papers on the table, ringed fingers shuffling pages like a card dealer. He occasionally glanced up at me. I couldn't help but think my new bosses threw me into this room with this guy to see whose jewelry survived. I was unaware I had just passed the Tim Dacey test.

Tim was our driver and assistant. He was the guy who "took your ass to court" and delivered you to the Cook County Criminal Courts building at 26th and California. Everyone there knew him. He didn't have a lot of patience, although he had been sober and "on the program" for decades. Tim grew up on Taylor Street around the old mafia, the "Outfit" guys. He himself could never be "made," being half Irish. He was a recovering heroin addict who had been to Leavenworth prison. Tim finally hit bottom after being arrested for shooting at police officers while speeding down Lake Shore Drive with a trunkful of furs (probably wearing a silk suit). He was a career thief. I was doing good by his standards—for a neighborhood girl.

Tim, dressed as he was, would drive Tom's Cadillac Brougham to be detailed at his "guy" at Grand Avenue and Ogden. Across the street was a shack that sold Italian beef sandwiches. Tim knew this guy, too. On his way to the courthouse to file papers, he'd say, "Gerda, I'm goin' to Grand and Ogden on my way back from court. You wanna beef?" Tim would return from 26th street with our sandwiches, simmering about something that happened at the courthouse. "So, this brahd . . . oh 'scuse me, Gerda you ain't a brahd . . . anyway, this brahd says to me . . ." Tim was "hot," often. He would get into arguments with the parking attendant in the open lot across the street where the two partners, Mitchell and Tom, kept their cars.

It was Mitchell's habit to pace in "la oficina" as he called it. Half into a cigarette, he'd walk out of his office, yell something to Sheilia, our secretary, head for the coffee maker, turn around, tell Sheilia to get him a coffee, and charge back into his corner office slamming the door. One day, Mitchell was in his paces, and he came into my office. "I don't know where Tim is. He took the Mercedes to get washed." Mitchell turned to the window facing the parking lot and looked down. "Oh Christ." He pulled open the window and began yelling out into the street below.

"Timmy, come on inside. TIM!!!" I looked over Mitchell's shoulder, and there was Tim in a staring contest with the lot attendant. Finally, after a few seconds, Tim took a step back. We waited and watched. Tim was still talking. He suddenly grabbed his silk suited crotch and yelled, "Oh yeah?! VA—FFAN- --CULO!!!!!(more Italian words, mixed with English)" He didn't look up at the window where Mitchell and I were both now yelling (and laughing).

The culture around criminal defense in Chicago was tight. The lawyers all loved to hate each other—it was competition gossiping. At my firm, we wouldn't take rape cases—others did that work, no problem. There were only so many high-profile cases and families who could pay for discretion. It was all about theater and getting a lot of cash up front from the clients. But there were also the bread and butter cases: DUIs, "juvie" cases, the occasional "stinky little gun case." Walking into the arena of juvenile court was like nothing else. Because of court rules, the corridors had to be clear. No congregating. I would find the client and go. There were angry gangbangers waiting to be "cut loose" so that they could get back to "their shit." I kept my eyes up and felt a certain pang from growing up where I did.

If I saw another professional woman in the courtroom, she was either the court reporter or the rare prosecutor (or even rarer judge). That didn't bother me one bit. It wasn't a beauty contest—focus on the law, the facts of your case, and do your job. My gender had nothing to do with my competency, and I was used to being around a group of guys with outsized egos.

A few times I had to drive myself to 26th street when Tim was engaged somewhere else with Mitchell. In my court clothes, I slid into Tom's black Cadillac for the first time. Tom asked me to put gas in the car. I had had a driver's license for about a year. I pulled into the gas station near the office and hunted for the gas cap on the Brougham. The Cadillac Brougham model for that year was "the largest American made vehicle in its class." A luxury liner of sorts. I had no clue what I was doing. The attendant came over, recognized the car and said, "You ever drive this thing before?" He walked around the back of the car and flipped the license plate. "That's where it goes," he laughed. It was the first time I had ever pumped gas into any car. It spilled on my hand—I was already toxic for 26th street.

I cruised past the parking lot at the Criminal Court's building as the attendees for the morning's sessions drifted by the car in small groups, flashing thumbs up and gang signs and blowing kisses at the window. "I want YOU to be MY lawyer," one or two yelled at the car. The others just mouthed the words and nodded. I imagined I could hear music somewhere, and that I was stuck in someone's video, gliding along in my ride.

Away from my professional life, my personal time was becoming more and more dependent upon Paul's studio schedule and tours. Ministry planned to tour the US for two months, starting on Halloween in San Francisco and ending New Year's Eve in Chicago. The band left a few days before Halloween. With Paul on the road, I began to record my thoughts about our long-distance relationship and why I held onto whatever we had, to understand why we were together and why we would stay together. I wrote in my journal:

"I spoke to you this afternoon, and it was no different from any other time when you have been away. Not really, although we are both reading Lolita at the same pace. I don't recall how many times I have read this book, only that I have made it a habit. I imagine this dialogue with Vladimir Nabokov, and how he is not interested in talking about his books at all. This of course pleases me immensely. Artists in general are bad at "explaining" what they do.

"When I speak of creativity and making art, I speak of course of the guy with the leather bolo tie who points to the left at the Dallas airport. I speak of the octogenarian woman I helped in her walk across three blocks on Clark Street a couple of years ago, a woman who was positive I would be a good lawyer; although, she didn't know scratch about me. I speak about half-second daydreams that consume me and everyone else.

"I can't ever believe that you're leaving. You're going to Cleveland. You're off to Vancouver. Who do you know there? I'm glad to see you go, and I am so convinced that I will never see you again as I have seen you today, and you know that that is the simplest of truths."

Sometimes I read these notes to Paul. Sometimes, I stored them away.

Ministry was on the road, and I considered possible dates for me to see the live shows. There were two: December 3rd in Chicago and December 22nd at the Holiday Star Theater in Merrillville, Indiana. I would go to both.

I preferred going early to shows, giving myself some time to talk to people at the clubs and get comfortable with the idea of being backstage. At times I caught glimpses of people doing things pre-show, post-show, and on the coach (the tour bus), things which brought on a feeling of embarrassment for me, rarely for them. One of the first times this happened was before Ministry's show at the Rivera on

December 3rd, at a time when the band was doing soundcheck—earlier in the day. The Rights of the Accused was opening for Ministry. Despite their name, they were a fun bunch of pranksters. The members of both bands were coming into and going out of the dressing room, and I wanted to get away from the growing crowd of bodies. I had the urge to leave the room and find a restroom, somewhere to be away from the smoke and people doing stupid things just to impress Al—or worse, sitting there staring at Al, waiting for him to do something outrageous. He had a habit of doing this campy dance like a drag queen in the dressing room, flapping his hands, pulling down his pants, constantly moving his body to limber up—didn't everyone?

I headed down the hall to a separate toilet. It may have been for the opening bands or the spillover backstage. I opened the door and looked in upon two stalls across the room. When I stepped in, a girl's head appeared slowly coming out from one of the stalls, then her full figure. She was fully dressed. Directly behind her, was one of the Rights of the Accused guys. Another band member stepped from around the corner of the second stall to get into the same stall with "Tammie," the girl I'd just seen. The three of them all looked up at me, then looked away not saying anything. I turned around and walked out, feeling a little nauseated.

I didn't have the slightest interest in knowing what they were doing. The expressions on their faces were all the same. They weren't drunk or high. No emotion. No smiles. No eye rolling, glassy eyes, or cocaine snorting sound effects, just a snapshot of human behavior I had no reference for, and one I couldn't shake loose. Need. Opportunity. Situational wants and fulfilling those wants. The undertow of the rock show. I hoped I wouldn't see Tammie again later on. It reminded me of punk rock club days at La Mere and outside at Neo's in the dead of winter. There was one girl at the clubs who would step out into the quiet, pitch-black gangway and perform her act while the soundtrack inside the club provided a muted series of background explosions. Her nickname: Blow Job Lucy. I found it all rather puzzling. Degrading. Why not be known for your own talents rather than glom onto someone else's fame or sexual desires. Get your own thrills. I never felt threatened by the girls who showed up backstage at

Ministry shows looking for companionship. Paul and I were into each other and nobody else came close.

After the Riviera show, Ministry was booked for a half-dozen shows out of town, heading to the east coast and swinging back to play Merrillville, Indiana's Holiday Star Theater. I was having dinner at Las Mananitas with my friend Sue a week before the Holiday Star show, when our waiter friend Manuel came up to the table and asked me if I was going out to Merrillville to see the band. I told him I had no way of getting there, not having a car, nor was I planning to rent one just for a night.

"Why not go with us?" Manuel and his boyfriend Guillermo both stood there at the table looking so formal in their waiter's black and whites. They went to every Ministry and Cocks show they could get to. They were loyal fans and friends of the band. I thought, "Sure. Why not?" They're nice people. Responsible, hard working guys. The weather forecast predicted heavy snow and blizzard driving conditions for the 22nd—there was my why not. But I didn't care. Manuel and Guillermo didn't care about the snow either. I wanted to see my future husband. It was Christmas week. I needed a break from lawyering and made the brilliant decision to head to Indiana with our friends. They would drive. It was an hour and a half away in good weather. I could relax, trade places, and let someone else be responsible for my wellbeing for a change.

It never occurred to me to not head off into below zero weather in a lightweight compact car with some extremely excitable Mexican guys who smoked pot as much as anyone else we knew, and who brought along their "cousin" to share the driving. I prayed they wouldn't light up a joint on the highway out. These guys were native Spanish speakers and LOUD. I deciphered every other word from their bantering and singing. I laughed with them at their jokes; although, I didn't understand most of it. Sitting in the back seat, I fell into the role of very white, potential legal counsel in the event we went off the road or were pulled over by cops needing to hassle some Mexicans. Paul and I loved those guys. It was a mobile party, the intersection of my legal life and my evolving involvement once again in the music industry. We were driving through a snowstorm. It was happening. I felt strangely happy to be alive. The singing was lulling my nerves. I closed my eyes and thought about Christmas and spending it with Paul. When I opened them again, we were at the venue.

Paul came home after the show. He was gone again the day after Christmas, bound for Dallas. I wrote him a letter, never mailing it:

"I'm embarrassed by the charms of Christmas. I'm embarrassed by the inventory of new toys that everyone is buying this year. There was a mild snowstorm in Chicago today, and I walked through the salt and snow to buy a winter squash. I feel like a lowcut dress this evening and no one else to enjoy it but me. I've gone through all the presents and find my lungs big enough to sing an opera. Simple things.

A camera. New cotton panties that leave me with the feeling I will only wear white from now on. Leather gloves that already fit . . . I recall now how I recited a line from Frank O'Hara's poem "Music." To you. On Christmas Eve. You were so nonplussed by that. I cannot recall very much verbatim—only that which I believe is worth remembering."

I didn't want to spoil the feeling of missing him. I put the letter away and went to sleep. I had work the next day.

13

You learn a lot about what motivates people to commit crimes when you practice criminal law. Often, it's not much more incentive than that's what they know. Their family history. Lack of resources. They grow up around gangs. Then there are the thrill seekers, the reckless ones who should know better. One of the singularly clueless clients we had was someone who wasn't a gangbanger at all. He was a white guy from the north shore, in his Porsche at a tollbooth outside of the city when some guys yelled at him from another car. He pulled out a gun and let go a round or two. Maybe he felt threatened. Or maybe he was feeling a little rebellious in his $80,000 sports car. Whatever his reasoning, it was a losing case. The toll booth had cameras, and our cowboy client was caught on film. Street smarts won't save you 100 percent of the time, but common sense is a plus. This guy had none.

In my first year with Mitchell and Tom, I soon realized that no matter how smart a defense lawyer I might be, most of our drug clients wanted a man to represent them in court. To them, I was a skirt with a brain. Nothing personal, of course. I couldn't do anything about other people's stereotypes or prejudices. This was business.

The clients wanted someone macho, a perceived even match for the prosecutor. This is what they found in Mitchell. I got that message loud and clear. Mitchell would see these clients into his corner office and call in our Spanish interpreter, Nancy Santiago. Nancy was a beautiful, curvy Puerto Rican twenty something who was there for the translation as much as for the mental undressing going on. I could hear Mitchell yelling once the door closed. I could hear him yelling in bastardized Spanish, and Nancy calmly keeping pace. He would say the arrest was bad, "what a tragedy to take this man away from his family and throw him in a jail cell for NOTHING." When the client interview was finished, there were smiles and handshakes to go around. Mitchell retreated to his office, coming out moments later with a jittery, "I can't take it. I'm taking heat from the clientes!" He was, of course, joking. I caught the smirk on his face as he closed his office door. It was theater. Mitchell was a brilliant lawyer, and the first one I knew who dared to bring in an expert witness on a case to illustrate the racial discrimination inherent in handing out stiffer sentences for crack cocaine than for powder cocaine. Mitchell was always looking for the new angle.

While preparing for my first visit to the Cook County Jail to see a client, Mitchell's partner Tom took me aside. "Ya know, the attorney/client interview room is the room they used to carry out executions back when guys got the chair. There are old blood stains on the floor." Our driver Tim lowered his glasses. "Yeah. Guys died over there." Fantastic.

To see our Spanish-only speaking client, Nancy and I took a ride over to the jail. We checked in, laid our briefcases on the conveyor belt, and rode the elevator down. We stepped out to a corridor lined with side by side, orange-painted metal lock ups. In the 1970s, marketing people had determined that the color orange for the interior of a restaurant encouraged patrons to eat more and have an enjoyable experience. The color orange confounded me. Putting men in identical prison wear and isolating them with nothing but orange to look out to through vertical mail-slot sized slits in their cell doors was my idea of "cruel and unusual" punishment. The salmon-colored suit I was sporting that day could have been the final straw, for some of them.

As we passed by the cell doors, some prisoners whistled. Attempting to stand out in this pageant of eligible bachelors, one inmate pushed his index finger through the window slot and chatted with us through up and down finger "nods." "Hi," he whispered. "How are you," he asked in an urgent tone of voice. I wondered what he was doing with his other hand. Despite the revolting, grimy uniformity of the jail, there was a new story waiting with each visit.

Ironically, what bothered me about being an advocate for the defense, and what was absolutely essential to being a "zealous advocate," was recognizing the power I had to boss my clients around.

"You want to see your kid again? Keep a journal detailing what you do in between your supervised visits," I told one client. I suggested she wear more feminine clothes to court and be polite and respectful with the judge and clerk. A bit of theater, a bit of lip gloss. She knew the drill. She was no stranger to the court system, visiting courtrooms like this one since high school. Out on bond with a heroin possession charge, she could barely stay sober.

This case, like every child custody case I worked on, reminded me of how lying in court was the dominant talent on all sides in cases involving children. Everyone lied—the clients, the social workers, DCFS (Department of Children and Family Services). It was all a matter of degree. This, for me, was the lowest you could go in a profession which required grace and integrity. I had my standards, until I played out the tape in my head of possible scenarios for a particular child's circumstances: If mom goes to jail, kid goes to foster care where anything can happen. If mom gets custody and no jail time, mom gets on methadone program and kid has a chance to see how the system works. Mom's character gets gussied up by me, despite that I maybe know she's not been sticking entirely to her bond requirements. So be it.

In law school I once made the comment to some classmates that someday a couple of us could be arguing a case in front of the Supreme Court. "You've gotta be kidding" was the consensus. They all had a bemused look, which made me feel as though I would never fit in with this legal clique who apparently knew more about the real practice of law than I ever would. I had a degree in English. Many of my classmates had studied history, marketing, or accounting. I felt somewhat vindicated when my boss Tom sponsored me to be licensed with the US 7th Circuit Court of Appeals after I'd been with the firm for a couple of months. Not everyone has those privileges. The 7th Circuit is one step below the Supremes. I realized again that not everything you heard in law school was true. During my first year of law school, I tuned out every voice I heard claiming they didn't study at all for finals. Sure thing.

My first appearance on a case before Richard Posner, Frank Easterbrook, and the other justices of the 7th Circuit would have been daunting for many young lawyers. I don't fully know why, but standing there in front of the panel felt familiar to me. Although I hadn't performed this exact task before, I was there as the one female lawyer in a multi-defendant drug case. Muscle memory kicked in. It didn't matter this was one step below the "Supremes." No time for hesitation, just stomach flutter as I imagined getting on a stage would be for musicians I knew. It was performance. You've warmed up practicing scales, now you're ready for the solo. It's live—your one shot for the day. You hear your cue from the judge, step up to the spotlight to use the force of your words, stir the court's attention and gut, the way music stirs us from the orchestra pit. Just another learning experience, not much different from arguing a case in front of the Illinois Supreme Court, something I'd already done at least once by then.

I recognized some of the local counsel. I also recognized F. Lee Bailey, one of the most famous lawyers in America. He was hired to represent one of the other seven defendants. He kept disappearing into (we guessed) the men's room. The justices listened to my spiel, with Justice Posner looking mildly amused. He later wrote the opinion in my client's case agreeing that yes, that kilo in the bag could have been any one of a number of grocery items: a five pound bag of sugar, a brick of coffee (Bustelo, anyone?). But alas, Posner decided the arresting agents had followed the law. I believe he even used the word "alas."

The variety of cases in my office and the speed with which most were resolved were the envy of my law school friends. Some of them worked sixty to eighty hours a week, pouring over contracts, drinking too much after work, and getting up the next day to do it all over again. I was appearing in state and federal court, writing appeals, and interviewing clients at Cook County jail and the federal lockup, the MCC. I was having a lot of fun.

The MCC or Metropolitan Correctional Center was a putty-colored, twenty-eight-story-high building in the shape of a right triangle, which sat in the south Loop next to el tracks on one side and not much else on the other. Irregularly placed vertical slits for windows ran up and down the face of the building to create a façade resembling an old computer punch card—a very modern 1970s era design. The MCC was meant to house federal prisoners waiting for court dates down the street and those serving short term sentences.

I had occasional client interviews at the MCC. The security guards on the ground floor would stamp my hand on the way in. On the way out, I pulled up my sleeve and held the stamp under a black light for inspection to ensure I had in-and-out privileges. It was like going to a club. But once in and out again, there was relief to not have to go back inside. The ripe pheromones of a client in a poly-blended jumpsuit, perspiring the whole conversation, gave the lingering impression he hadn't showered in days.

It seemed like a joke whenever the feds filed for civil forfeiture on our clients' properties and their cars. With case names like US v. One 1967 Chevrolet Corvette, you couldn't help but smile at the battle imagery invoked by those simple words. One of the few forfeiture cases we had which had a very good chance of being thrown out of federal court involved a client who was just a young kid, still in his late teens. His family was perpetually rumored to be kingpins of the local heroin trade. The family name was well known in certain circles. The kid himself didn't do anything illegal, but the burden of proof for forfeiture cases was so low, and the US Attorney's office was so primed to get him to testify in federal court, presumably to rattle him on the stand. I was set for a trial date on the car case, when at the last minute a call came from a family member. Forget about the car. They didn't want their boy going anywhere near a courtroom.

Paul and I had begun telling the rest of our friends we were getting married. We decided we should have platinum wedding bands, the most precious of metals. Neither of us ever wore gold. Not even gold and silver side by side—how gauche. We had no idea jewelers had to special order platinum. The universal standard for wedding bands was gold. Everywhere. I couldn't believe I missed this fashion "classic." I wandered into Tiffany's on Michigan Avenue and asked to see what they had available in platinum.

"We don't do platinum." The clerk didn't bother looking up from his appointment book. Priggish twit.

I asked, "Why not platinum? I don't wear gold. This is Tiffany's. Don't you offer your clients options to gold?"

Realizing I wasn't budging from his field of vision, the clerk raised his voice slightly, still looking down and said, "No one wants platinum." In other words, I was a no one. Tiffany's could now assure itself that this no one would never be a customer.

"We'll have to get creative with the rings," I told Paul later. I mentioned our plight to my boss Mitchell. Mitchell called around to our clients who owned jewelry stores near Humboldt Park. Side businesses. One client offered to custom make our bands. How ironic. My old working-class stomping grounds would be the source for uncommonly rare wedding bands.

Our plan was to drive to Las Vegas and get married inside a casino. We were gambling with our futures together, so why not throw in a sideshow? Michael Short and Ellie Fairey were game for a trip to Las Vegas and asked if they could join us. If the shows were lousy, we could all read a book together poolside and flirt with the bartenders. Paul's brother Roland was coming from Seattle with his wife Lisa. We went ahead and booked rooms at the Golden Nugget off the main strip.

Paul never ceased to surprise me. I didn't have a clear idea of how we were getting to Las Vegas, when he called me at work and said he'd bought a car. He said it was the perfect ride for "cross country . . . uh, driving! Yeah." I trusted his taste.

In June, a few days before our wedding date, we set off for Las Vegas in an olive green 1970 Plymouth Fury III convertible with the top up for most of the ride. A big American car. My driving skills were still fairly underdeveloped. I had successfully avoided getting a license for years, but I was an adult now. I wanted to learn to ride a motorcycle. Paul's influences were rubbing off. So, being possessed once again of only a driving permit issued in Illinois, I was a moving target in probably five or six states. Growing up in Chicago I never really needed a car and managed to ride trains and buses at every hour of the day. It was part of my rhythm, my schedule, my day to day. Maybe it was time to branch out of my comfort zone in this rather large way.

We coasted into Las Vegas early on June 20th and discovered the Golden Nugget would not check us in before noon. It being 9:00 a.m. or so, we decided to investigate City Hall or the county courthouse or wherever it was that the real people of Las Vegas worked and issued marriage licenses. In Vegas, there was no particular blood test to take and no waiting period. Their motto, obviously, "Let's be generous."

The process of getting married had always seemed so stingy to me, so tight, so perfectly orchestrated. It was opposite to what was going on in our lives. I was ecstatic to be marrying the most generous, kindest, handsomest man I had ever met. He made me laugh and think about art in new ways and made me feel good to be myself. There was nothing perfectly planned about wearing a sculpted, strapless Victor Costa floral cocktail dress I ordered over the phone two weeks before our trip after seeing a photo in Vogue in an ad of a dress I thought I could wear. The dress arrived the day before we left town.

There was nothing stingy about lying poolside in a black bikini and little sunscreen or throwing away twenty-five or thirty dollars on the slot machines, when what you started with was ten. Paul and I decided to get married in Las Vegas because both of us were spiritual souls, but neither of us were attached to any organized religion, and we both wanted a road trip with an excuse to go to Las Vegas. I had never been. The idea of lingering over a blackjack table had gotten into his head. I imagined he was simply obsessed with the word—black . . . jack. It made a nice staccato point.

Paul's brother Roland arrived in town for the event with his filmmaker wife Lisa. Lisa shot Super 8 film of us sitting on the headrests of the backseats in the Fury with the top down, cruising the drag in front of the casinos. Michael Short, Ellie, Paul, and I formed a human flotilla in the pool at the hotel, all of us wearing the darkest shades we had and baring our skin and souls. I was the only one without a tattoo somewhere. We were all disappointed when we learned Nudes On Ice was no longer an active show to see. The appeal for us was acknowledging retired showgirls hired for this gig—presumably they could also skate. Drinks and more drinks and surprisingly not a good meal to be found anywhere. We guessed eating delicious food was the lowest priority on the minds of gamblers and tourists thinking of winning it big.

Romantic feelings aside, we wanted the ceremony itself to fully embody the gamble of marriage. We sought out a chapel intentionally situated inside a casino. There were dozens of options for couples in search of a theme in Las Vegas, but only one casino had what we wanted—Circus Circus. There, the dearly beloved gathered at "The Chapel of the Fountain" nestled inside the casino, tucked away discreetly like a chapel embedded in a hospital. The namesake fountain suggested a martini glass, multi-tiered monument to flowing champagne excess. The actual fountain turned out to be not much more than a garden hose hooked up to a ceramic wall sconce. Maybe it wasn't even ceramic. On this day, nothing was kitschy as we ditched our design snob ways to make room for the transient Las Vegas way of life.

We were married on the summer solstice, the longest day of the year—June 21st. I had no doubt in my mind I would be happy to wake up every morning and see the human being I chose to marry lying next to me. He was almost giddy at the altar. Paul looked so anxious to put the ring on my finger I was worried he would let loose with a "Fuck, yeah!" when the minister asked, "Do you, Paul Gordon Barker . . . ?"

The minister asked me if I would be taking my fiancé's last name. I said yes. Before leaving on our trip, we had discussed the pros and cons of the name change. For me, it was a career decision.

"In court, my name is weird enough. 'Gerda Serba'—do you know how many times I get the incredulous look like, 'You playin' with me,' from the court reporter while their fingers are tapping away? If I change it to 'Barker' it will make their job a little easier," I told Paul. And that was that. I became Mrs. Barker—"Gerda Barker" for the stenographers.

It seemed odd to me that Al and Patty Jourgensen either weren't interested in coming to our wedding or couldn't make it. Paul didn't care. He was relieved to be away from the studio grind. It was a pleasure to be married in the company of four people we adored, who wanted to spend the day with us. My new sister-in-law documented our journey down the aisle in Super 8, and it was back to sightseeing on the strip.

Always in search of vintage or unusual jewelry and watches, we targeted the pawnshops, the most likely places to find real fortune abandoned in exchange for a few more dollars to burn. In a place devoted to thrills, people around us were indeed abandoning their heirlooms to win at the tables and slots. For the really desperate and discouraged, the free ad papers at every corner box were filled with hotline numbers for hot dates. Paul and Michael flipped through one after another and asked out loud, "Who calls these places?"

Our stay in Las Vegas was brief but left a red-carpet impression. Michael and Ellie flew back to Chicago. Roland and Lisa were off to someplace else, possibly Seattle. Leaving Las Vegas behind, Paul and I headed to the west coast to see friends in LA, San Francisco, and Seattle before swinging back to Chicago in that boat of a ride. At every stop someone had to ask, "How does this work, you being a lawyer and him being a musician?" It wasn't about career choices and cliques. I had met and known a lot of musicians in my life and couldn't have pictured myself in a meaningful relationship with any of them until now. I saw Paul as a human being, as a man, first. The musician part added color. This would be an engaging life-long partnership, we told ourselves. It was nobody else's business why we were together, how it "worked." The image of being with anyone else was unthinkable. We had more fun together than we did alone.

In LA, we rang my old friend Rick Buscher and gratefully slept on an air mattress in his apartment for a night. Rick had recently moved to LA from his hometown of St. Louis. Our bohemian honeymoon was taking on more adventure in the chase than any tour package of Hawaii or wherever other people spent days after their weddings. Paul and I didn't care what other people did. We had our own fun. Having coffee at Rick's, I admired a painting he'd done hanging on one of his walls. "That's pretty nice. Self-portrait?" I asked. "Yeah. You want it? I didn't have money to get you guys a present for the wedding." I could have wept. I could never refuse original art. The canvas was locked in the trunk of the Fury, and we headed north for San Francisco.

Paul drove in circles at the Presidio searching for a parking spot big
enough to accommodate the Fury. "How long do you think this marriage will
last?" I jokingly asked my new husband. He looked wounded by my question.
"How long? Forever! What do you mean?! . . . This is hopeless . . . FINDING
PARKING—not our marriage."

We visited Seattle for two days and stayed with Paul's aunt and uncle,
the people who raised him. Paul and his brother Roland had spent childhood
afternoons sometimes playing croquet on the grassy lawn around the old house
with their cousins or inside playing cribbage and Scrabble for hours out of the
rain. It must have been a Seattle thing—not something I grew up with. Paul was
raised in a houseful of kids who were mostly not his siblings. It must have been
a detached attachment. Life. Paul's uncle Charles painted some of the pictures
hanging in the house. How wonderful that my partner and I now had this in
common too, something so intimate as the ability to rest our eyes every day on
original family art. It was with these realizations in my head we left Seattle for
the drive back home.

Somewhere, sometime, I read about the "hidden life," one that generates
thoughts in a person which seem out of the norm. I felt nothing was hidden in
my life, even if it was beyond vocalizing. I would habitually ask Paul, "Was
denkst du?" (What are you thinking?) It was the beginning of a decades-long
examination into his thought process and my own, when there was nothing solid
for me to say, but acknowledge that I was there, looking at him and curious about
what he might be thinking, something concrete I could riff on with my own take.

About a month after returning from our Las Vegas road trip I mentioned
to Paul that I kept seeing his friend Eric Werner's face while I was awake and
working. I met Eric in San Francisco on our trip. He was the singer in Paul's
former band, The Blackouts. There was some connection I felt with Eric. Paul
and I met a group of his old San Francisco friends—Eric, Lisa, Tenta, and Gigi.
Lisa asked me what I expected to accomplish as a lawyer. We were all sitting in
the outdoor back of a biker bar and my eyes went to Eric, who was sitting next
to Lisa. He leaned into our conversation even though his head was turned to Gigi

and her storytelling. I told Lisa, "I just want to be good at what I do. Be useful in that world." I distinctly felt this was a conversation between three people, not two. I did wonder what Eric was thinking about. I was mixed in with this group of artists in a bar in San Francisco, telling them my story, like I was a visiting somebody. Perhaps all of these people were curious as to why their Paul had chosen to marry me. It occurred to me much later that he probably slept with some or almost all of them at some point. Funny thought. Although Paul was the only man I anticipated being intimate with now that we were married, others I met gave meaning to my life too. Up to this point, most of my friends had been men. That wasn't going to change.

The vetting of friends, vetting of family. The escapades of our past—we try and clean them up and show those people we are doing just fine, thanks. I felt this was part of what was going on in San Francisco, why Paul took me there to meet that group. Did I do this with Paul? Many of my friends already knew him or of him before we were married.

My mind wandered to thoughts of our twenties, and how in our collection of friends and co-workers and lovely people to party with, there were those moments when people got together, hooked up for a night. I couldn't remember doing that more than once, with Greg Pickett at Wax Trax. Greg was in between girlfriends; I routinely wasn't seeing anyone at the time. We were both soul and funk fanatics. We talked about how cool and funny it would be to go out to Dingbats, the local old-school black disco. I hadn't been there since Mr. T. was a doorman and I was seventeen years old with a fake ID. Greg and I decided to make a date of it, go somewhere outside of our regular haunts.

At Dingbats the dance floor looked the same as it had in the 1970s. We were the only white couple in the place, out of step with the body hugging knits and gold jewelry many of the patrons wore so well. It was an older crowd, ten or fifteen years older than we were, easily. Greg stood out at six feet tall, wearing cowboy boots, blonde baby curls edging over his forehead, with his white, almost translucent skin and zero facial hair.

We sat at a small, round table on the edge of the dance floor. Couples danced together with a studied formality I normally didn't see at clubs. It reminded me of salsa dancing with my high school crush, Marvin Garcia. The couples seemed so "adult" together, not loose and chummy the way couples I knew were. The atmosphere in Dingbats was far more interesting than the sameness of Neo's or the neighborhood bar atmosphere of Lucky Number. It was a place that made you think you were still wrong about a lot of things.

Greg and I didn't dance at the club. We sat and watched the bodies on the dance floor performing their slow seductions, step by step. We had drinks, watched the show, and went over to Greg's apartment afterwards, a place I'd never been before. I was happy to sit around and talk for a couple of hours, but that wasn't really why we were back at his place. I was conflicted about what I was doing there and hated to think I felt obligated to pursue sex with someone I really only wanted to be better friends with. I had a passing notion that I should stop thinking so much and try to enjoy what was right in front of me, instead of wondering whether or not I'd spend a good portion of my adult life alone.

My one-night stand with Greg ended with my taking a quick glance for the last time at the full-size American flag tacked to the wall at the head of his king-sized bed that looked so inviting and quietly slipping back into my street clothes. I could hear Greg saying, "You don't have to go do you?"

I didn't. I didn't want to tell Greg I wasn't interested so much in him as I had been in revisiting Dingbats. "Gotta work in the morning." I didn't know how to negotiate these one-night things. That was clearly all it was ever meant to be for him. Fun. But now I had to pay for a cab ride home. Greg was a sweet guy. There was no passion there. Just something to do.

Jim Nash of course knew we were having a night out. I thought it odd that he didn't ask how it went, afterwards. Jim was off the gossip train for once in his life. Maybe he liked the two of us too much as individuals. Or maybe he knew nothing would come of it.

I thought about Greg and had the distinct feeling I had nothing else in common with him. In my life now, with Paul, I had everything I needed. And, I was grateful to be unburdened from having to process one-night stands or short term, convenient relationships.

Paul and I were a married couple when we arrived back in Chicago on July

2nd. I went back to my office on the third, and on the Fourth of July, we rode the Morini to Franke Fun's apartment, where he and Dave were having a barbecue in the yard. Cynthia Plaster Caster was there with Giulietta (one of the Karras twins, old friends from PRAXIS days). Franke's Thrill Kill Kult bandmates Marston Daley and Jacquie Black were sipping drinks and making small talk with Jim and Dannie from Wax Trax and most everyone we loved in the world. Franke's Belgian hare "Satan" was confined to his cage in the house as watermelons were tossed to the ground from a second story window in back, and we watched Franke and Chris Connelly eagerly forage through the juicy red flesh shattering into chunks on the patio.

I looked over at Paul. He was smiling, watching me, and talking to Jim. We were married now and nothing really looked the same—even if it was.

14

It was July in Chicago, two days following the Supreme Court's decision in the Missouri abortion case, Webster. I happened to be researching case law at the Daley Center that morning and left around noon to go back to my office at Hubbard and Clark. As I left the building, I could see across the street in the plaza of the State of Illinois building, next to the good-sized Dubuffet sculpture, a small crowd of television reporters and women carrying signs that read, "Keep abortion legal and safe in Illinois." In the center of the plaza was a massive scroll addressed to the governor of the state and signed already in differing colors of ink, by hundreds, perhaps thousands of people.

It was the first time I signed my married name to anything. It was the right thing to do on this warm day, with Picasso's Woman sculpture etching a shadow behind me. Abortion in the United States became legal in 1973 when I was in high school. It was crazy, sixteen years later and we were still debating. In the plaza most of the women carrying signs were in their early twenties. People lining up to sign the petition to the governor were largely older men and women carrying suit jackets and briefcases in the heat and pausing briefly to sign their names. This is absurd, I thought. Absurd that there should be any question as to whether women are qualified enough or have the right to decide when they will have children. Women are the only people capable of bearing children and yet the least qualified to make that choice?

Back at the apartment that evening, I answered calls from friends leaving RSVPs on our answering machine to let us know they would be attending our after-wedding party coming up. A month before we'd left for Las Vegas, Paul and I decided to host a small cocktail party at our Logan Square apartment for our friends and family who couldn't join us for the actual ceremony. We'd have people over once we were back in town. We looked into hiring a chef friend to cater for us and fifty of our dearest co-conspirators in life. Rich Ladd, my old friend from restaurant days, was available. There was a lovely synchronicity in hiring Rich, who had in fact been the chef at the restaurant where Paul and I had our first date in the spring of 1987.

A couple of days before the party, Paul and I drove to O'Hare Airport to pick up my dear friend Sunny Chapman, the jewelry designer. She was in town to help us celebrate. Sunny and I rarely saw each other anymore. She was starving after a long flight, and the two of us set out for a short walk to Abril, the Mexican restaurant on Logan Boulevard around the corner from our apartment. Paul walked out with us, heading back to the studio for the evening. He was making some time to work on new Lead into Gold material, his solo project.

Paul insisted upon showing Sunny our wedding car, the Plymouth Fury, parked outside. He got in, all smiles, and turned the key. It wouldn't start. Frankly, I wasn't surprised. It seemed Paul routinely had problems with his vehicles. Ironic, considering he'd worked in the motor pool in the army and he just knew engines. Some would call that being a gearhead. These stalled engines became a kind of running joke in our house, although I never thought it was funny when we were ready to go, go, go somewhere and the machine of choice was at a dead halt. I adored his patience at times like these. He could analyze the problem and get the thing running "in no time." I trusted Paul's ability to make things work on levels very foreign to me. Once the car started up after some minor tinkering, I was relieved to see him go off to make noise that would make him happy and had little to do with Al Jourgensen or anyone else.

*

"YOU need a champagne fountain for your little shindig, Gettagirl."

My friend Ruth wasn't about to argue the point, either. The day of our party had arrived. It was Ruth who'd convinced me to be a woman already and finally pierce my ears. Who was I to disagree with her now? She arrived at our apartment early and began stacking plastic champagne glasses into a tower of Vegas-like splendor. "Pour from the top tier and watch the champagne cascading down."

"Very CLASSY," I said, putting extra emphasis on the short a in classy—a nod to the north-side Chicago accent I spent years consciously trying to dissolve. Our friends treat us so well, I told Paul.

Our chef was on the enclosed wooden porch in the back, firing up the grill for Thai shrimp kebabs, and I wanted to kiss him for not getting insulted by my father, who insisted he wouldn't pay the balance on the catering until he saw the results. I told him my dad was a control freak of many decades and, thankfully, shrimp platters and cheese frou frous were the last controlling elements of my life he had left, now that I was officially married. Guests began to arrive. I slid into my strapless floral dress and fuchsia heels. Paul helped with the side zipper, as he worked into his own outfit for the night.

"I quite like that jacket on you. And it does cover your 'dupa,' whatever there is of it" I said, waiting for him to feign a look of outrage.

The reference to Paul's posterior harkened back to our visit to Marshall Field's men's department on State Street, while looking for a suit jacket for the wedding—something rather unconstructed, in teal-blue silk blend. The jacket had a hint of Anthony Price styling. Shudder to think my husband was sporting something remotely Duran Duran-like. I preferred to think it was Bryan Ferry-ish. After all, Duran Duran had borrowed their look from Ferry (and his tailor) and not the other way around.

As serendipity would have it, the head men's tailor at Marshall Fields was Polish. He had Paul try the jacket on and spin around in it, at which point the Polish one quietly acknowledged to himself, "Good—covers the dupa" (the ass). I spit out a laugh. I, of course, have hearing in the canine range, despite attending hundreds of rock shows. To compensate for terrible eyesight since childhood, I had finely calibrated my ears to near international spy levels of eavesdropping skill. The Polish tailor looked embarrassed. His eyes went back and forth over my face, undoubtedly now seeing my cheekbones as the real Slavic thing, and not cosmetic contouring.

Paul and I were dressed, loosely color coordinated, and ready for a receiving line, were there one. Guests were allowed in with the assistance of our bouncer/door person for the evening: the inimitable Sunny Chapman. I was confident she wouldn't allow in any stray, "unauthorized motherfuckers," considering her history of bouncing thieves from her booth at the trade shows. To think, this woman had custom designed my pale green and metallic gold earrings and bracelet to go with my dress.

The lawyers from my office were caravanning over. My boss Mitchell and his wife Edie arrived, looking every bit as casually young, suburban, and elegant as they needed to be in our little apartment in reluctantly gentrifying Logan Square. Everyone I worked with understood the unusual marriage I was getting into—with a rock musician ("So what's it like, you being a lawyer . . .")—and they liked Paul. Tim Dacey had Lucille on his arm, his companion and lifelong friend from the old Italian neighborhood. The gold jewelry count between the two of them was staggering. But not too much—showing respect for the new bride.

Watching the champagne tower go up, it occurred to me I was now part of a unit. I wasn't solo anymore, and that was new. Hand-lettered invitations had gone out in the mail. All of our friends trickled in: Judy Pokonosky, who'd introduced me to Paul at Wax Trax; old friends Marston Daley and Franke Fun from the band My Life with the Thrill Kill Kult stood side by side with newer friends, Brian and Mike from the band Rights of the Accused; Cynthia Plaster Caster; Jim and Dannie, my old bosses from Wax Trax and the rest of the Wax Trax contingent; Brian Shanley, who'd I'd known since his early photography for PRAXIS magazine; my parents, my brother, my sister, my law school friends (some with impulse-challenged spouses); Keith "Fluffy" Auerbach, one of Ministry's studio engineers; my friend Sue Bowman, volunteering to be official wedding photographer; Manuel Partida, one of our waiter friends from Las Mananitas, who bestowed an original painting upon us as a wedding gift. I had forgotten he painted—beautifully. Finally, Al and Patty Jourgensen arrived—they couldn't make it to the Vegas wedding, but the party after was an easier commitment.

For once, I let everyone else run the drinks, pu pu platters, and the music. I was a real hostess now and with "help." It felt wicked to be the center of attention in my Gaugin-inspired summer colors flowing down the bodice of my dress. What a civilized gathering, I thought, as an hour or so passed and the sense that Paul and I were official now to all of these lovely souls gathered on our behalf.

My reverie was interrupted by the doorbell, ringing once, twice, again, and again with one long insistent drone. Giulietta Karras—one of the twins I'd honored with an eighteenth birthday celebration in direct contravention of her Jehovah's Witness upbringing—was grabbing my arm. "The police are downstairs."

Paul looked at me with a slightly tipsy, raised shoulder pads shrug. "Let me deal with this," I told him.

Stepping out of my fuschia heels, and hooking them with two fingers, I sashayed sideways down the hall stairs, pinching my dress upwards with my free hand. I opened the door. Two uniforms greeted me with all the dull, vaguely suspicious routine phraseology they could muster.

"Got a call about a disturbance. Neighbors complaining about the noise. You the resident here, Miss?"

"Hellooo, officers! Yes! It's my apartment—well, actually mine and my husband's—we just got married in Las Vegas. Having a little party." I told them I'd sent advance notice to the immediate neighbors and the landlord downstairs, who was gone for the week. The uniforms eyeballed my shoes and looked over my shoulder up the stairs. "Music's too loud." They stood there again looking past me. Not feeling compelled to invite them in, it was time to bring this little tete-a-tete to a close.

"C'mon you guys, I'm an attorney. I do criminal defense work downtown. My bosses are upstairs, too. We'll keep it down."

Perhaps the pink cha-cha heels dangling before them, the lack of unconscious waifs deposited on the stairs behind me, and the absence of any incriminating aromas charging the air left the lawmen satisfied there were no "indications of crime present." They were possibly thinking, thank god—who needs to trek up those stairs? They gave me a knowing nod, stepped back, and turned towards their patrol car. Neighborhood kids were gathered on the sidewalk whispering and smiling, then dispersing like ants.

I ascended the stairs to the top of the landing, snapped my pumps back into place, and rejoined our guests. Paul and the "Rights" boys were cracking stupid matrimony jokes, everyone else was smiling, toasting, and spitting shrimp tails onto paper cocktail plates. I noticed Al and Patty had once again disappeared from the party and locked themselves in the bathroom. Again. We had only one bathroom in the apartment. Our apartment was in an old graystone two-flat— three bedrooms, one bath. For the few hours they were with us celebrating, Patty and Al made several stops into the facilities, causing our other guests to linger patiently in the kitchen or admire the Marnie Warren painting hanging in the dining room. Patience. I had a lot of it.

I wondered if our guests were having a good time, but Paul looked happy and relaxed, so that was enough. My father finally removed his suit jacket and was chatting with my law school friend Mary's husband Mike, a veteran tax lawyer. They were the two oldest men in the room. Our catered menu was a hit, save for the kosher crowd. I looked at Marnie's painting again and realized Paul and I didn't have much in the way of worldly possessions, aside from a few chairs and tables. What we did have were so many people who really cared about us as individuals and as newlyweds—a unit. And we had each other. That was enough. Life on life's terms.

***

I told Paul I wanted to learn to ride a motorcycle on my own. Sitting on the back of his bike was getting old. I wanted to try something new, something physically challenging. I was inching my way into Paul's world, assimilating closer into something he knew and loved to do. I implicitly trusted his skill as a rider, but I wanted to try it for myself. He took that to mean I should own my own bike.

During those enterprising hours of downtime from the studio while I was at work, Paul searched out a bike for me that matched all the criteria for happiness in our household: it was beautiful, vintage, and a challenge. I soon became sole owner of a 1972 black and silver Ducati 250 Mach III. It was the perfect size and fit for my five foot-four frame. It looked good in an Italian vintage cool way, slightly curvy and dark. Paul thought it might have been manufactured in Spain. The gears were in reverse order, which didn't seem to be a problem for a novice like myself. There was nothing to "unlearn" about standard shifting. I did however have to learn to kick start a bike. I secretly thought my husband just wanted me to work for my fun. Being in the studio with Al for days on end was a complicated dance. Did this idea of constant struggle have to spill into every area of his life?

Michael Short was finally taking his motorcycle riding test at the DMV to officially get the m classification on his license and quit riding around illegally. Michael borrowed Paul's Morini and left his Laverda in our garage. Paul removed the plate from Michael's bike, slapped it on the back of my new little Ducati, and the two of us rode around our neighborhood flouting the law, riding with "fictitious plates" on the back. I needed something to practice on. We rode to the parking lot at Montrose Beach where I could practice bump starting the bike and riding around in circles. My new motorcycle was fun and black and adorably stylish. Paul was apparently so taken by the design elements of my new ride, he had Brian Shanley photograph it. Paul used one of the images on the cover of his Lead into Gold EP, Chicks and Speed: Futurism. Art once again mirrored life.

Two weeks after our party, I was home playing the new Lead into Gold tape Paul left for me. He was at Chicago Trax finishing up mixing his Age of Reason album. The night before, we sat in the kitchen of our apartment, listening to the songs echoing from the high ceiling in the room, down to the black-and-red checkerboard linoleum tiles on the floor. It was the room in our apartment with the best acoustics. I sat and wondered "How do these things get done? How do you know when the songs are ready?" I didn't mean the actual recordings.

I meant the songwriting process itself. Art doesn't come out of the blue. Paul focused a lot on dreams. Daydreams. Lead into Gold was his project, his up and down of his own vision. It had a different aesthetic from Ministry. Surely the process was different. Paul and Al as a team seemed to labor over Ministry material more than anything. I suggested to Paul at one point that he should just tell Al a Ministry song was done and leave it where it was. He liked that idea. It was something we talked about quite a bit. With art, you just know when it's ready. With collaborations, that was more difficult. It seemed to me, anyway.

"Do you like the lyrics?" Paul was asking about the new Lead into Gold songs. It was a question I really didn't want to answer. Lyrics in songs were not supposed to be poetry or even "good." They expressed a mood, if anything.

"I like them just fine. They sound like you." That was my honest assessment. I wasn't going to say: it sounds like you're trying to be Scott Walker or something. That wasn't true anyway. I simply wasn't accustomed to his style of singing. His voice sounded vulnerable, and that was a good thing.

Paul obsessed over his own lyrics. I told him more than once, "Stop trying to say anything. The words will come on their own. Don't force them. It won't work."

He looked at me with a wild expression. "'Fell From Heaven' is about you, you know."

Really. Okay, I could die right now and be happy for the life I had. Paul made a song, a genuine solid piece of creative labor, and it came together because of me.

"And what did I do to achieve the honor?" I asked.

Judging from the expression on his face, it took tremendous effort for him to even tell me this much. He didn't like to analyze his feelings too much. Impulse seemed more exciting.

I was discovering Paul's impulsiveness at times overshadowed his common sense. On one of the nights he was back in the studio, he met a young rap singer, a friend of someone else hanging around at Chicago Trax. The rapper might have been waiting for a budget to record in the B room. The details of their meeting were slim. In their conversation, the rapper asked Paul about our Plymouth

Fury III parked outside the studio. He was interested in buying it. We wanted to unload the car. It was an impractical beast in the city and winter was coming. They agreed on a price. Paul was happy to sell the car so conveniently and not have to think about fighting for a parking space in the snow in our neighborhood or anywhere near Chicago Trax. The Fury had fulfilled its purpose as a cross country parade car, a banner announcing the arrival of the newlyweds (us) to our west coast friends. We could use the sale money for something a little more useful than a convertible "semi-pimpmobile."

I was highly entertained when Paul brought the car home for the first time. It was a surprise. I was equally surprised to see it leave our possession so quickly. A little too quickly. In a classic example of rushing into something without thinking, Paul accepted a check for the price of the car.

"You took A CHECK?! You don't even know the guy." I had just come home from work when he told me.

Paul seemed so trusting in the inherent goodness of other people, or in this case, didn't think anyone he met at Trax would con him. It was an unwritten rule of adulthood for me. You never take a check from a stranger. I would come to know that Paul had a proclivity to trust the wrong people. This was the first of countless times when my husband would tell me, "Beautiful, you were SO right." I didn't want to be right. I wanted Paul to be more discriminating with his trusting nature.

The check bounced. Paul was pissed. He saw the rapper again at Trax, who told him to deposit the check again. His girlfriend must have withdrawn some money from his account, he said. Once again, the check was no good.

In my fresh out of law school lawyer's mind, I thought we should report the bad check and get our money back. The rapper was already tooling around town in the car with the top down. In the end, it seemed such a hassle to seriously go after such a jerk. It wasn't that much money. It was the principle involved that bothered me, and I assumed it bothered Paul, too. On the other hand, we both knew the Chicago music community was a small place, especially at Chicago Trax. Let someone else vent on this thief. Paul and I were both comfortably making our livings working. Live and learn. Bad karma moment. He let it go.

Several weeks went by. Paul and I were at a party for the record label, Invisible Records, at their new loft in the south Loop. I went outside on the roof of the building with Leila Atkins, the owner of the label, along with some other women friends who were there. While we admired the view, the surrounding landscape of industrial buildings, someone called me over to the edge of the roof. "Hey, isn't that your car?"

I looked down, and there indeed was the Fury parked on the street with the top down, unoccupied. Someone else in the neighborhood must be having a house party, I thought. Everyone we knew knew Paul had been stiffed.

"No offense, Leila," I looked up and down the deserted street below, "but you live in a pretty dangerous area for someone to leave a sweet ride like that unattended. Know what I mean?"

Since it was a party, we were all up on the roof with refreshments in hand. Bottles and bottles worth of refreshments. Without much discussion, a coordinated relay of arms went up and sacrificing one after another, a stream of open beer bottles hit their mark exploding silently into some vulnerable upholstery below.

***

In August, Paul and Al were locked in the A room at Chicago Trax finishing up the new Ministry album. The world outside the studio didn't exist for them, and the work was taking a toll on Paul's mental faculties. One night at 12:30 a.m. he called me just to complain about having to work in a "filthy studio." He was tired of it. The next day Paul wandered around our apartment singing a Dusty Springfield song. I said, "Dusty . . . nice. I love that song." It was a familiar hit, written by Burt Bacharach. Paul only knew the lyrics and couldn't remember who had done it—this, coming from someone who had the Burt Bacharach/Hal David song catalogue etched into his memory like a subset of music theory. I was worried about him.

The Warner Bros. art department was already leaving messages that they needed artwork for the album cover. Ministry had free reign over what to say with images and artwork representing the band and who to use to execute those ideas. Al got into his head the image of a human skull x-rayed for the cover. Paul envisioned something else, something not so literal a reference to the album title, The Mind Is a Terrible Thing to Taste. It was a great title and pun. I liked a sweet pun more than most, especially this one encapsulating the vagaries of wasted minds on drugs, and it was a direct assault on the old "mind is a terrible thing to waste" anti-drug campaign from the '70s. Al, like a punk rock court jester, was automatic with puns. But the x-ray idea seemed old and lazy for Ministry. It reminded me of why I disliked the photograph for their Pailhead single "No Bunny," which incorporated a stuffed rabbit. It seemed a dumbing down. Al insisted on the skull x-ray. Al had the final word.

Patty Jourgensen and I were becoming a little more friendly. We met Ruth from Wax Trax and a couple of other women a few times for high tea at the Drake Hotel. We were not necessarily chummy, but Patty and I got along well enough to share laughs about ridiculous things happening at the studio and in our lives. Patty's life revolved around Ministry business. She didn't have much time to socialize outside of that world. Otherwise, she had her daughter Adrienne to take care of and Ministry. I had a full-time career practicing law. Patty and I had our personal connections—the obvious ones, and she had, of course, pierced my ears. Patty also knew Paul before I did. They met in Boston when Al and Paul first met. Patty's best friend in Boston dated Paul after his old band the Blackouts moved there.

With both of our husbands in the studio, Patty and I would talk on the phone. It was summertime. She told me she had a friend in town who was also a mom, someone really active in her kids' lives. "Brazilian Ruth" was what everyone called her, possibly to distinguish her from the other Ruth we knew at Wax Trax. Brazilian Ruth was in fact from Brazil and seemed like a lot of fun to hang around with when I eventually met her. She had a buoyant, positive view of parenting, the kind of person you imagined found real joy in doing art projects with her kids and not just going through the motions. She was genuine, very Brazilian. And for some reason I never could understand, Al didn't like her.

I was on the phone with Patty getting the new address for Manuel and

Guillermo, our waiter friends who'd moved back to Mexico. I wanted to send a thank you to Manuel for the painting he'd given to me and Paul as a wedding gift. Patty seemed distressed on the phone. I asked her how her day was going. She said she'd been talking with Al about Brazilian Ruth.

"I don't think he wants me to have friends. He said I need to choose between Ruth and him."

"That's ridiculous," I said.

Was Al that insecure? How much more could Patty do to make his life easier? Did he require 100 percent of her free time? It riled me that this brand of emotional slavery still existed. I felt grateful for the relationship I had, one that was free of such jealousy. But I didn't want Patty to think I was being flip about her dilemma.

"I don't think Al really understands much about women if he feels threatened by your friendship with Ruth. We all need our girlfriends," I told her, and we went back to gossiping about our waiter friends, Manuel and Guillermo.

15

In 1989, the Star Top Café was the number one restaurant for everyone we knew in the music business in Chicago. Not long after we were married, we had a few dinners there with Leila and Martin Atkins. Martin had played drums with Public Image Limited and Killing Joke. Martin's band Brian Brain was active, and he knew a lot of musicians Paul and Al knew or would come to work with. Leila and I shared a healthy skepticism about the music industry having both worked in record stores, and we became chatty friends. She was from Milwaukee and possessed that brash Midwestern way of verbally tackling an opponent when they least expected it. It was an attitude of calm urgency peculiar to the upper Midwest, where in winter you knew you had to keep your body moving—if you stood still in the cold for too long you risked getting frostbite. I could see why she was good at managing her husband's affairs. I could easily see her telling a club owner, "Life is hard, but Martin will get paid, dumbshit. Get over it." Leila and I both had partners whose music we liked, and often project personnel would overlap.

Martin and Leila had moved around a bit, to the east coast, then to Chicago. They introduced Paul and Al to some of the musician friends they'd made in other cities. One evening in the fall of 1989 Paul and I had dinner at the Star Top with Martin, Leila, and two people I had never met before—Trent Reznor and Richard Patrick from the band Nine Inch Nails. Trent and Richard were sitting with some music industry types ("assistant to," "personal manager for"). Nine Inch Nails (NIN) were in town to shoot the "Head Like a Hole" video at Exit on Wells Street. Martin was hired to be the drummer for the video. Martin and Leila were friends with Trent for some time before any of the rest of us met him or Richard. For dinner, we were all seated at a long group table in the center of the dining room.

I sat across from Richard and Trent. Trent seemed slightly guarded until I joked about the exotic choices on the menu in front of them. We were soon immersed in a conversation about less sophisticated dishes from our childhoods. For his part, he could still envision those chipped beef sandwiches swirling around his palette. For me, nothing could rival Jello 1-2-3, a three-layer parfait that built itself by magic once placed in the refrigerator to cool.

I had heard from other people we knew that Richard Patrick was an excellent mimic. As dinner and multiple cocktails were winding down, I looked up at Richard and saw him miming an impression of Paul to a person sitting next to him. It was quick—like a snapshot of Paul in professor mode—and it WAS funny. I didn't say anything and didn't mention it to Paul. I forgot about it until fifteen years later when Paul and I moved to LA for a few years. We had mutual friends there who worked with Richard. I casually asked someone if he still did impressions and told them about Richard's spot on impression of Paul. This revelation made its way back to Richard, who apparently was mortified I had caught him in the act.

During our Star Top dinner with NIN, Leila invited us to come see the set where "Head Like a Hole" was being shot and to watch Martin play. It was a treat to see the dance floor at Exit covered in black reel to reel tape while Martin banged away. Eric Zimmerman, the video's director, later directed Paul's Lead into Gold video for the song, "Faster Than Light." Eric's company H-Gun produced several Ministry and Wax Trax videos and was getting popular working with NIN and other bands. While Trent was in town on this trip, Paul corralled him into making a cameo appearance for Lead into Gold. The checked windbreaker Trent is wearing in the video was pulled at the last minute from our closet at home on the day of the shoot.

Leila and I often talked about her managing hers and Martin's new label Invisible Records and about Martin's career. She was a little perplexed by the fact that Martin and I could talk about poetry and language and she couldn't. Not in the same way, anyway. It was really a mental exercise, a dance step between me and Martin. I talked about language and writing with anybody who had something to say about it. Martin had a lot to say about it. I never felt our conversations were threatening to our respective marriages. I wasn't interested in him other than as a good foil, someone happily ready to take a semi-drunken mining expedition into the world of modern writing. We would all meet at the Star Top for dinner and drinks and that was all. That was the place to be. When Paul and Al had finished vinyl—Revolting Cocks, Ministry, or a side project—we would drop a copy at Star Top and let Michael Short decide whether to play it or not. He never turned us down. Paul would step onto the window platform and deliver the first public airing of the songs—on a hi fi. Perfect.

***

Ministry's The Mind Is a Terrible Thing to Taste album was released right before Thanksgiving. A tour schedule was coming together. I felt like a bystander, waiting for the next space launch. Although I was a lawyer now, my free hours were chaotically calendared, always dependent upon Paul's studio schedule or touring. I still needed to spend time every day being quiet with myself. Restoration. Read. Write a few pages.

It was December, six months after Paul and I were ritualized into marriage. Bill Rieflin, Paul's good friend and Ministry's drummer, was staying at our apartment on Albany. I was adjusting to the idea that when Paul was preparing to go out on tour sometimes one of his bandmates would stay with us for a brief time during rehearsals. Bill was someone I was still getting to know better.

A week before Christmas, we all went to the Wax Trax Christmas party at

Jim and Dannie's. Afterwards, back at our apartment, Bill was sitting in the kitchen, drumming his fingers on the table. "You do that a lot," I told him. It was an observation, it wasn't disturbing me. It seemed almost a meditative tic of his. I noticed it every time I saw Bill—here, in a restaurant, and at the Wax Trax party. Always practicing, notating.

Someone else might have been uncomfortable with the fact that as a newlywed bride I had to accommodate visiting male friends in our apartment for extended stays. I accepted it. Sometimes the lack of privacy was a drag on our relationship, but this was part of Paul's life and now my life, too. I was more annoyed by people still asking what it was like as a lawyer to be married to a musician. I felt like saying, "Aren't you happy for us?!" It seemed such a political question, as if I were married to someone of a different race. Depending upon who was doing the asking, it really seemed like a question directed at class and stereotypes. Wasn't I, as a lawyer, supposed to be aiming higher than this? And what fun was Paul, as a rock musician, hoping to have with someone whose job was so connected to law and order—the antithesis of a (presumably) chaotic, exhilarating, creative life. It really was nobody's business, but plenty of people seemed perplexed by our choice of partners. I didn't care. Neither did Paul. Neither did Bill Rieflin. We sat in the kitchen of our apartment and Bill and I started debating the word "proud." Bill asked what I would think about his statement that he was "proud" of the way his drum playing was going on, evolving.

"Pride has a very nationalistic sting to it," I said. Bill looked annoyed by my answer.

"Forget the idea of nationalism. What does it mean as far as I'm concerned?"

I responded, "When you state that you're proud of something you've done, you're removing yourself from something which is inherently personal—what you DO." I didn't know where that came from, but I liked the way it sounded. Paul was in the habit of telling me I was wise AND the smartest person he knew.

Bill looked mildly annoyed by my comment. He said he'd "BEEN wondering" how his playing was viewed by others. Bill pronounced the word "been" with a long e like "bean," an affectation of his that exaggerated his Pacific

Northwest accent. I told him to settle down, his accent was showing.

"You're the first person to ever tell me I have an accent. What do you mean?"

I illustrated the point by asking him to pronounce the word "grocery." He said "growshery," exactly the same way Paul pronounced the word. Bill had to agree with me. He hadn't recognized something so subtle in his speech. At that moment, I felt a little less as though I was just biding time tolerating yet another musician Paul worked with.

Following our regional phonology discussion, I was even more interested in hashing out ideas with Bill. He was one of Paul's oldest friends, and I was getting to like Bill, except when he complained to me that the toilet paper in our bathroom was too rough. I wanted to say, "This isn't a four-star hotel, buddy," but instead, I just gave him a look and changed the subject.

I told Bill I had eczema on my hands all through childhood. The skin would crack and bleed, and my mother bought prescription salves for me and wrapped gauze around my fingers to keep them dry and clean. Bill knew exactly what I was talking about. He told me he had eczema as a child, too. It went away for both of us at the end of our teenage years. We realized we both felt self-conscious of our hands growing up. But my eczema didn't deter me from believing someday I would be a writer. Bill's hadn't interfered too much with his ambitions either.

I don't imagine Bill could have become such a powerful drummer had his skin condition stayed the same. The constant itching, the "pins and needles" sensation would have distracted him from focusing on the instruments he used with such stridency now in his art, his playing. As a child, it was difficult for me sometimes to hold a pen or pencil and write. The relatively soft flickers of motion in the act of writing were enough to trigger pain receptors in my fingers and warn my brain to distraction. But, no more.

During his visit, Bill practiced tai chi in our yard. His movements were graceful and exacting like his speech. He wore black cotton Chinese shoes. Bill seemed almost too measured. Maybe it had something to do with being a drummer. A great drummer. We had a mutual admiration for words and how they could be intimidating or benign. Bill read a lot. He was, after all, one of

Ministry's "Book Club." I sometimes wondered why Al coined that moniker with such derisive intent, likening his band mates to a sewing circle of literate snobs. Al was literate and a good storyteller. I imagined he simply didn't like that the other band members were more interested in exploring other distractions available to them in their free time—everything that wasn't a mind-altering substance.

I was getting a shopping list together for our own Christmas dinner coming up, and feeling energized by my conversation with Bill, I finished recording a message on our answering machine at home that went like this: "During this holiday, while you are all rereading some of your favorite books, I am reading Francis O'Hara—commonly known as Frank. FRANK for obvious reasons . . . BYE!" It was a little cheeky, but definitely me. I was amused that Bill and I were simpatico to some degree.

The Mind tour began after Christmas. Paul was once again on the road. Our long-distance relationship over the phone from hotel rooms, lobbies, and airport terminals seemed casually sexy —as if he were still just my runaway boyfriend. I had always imagined not being married at all, unless I found someone willing to agree to an arrangement whereby we would see each other six months out of the year, like Georgia O'Keeffe and Alfred Stieglitz had managed to do. The rest of the time would be to recharge. I was getting what I wished for.

Patty Jourgensen and I met again for drinks at the 95th in the Hancock building. We were having a girl's night out again, building a rapport. It was her idea. Patty looked relaxed for a change. She was wearing a skirt—an outfit almost, not her usual jeans and T-shirt for when she was doing Ministry business around their house. It felt cliche to think about, but we were band wives currently without the spouses. The conversation inevitably came around to my new married life.

"You got the better guy," she said.

I couldn't believe she was seriously comparing those two, like racehorses. They were different personality types. I wondered what was on her mind, what prompted that thought now that our spouses were safely away on the road. Al was a super talented guy, smart, funny. So was Paul. Was she finally weary of Al's showboat antics? They had been married for five years, enough time for so many things to wear thin. I couldn't imagine what it was like living with a normal guy, whatever that was, but Al must be a special case.

"What do you mean I got the better guy? What's wrong with Al?"

Patty looked at her drink. After a few silent moments, she told me Al had shoved her around once or twice.

"OH. That's unhappy news," I said. "What did you do about it? "

"Nothing."

Unbelievable. Nothing. For all the personal sacrifices she made moving to Chicago, organizing and managing the band's business affairs, and now taking care of Adrienne, she did "nothing"? Then I remembered Al's "problem" with Patty's friend Brazilian Ruth. He didn't want Patty to have any friends, it seemed. That was one of the hallmarks of an abuser. Poor Patty.

From what I knew of Patty's life, she had a fair amount of early experience booking bands in Boston and New York and knew her way around egos in the music industry. She was nobody's arm piece. Before Paul, I had no experience of day to day living with a performer. However, what I did have was visceral experience with the depths of human behavior. What could possibly have led to such rage in Patty's spouse?

Patty collected her thoughts and assured me it wasn't a big deal. As some kind of proof she told me she and Al had had dinner with some of Al's relatives afterwards and she set her husband straight on the ground rules of their relationship. One of the men at the dinner was slavishly attended to by his female companion, and Al seemed to be eating it up. Patty looked at Al and told him he could forget about that kind of "Cuban macho bullshit." She wasn't going to play that game. I wanted to believe her. Why had she told me any of this? I was happy she did, but there was nothing I could do but listen to her story.

The Mind Is a Terrible Thing to Taste Tour was becoming a turning point for Ministry as a spectacle, as a band taking not only musical risks, but risks with audience provocation and audience participation. The press was all over it. Ministry began their tour on the east coast with eight band members, including two drummers. Bill Rieflin was one. Martin Atkins was hired as the second drummer.

Not satisfied with filling the stage with bodies, the band commissioned someone to create visuals on a screen behind them and construct a massive chain link fence in the front of the stage. The mosh pit enthusiasts at the shows began climbing the fence and diving back into the audience like Wizard of Oz monkeys on fire. The Mind tour was morphing into "the fence tour" in the minds of fans, historians, and the press. I made plans to go to New York to see the show with Patty Jourgensen and fly back from Boston with Martin's wife Leila.

Before leaving town for the east coast, I invited Leila out for dinner. She was alone at home, as Patty and I were, and could probably use a break from thinking about the music business. Too much of anything is unhealthy. I could count on Leila to keep up with juicy gossip involving people I didn't know or care much about in the nascent industrial music scene. I just liked listening to Leila's raspy, smokey voice and her laugh. Leila and I put on our best jewels and headed over to the Rosebud restaurant in the old Italian neighborhood on Taylor Street, where we watched middle-aged gangsters arrive for dinner with twenty-one-year-old concubines in tow. We marveled at the outfits: sharkskin suits on the men, toned-down prom dresses on the girls—so as to appear classy. Inevitably, his money clip made an appearance at the table. For us, it was dinner and a show. So much fun. In the back of my mind I couldn't help wondering if Patty was okay. I cared because she was a good person, and not because we were sisters in this ragtag sorority of "rock wives."

*

On the flight out to New York, Patty and I were having a little too much fun ordering and immediately downing cocktails. We were priming ourselves for the evening's circus show. "Waitress, do me another!" More libations for the ladies, and the flight crew had had enough of us. I got up to use the restroom. There was sudden turbulence, the seatbelt sign came on, and a flight attendant walked over, put her hands up in my face, and said coolly, "If I have to sit down, YOU have to sit down." I probably deserved the guff, but I was anxious to see Paul and really happy it would be in New York.

We arrived at LaGuardia and took a cab over to the Omni Park Hotel. "My husband is here with Ministry. It's under 'Champale Chiffre,'" I announced at the front desk. The desk clerk looked up at me, then on her list of aliases, and handed over the key. I was slow in getting used to these meetups with Paul and the discreet hotel bookings. Of course it made sense, to keep fans and groupies at arm's length.

It was just after 1:00 p.m., and I entered an empty hotel room. Almost empty. On the night table was a wrapped box—"For Gerda. HAPPY BIRTHDAY." A shoebox(!) from what I could tell. Paul had missed my thirty-second birthday a few days before playing a show in Canada. I tore at the wrapping and decided if Paul didn't show up soon, I'd have to clomp over to the Museum of Modern Art by myself in my new Montreal shoes. It did seem a little presumptuous of him to buy me shoes, but Paul knew my style, and they were excellent black leather brogues.

I eventually did make my way over to MOMA, losing myself in room after room of fabulous art for an hour and a half. This seemed an extraordinarily, scandalously short time to look at anything there, but I already knew what I wanted to see—Matisse's Piano Lesson. In the process of looking, I came upon some surprises. MOMA was always full of them. Matisse's (The) Back – I through IV, a series begun somewhere around 1909 and ending in 1931. "MOMA is a sexy place," I wrote in my journal, and headed over to the Ritz where Ministry had played the night before and were doing press for the night's show coming up.

MTV was setting up to interview the band. People were milling around—Dave Kendall from MTV, road crew, band members. I saw Paul standing with Martin and Leila Atkins. Aside from the core Ministry members—Al, Paul, and Bill—Chris Connelly, Mike Scaccia, William Tucker, Martin Atkins, and Ohgr from Skinny Puppy were with them on this tour. Dave Kendall was determining who would be in on the Ministry interview for MTV. Al, of course. And suddenly, Martin and Ohgr were enlisted to be part of the on-camera "voice" representing Ministry.

Paul looked pissed off. I asked him why he wasn't in on the interview. He and Al were the majority songwriters on the record, and they had co produced it as the "Luxa/Pan" production team. But Dave Kendall was a huge Killing Joke fan, and it was easy to see why he wanted to have Martin included. I guessed Al wanted Ohgr there as a heads up to Skinny Puppy fans. There were the three "stars" camera-ready to explain why the novel stage set-up, with two drummers and that fence. Paul continued to look pissed off. Martin was just a hired gun for this tour, and Ohgr had songwriting credit on just a couple of songs.

"Let's get out of here," Paul said. We left the club and headed off to dinner with our friend Sunny Chapman.

Returning later to the club, Paul got ready to warm up before going onstage. I knew the routine. We (being wives, girlfriends, groupies, fans, and friends) were all welcome in the dressing room until the last twenty minutes or so. Then Ministry did their final secret handshakes or whatever yoga poses necessary to get into performance mode. As I walked out of the dressing room door I leaned over, kissed Paul, and said the simplest thing I would say at every club, "Have a good show." It was ordinary, and I hoped, calming, reassuring. As if he needed it.

I caught up with Leila who was with a handful of other women, and we began looking for the way to the backstage at the Ritz, to secure our places for the show. Depending upon the club, it could be really obvious or impossible to make a clear dash from dressing room to stage. At the Ritz, it was like entering a board game:

Behind door number two sits a stocky black dude wearing a blue Philadelphia T-shirt and jeans, telling you "Let me see," as he gets up from his folding chair, turns in all directions behind him, and stares at what appears as a maze of boilers and low hanging pipes. "Not here. Down that way," as he points you out the door you came through. You see a couple of unionized, middle-aged women pushing what look like drink carts. They signal to go "that way," and the adventure continues. You get the sneaking suspicion this happens all the time, and this time it's at your expense. You've now spent more than ten minutes in the guts of an aging rock venue introducing yourself to people who couldn't give a shit that you're running out of time as your husband has by now left the dressing room and is being led down the perp walk to the stage by someone holding a Maglite who works for the club and is on a schedule. You finally get lucky and run into a familiar face from the touring company, and they're waving and mouthing "Over here!" as you take your position offstage. The intro music—Hank Williams— is starting. The crowd is getting increasingly more agitated as they fix their anger upon the fence facing them onstage, out of step with the slow country ditty pinging loudly now in the room. Your husband takes four or five steps onto the stage—no hurry— and you hear "YEEEAAAAHHHH!!!!! FUCK!" from the audience pit, and one by one every other band member comes up, is acclimated to an invisible workspace, absently checking guitar strings, water bottles, drumsticks, microphones, and cables on the floor. You want to be on that platform and know for a split second what it means to be adored like this. But you never will. That is him. Not you. You don't need to be baring yourself for a crowd. That is him too. The show begins.

If there had been friction between Paul and Al about the MTV thing, it was gone now. The show was all that mattered at the moment. I stood with Leila in that sequestered space away from the audience and tried to visualize how different the sound up here was from the sound at the back of the venue or even right in front of the stage. It was a 360-degree meditation process, and I was still getting used to the idea I was privileged to be standing where I was. Paul was having fun. Al was circling around the stage like a sumo wrestler, stomping his boot down before grabbing a microphone and exhorting the audience with one invective after another.

Later after the show, we had a short night's sleep and a 10:30 a.m. coach call. Leila and I rode with the band to Boston. Ministry was playing The Channel next.

The infrastructure of touring was unfolding in real time in front of me. I was on the coach (in common parlance, the tour bus). Coaches are all different. Different clean smells. Different professional drivers. I had a conversation with the driver of the bus taking us away now, and I came to realize many of the drivers actually liked touring with Ministry. They liked the people. I wondered what other bands were like on the road.

We arrived in Boston and headed over to the club. At showtime, the air inside The Channel was sweltering, and I could barely breathe—in January. I was close enough to the stage, I could see the ceiling dripping onto the band. Paul came out with no shirt on under his leather. There was little room for him to move. On the larger stages, he was often the first band member to appear. The audience would see the image I knew so well—the tall, straight figure coming into the light, the long, slow strides onto the stage, picking up his instrument and draping the guitar strap across his chest methodically—like a matador. Everyone else would follow, with Al finally emerging like a bull in the ring. The Channel's tiny stage crushed that dynamic instantly.

A woman photographer from B-Side magazine told Paul after the show, "It was so sexy when you took off your cabretta!" I hoped she got the shot she was after. Yes, quite the spectacular look: no shirt, black jeans, engineer's boots, sweaty hair, and specs. Yes. My "sexy" husband was killin' it. I felt lucky to be able to travel and see Paul doing what I knew he loved best—performing live.

This tour was loud, visually and sonically, and the physical barrier seemed to incite tempers onstage and in the audience. Al tossed water at the crowd and the occasional beverage bottle of his choice. I was getting phone calls at home, complaints coming back from the venues about audience members getting hurt and looking for someone with a deep pocket to blame for their injuries. One woman tried to sue the band for allegedly getting hit by a beer bottle she knew Al aimed directly at her. Someone else claimed Al threw a bottle at them. Lawyers were hired to make these sometimes real, sometimes fictitious claims go away. No one was seriously injured. It seemed some fans were seeking their own notoriety at the band's expense. Live shows are inherently unpredictable. Ministry's fence tour took that axiom to a whole new level.

I needed to get back to Chicago, back to winter and my law reality. Leila and I waited for five and a half hours at a snowed in Logan Airport, yucking it up and reading the Sunday paper to kill time. Sunday in Boston is a dull, dull day, she said. I imagined the band on the bus again, duly occupied with brain teasers (other than groupies and drugs), things like memorizing the capitals of each of the fifty states. It was something Paul mentioned in passing when I asked him what they actually did to make use of their long bus rides between cities: watch movies, listen to music, read, memorize state capitals, write postcards. "And the capital of Maine is NOT Bangor."

Paul called every day from the road, when he knew I would be home from work. Sometimes more than once a day. He would call me and not the other way around. It made sense. I was the one with the stable, straight job, and cell phones were not available yet. The only people I knew who had pagers, let alone car phones, were lawyers or drug dealers—some were my clients.

When he called, Paul would recite fun facts from the road. "There's a city called Defiance in Ohio. Let's live there!" He couldn't wait for me to be comfortable riding my own Ducati. We'd find the time to practice in the spring when the snow melted, he said.

In one of our phone conversations, Paul mentioned getting out of town, just the two of us, when this tour was over. He was a fan of Grand Prix racing and knew there was an American stage of the Formula One race coming up in a month. It wasn't every year that Formula One came to the US. The venue this time was Phoenix. I thought it would be great fun watching fast cars and international racing groupies getting blanketed in dust trackside. The day before Paul's birthday, I booked our flights as a present to him.

While he was out of town, I wondered what this tour would mean for Ministry's growing reputation. The MTV metal crowd was pumped for the shows. The fence brought even more drama to the live show, on top of the dual drummers, precision playing, and impossible decibel levels onstage. The reviews were all wildly positive. I pondered where they would be going next—literally, on this tour, and professionally, when the tour ended. I had the itinerary, which told me there were sold out shows three nights following Paul's birthday on February 8th—the 10th, 11th, and 12th- a long stretch in Denver. Paul could amuse himself with local museums and books. He was a member of what Al called Ministry's "Book Club": Paul, Bill, and any other like-minded souls who'd rather read than obliterate their brain cells with substances. Rockstar clichés were boring. The Book Club wanted more than to get high all day long on the road or entertain groupies every chance they had. They wanted to make the most of their time. That's what everyone was told. I believed the hype, too. The Book Club had a better ring to it than, say, "The Shooting Gallery."

It occurred to me I should call Paul on one of their nights in Denver on the off chance I'd actually catch him in the hotel room. Surely there was plenty of down time between the three performances, with no coach call to make or new club to rehearse in for the first time. I heard the phone ringing and Bill Rieflin answered. After a brief hello and some muffled conversation on his end, Bill handed the phone to Paul. I was exhausted from work and happy to hear his voice. We said a few things back and forth for a minute, when Paul finally said, "I fucked someone last night."

***

I thought he was kidding. "What?" I started laughing. The two of us weren't beneath the inappropriate or politically incorrect outburst now and then. When we first met, he told me he had briefly worked as a gigolo when he lived in Germany. Sometimes it was hard to tell fact from fantasy with his history.

He wasn't kidding. My knees collapsed, and I sat down. This wasn't happening in my perfectly charmed world of hopping planes to New York and San Francisco. I didn't sign up for this. My ideal partner, who was "the nicest guy," was quiet on the other end. It hadn't been a year since we were married. I felt nauseated.

My nights were played out in numbers, in "wait times": Paul's coming home in four days, three days. His flight is in at ten o'clock. "Wait for this intro to finish." So much waiting. All the waiting around for him. Wait for the phone call. Wait at the airport to pick him up. Wait for him to leave Chicago Trax for a few hours. Wait for the tour and press schedules to plan when I could see him, when he wasn't busy building his reputation in the music circles we traveled. "The nicest guy in the world." Mr. Nice Guy. Patty Jourgensen had told me I "got the better guy." I felt safe—always—because I was NOT the girlfriend, the groupie, or the mistress on the side. I was his wife. I was his best friend.

What a load of nonsense. Did he get high with Al? Was this an ego thing, a birthday present to himself? So many clichés. My gut told me, stop giving him the benefit of analysis, of "How could this happen?" In those few seconds, I wished I could simply disappear. I hung up the phone.

I felt someone else had taken over my identity, had taken my place and wrapped themselves in it. It was sickening. The colors of the canvas were shifted. The family snapshot—me, Paul, MY Paul—displaced like liquid spilling over the edge of a martini glass. This other. A stinking olive thing thrown in the glass. I hate olives in martinis. I was drowning in my own delusion of happiness. Was I? I went for a walk to think. Was this the beginning of something really disgusting? Did other women now think he was famous and fair game? Is this how it begins?

I never understood the concept of men as a separate species. Paul was possibly the first person I intimately understood as a person. I accepted him in all his imperfections and insecurities about his own talents and worth. I thought he accepted me with all of mine. I understood his need to create, put something on a page or into sounds. It's who you are as an artist. I got that. I understood him. I understood that vulnerability. What I could not understand was this other base need or impulse to have sex with a stranger. I didn't want to understand it, either. Maybe there was no explanation, there was nothing more to see, nothing more to understand.

He could have said nothing about it. Why did he? That question stayed with me, kept me sane for the next few hours, kept me considering my fondness for Paul. I told myself, keep it together. Keep it in the frame, in the snapshot. He could have said nothing.

Ministry had another week and a half of shows. Paul kept calling. He was sorry. He felt like an idiot. Words. "I don't know why I did something so stupid." Had we not been married, my attitude toward him would have been different. I would have ended our relationship. But there was so much more involved now. I loved him in ways I had never loved anyone else before. We were planning to move out of Chicago at some point. He and Al were beginning to talk seriously about building their own studio. We had plans, mutual desires to fulfill.

Paul had no explanation. Lust. Really. There is no accountability in simply naming your weaknesses, I told him. Love is a weakness. Lust is an impulse, an action you choose or ignore. "I love women" rang in my head, his line from our first dinner together. Did he even give it a second thought before losing himself completely in the act? We would talk face to face soon. I needed an explanation.

Paul came home at the end of February with some other news about his foray into sex with a stranger. She told him afterwards she was HIV positive. Now I was scared—for myself and for him.

I had more than a few friends die of AIDS. All of them were gay or bisexual. I didn't have sexual contact with them or any IV drug users. I felt secure until now in my own partner's vetting process and body integrity, disengaged from the drama of fatal diseases. In the gay and straight communities, everyone was bombarded with PSAs promoting condom use. You used a condom because of the remote possibility you could get infected by someone who'd slept with someone else who was a casual drug user who'd shared a needle or a bed with some poor HIV positive soul. I knew Paul didn't have condoms and wouldn't use them. Or maybe I was wrong about that, too.

What I was certain of was the fact that AIDS was still very much an active disease. It wasn't until 1987 that a "cocktail" for HIV/AIDS patients was available to give them hope. Not enough time between then and now for anyone sexually active to forget the virus was deadly and everywhere. When I was at the ACLU, I read through footnotes, exhaustive reports, and comments on proposed AIDS legislation around the country. I was very familiar with the nuances of transmission, incubation, poison spreading over your body. It happened sometimes quickly. You heard "plague," "gay plague," and "death sentence" whispered in the bars and amongst friends, reiterating the finality of being "positive." With all this information as backdrop, I asked myself, how could Paul— someone so alert, so aware, so smart—how could he be so reckless? Even if his one nighter was a "lying piece of shit," this wasn't herpes for god sakes. I told Paul to stay away from me until he got tested.

Irony sometimes creeps in to bite us in the ass. When Paul came home from tour, he made an appointment with a men's clinic around the corner from Medusa's, the club where I had seen him sing onstage for the first time. It was a sweet reminder of more innocent times.

Tests and results at the clinic were confidential. Enough time had passed since potential "transmission." We waited for his results. All I could think about again was getting away from him. I hated the drama of waiting. More fucking waiting. I still couldn't stomach that he had sex with someone else.

The test came back negative. My next thought was this groupie must be a real whack job with a need to leave a lasting impression. Maybe. But this girl had a perfectly willing accomplice. I was so angry and at the same time relieved Paul was okay.

Perhaps I should have left him then. But the thought of leaving him was paralyzing. Taking the el downtown to my office over the next few days was a great relief from the disappointment and hurt feelings I couldn't ignore. I reminded myself Paul worked in a business full of excess and temptation. This dalliance with a groupie was his wake up call that our marriage was a sacred place, where boundaries were serious and real. There wouldn't be a next time.

Bill's girlriend Frankie once told me she would leave and not look back if Bill ever cheated on her. But I wasn't Frankie. The longer Paul and I knew each other, the more we talked about not being like other people. The longer we knew each other, the more often he said I was his best friend. I felt I had to forgive him—this one time. I didn't have time to rationalize something so irrational coming from the one person who I thought was my best friend. I couldn't bear the loss. But now, I needed to get out of town. I couldn't get over feeling I'd been taken for granted by my own husband. The balance was off. My companion Paul needed to get out of tour mode.

16

It was the beginning of March 1990, and as it was, we had airline tickets for
Phoenix to see the Formula One race. I had innocently booked the trip while Paul
was still on the road. A week after his HIV test results, we were on our way to
the airport. Yay. We were going to an event that would be louder than a Ministry
show and perfect cover for him for any serious discussion about marital cheating.
Not exactly a romantic getaway on any level. I still had his infidelity haunting my
thoughts and took every opportunity to tell him it would not happen again.

Paul was a huge fan of motorcycle and car racing and had only watched
Grand Prix races on television. I had to admit I was excited to go, even if it was
again all about him and what he wanted to do. It was still winter, so that meant
going somewhere warmer than Chicago. It would be an adventure into the
pinnacle of racing. It was a cheap flight away. This was a step toward healing a
rift, a shift in the boundaries of our relationship.

There was a separate ulterior motive to this trip. An art collective was staging
its own Formula One-style event the day before the real thing. An alternative
race, "Crash Grand Prix" was setting up at Ice House, a performance space
in town. The event was a kind of industrial art car race. I imagined the art car

drivers as "Those Magnificent Men Flying by the Seat of their Pants." There was something so absurdly wonderful in that idea, and it reminded me of all the studio work Paul and Al were endlessly doing together.

Our flight to Phoenix was one extended conversation about the historical underpinnings of a race meant for the jet set, AND how many clowns can you fit in an art car, anyway? The venues for each stage of the Grand Prix (Monaco, Brazil, Italy, Japan, and Australia) were places we had only dreamed of visiting. For now, Phoenix would have to do.

When we arrived in town, we discovered we'd missed the Young Gods performing at Ice House the night before. Wax Trax had released one of their records. As a consolation, Paul convinced me we should take in a quick side tour and a cocktail at the historic Biltmore Hotel in downtown Phoenix. The Biltmore was one of those architectural wonders I loved to explore in a new city, having grown up with the Chicago skyline and its rich architectural history. Good. Let's look at a solidly constructed beautiful building. I liked the symbolism in that. The building was a reminder of the fragile beauty of life and our places in it. I was confident Paul was consciously thinking of my interests now, actively trying to repair a wound he had inflicted.

When we arrived at the historic hotel, I marveled at the exacting attention to form in the textile block-design stonework fortifying the exterior walls of the structure like a temple. The obsessive attention to small decorative details was reminiscent of some Frank Lloyd Wright buildings, but on a much more sprawling scale. The Biltmore's designer had in fact apprenticed with Wright, and Wright consulted on the hotel's construction. We finished our drinks, storing these peculiar architecture history facts in our brains as we headed over to Ice House to watch the interactive art show getting underway.

Ice House was in a steel factory space once housing an industrial fabricator and since used for the arts and artists' exhibitions. There was that familiar din of metal and machines in the air. It was as if Paul were back momentarily at Chicago Trax twiddling knobs and beating sounds into submission.

The "Crash Grand Prix" drivers were outside of the building tinkering with their vehicles. In the dark, dusty air, Matt Heckert's "Walk and Peck" entry stood off to the side as if balancing on a ballet barre, its metal aquiline skeleton head reaching ten feet into the air and poised for "pecking" at the road. Brett Goldstone's "Steam Powered Car" looked suspiciously like something not meant for speed at all. The structural components on the car: one factory-grade hot water heater strapped horizontally onto a plank with small wagon wheels underneath. In keeping with its theme, large gulpfuls of steam randomly blew out from the sides. Finally, there was Eric Werner's "Ramcar," with a side arm running the length of the machine and equipped with a medieval, mace-like weapon on the end. Paul talked to some of the crew who, we were not surprised to find out, were Ministry fans. Industrial meeting industrial. No one really raced. No one really "won." The entries were amalgamations referencing cultural, environmentally destructive wars on civilization. A slow-motion antithesis to the weekend's international jet set speed race, the art cars were theatrical anti-fashion statements moving at their own pace.

The following day we went for a quick breakfast at the diner attached to our motel. The Kon Tiki Motel, with its oddly tropical name in a city far from the Pacific Ocean, was suspiciously non-Hawaiian in décor and aloha spirit. Phoenix was a warm and dry place.

I was deferential to wait staff everywhere we went, having been a waiter for years as a student. I was so looking forward to coffee and hot biscuits that morning, I could already taste the butter melting into the jam. I ordered "Biscuits, no gravy." The middle aged waitress gave me a look. "We don't serve biscuits without gravy," she shot back. "You can't get them without the gravy." I hope to get them without an attitude, I wanted to say. But I was hungry, held my tongue and ordered toast. "Welcome to crusty, dusty old Phoenix," I mumbled to Paul.

Paul was in a hurry to finish his breakfast, unusual for someone so committed to savoring every bite of every breakfast, toast, and coffee combination put before him. Food rituals were a constant reminder that my partner, despite being so quick to note his "fifth generation Californian" ties, was often micromanaged by his French lineage. He, like I, couldn't embrace the idea of eating while walking or even smoking while walking. These necessary pleasures needed "one's full attention." Thankfully, I disabused him of the habit of saying, "One (does this and that) and 'one never knows.'" I would ask, "Who the hell is this 'one' you keep talking about? Is it YOU? Then say so." My husband was now paying the bill and halfway out the door in a rush to get over to the track. Hm. Slow down there, Mr. Andretti.

We arrived at the race track in our cheap rental car. Paul checked to see if we had earplugs for this thing that would be louder than some rock shows we'd been to. We were both anxious to get to the track and catch some of the pre-race celebrity laps. As we hurried away from our parking space, Paul realized in his haste he had locked the keys in the car.

Exasperated, trying to decide if we needed a locksmith now or should it wait until after the race, Paul studied the car. "Cheap fiberglass piece of shit," he said tugging at the molding on the driver side door. More tugging and frustration taking its toll and we could see the "cheap piece of shit" car door was flexible enough that while Paul pulled, I could squeeze my smaller fingers into the space and quickly pull up the door lock. What a relief. We hurried to the track in time to see the actor Paul Newman speed past us and around the course. We wandered through the crowd trackside, catching glimpses of David Letterman, a big racing fan, walking the adjacent chain-link fenced path separating the rich from everyone else there.

"Gorgeous, at some point we'll follow the whole circuit, every stage, every city—or I'll be so pissed!" Paul addressed me now as "Gorgeous" with fantastic regularity, much to my delight. It was an afterthought, as if my name had simply disappeared. He seemed to be in repentance mode from what I could tell, and I wished he would stop. Sure, fantasizing about the far off future and his pop star status in it was fun. We would be part of the jet set ("Yay!") But we were (for now) in the very real present world of racing, and of course, surrounded by big loud engines. Earplugs in, faces forward, the dazzle of a Ferrari whipping by was intoxicating. Onward.

When we returned to Chicago from our trip, I eased off from examining Paul's infidelity. It was one time. Life was bigger than that. Paul buried himself back into the studio to do production on the live Ministry record, In Case You Didn't Feel Like Showing Up.

I felt fortunate to know the people I knew and those I was starting to know better through our regular wild dinners at the Star Top. Socializing with Leila and Martin Atkins over dinner and Funkadelic was becoming routine. It amused me that out of all of our friends, Martin was the only one who still resembled a rambunctious child. It wasn't in my nature to employ theatrics, to thrust my arms toward the sky to make a point and show everyone else I was as big as a grizzly bear so "back off," but Martin seemed to get that result just walking into Star Top with his disheveled platinum hair and his long sleeved striped tee, eyes looking around wildly then ordering his usual, "Newkie Ale."

Having sipped a martini and smoked a cigarette, my mind always wandered to language of the written kind and not of the body kind. I wasn't obsessed with the physical projection of myself. There were plenty of narcissists of that ilk in the legal world I inhabited. Showmen, waving their props in court like preachers in the pulpit wave their bibles. Drug dealers and murderers were often at the top of their own political hierarchy, as opposing counsel from the State's Attorneys' office were on top of theirs. I was pulled in one direction towards consciously ignoring the larger than Cadillac egos in court, just to get my job done. But when it came to my place in the music scene, that had more to do with stepping away and watching the egos fly, good or bad.

I once told Leila that I liked talking to Martin about writing, words, and our own ancestors' influence on our aesthetic. Growing up in my parents' house, if a picture was on a wall, it was painted by someone in the family. Martin and I had several extended conversations about writing and poetry, making art and the function of art—if it had one. In spring of 1990 during one of our tete a tetes at Patty and Al's place after a Nine Inch Nails show, I must have diverted the attentions of a very inebriated Martin for a bit too long to spark a little trouble in paradise in the Atkins' household. A week later, I was having drinks with Paul, Chris Connelly, Chris' friend Gillian, and Martin and Leila at the Crash Palace, a bar across the street from the Star Top. Leila came up to me at the bar and said, "Oh, I've been telling Martin, every Saturday you and Gerda really should get together and have your usual chat about the mystery of life." I must have really set her off that night, somehow. Sometime later, there was an empty seat next to me, and Martin brought over a vodka and soda for me and this message from a fortune cookie:

"Your mind is creative, original, and alert."

He sat down, and we talked about motorcycles and visiting St. Thomas and watching iguanas in the trees there undisturbed. I didn't have to explain to Paul my little friendship with Martin Atkins. It didn't matter. I wasn't attracted to Martin, and besides, even if I were, I took marriage seriously—mine and my friends'. I had enough drama in my life. I was busy keeping people with names like "Flaco" and "Junior" out of jail. Cheating on my spouse never crossed my mind. I was not like other people I knew.

1990 was building up to be one milestone after another. Paul and Al went back into the studio to finish some of their side projects. The single for 1000 Homo DJs cover of Black Sabbath's "Supernaut" was in the final stages of production. Having time to spare from his Nine Inch Nails gigs, Trent Reznor was also back in town and had dropped by Chicago Trax. Al asked him if he would lay vocals on the "1000 Homos" track. Trent was more than happy to oblige.

In July, with 1000 Homos finished, Paul and Trent had the brilliant idea to get together, to play around with some musical ideas—just the two of them. Trent had by now moved to New Orleans, where he was renting a house. He invited Paul to come down. I had only been to New Orleans once before with Paul. Since my husband was going away to work on music for longer than a week, I decided I was finished missing him. Tired of waiting around. So much time in the studio, sometimes twenty-four hours straight, and now off from tour, he was leaving town to work somewhere else? I booked a weekend round trip plane ticket for myself, and Paul had no objection. I should get out of town, too.

***

When I arrived in New Orleans, I was greeted at the airport by Paul and Trent. Trent and his girlfriend Beth were renting a frame house near the Garden District. When we walked in, the first thing I noticed was the workout and weight gear taking over a good chunk of floor space. A set of bicycles stood in the hall. Seeing all the gear, I felt inspired to head out for a walk, get acclimated to the humidity, and that would give me and Paul a chance to explore this small sector of New Orleans. We had considered moving to New Orleans after Trent moved. Both of us were tired of Chicago and wanted to find a quieter, cheaper place to have a studio and raise a family, were we so lucky as to have one.

On our walk we discovered a little neighborhood grocery. From the sagging exterior, it looked as if the place had been there for decades. Humidity and age had settled in with the realization that the neighborhood needed this place, and it wasn't going anywhere so why spruce it up. I looked over their limited bins of produce hoping there would be a red bell pepper. There were none. My idea was to make a summer pasta salad for the house as a thank you for the weekend hospitality. Bell pepper was one of the handful of ingredients for the recipe. This was New Orleans, land of the "holy trinity"—celery, onion, and bell pepper—and the only colorful peppers on display were small and yellow. "Scotch bonnets." The name sounded innocuous enough and we bought a few.

Back at the house I cooked the pasta, grated the parmesan, and began slicing the peppers. I was wearing my contact lenses. My right eye began to itch. I closed my eyes and rubbed the eyelid. Not wanting to be too surprised by the flavor of the peppers, I tasted one to see how it worked with the other ingredients. Just at the moment when my tongue picked up the full velocity of the thing in my mouth, my eye began throbbing like someone had stuck a needle through it.

Unknown to me at the time, the Scotch bonnet is sometimes called the "ball-of-fire" pepper—and for good reason. It has the singular distinction of being 140 times hotter than a jalapeno on the Scoville scale. I was unaware of its eminence. I could barely see through the stinging, tearing, and squinting. I stumbled over to the sink, about to vomit from the pain.

I had somehow forgotten to pack my clear eyeglasses for this trip. My only option for replacement eyewear was a pair of prescription sunglasses I brought with, in the unlikely event I lost a lens. I rinsed my hands and pinched at my lenses to pull them out. The chili oil was now on both lenses.

No matter how many times I rinsed them, my contacts were tainted for the rest of the weekend. My amber lensed cat eye sunglasses would have to fill in. The frames looked vintage, of a different era. Being extremely nearsighted and recovering my full clear vision slowly, I imagined myself navigating through the city's streets with a great deal of trepidation, looking to all the world like a fashionable blind woman.

That night, Paul and I slept on a mattress in the living room. I fell asleep with my sunglasses on, reading some tourist brochures. Being a light sleeper with excellent hearing capabilities, I heard the house door open. Trent had been out for hours while we shopped and attempted to cook. He came into the living room, and I could tell he was studying my choice of late night eyewear. He had a devilish smile on his face and said, "So nice to see you again . . ." and took off to another room in the house.

The next day, Paul and I ventured out to explore further into the city center. Eye poisoning or not, I felt much joy lingering over the architecture of New Orleans through the sepia screen of my specs. There was something just right about that—a faded postcard view. I loved being there, the sounds, the hawkers outside the bars, the lazy Old World feel to the place. We investigated a voodoo bookstore like tourists and felt the breeze from open windows on the trolley ride past Tulane. We walked everywhere else, satisfying my need to feel the city with my own two feet. Paul and I were reconnecting. Walking together realigned the rhythm of our waking hours.

Before leaving town, we all went for drinks at the Top-of-the-Mart, the revolving bar crowning a building downtown overlooking the Mississippi River. It was my and Paul's predilection to visit every revolving lounge in every city we found ourselves in. What could be more stimulating than vertigo and martinis to get an evening rolling? As much as we all debated how drunk you'd have to be to lose your balance stepping off the thing, the revolving lounge spun much too slowly to propel a body off balance. Paul and Trent had their few reels of music in the can—something to revisit later. That was something we could all celebrate.

Paul and I flew back to Chicago. Summer 1990 was in full swing. Rehearsals were starting for Paul and the Revolting Cocks' month-long tour in August to promote their new album, Beers, Steers and Queers. I learned early on that it didn't matter to Paul and the friends he worked with whether they were doing one show or one hundred shows—the rehearsals were equally rigorous. The Cocks' first show was coming up in St. Louis, with the band returning to Chicago to play at the Rivera Theater and then out on the road again.

More touring. Touring was something essential to Paul's livelihood, something he had to do. There were times of the year when it made more sense than others. As a counterpoint to all of this tour talk (and perhaps to consciously make an effort to maintain a peaceful marriage) Paul suggested we should go on a honeymoon, and I, of course, couldn't say no. It was a year later, but we weren't like other people, were we? Our wedding was dashed together informally to compress our personal lives into his schedule of recording and touring. A honeymoon now would be a renewal of our vows—somehow. It was a great idea. The question was, when could we go and where.

Paul suggested Hawaii. I would have chosen Italy, but that required so much more planning, passports, and such. The Paradise State had its own kitschy appeal, but the underlying point to going there was to see Paul's dad. Gordon Barker lived on Kauai. I'd never met him. We could stay at Kay Barker's Bed & Breakfast, the family business his grandmother had started after retiring to the island. Paul talked about his dad often. "He's kind of like James Garner during his Rockford Files period."

Really. A Hollywood icon and TV private eye. I couldn't wait to meet him. If he was as good looking as his two sons, I could wager a small fortune any kids we might have of our own would be gorgeous. I decided to satisfy my curiosity about a related question that crossed my mind.

"So, when we decided to get married, was it important to you that I was physically attractive?" I asked.

"Of course. I didn't want ugly kids," he said without any hesitation. Now I knew. Although his resolve to get married seemed spontaneous, he had already prioritized the deal points. He had already hashed it out in his own mind before we had our talk in my old apartment. He didn't want ugly kids. Fair enough. When Paul finished his August tour with the Revolting Cocks, the two of us would fly to Kauai, and I could meet my new father-in-law.

The Cocks tour was underway. In the late afternoon on the day of their Chicago show, Paul and I searched through our collection of table linens for something to wrap around his body, toga style. Al wanted everyone in the band dressed in pseudo-Roman garb in keeping with the album cover art. I found a vintage white tablecloth with minimalist cave drawings of deer and naked huntsmen carrying bows and spears. It was perfect.

We arrived backstage at the venue. I unpacked a bottle of olive oil and the tablecloth Paul would wear. I rubbed and massaged Paul's front and back to achieve a sweaty, muscular, workhorse stance for the show. The stage set would include female go-go dancers—the Revolting Pussies—friends of ours, lazily grinding themselves into the floorboards.

The band came out and shortly into the first track, Al tore off his toga and performed the rest of the set in his street clothes and boots. Paul kept his toga in place. One of the Revolting Pussies was already under a keyboard stand, appearing to pleasure Michael Balch with her free hand. Yes. This was a Revolting Cocks show. Bacchanalia and babes.

Jason Pettigrew, an editor for Alternative Press magazine, convinced his bosses he should tag along for the Cocks tour. The Revolting Cocks were, after all, Ministry's alter ego—mostly the same band members. If Ministry had gone out the previous year with a massive chain-link fence fronting the band, who knew what the same people, dressed as the Revolting Cocks were capable of pulling off? This was the Cocks, a whole different universe from what Ministry represented. Ministry made dark, urgent, angry sounds. The Cocks were Ministry in their down time. They were the weekend dance party—dance music for hillbilly, lampshade wearing, cattle rustling, hooker pinching, pimp clothes donning court clowns. It was only for a month—August—would cover a smattering of cities in the Midwest, east coast, parts of the southwest, and west coast. Why not capture the relentless momentum of Al Jourgensen and his merry band of low lifes and spend twenty-four hours a day with the freakshow? Pettigrew tagged along to capture the before, after, and sometimes during show lawlessness and complete rejection of protocol required for this tour. His tour diary for AP became required reading for anyone interested in learning what touring was REALLY like or for someone ready to become thoroughly disenchanted with "making it" as a music journalist.

Jason Pettigrew's dedication to his craft seemed to be rewarded with all sorts of abundance. Trent Reznor joined the band in Cleveland. In Tulsa, Paul, Trent, and their friend Fritz Michaud muscled their way into Pettigrew's hotel room, raided his toiletries, doused the hotel rug with aftershave, and promptly lit it on fire. "Volunteer firefighter" Paul, accustomed to cleaning up his fellow band members' messes (literally and figuratively) came rushing forward with water to douse the fire, dumping a mess onto Jason's bed. As Jason noted in his report, his bed was nowhere near the actual fire. But Paul (being The Tall One) had a commanding presence and could take charge of any (fabricated) situation he put his mind to.

The band's stage set up was initially five Revolting Cocks flanked by two or three Revolting Pussy dancers pulled from the audience to dance free form next to the band. As the tour progressed, Al encouraged more audience members to get up and "dance with the Pussies." Once onstage, audience members displaying varying degrees of natural rhythm grooved to the music, or deciding better of that idea, simply stage dived. At one show, audience participation swelled to a twenty-eight person juggling act on the stage. It was a tour manager's heart attack moment waiting to happen.

As the tour continued, an inflatable sex doll made its way onto the coach, a token of the band's affection for my old friend Sean Joyce, who was stage managing this tour and had just gotten married. Buses arrived late, guitarist Mark Durante earned a stint in jail for throwing rocks at a cop car, and familiarity amongst band members grew to mere tolerance, or so it seemed. For a month-long tour, it seemed to garner the headaches of a world-wide attack. More press, more spectacle.

Paul was losing his patience with interviews by journalists who asked the same questions over and over, or who weren't familiar with the Revolting Cocks or Ministry, or seemed to confuse the two bands' histories entirely. When Paul's usual love for playing live had finally left the building for good, after being asked once again about "the band's" (which one's?) drug excesses—real, and in his case, imagined—he'd had enough. An interviewer asked, "Paul Barker, what's your favorite drug?" The usually cautious Paul Barker, whose tone in interviews was measured and thoughtful—that Paul— replied, "My wife sitting on my face."

Jason Pettigrew dutifully captured the quote in print. After all, it wasn't as if Paul had shared this revelation at a twelve-step meeting, was it? I soon heard all about my husband's confession, over and over from friends and especially, Michael Short and Ellie at the Star Top. Ellie would see us coming into the restaurant, run over, tilt her head coyly, and inquire, " Paul . . . what's your favorite drug?" And Michael would burst through the kitchen doors yelling, "PAUL BARKER! What's your favorite . . ."

Jason Pettigrew and I would become friendly pen pals after this and occasionally chat on the phone. He told me on this tour he'd overheard an angry Al yelling, "What is this shit?" as he tossed some groupie's poems into a dumpster near their bus. Jason, ever so vigilant in his pursuit of all things "verité," climbed into the dumpster when no one was looking and read through just one line: "I dream I'm a tiger . . ." and at that point, gleefully perused the rest of this Nobel contender until finally screaming, "Enough!!!!" as the papers flew right back from whence they came.

Jason wondered why Al liked to talk about being a Cuban expat from pre-Castro Cuba. Al liked to fantasize about a lot of things, I said. I told Jason Al's immigration history and his growing paranoia were all just a continuation of the "anti-new wave Al" he'd been cultivating since splitting with Arista Records. To my eyes the expat shtick made him seem more rebellious—or something. (The idea that he pushed his wife around might have been at the back of my mind.) I told Jason I now refused to call Al anything other than "No Lo Molestre." Yes, I had effectively reduced Al's stature to a hotel door hanger. In Spanish. He was Cuban. In my world, there were no sacred cows. Not ever. Jason eventually took to calling me "Beyoncé." Was it my looks or was it my "reputation" in the press?

The Revolting Cocks were gearing up for a European tour directly following this one, and suddenly the tour was in limbo. Some enterprising journalist/ PR person had alerted the UK press that the Cocks stage show included not only strippers, strippers, and more strippers performing lewd acts onstage, but also (charmingly) a herd of live cattle. A member of the British Parliament caught wind of this press gossip and introduced a measure before that esteemed body banning the Cocks from performing. Did someone take Beers, Steers and Queers a little too literally?

The Cocks were idled stateside with this change in plans, and it would be January before they finally arrived overseas with work permits in hand. No cattle were harmed or rustled in the intervening months. Paul and I spent our free evenings having dinner at the Star Top, enriching our culinary vocabulary, and further solidifying our friendship with Michael Short and crew. I had the impression that if Michael honestly didn't like someone, he would honestly let them know it. The opposite also held true. He could intuitively sense the humor and absurdity in time wasted trying to please other people and wanted no part of it. You were either with him, or you were "eighty-sixed."

Paul's friend Fritz was in town beginning work as a soundman for Nine Inch Nails or soon to be. Fritz stayed at our place briefly, and at night Paul, Fritz, and I had dinner at Star Top, afterwards crossing the street for drinks at the Crash Palace. Michael Short followed us over.

Inside the front entrance to Crash Palace was a pinball machine. Paul and Fritz took to challenging one another, standing momentarily at the controls together while the music in the bar was shifting to some funk number even I wasn't familiar with. I took a seat at the bar, looked over at Fritz, who was tall and lanky like Paul, and both of them began unconsciously, almost involuntarily, bouncing their right legs in time together with the beat in a "tall guy" leggy display of solidarity, while their bodies remained bent over their pinball duet. Michael Short was eyeing them at that moment too and unable to contain himself turned to look at me in the crowded bar, pointed at Paul and Fritz, and we both yelled in unison, "LINE DANCE!"

***

With no shows scheduled from September until the end of the year, it was an opportune time for me and my husband to fly to Hawaii and for me to finally meet the new father-in-law. My bosses knew we hadn't really had a honeymoon. They also knew Paul had an insane work schedule. I was able to take a week off at the end of September, and off we went.

For the trip, we flew from Chicago to the Big Island, connecting there with a much smaller plane bound for Kauai. When we arrived in Kauai, we followed a few other young couples off the plane and walked onto the tarmac of an airport roughly the size of a corporate airstrip. Inside the airport building, I studied the faces of several men walking in our direction near the gate. I was looking for someone who resembled "Jim Rockford." I noticed a dark-haired middle-aged man whose physique was reminiscent of James Garner, and I felt confident this must be my father-in-law.

"Hi, Dad," I heard Paul say, walking in the opposite direction of where I was facing, and toward a man shorter than I was expecting. This man had slightly cropped, graying, kinky hair. He walked toward us with a kind of stomp to his gait. He looked like a surfer—the aging face of one who had been ruggedly handsome twenty years before, who now bore the fatigue of the sun and wind and too many parties on his dusty tanned face, neck, and arms. Faded Hawaiian shirt. Faded beach shorts. Washed out tennis shoes from which the laces had been removed. Private eye and natty dresser "Jim Rockford" was nowhere to be seen here. Instead, the expression of a man hanging onto a simple set of rules governing his daily existence, a man whose prime had passed, but was content with what he had left.

"Had to put a shirt on today," he said, smiling broadly at his new daughter-in-law.

Paul hadn't seen his dad in a long time. It was possible he remembered just photos and self-conjured images of his father from when they spoke on rare occasions by phone.

Gordon Barker was retired from his career working for a defense contractor, a job that had required him to live at varying times on Guam and in the Seychelle Islands. Island life had appealed to him for most of his adult life, but not so much apparently to Paul's mother. They were together for such a short amount of time; it was not something I cared to discuss now, but it was something I thought about.

Gordon seemed perfectly content living on Kauai and staying busy managing the bed and breakfast business he'd inherited from his mother after her recent death. He'd helped her with the business for several years already. When Paul and I booked our flights, he called his dad who was looking forward to our visit and happy to have us occupy the last remaining available bedroom in the sprawling ranch house known as Kay Barker's Bed & Breakfast. I felt welcomed like family when we dropped our bags at the house.

I stepped outside into the backyard. I couldn't help but notice the walking path beyond the fence that led directly to the base of the Sleeping Giant. The mountain was right there, on the edge of the homesteads and small farm plots scattered below it.

"We'll have plenty of time for a hike," Gordon said, noticing my wandering eyes. "You kids need a drink?"

My father-in-law enjoyed his liquor. It seemed to be a daily habit, which endeared him to the local bartenders near the beach, one of whom became his companion for a time. Women on the island were drawn to him for their own reasons, but I could see he was a talker with a colorful history and sense of adventure—a man's man. And he could cook. Before a day had passed, he invited us over to his separate residence a short walk away, past a few neighbors' houses. There, Gordon prepared a restaurant-sized stockpot of cioppino, a hearty fish stew, for us and for himself for dinner. He moved around his own airy sparse kitchen like a seasoned chef, stopping to pour himself a drink or add wine to the stew. I understood why some non-natives such as himself adapted better than others to island life. My sister and brother had opened their own café on St. Thomas in the US Virgin Islands and lived there for over five years. I couldn't do it. City life was too precious a draw for me.

After dinner, Paul and I walked back to the B&B and discussed Vernon and Kay Barker's banana plantation here in the early days, and the later decision to open Kay Barker's Bed & Breakfast as a business. I felt lucky to be a part of his family. I felt lucky to experience this lush Hawaiian landscape, where the patio was called the "lanae," and common words were full of repeated vowel sounds as if to gently remind you to pause and linger over what you have to say.

In the morning, I was surprised to see Gordon already in the kitchen with an apron on pulling something out of the oven before I'd even asked about having coffee. Whatever he had in his mitts smelled fantastic.

"Poi bread," he said, without waiting for me to ask.

Paul and I soon discovered breakfast at the B&B meant Hawaiian coffee, Kay Barker's signature poi bread, and freshly cut fruit. Poi—a staple of the Hawaiian diet—made from cooked taro roots mashed to the consistency of a batter the color of purple eyeshadow. The bread made with poi was dense and sweet like banana bread but carried a milder flavor closer to a zucchini type bread. It was delicious, in its oddly Easter-egg colored way. I was happily falling in love with this tropical place for all the right reasons—without ever having a lei tossed in my direction for good luck. Aloha . . . indeed.

Gordon's current girlfriend managed a business on the island that offered guided tours by boat and by helicopter. Kauai was the Garden Island and had little commercial development on it. Unlike most of the other Hawaiian islands, there were remote hikes and natural pools to satisfy our lust for discovering things off the beaten path. The Napali Coast was pristine, home to the Hidden Beach, a site used for at least one movie and some award-winning photography layouts in the past. The best way to see these sights on Kauai (according to Gordon and his girlfriend) was by helicopter. Gordon had prearranged a helicopter tour for us as a belated wedding gift.

I wasn't as eager as Paul to defy gravity in a three-man aircraft wavering and dipping near cliffs and endless ocean, but I loved the adventure in trying something new. Why not? I hadn't watched Apocalypse Now nearly as many times as Paul, but the cinematic "feel" to those scenes, where the characters are in close proximity to helicopters touching ground and taking off, was enough mental preparation for me, I thought. Art imitating life—sure thing. We headed out to the helipad.

"Keep your head down approaching the craft and when disembarking," the pilot said, with a formal hello. Such rules. Such language protocol for just two passengers out for a joy ride. I suppose it was all necessary to avoid liability claims from lightheaded newlyweds having their honeymoons literally cut short by blades spinning overhead. I held my breath, slipping headphones over my ears to muffle the noise. The pilot pointed to where he wanted each of us to sit according to weight—ours and his. I looked over at Paul and winked, and we were off.

"Nawiliwili Bay over there . . . Wailua River . . ." the Hawaiian names were melodic and wonderfully distracting for a language freak like me, as I tried to calm my anxiety hanging so precariously high in the air. I wanted a Hawaiian dictionary as soon as we were back on steady ground.

Paul had an urge to play tour guide himself following our helicopter flight. He knew so much about the history of the island. I couldn't believe he had actually been here many times when his grandparents were still alive. I had a difficult time picturing him as a school-age child. What I knew of his formative years centered mostly around his desire to get away from his family.

"That's where I played golf with Grandmother," he said, pointing to a busy course along our ocean drive. I couldn't envision golf attire nor the posture on someone with his frame and temperament. "She played there all the time with her girlfriends."

"Really? And where did the ladies go for lunch?" I asked, intrigued by these island Barkers who lived a life where women played golf and men cooked dinner.

"Where did they go? Coco Palms, of course. Let's do it."

The name alone "Coco Palms" had a jazzy ring, and the place had a storied past. I discovered that The Coco Palms hotel was host to Hollywood productions and crews for 1950's Pagan Love Song, 1956's Voodoo Island, and 1957's South Pacific. Elvis Presley's Blue Hawaii chapel scene was filmed on the grounds in the coconut grove. Famous authors like James Michener had stayed there, and celebrity sightings were common by the late 1960s. It was reputed to have the most authentic Hawaiian vibe of any hotel in Hawaii. Coco Palms was where the nightly torch-lighting ritual performed by native Hawaiians in loincloths began.

Paul and I ordered lunch and drinks with floating fruit and paper umbrellas, sitting in a dark, wood-paneled main dining room, and taking in the well-worn

Hawaiian themed interior. The coconut shell motif everywhere, on the tables and around the necks of the waitstaff seemed appropriate in light of the natural coconut grove just outside the restaurant's doors. If cheesy had a rich older cousin, this was it.

After lunch, we made the obligatory stop at the ABC souvenir store to buy new flip flops and locally made plumeria body lotion. It was just like us that the last place to visit for the day would be the beach to experience the full-on Hawaiian sun. I told Paul we would have to get prescription goggles for snorkeling on our next trip. So many coves to explore, so little time to pause. We had just a couple more hours of sunlight. But as I laid my things on our beach towels, tightened the bolo string under my giant straw sunhat, and adjusted my newish "sunflower" colored J. Crew bikini top to read the History of the Hawaiian Language, Paul ignored his immediate impulse to dive into the ocean.

"Look up, Beautiful," I heard. When I raised my eyes from my book, there was Paul snapping a Polaroid picture. And then, another. I really am adored, I thought. He loved his Polaroid camera. That image on the beach stayed with me.

17

Paul and I had been married for eighteen months. Before the wedding we discussed what we would do in the event we had children, but that was never a given for either one of us. I wasn't in a rush to "beat the biological clock." I never thought about it. I was thirty-two and Paul thirty-one. We were back from Hawaii, the Cocks were on break until December, and Paul and I could spend some quality time at our apartment alone in the evenings doing nothing but enjoying each other's company. I soon discovered I was pregnant.

This wasn't planned. It was a nice surprise. I didn't tell anyone but Paul and my doctor, being superstitious about early announcements with such fragile possibilities at play. I had been pregnant before, but being pregnant now was a welcome adventure—going somewhere new for the first time. I had no idea what my life would be like with a child around. I felt at home in the stories and drama associated with doing my job, and started conjuring vague scenarios of myself walking around the courthouses with extra weight and expanding waist. Being pregnant seemed such a fantasy at this stage. Before I'd met Paul, I had never entertained the idea of even getting married or let it enter the narrative of my life at all. Now pregnant, my home life seemed like a daydream—not quite real.

Each day for the next two months, I went to work, pausing in the day to conscientiously consume an extra yogurt or half sandwich to add calories into my diet. I sent my secretary Shelia to Popeye's a few streets away, to pick up red beans and rice. New Orleans food was suddenly on my mind again. Physically, I felt no differently. If anything, I wasn't hungry at all and didn't have bouts of morning sickness. I felt light headed and distracted. Did it matter when we had kids? With the exception of Al and Patty, few of our friends had children. But Paul and I were so close in what we wanted out of our lives and experiences that whatever came along, we were prepared.

Early in December I rode the el home and felt a kind of migraine coming on. I had not had a migraine headache since weaning myself off of the pill in my early twenties. I began walking slower than usual from the Logan el stop to our apartment. Climbing the back porch stairs, I felt dizzy and had to stop—something's wrong. A trail of fluid was trickling down my stockings. I made it to the top of the stairs, called my doctor and Paul and a cab to take me to the hospital. I was told I was quite possibly having a miscarriage. This too was new to me.

I woke up on an emergency room bed with Paul standing there looking in my eyes trying to gauge what I was feeling, what he was feeling, and what did it all mean. He looked puzzled. Finally, he said very quietly, "Gorgeous, you have a mustache."

I felt like screaming. It was as if he had no filters for what he said at times. He looked baffled by his own words and probably the expression on my face. What was he supposed to say? Some comforting words, maybe. Maybe? My emotions were currently on hold in a liminal state. My physical appearance was the last thing on my mind.

You can't give what you don't have. Where had I heard that expression? Psychology class in college. You can't show empathy for others around you if you haven't seen it yourself. Paul wasn't raised by his parents. He was raised by two busy relatives who were also trying to raise their own four kids as best they could. Paul stood next to the bed with a look on his face as if he wanted me to feel better or wanted to understand what had happened to me. He wanted to know how it made me feel and how he felt as my partner, but he lacked the language, the words, to express it. He was deflecting.

He apologized for upsetting me, but I still felt as vulnerable at that moment as he must have felt embarrassed. Was it any wonder my facial hair had gone rogue, along with my hormones? It was my body, and I had no control over what was happening to it.

Discharged from the hospital, we headed home with this new feeling of loss between us. It was an awkward walk back to the hospital parking lot. Silence. I couldn't convey what I was thinking to Paul. I couldn't even clarify my thoughts to myself. Christmas was just a few days away. Paul went back to rehearsing for the Revolting Cocks' New Year's show coming up at the Vic. It was an odd return to normal.

I didn't know how I felt about losing the baby. Was I feeling enough? Was I depressed or sad? I wasn't sure how Paul felt either. He was not inclined to discuss it. Childbirth books I bought were silent on the topic of miscarriage. I read all sorts of viewpoints going so far off the usual discourse as to read some of Paul's Jane Roberts's Seth books. He used them often, when he was looking for answers to life's conundrums. But I found even those books didn't address miscarriage, only abortion. There was a choice involved in having an abortion that was lacking in this case.

As a welcome distraction, I was slowly warming to the idea of musician friends staying at our place to prepare for the New Year's show. It was strange to me that so many tour personnel had gathered in town preparing for the show, and they had no place to go for Christmas dinner. I offered to cook, feeling a little sorry for these food orphans, and at the same time wanting to get more comfortable around this configuration of the band. I needed to celebrate something in a big way. No longer eating for two, I was now cooking for thirteen people.

There was something hopeful and positive in having a family dinner, even if the only actual family would be Paul. I decided to go all out and be useful to others instead of feeling sorry for myself. I planned an elaborate menu: turkey with sausage, apple and cornbread stuffing, sautéed Brussels sprouts in a nutmeg-spiked roué, mashed potatoes and sweet potatoes with banana puree, homemade cranberry sauce, cheese piroshki as an appetizer, and lemon raspberry muffins, pumpkin pie, and ricotta cheesecake for dessert. My friends thought I was nuts to be cooking for that many people, but what the hell. All the food prep would take my mind off of my healing body. Cooking for a crowd wasn't really new to me. I grew up in a household of seven and often helped my exhausted mother in the kitchen. I was always a huge fan of magazines, and my latest obsession was cooking mags—Food & Wine and Bon Appétit. This dinner would test some of those WASP perfect platters regularly featured in the photo spreads.

I invited Michael Short to join us for dinner. He had holiday time off from cooking at the Star Top. But it being Christmas, it was his tradition to go see a movie opening and brave the weather in line. No Michael this time. I was on my own with cooking duties. Paul was still rehearsing.

An hour before the turkey was set to come out of the oven, Michael Short appeared at our door. The nine degree weather outside was apparently too much for his wool army coat, boots, scarf, gloves, and a flask. I secretly thought he just wanted to hang out with everyone and make sure the meal wasn't a complete disaster. Michael knew I liked good food, but was ignorant of my kitchen skills. We went to work in tandem prepping the turnovers. Michael made a dipping sauce with whatever I had in the fridge. He paused and sniffed the air, which by that point was thoroughly turkey infused: "What's in the stuffing?" he wanted to know. I went through the ingredient list and told him there were three kinds of bread: homemade cornbread, wheat, and torn French. "BLESS YOU," he stammered, bowing and kissing my hand. I had our home boombox turned up to high volume, and we yelled back and forth at each other as dishes were coming together, reminding me that I always did get along with the chefs in restaurants when I waited tables—even if only because most of them were gay, and we went to some of the same clubs to dance.

The turkey was ready to come out of the oven and rest. I looked around for a surface to clear for the tray. There were serving platters already covering every inch of woefully minimal counter space. Michael noticed the open door to the bedroom directly off of the kitchen with its beautifully polished hardwood floor.

Bill Rieflin was currently staying in that room waiting for the tour. Michael lifted the roasting tray, set it on the red and black checkerboard linoleum tiles in our kitchen, and gave the turkey one long shove with his foot, as it sailed across the kitchen floor and into the guest room.

"There we go . . . now let's do these awful green things."

Michael Balch and Chris Connelly from the current Revolting Cocks lineup, Michael Short and his girlfriend Ellie Fairey, Lee Popa, Ministry's head live show soundman, and a handful of stragglers joined us for the feast. I knew Chris was a vegetarian, but there were plenty of safe side dishes prepared in my overly enthusiastic first try at entertaining a crowd. Everyone toasted the cooks. These Cocks band members and crew looked relieved and grateful for a home cooked holiday meal. It was my first, and would start a tradition of sorts, even at times when there was no holiday, just friends visiting on tour.

The Revolting Cocks were playing the Vic Theater on New Year's Eve. It was becoming routine by now in our world that Paul was doing a show somewhere every New Year's Eve with a revolving collection of players assembled to represent one of his and Al's projects, usually the Cocks or Ministry. It was always mind-shatteringly cold outside, and it made the trek to the shows seem like too much work for such brief pleasure. I bundled up and went, each time. Someone we knew would be there to talk to. Franke and Marston's band, My Life With the Thrill Kill Kult, were playing at the Metro a few miles up the street the same night and there was a party bus going back and forth between the shows.

I looked around the apartment for the envelope of Hawaii pictures from our trip. Paul had a funny way of scooping up new pictures and slipping them into his wallet, his drawer, or some empty envelope to keep for another day. I found the pictures and headed to the venue.

I made my way to the backstage area of the Vic and walked in on our friend Ellie Fairey who was making small talk with a handsome blonde guy who appeared relaxed and comfortable in his own skin, and who had the piercing eyes of either a philosopher or a professional ball player. I surprised myself sometimes with how accurately I could size up what someone did for a living, sometimes simply by studying their choice of footwear. Ellie's new friend extended his hand.

"Hi, Mark Grace," the blonde one said, introducing himself. As I stood there absentmindedly coding together what he did for a living, a small panic of recognition fell into my thoughts, and I realized I was gripping the very real hand of the first baseman for the Chicago Cubs.

I made some stupid joke about Mr. Grace being "out of his league" at a Cocks show, but he was incredibly humble and good natured.

"I'm just a country boy at heart," he said.

I remembered the Hawaii pictures in my bag. Ellie was one of the few people who attended our wedding ceremony in Las Vegas, and I thought naturally she would welcome some silly tourist beach shots from my "honeymoon." I handed her the envelope. Ellie had that wicked smirk I loved so well, working its way into place as she squinted at the Polaroids in her hand.

"Wow. Nice tits, Gerda . . ."

Yeah. Not quite the critique I was anticipating, but appropriate coming from this fan of Martin Amis.

"You know, that's exactly what I was thinking. But I didn't want to say it," said the country boy standing next to Ellie and looking over her shoulder. Sweet. I thought of some dumb major league "win" metaphors but let this one go. Mr. Grace was clearly a fan of the whole family now, and it was a funny moment. We chatted some more, and he mentioned living somewhere in Lincoln Park. He seemed genuinely funny and interested in Paul's music. By the time the Cocks were onstage, I had Mr. Grace's home address, phone number, and an open invitation to come by (with my husband) for drinks. I folded the note and slipped it into my bag.

It wasn't news that Ministry and the Cocks were attracting the attention of major league sports figures. It was just funny to put into perspective. More than one source had told Paul and Al that "Black Jack" McDowell, the pitcher for the Chicago White Sox, had a ritual of putting on headphones and listening to Ministry while warming up for games. Aggressive conditioning or aggression venting—which was it? Our "inquiring minds" wanted to know.

A few days after the show and before the Cocks left for Europe, a group of us gathered for Indian food at Moti Mahal on Belmont. It was Marston Daley's birthday. Bill Rieflin and his girlfriend Frankie, Franke Nardiello and his boyfriend Dave, Marston, Chris Connelly, and Paul and I all sat together at one long side table. We all loved having dinner at Moti, the place where I had first cultivated my appreciation for Indian cuisine. We also greatly admired the host at Moti—"The Colonel", as we called him. He was an elderly gentleman with graying temples, military style jacket with epaulets, perpetual scowl pressing down on his face, and a consistent rude manner as he "greeted" diners and those waiting for tables. We imagined he was of an upper caste in Indian hierarchy and entirely unhappy to serve the public in any capacity. He may have been the owner or their father or the crazy uncle of the restaurant. He was a character to contend with, a look of utter outrage on his face at each new table coming in.

At Moti Mahal, when anyone passed through the kitchen doors out into the dining room, you could see an enormous standing mixer constantly in operation, but so much larger than a commercial mixer. Perhaps the family had brought it over from India. It looked capable of grinding a human body's full form. We dubbed it the "Corpus Crusher." Or as Paul and Bill liked to pluralize, "Corpii Crusher." Despite the cheery faces of my dinner companions, and the usual Colonel jokes, I had the feeling I was sitting with a tableful of complainers. I couldn't tell if it was their pre-tour anxiety, my lingering thoughts about my miscarriage, or just the usual "January in Chicago" blues.

The following day, I was recruited to be an airport-van driver for the Cocks. I guessed everyone thought my spectacular Christmas dinner spread was an indication of overall excellent health following a miscarriage and thus qualified me to drive to O'Hare. Paul, Bill, and I waited in the apartment for the others. When Paul left the room to answer the downstairs door, Bill turned to me and said, "I hope everyone's a good boy for this tour."

I was surprised by the comment, coming from someone who normally maintained a calm, nonjudgmental zen face. I didn't really know what he meant, other than the obvious—some in the crew doing too many drugs and others too many "dates." I found myself wondering now if I needed to worry about Paul chasing other women on this tour. I nodded in agreement with Bill. He was Paul's oldest friend and probably knew him better than most. "Yes. I hope so," was all I could think to say. I wondered also if Bill had perhaps leaned on Paul that night in Denver and convinced him to tell me he'd had sex with a groupie. Did I need this?

Paul, Bill Rieflin, Chris Connelly, Mark Durante, Sean Joyce, and Critter (Jeff Newell, the Cocks' studio engineer) were packed into our new silver van with all their belongings for the month overseas. I drove somewhat clumsily. It was dusk, my contact lenses were dirty. I hadn't driven on the highway in a long time. I had never pictured myself as a "soccer mom" until that moment.

"Just another day in my glamorous life," I said to the shadowy figures crouched together in the back.

The drop off curbside seemed almost perfunctory as I kissed Paul goodbye. I knew he was already "gone," thinking about the upcoming shows. I drove home, wishing they had taken cabs, and hoping my contacts would clear up—I was testing out new "extended wear" lenses, extended presumably for convenience.

I walked into the apartment and called some friends—Rick Buscher in St. Louis, Leila Eminson, and Patty. I wanted to feel some sense of camaraderie of my own, before heading back Monday morning to the legal dramas at work. I put on Al Green's Greatest Hits Vol. 1 a Christmas present from Paul.

Bill's girlfriend Frankie called. She was back in Seattle. I liked talking to Frankie about painting and women artists like herself. She spent a good deal of time staring at the painting hanging in our living room during this last visit. It was my friend Marnie's painting of another painter, Jim Brinsfield, with a piece of one of his canvases creeping into the frame. "She's a fantastic painter," Frankie said. "Someone who can really draw, too. These days, that's rare." She wanted to talk about the European shows and "the guys" being on the road. She let me know again if Bill ever cheated on her, she'd "walk." Thanks. A little late for that advice, but the two of them weren't married, either. Something else seemed to be pressing on her mind.

"You did know Al practically OD'd on New Year's, right?" she asked.

No, I didn't know about Al. Paul neglected to tell me.

Why wouldn't he mention that? I made it clear to Paul I couldn't be around when Al was actively using or getting ready to. I didn't want to lose my law license. On the other hand, I certainly needed to know if he had avoided becoming a statistic on a coroner's report a few days before they were set to leave the country.

What else was Paul not telling me? Was he concerned we'd been through enough emotional turmoil before the holidays? Was he afraid I'd run away if I heard any more salacious details about Al? I knew Al—and of Al—five years before I ever met Paul. No surprises there. Or was Paul thinking he would somehow insulate our relationship by not saying too much about Al's habits.

Now I understood why everyone seemed "off" at Marston's birthday dinner the night before. They were nervous about going to Europe to do the shows with Al. Perhaps Bill's comment to me before they left, about everyone being a good boy on this tour, had more to do with Al than Paul's past infidelity. Or was it a combination of both. Did I need this?

Al. What a guy. I went back to listening to the "other" Al. "Forgive me baby, if I do wrong . . ."

63

Photo credits:

on the sand, Lake Michigan, 1959;

all the siblings and Ma, south side harbor, 1963;

with Larry Crandus & Gary Jacobson, Wax Trax, early '80s;

with Ruth Pellicore & Lou D'Angelo, Wax Trax, early '80s;

with Sean Joyce, Wax Trax, mid '80s;

with Paul, Smart Bar, Chicago, 1988;

wedding invite, fall 1988, photo by Susan Bowman;

wedding at Chapel of the Fountain, Las Vegas, June 21, 1989;

witnesses Michael Short & Ellen Fairey, Las Vegas, June 21, 1989;

somewhere on the west coast, post-wedding, June 1989;

Paul at Grand Canyon, June 1989;

with Paul, Kauaii, 1990;

with Paul & Jane McIntyre, backstage Glasgow, 1991;

with Sunny Chapman, feigning intoxication, early '90s;

with Paul & Ursula, August 1992;

with Rick Buscher, waiting for Ursula, August 1992;

with Claude Gordon, Austin house, 1994;

Paul & Eddie Vedder, Bridge School Benefit, October 1994;

with children, Werckman wedding, August 1997;

Paul with children & Ogre Nivek, Ogre's wedding, September 1997

18

On some occasions backstage at a club in Chicago or over at Patty and Al's, Al needed to get high. At the first sight of a syringe, I had to leave the room. I didn't need to jeopardize my years of law school and my practice for Al's personal adventures. And he had no qualms about being very public with his drug use when other people were around. I'm all for enjoying the grotesque, but not that.

It's pointless to speculate about the years Paul spent watching Al get high on and off stage—their professional relationship worked. They were a writing and production team as Luxa/Pan Productions, and as long as that produced meaningful work, the relationship kept going. I usually laughed it off when Al would get onstage and a full bottle of Bushmill's waited for him, along with the water bottles. Somehow, alcohol seemed okay to use. We didn't socialize with Al much at all. Paul constantly told me Al didn't really want to do much of anything except stay home. It seemed the suburban ideal was ok with him. If we were over at Patty and Al's place, it was usually prior to a tour or for a celebratory band dinner that Patty arranged catering for.

The Revolting Cocks were back from Europe in February 1991. Al and Paul were getting offers from people looking to manage Ministry. Patty and Al wanted to discuss the offers. The four of us got together at the Jourgensen's loft space on Berniece to talk about a contract sent over by Crazed Management. Jon and Marsha Zazula, the owners of the company, had managed Metallica as they were coming into their notoriety, and that was a selling point for Al and Paul's own "Five Year Plan." Paul actually called it that. That was their goal, to have their own studio and to keep making the records they wanted to hear.

Al made jokes about the "greaseball" New Jersey couple wanting to manage Ministry. I didn't care where they were from or what kind of accent they had, as long as they cared about the band and were qualified to pound the proverbial pavement on Ministry's behalf and make a decent living for everyone. I liked that Crazed Management had organization and actual strategies in place. They had the track record. Al and Ministry had survived with the least amount of focus on attainable, tangible success so far. They were lucky. But merely guessing a record or tour was going to be profitable and make all the band members happy wasn't enough anymore. What they needed at this point required more structured promotion, advocacy, accounting, and knowledge of industry standards in dollar amounts. They were attracting bigger crowds and more press attention than ever. Jon and Marsha Zazula also made it clear they wanted Al and Paul both on the management contract. It was a smart move for them, a way to ensure someone other than Al alone was accountable for the band.

Al habitually didn't want to bother with details. He cringed at the thought of signing his name to anything, having the bad taste of his experience whoring himself out for Arista Records to thank for that. The former Boy George-ish look, fake English accent, and electro pop music of his early records, all of that was history. In the present moment, there was a new management contract to accept or reject, and I was the only lawyer in the room to make sense of it.

"Well . . . what do you think?" Al looked at me. He wanted to know if they should sign it, and if there were anything approaching a slavery clause in it—that's all he wanted to know. I had everyone's attention and wanted to hold onto the satisfaction of contributing something tangible to Paul's and Ministry's success. Of course I had gone through the contract by now, line for line. There was one problematic clause in it that immediately came to mind. It allowed management to buy life insurance on Al and Paul to cover management's costs if some tragedy occurred. I told Al it was a boilerplate clause, and they should strike it from the document.

"Yeah! Strike it! That's bullshit," he said.

Al's favorite word at the time was "lambast" ("We're gonna lambast that guy!"), so the idea of getting physical with contract language was hilariously apt. He and Paul thought life insurance was a scam under any circumstances. They looked absolutely bemused at the idea of demolishing a whole section of a contract just because "their lawyer" told them it was alright. I wasn't their lawyer, technically speaking, but my own self-interest required me to be available for interpreting contracts and the language in them. Crazed Management of course had no objection to the change.

It then became a running joke for Al; if anyone even entertained the idea of screwing the band, "Paul's wife" would "slap an injunction" on them. Al clenched his cigarette between his teeth, raised both hands up waist high, and WHAM!—one arm went up and came down to hammer (in theory) the poor soul standing there. Yes, that was me. I was now Ministry's enforcer, or at least in Al's head. I toyed with the idea of giving him an explication of the Latin meaning behind the "writ of habeas corpus"—a command to literally, "bring forth the body" of an accused—but I did have a legal duty to safeguard an unsuspecting general public from the kidnapping spree which might have ensued.

The remainder of the management contract seemed reasonable. Paul and Al were pleased with the deal Crazed Management was offering them. There were guaranteed dollar amounts management would strive for when negotiating recording budgets, merchandise advances, and touring profits. It promised more money than any of us had ever seen. In Al's words, "We're gonna be nigger rich!" Well, that settled it. We all laughed, and Al got up and went over to the wet bar. After a minute of fumbling at the bar, there were no more jokes, and he was quiet.

I looked up from my notes and realized Al wasn't mixing himself a drink. He was preparing to shoot up and getting frantic in the process. He and Paul were both behind the bar now, and Al was nearly in tears, pleading with Paul to help him. I glared at Paul. He knew my rules. I closed my notebook, walked out of the room, down the stairwell, and out into the air.

Was this the norm now? I couldn't understand how Al, such a hugely talented, funny guy could be so debilitated by a drug habit. Where was this going? Why couldn't he quit? Paul wasn't an addict. He wasn't a drunk. Why was he helping him? As ugly a thought as it was, it occurred to me at that moment that Paul's attachment to Al, and why he stayed working with Al, was more than just believing they would make ultracool, groundbreaking music together and maybe become notorious in the process. There was a lot of money at stake. New management promised them greater exposure and bigger budgets to play with. Endless studio time. Paul was assuming the role of responsible adult in the band because it made good business sense. I let that thought sink in.

Ministry signed the deal with Crazed Management. Al authorized Paul's publishing entity, Spurburn Music, to represent him as a songwriter on their joint compositions, and Crazed Management latched onto the Ministry momentum with every ounce of their experience with Metallica pushing the pitch. As a bonus, toward the end of the year, Paul, Al, Patty, Mike Scaccia, a handful of other touring band members, and I were invited to see Metallica at the Rosemont Horizon near the airport. Crazed Management arranged for us to be on the guestlist for the show. We all piled into our van, inventing hallucinatory scenarios for what we'd do when we met the great Metallica. Somewhere along in the conversation I mentioned to Paul about being at "The Jail" that day to meet with a client who had the usual tale of "whoa'" to tell. Al looked amused. He tapped the visor on his Chicago cop hat, knocking it off his head. As we drove north on Broadway, Al leaned over, planted his hat on my head, and crowned me "GForce!" then started again preaching to everyone present how I routinely spit out injunctions like baseballs in a batting cage (or something close to that). I had a new superpower. I radiated authority and THE LAW. I thought with my new headgear I probably looked the part of an S&M pinup surrounded by my leather boys, with Driver Paul steering, directing the show. It was a rare, vaguely personal moment between me and Al. A bit of Helmut Newton—a photographic slice of life.

We didn't usually see shows at Rosemont and hadn't considered the band might actually hit the stage on time. When we arrived at the venue, Metallica were already on. We were told at the door we'd have to wait until the "after party" to meet the band. I stood in the lobby with Paul and a few other people, and we could hear Metallica playing inside. It wasn't too long before the same idea began floating around in our little collective—the music coming through the walls of the packed venue sounded surprisingly uninspired. Sure, it was loud. It was Metallica. But Ministry shows were better than this.

Here we had driven forty minutes out to Rosemont to see and meet the great Metallica, and the show's sound was thin. And we would have to sit through their entire set. At that point none of us seemed willing to linger in the lobby and wait for a personal introduction. I couldn't take it anymore. I wanted to leave, as did most everyone else. Mikey (Scaccia) wanted to stay. I never cared about meeting bands anyway, and having a healthy skepticism about live shows, I was happy to go.

We piled back into the van, and I let my thoughts wander over the institution that was now Metallica. Did I even care? Was it fashionable today to say you were into Metallica? Into Ministry? Fashion, fashionable, what did it mean anymore. Somehow making a giant leap in logic (I was a lawyer), I realized I'd never actually owned a black leather motorcycle jacket. Paul had at least one. Black leather was timeless. The periwinkle blue leather I was wearing was broken in with the grime of the city permanently dimming the color a few shades. It looked fantastic, but it was time to spend some serious cash on myself and Paul, and we could finally afford it. Together. Paul agreed. More leather. Screw Metallica.

***

"The problem is, I have long arms, and I need to lean over on the Morini."

Paul had a habit of beginning sentences with "The problem is . . ." We were both odd sizes and didn't really fit well in clothes off the rack.

"You say, 'The problem is' so often, I'm beginning to think your life is beset with problems and maybe they have something to do with me," I said.

I was joking, of course. But catch phrases and clichés were conversation death for me. And now that I was practicing law, there were no problems that couldn't be fixed.

"Not everything is a problem, okay? Where does 'one' go for custom leathers, 'Mr. I've Been Riding Motorcycles My Whole Adult Life'?" I was having my fun perfuming the air with fake titles for the man in my life.

Paul subscribed to Cycle World and Motorcyclist magazines. What did they recommend to their motorhead readers? Langlitz Leathers in Portland, Oregon. The shop had been in business, custom fitting riders since the 1940s. Paul called and told them we wanted to order jackets. Langlitz sent out a catalog and measuring kits with paper tape measures for us to tick off the inches of our wrists, necks, backs, fronts, torsos, and arms. We played tailor's models in T-shirts and underwear as the two of us methodically calculated each other's bodies in this new way. How much distance riding equals more "give" for the elbows? I needed a lipstick pocket on my left forearm like the one I was accustomed to on my blue leather, and besides, Langlitz was serious about riding comfort, yes? What we won't do for glamor.

Our jackets came months later, stamped inside with our full names and year of completion. It was one small way to prevent them from getting nicked. Bill Rieflin followed Paul's lead and ordered a jacket for himself. Sadly, Bill's jacket disappeared from a dressing room on the next tour. So much for branding them on the inside.

***

Paul and I made every attempt to travel together as much as possible, depending always upon business—his. My immigrant mother called us, "buncha gypsies". We were happiest when the trip didn't involve work. I had never been to Mexico, and in November of 1991, Paul suggested we visit his mother's father in Cuernavaca while there was still time. Roland Du Luart was in his nineties. He was one of the few male role models in Paul's early life. His grandfather had financially supported Paul and his brother Roland when they were very little boys after the early breakup of their parents' marriage. As an infant, Paul and his brother had in fact moved to Mexico with their mother for a brief period.

Paul was convinced his first language had been Spanish. He told me he discovered his favorite fruit was "mel-loan" as the word was pronounced in Mexico. He also told me a story about how when he was barely two, he and his brother Roland walked themselves into a church in Mexico, and Roland baptized them both with holy water. Where their mother was during this ceremony remained a mystery. It defied common sense that anyone would allow two little boys to wander outdoors alone in a foreign country. I assumed Paul's lack of formal religious upbringing created some need in him to fashion a hero's story of self-redemption. Whether the story was true or not, Paul's brother backed him up on it. The veracity of childhood memories in general was an open question, but the self-baptism tale wasn't the only hazy marker in my husband's early life. He also told me after he was born in Palo Alto, California, there had been some confusion amongst the relatives as to his actual birthdate. Some thought he was born on February 8th, while his grandpère in Cuernavaca was certain it was the 7th and sent him cards every year reflecting that date. I found Paul's boyhood stories of identity crises charming in their guilelessness, his imagination trying to make sense of rituals and customs of two cultures. In the end, when caring for her two small boys in Mexico became unmanageable for his mother, Paul and Roland moved to Seattle, where they were raised by their aunt and uncle. But their grandpère, Roland Du Luart, regularly took care of his grandsons' expenses and schooling costs.

Mexico. For me, the privileged spontaneity of another break from impending winter away from Chicago weather felt so . . . glamorous. But it was important to Paul that I meet his family. The two of us were our own family now, and I should know his history. We should understand where we came from and where we were going. My side of our family was quite small. Aside from three siblings—only two of whom I was in contact with, the other having divorced herself from the family and converted to Judaism—and my parents, nearly everyone else lived in Germany or Poland, and we weren't going there anytime soon.

Paul and I flew to Mexico City and rented a car. It was an hour and a half drive to Roland Du Luart's place in Cuernavaca. I picked up some tourist brochures and discovered Cuernavaca had the distinction of being the number two city for pools per capita in the world. It was lush, and a place where Mexico City's rich went to get away from the noise and smog.

Paul's grandfather greeted us through the wrought iron gates of his courtyard. He was tall and thin and looked to me like the final page of a flip book on the physical evolution of Paul Barker—my husband. Roland Du Luart held a title as a marquis in the strange history of French aristocracy. He would have been a duke had he not married outside of his religion.

Roland Du Luart was almost ninety-five. He seemed to have avoided much of the body deterioration and intellectual decline of those still alive of his generation. Genetics were a part of the picture, but he also lived leisurely and swam in his pool every day. He had designed his house, a single-level ranch house constructed into a V shape to surround the outdoor pool. A flower garden with a stone wall framed the rear of the property, which appeared in size to be two acres. The house was set into a private subdivision outside of the city center. Roland was the epitome of elegance as he introduced himself and asked me to please call him "Grandpère."

Every morning during our stay, Grandpère drove himself to the newsstand and to buy some "pan dulce" (sweet bread) for breakfast. This, despite having staff on hand daily to cook, clean, and maintain the grounds. He had a steady companion, Michaela, who was in her seventies. She lived nearby in an enormous villa, the back of which revealed sumptuous verandas—three tiers of them—stretching down to three separate swimming pools. Michaela was a widow who had inherited the Coca Cola franchise of their state when her husband passed. Her looks and composure reminded me of the ballerina Maria Tallchief—regal.

Grandpère sat smoking a cigar poolside at Michaela's and offered us drinks from the wet bar on the patio. As a young man, he had been conscripted into service as an officer in France and was placed into the same unit as the American composer Cole Porter. Later, after the end of the second world war, he had managed to leave France and in the 1950s, became a stock broker and made a very comfortable living for himself in Mexico. He clearly had had an extraordinary life.

I carried a camera to catalog the colors of Cuernavaca, the outlying architectural ruins, and the faces of the natives. Grandpère sat in profile next to me, smoking a cigar. "For someone who already knows two other languages, why did you never bother to learn French?" he asked me, somewhat scandalized by my cultural oversight. I pointed the camera at him and snapped a picture. "Oh for heaven's sakes," he said, straightening up slightly in his deck chair. "Must it be from the side?!" Grandpère had a most distinguished French nose. He smiled for the camera.

Michaela called to me from the house, and I left grandfather and grandson to smoke in peace. Michaela wanted me to see the main house, filled with photographs of her childhood in the Morales state. She had grown up poor. She was stunningly beautiful. She worked hard to make a life for herself before ever meeting her now deceased husband. She turned up her nose at the ugly gossip, a steady backdrop to her marriage to such a wealthy man clearly outside of her class, her station in life. As we walked through the corridors and I listened to her stories, Michaela gathered her maids and introduced them to me one by one. She wanted them to feel valued. She was a hero to these women. While she spoke, I felt a connection in our histories. My childhood had not been privileged, my dreams now coming to life as an adult with an ever changing perspective on beauty and living a passionate life. We made a pact that she would come visit us in Chicago and continue our conversations.

Paul and I returned to Grandpère's for the night, our heads filled with images of European conflict, Cole Porter, ancient ruins, and romance. Patterns of regionally crafted bird images were woven into the rugs in our room. The dark paneled walls were filled with handsomely carved, built-in wooden cabinets created to last and age along with the owner of the house. I looked at Paul and said, "Dip me," my cue for him to support his dance partner as she collapsed backwards and onto the bed. His smile assured me we were both restless, renewed in spirit, and more in love at that very moment than either of us could have ever imagined. We were so lucky.

The next day we drove with Grandpère and Michaela to the small mountain town of Taxco where silversmiths and artisans forged fantastic jewelry for hundreds of years. I bought a silver bracelet of tiny mesh sombreros linked together waiting to be flung in the air for a fiesta. We ordered tacos at an outdoor café and watched a tour group of Japanese senior citizens strolling in a circle around a fountain in the square. They wore identical white cotton hats, petal shaped as many infant sun hats were fashioned and tied at the chin. The petals lifted with every gust of wind. On the drive back Grandpère took us to see abandoned temple ruins nearby, which were in desperate need of preservation. He told us, "It's a shame there is no money available anywhere to restore and save these monuments, and in time who will care?" Paul took photos of me standing with Grandpère on opposing sides of some temple steps. Generational differences didn't matter when each of our figures created shadows of the same size. I was already missing this place.

We returned to Chicago just before Thanksgiving, satisfied in knowing a little bit more about Paul's family history. Paul once again climbed back into the cave of Chicago Trax to work with Al. I was back to suiting up in the best fabrics and shoes I could afford, always mindful of courtroom dress protocol. Mostly, I didn't want to look like anyone else. I owned one gray tailored suit. The rest were plucked from the racks and in varying patterns, colors, and cuts to accentuate my reddish-blonde coif and Chanel slicked smile.

I spent some mornings on the el wondering whether I was doing good work, whether I was satisfying my goals. I was part of a system now of behaviors reined in, judged, sentenced, and appealed. I thought about the other players. What does it take to want to be a Chicago cop? I thought about this many times walking into the courtroom at Belmont and Western where my firm routinely had pending cases. There was no right answer. What does it take to be a lawyer for the defense? As a criminal defense lawyer, you put aside your personal feelings about your client, do your job, and get on with the day.

Entering a courtroom at Belmont and Western, I could see the front rows filling up with ten, twenty police officers making their appearances on misdemeanors and traffic violations. "How you doin', counselor? After you, counselor." These were men (primarily) who didn't know me personally, but mutual acknowledgment was the norm, as the cops filed in and the attorneys made their way to the judge's clerk. Cops have lives. We all have lives away from our roles. A typical conversation between two uniforms greeting each other in court:

"Hey, how you doin'?"

"Oh, not too bad, not too bad. Can't complain, can't complain. Same old same old . . . so, how you doin'?"

"Not too bad, not too bad . . ."

A sparse vocabulary ping ponging back and forth, the same words exchanged, the same meaning derived: I'm alive.

Early in the summer, one of the partners in my office returned from federal court one day and mentioned an undercover narcotics officer he dealt with on and off in our caseload. The officer needed a lawyer to represent him in his divorce case recently filed by his wife. The officer was due in our office later that day. It was my task to interview this new client and build up the file to represent him. It was easy to switch gears to take on a non-criminal matter like a divorce, just as I would advise criminal clients in real estate closings, personal injury cases, and civil forfeitures. You separated the person from their daily "work."

The new client arrived with his girlfriend, someone he'd been to Sturgis with, someone he carried on the back of his motorcycle. I interviewed the new client and began the process of becoming familiar with this man's life, personal and professional. He was a veteran cop with a pension, a lengthy career, and many years of marriage behind it all. He and his wife had a handicapped child.

The client told me he trusted Mitchell and Tom as lawyers who did their jobs with integrity, even though they had been on opposing sides in dozens of cases. He was entrusting this personal matter to us, and I felt a great deal of compassion for him, especially in light of his son's condition. We ended our conversation weighing the stylistic advantages of Italian motorcycles over Harleys like his own.

I had my doubts about the ethical considerations with this one, although we didn't have any current pending cases in common. I came to refer to this client as "my motorcycle cop." I could understand the appeal of wanting to get away on a bike and just ride—Paul and I did it as often as his schedule and mine allowed. We had that degree of trust and closeness and silence necessary to ride in the city, unable to communicate except for hand signals and squeezes to the waist and thighs. It felt safe. I could empathize with my motorcycle cop. Police work wasn't easy. Riding a motorcycle on and off the job would make the segue to life after retirement and divorce easier. Seamless. The more I came to know him, the more he appeared ready to accept responsibility for his marriage breaking up, move ahead with his life, and take care of his child for the future.

After two meetings in the office, I organized my file for court appearances coming up, made some calls, and researched union benefits for police officers. I was surprised by how generous they could be. My client had issues to resolve still with his wife over his pension and permanent care for their son. Their son was his highest priority.

I took the el home from work in early December, thinking again about our recent trip to Mexico and thinking about Christmas. Paul had two tours coming up. I was making travel plans to meet him on the road. I headed up the stairs to the apartment. Unloading my briefcase onto the kitchen table, I leaned over to turn on the television and listen to the news while I made some decisions on what to eat, what to cook, if it should be just for me or Paul too. I never knew from day to day when he would be home. I had gotten in the habit of listening to the local news while preparing dinner and clearing my mind of any lingering, aggravating phone calls or exchanges with court personnel during the day. I cherished that free time. Riding the train home each day, going underground for much of the ride, had its limited appeal. It felt so confining. Sometimes, when the weather was warm and dry enough, I'd walk half way home from the office just to pass familiar landmarks on Clark Street along the way.

My thoughts were interrupted by the news on the television. I heard my client's name. Then, "Chicago police officer dead . . . partner shot . . . police station . . . apparent murder-suicide." I called Mitchell and Tom.

"Yeah I know! I'm in the car. Jeez. It's all over the news."

For personal reasons ultimately known only to himself and his partner on the job, my client killed a fellow officer, then shot himself. My motorcycle cop had in an instant disappeared from my narrative.

Each day, when I walked across the Daley Center plaza downtown heading to the courtrooms or the law library, I would glance over at the Picasso sculpture to see if anything had changed in her face—from my point of view. On this particular day, after my client took himself out of my world, I felt as though Picasso's Woman was a constant, reminding me to do my job and not get emotional. I thought about my old roommate and friend Carol who had taken her own life. Such pain was frightening to imagine.

I headed into the building, flashed my sheriff's ID at the deputy manning the security line on the ground floor, adjusted my silk blouse, and fed myself to an already packed elevator going up. My client, the motorcycle cop, was dead. His wife now had to grieve for her husband and his partner. I handed the paperwork to the judge's clerk. The judge had already heard the news. I made my motion to withdraw from the case and was back out on the plaza before lunch.

A week or so later, I dropped off a couple of suits and silk blouses at the Korean dry cleaners by the el and headed downtown to my office. Things there were always in perpetual motion, shifting our schedules to accommodate new cases and trips to bond court. But that was the beauty in working criminal cases, which came and were resolved much more quickly than the average civil matter. My concentration seemed off. It took longer for me to reacquaint myself with our files. In sorting through Juan Rivera's appeal, which really needed my attention, it occurred to me I had missed getting my period. I felt anxious enough to buy a kit at Walgreens, which confirmed what I already knew and had known after that last night in Cuernavaca when the bird images in our room once again filled my head with lightness. I was pregnant. The baby was due in August. Paul had two tours scheduled for the coming year—Ministry's Psalm 69 tour and Lollapalooza. Fantastic.

***

As a lawyer you compartmentalize, observing other people's problems under glass until the day they are no longer your problems. After my client's suicide, I felt physically ill. Not from being pregnant—I never experienced morning sickness or any other physical symptoms, aside from the extra pounds and constantly feeling full. I felt ill because I couldn't "fix" this one. I felt robbed of that part of the story that I didn't see coming. My client had had enough of his personal life and something just snapped. Being a lawyer didn't stop me from being human and feeling empathy. As human beings, there are stories that we're glad to hear and those we wish we hadn't. There was nothing happy about this story.

I was pregnant, again. It had been over a year since my miscarriage. Liminal images of my client's last minutes of life crept into my thoughts. After my first full checkup, my ob-gyn, the very mildly tempered and very direct Dr. Arekapudi, had an unnerving diagnosis about the current pregnancy.

"You have an incompetent cervix," she said. "You will need to have a stitch."

Come again? Incompetent cervix. What? How often did that happen? I couldn't think of a single time when someone questioned my competency in anything as an adult woman.

Dr. Arekapudi's clinical assessment came from years of practice with me and other patients. My carefully tended to corpus was exhibiting signs of feeble strength in actually providing a reliable womb for a baby to develop in and stay in place. A simple stitch on the cervix would ensure the baby would stay put. The stitch would also ensure my sex life was about to contract into a smaller world of physical possibilities.

Why did there have to be extraordinary physical obstacles piled onto the usual nine months of limited mobility I was fully prepared to experience? There was no way around this impediment either, without the strong likelihood I would miscarry again. My mother had four miscarriages during her childbearing years and gave birth to five healthy babies. She also had one illegal abortion, that I knew of. Mine was legal, but outside of marriage. I couldn't beat myself up for it and attach any correlation to my body's current state, but I thought about it briefly. There was no connection, according to my doctor.

I had to tell Paul I needed surgery and why. He didn't seem too distressed by the limits imposed upon our relationship as a result of the surgery. He was more concerned about me, and how I was going to handle it on my end.

"We could be creative, couldn't we?" he asked, as only a man could, whose own bodily integrity was not being compromised—not to mention his emotional or psychological health.

I rarely compared myself to other women, but my mind went there trying to rationalize how fortunate I really was:

"Other women develop diabetes and high blood pressure when they're pregnant. Some get acne, depression, all kinds of problems." Yes. What was 75 percent of one year's time avoiding full intimacy with my husband, when it meant taking 100 percent care of another growing life? As a bonus we wouldn't be forever on alert for another miscarriage and all of that anxiety. I still cursed the universe for throwing out a curveball. I got the stitch.

I continued working full time. My job as an attorney was satisfying in its own intellectual way, and in my personal life I was adjusting to a lot of new things, not the least of which was the constant Ministry related calls and mail when Paul was not at home. People calling about the tours, merchandise, artwork approvals, or simply to reconnect with their long-lost (second) cousin, Paul. Paul and Al were nearly finished with the new Ministry album, Psalm 69.

After the new year, someone in the Chicago Blackhawks organization (who was a Ministry fan and friend of Al's) gave Paul a pair of tickets to see a Blackhawks game at the Stadium on the south side. Choice seats close to the ice. I hadn't been to the Stadium since seeing The Jacksons' Triumph tour there with Steve Miglio and all of my art crowd friends. Going to watch professional sports was a rare mindless spectacle, but a welcome break from routine. Paul and I had ridden the Morini to Wrigley Field a few times to see the Cubs play, stopping first to pick up steak burritos on Chicago Avenue. Unlike the bleachers at Wrigley, the seats at the Stadium would be closer to the action and inside.

On game day, we headed to the Stadium, found our seats down by the ice, and watched a few warmup plays, getting accustomed to keeping an eye on the puck and the direction it would go, accelerating at one hundred mile an hour speeds. I could do without an unscheduled tooth extraction, thank you very much.

Before the game got underway, Paul remembered he had to call Tom Baker in LA. Tom Baker was deep in the process of mastering Ministry songs for their new album. Paul needed to find a public phone somewhere quiet in the building to make the call. I got up with him to find the ladies room, knowing now that I was pregnant my bladder was operating on overdrive and I couldn't wait in lines for anything. Paul headed for a bank of phones on a wall in the lobby. When I came back to find him, he was still on the phone. He had that look of someone trying to figure out a word in a crossword puzzle.

"Okay. Tom, hang on . . ." Paul put his hand on the receiver and said to me, "We want you to listen to this track and tell me what you think we should call it."

I looked at him. "Seriously?" Something about his smile made me realize yes, with all my literary, music, and art background, I was being asked to exercise my judgment in this crunch time for titles. It was a Dada moment. What fun. I took the phone, said hi to Tom, and waited for the intro to begin.

There were no vocals. This was one of two instrumental tracks at the end of the album, and from what I gathered, it was up to Paul to write and finish them. Listening to the song left me with the impression of floating in a wind tunnel. It was a familiar wall of sustained noise.

"It sounds like grace," I told him. A fine ambiguous choice. Paul looked pleased. He took the phone back. "Tom, the track's called "Grace.'" He hung up, the Blackhawks game was back on, and we descended into the darkened arena to reclaim our seats.

My opinion would become quite an asset as time went on and songs on other records went through stages of completion. I was flattered and humbled whenever Paul needed a second set of ears to listen to playback. This all mattered. It was the stuff of a trusting partnership and brought us closer as time alone together became so precious and unpredictable.

Gibby Haines from the band Butthole Surfers was brought in to work with Ministry on a single for the new album. It wasn't a formal request, but not as grab 'em by the collar and throw 'em in front of a microphone as Al made it seem in interviews. On a basic level, Gibby was tasked with improvising and singing lyrics over a piece of music, and then appearing in the video for the song. Paul and I drove out to O'Hare to pick him up when he arrived in town. When I first saw Gibby I was surprised at how tall he was and physically big, like an ogre. He didn't smile. The session went fairly quickly by Ministry standards. Afterwards, the fun began.

Gibby wouldn't budge over what he thought he was entitled to as the lyricist. The haggling over songwriting splits (and ultimately, the royalties) became the first time I could think of a collaborator demanding "industry standard" for writing lyrics.

"Fucking guy wants more than anybody else," Paul said. Paul and Al took for granted the loose democracy between themselves and other songwriters on Ministry, Revolting Cocks, and side project sessions. With Pailhead, all splits were equal. The same with Lard and Acid Horse. The Revolting Cocks and Ministry were decided song by song, and the splits went all over the place. Sometimes Al would get 61 percent, others would get 13 percent or Paul would get 80 percent and Al 10 percent and 10 percent to someone else. Or the reverse. Sometimes Al received credit on songs he had very little to do with. I was amused by Paul and Al's outrage over Gibby's prima donna act. He was singing "nonsense lyrics." What was that worth?

I could see Gibby's point. It would be a different song if they'd used a different lyricist. I knew enough about copyright law to recognize he wasn't just being greedy. But he was asked to contribute on someone else's project, and he wasn't exactly "Scott fucking Walker" or Leonard Cohen. But money is money, in the music business as in any other. Gibby got what he wanted, and Ministry started rehearsing for tour. The single, "Jesus Built My Hotrod," the song Gibby rapped nonsense lyrics over, became Ministry's biggest charting single.

19

I was pregnant with our first child and still going to court. I refused to buy any pregnancy clothes. The options were hideous—"cute" fabrics or reengineered regular pieces expanded into SUV versions of the same thing. I looked for creative ways to feel comfortable at work and still retain a sense of decorum and style. I wasn't trying to hide my pregnancy, but I was unwilling to draw attention to it by wearing anything tent-like or cute. I bought black cotton and lycra swing tops at a fitness shop and wore those over a tailored skirt held together by a large safety pin on the side. The pin was out of sight. No elastic waistbands for me, thank you. I was slowly gaining weight, all apparently in my mid-section. I had no appetite. No cravings. My ob-gyn would tell me to eat more fruit and protein bars, something palatable that would add calories and weight. Some days I felt I was forcing my hand to put something in my mouth.

There was no joyful, carefree indulgence in it. It was all calculation. I wondered how many pregnant women felt the desire to take a break, just for a few hours, and do nothing calculated to bring "optimal" results to their pregnancies. Then I wondered if I was just thinking too much, getting overly emotional or sensitive, and I should just accept this new fate that my husband and

I had designed for us.

My work schedule was slowing down—a walk to the Daley Center to research and make the odd court appearance. On one of the court days in the spring, I argued a motion in a Domestic Relations courtroom and was finishing up at the bench. I turned to leave and saw my old friend Ross sitting in the back of the courtroom. I hadn't seen Ross since I had the abortion, which effectively ended our friendship. He was dressed like a lawyer. He followed me out to the elevators. It had been five years.

Seeing a friend's familiar face after a lengthy absence was different from seeing someone with whom the friendship had dissolved. I was open to anything he had to say. He was happy to see me at work in a courtroom. He felt compelled to reach out and see how I was doing. I was obviously pregnant. Could we meet for lunch? Why not. Let's make amends. If he was here in the building on this day, I might be seeing more of him around the courthouse and on the street. We agreed to meet for lunch.

A few days after our chance meeting, I found myself sitting across the table from Ross at a restaurant not far from my office. He leaned in as if to tell me a secret and said the sandwiches here are really good and not horribly expensive for junior associates on a budget. He smiled at me in the same boyish, shy way I remembered so well. He told me I looked great. He was happy for me and Paul. He was very happy we were expecting our first child. Ross had a job with a medium-sized law firm downtown and was thinking of finally joining his sister in Florida and opening a practice there. He wasn't involved in music at all anymore. I listened for a long time, feeling grateful things had worked out for my friend and grateful he had chosen to approach me at the courthouse instead of turning away without a word. We didn't discuss the past, just our current lives and the immediate future. Something began to feel lighter between us. I hoped he sensed it, too. We exchanged business cards and went our separate ways once again.

***

The publicity hype for Ministry was accelerating with the Psalm 69 tour and

Lollapalooza dates coming up. The album was scheduled for July release, just in time for summer touring frenzy. Andre Barzinski, a journalist in Brazil, was in contact with Ministry's management and asked Paul and Al to come to Rio de Janeiro for a book promotion. Andre was the entertainment editor for the major Sao Paulo newspaper. Andre had written a book featuring his favorite American bands. His publisher was funding the book release party and scheduled events in Sao Paulo and Rio. Andre's book covered an eclectic range of his personal American heroes, like Ministry, the Cramps, and the Dead Kennedys. He had gone to see Jello Biafra in San Francisco a few years before, and everyone at Jello's label knew he was legit. The trip to Brazil would be good PR.

Patty and Al decided they couldn't risk flying to Brazil. Al was convinced he'd either be arrested with drugs or not be able to find what he needed once we arrived there. More paranoia—would it ever end? Paul and I didn't have such issues hampering our foreign travel plans. We weren't passing up a free trip to South America, either.

Paul was on his own representing the Ministry/Luxa Pan team. By this time, I was six months pregnant. I was given the ok to fly by my doctor. She said another few weeks and I could forget about long flights and concentrate on finishing my pregnancy in less physically stressful scenarios than being confined to a pressurized cabin thirty thousand feet in the air.

The featured artists making the trip to Brazil were Paul and Jello Biafra. Ministry's publicist Maria Ferrero and Michael Mazur her photographer were to meet us there. Alternative Tentacle's label manager Greg Werckman was accompanying Biafra from San Francisco. Greg was already friends with Andre Barzinski, and Paul and I were both excited to be plopped into a country where everyone spoke Portuguese and very few spoke English.

From the moment we arrived, it was apparent that only the journalists we met spoke any English. It didn't matter. Andre arranged interpreters for us. Andre's own English was perfect, but I had never met anyone so hilariously out of whack with his use of the language. The arrangements of words emanating from Andre's mouth at times were like surrealist paintings.

He made grand statements: "I had a funny meeting with Russ Meyer.

I laughed so hard, my eyes fell into my hand." Andre was so charming, we believed him. Paul and I couldn't get over his outrageous hyperboles to describe mundane things. It was hard to tell if it was his Brazilian point of view skewered in translation or just Andre being Andre.

As we drove from the Rio airport to our hotel, we saw unblemished new houses on the side of the road partially blocking our view of shacks clustered in a dirty mass behind them—expedient gentrification. Andre clarified for us how a lot of money had been invested in sprucing up slummy parts of Rio in preparation for the Earth Summit happening the following month.

Historically, very few American bands played Brazil. Like Australia and Japan, the market was there, but the headache and expense of traveling to such less trodden venues was not worth the planning. Andre had visited the San Francisco offices of Alternative Tentacles a couple of years before to meet Jello Biafra, and the idea for a book came together at that meeting. From what we gathered, Andre wrote the book as a ploy to get his favorite artists to at least visit Brazil before the height of touring season, with all expenses paid for by Andre's book publisher. It was a fantastic mini scam complete with nice hotels, car service to clubs, and the odd MTV green-screen interview. For Paul, the trip to Brazil was also a good excuse to hang out with Jello Biafra and our friend Greg Werckman (who I called "Wreck-man") as he attended to Biafra's needs. We all knew each other to some degree for years, but Jello kept much to himself. When he was feeling sociable, he was happy to discuss Brazilian politics and the government's rush to throw some cosmetic touches upon the local slums just in the nick of time for the observant eyes of dignitaries flying in to talk about the health of the planet.

Greg Werckman had a perpetual "Oh God, Biafra's a freak" look on his face. It was a running gag; although, I occasionally heard about Biafra's peccadillos from other people we knew. Jello had his quirks. During one of his stays at Patty and Al's loft on Berniece in Chicago, he went about in his underwear doing a calisthenics exercise routine, which in the privacy of his own place was one thing. But there was the presence of the Jourgensen's young daughter Adrienne to think about, and she had the run of the loft space too. Cute. It wasn't cute to Patty.

When I heard that story, I too thought it at best irresponsible, at worst, just plain weird. But something about Biafra's whole self-possessed public demeanor made me reevaluate even that scenario. He didn't have kids, so what did he know about being a parent and having to childproof your friends? It occurred to me Jello was simply trying to take care of himself. He needed the exercise. He was a performer—front and center onstage for a punk band and his spoken word gigs.

When Paul and I first encountered Biafra in Rio, we couldn't help but notice the curious hue of his skin before we'd even hit the beach on this trip. His face was a light shade of orange. Greg had all the answers, of course, having to attend to his charge's daily regimens and needs. He pulled us aside. "Jello's been taking too much spirulina. I think he's really overdoing it. (Pause) God . . . he's such a freak." Watching the two of them was pure comedy—Biafra obsessing over what magazine to read, Greg behind him rolling his eyes. Greg wasn't one to kowtow to his star's needs. He protected his own sanity first and foremost. I respected that.

Our host Andre had a loose itinerary planned for our stay. In Rio, it seemed to be mostly business. Maria Ferrero (Ministry's publicist) scheduled Paul for an interview with MTV Brazil. I watched from the sidelines with Greg as we traded comments on how annoying the woman "VJ" was. Maybe "annoying" was part of the job description to work at MTV. The interviewer wanted to hear all about Ministry's new record, and "why wasn't Al here?" I was simply fascinated by the green screen behind Paul. That was a first, for me anyway.

We were secretly hoping Paul would say something about the scam that brought us to Brazil in the first place or the fact that Al wasn't ready to be sitting in a Brazilian jail. It would have made for a livelier interview. MTV was a necessary evil for any band's exposure. But the on-air hosts usually came across as so painfully hip.

Paul was grateful to get out of the TV studio with his integrity intact. And what better follow up to self-promotion, than a visit to see Christ the Redeemer—the statue, that is. Paul, Greg, Maria, Andre, and I rode a cable car up the hillside where the world-renowned monument stared down at us. The sheer size of Jesus on the hilltop was enough to quiet Paul's ego for a while; although, he couldn't help pantomiming the outstretched hands of the giant savior upon our ascent. Despite his on again/off again insecurities, I was, in fact, married to a ham.

Later in the day, Paul and I were advised to stay close to the hotel. Crime was a big problem in parts of Rio. Ironically, we were also encouraged to visit the many Satanic worship shops around. A spell and amulet for every need, it seemed. A life sized devil statue with horns painted a sunburned tomato red greeted us outside one open air shop. We visited one or two others, were handed tapes of "spiritual" mantras and music scores, but I was not in the mood to unduly influence our unborn child with anything but our own voices—that and the occasional Patsy Cline or Eric Satie tape for the time being.

Despite the darker elements lurking in the back streets (and on sale in certain shops), I soon felt this country had in it the most beautiful women I had ever seen. One stunning face after another on the street, as if every modeling agency in town had shut down for an emergency that day and all these leggy ingenues were left to fend for themselves or fetch a cup of coffee somewhere at a street café. Perhaps being pregnant fundamentally rebalanced my brain chemistry, but it seemed to me as though all of these women were "unattached." Many of them stared at Paul when we were out together walking. Women stared at him all the time. But here, with motherhood advancing in my direction, it certainly didn't help my self-esteem to recall the Brazilian idea of a bikini was closer to an eye patch than the two piece J. Crew number I had buried away for post-pregnancy wishful thinking. Greg managed to cultivate a new "friendship" with a beauty he'd met while we were all out with Andre and his Sao Paulo posse. I was happy for Greg but surprised, considering the number of hours in the day he was required to tend to Biafra.

Andre and his publisher arranged for all of us to have dinner at a classic Brazilian steakhouse. We were seated family style at a "ten top" roulette wheel of treats. Gauchos swooshed by, circling our party table, and ceremoniously displayed cuts of meat skewered on swords they held high before moving on to the next table. I sat next to Jello with Paul on my other side. I accepted a glass of red wine offered by the roving waiters.

"Are you SURE you should have that?!" Biafra looked alarmed. It was the first non-political utterance I'd heard from him so far. I was touched that he was thinking of my health in this obviously pregnant body.

"It's okay. We're eating a lot of red meat. One glass of red wine will help my digestion." I was fumbling for an explanation, but it was true from what I'd read.

Biafra was an enigma. I had met him a few times when I worked at Wax Trax, giving him a ride to O'Banion's once when the store was closing for the night. I absolutely adored him as a champion of the First Amendment and respected him as an artist. I was happy to be in his company as much as the rest of our party. I still thought he needed to lighten up. We were going to be driving to the beach soon enough. I was curious to see if Biafra's rhetoric would be subdued once surrounded by the white-sand beaches of the Brazilian coastline— and of course, all those bikinis.

On the second leg of our Brazilian visit, we arrived in Sao Paulo, and it was back to focusing on the real reason we had come this far: to generate fanfare for Andre Barzinski's book. Our driver spun through loose traffic patterns in the city center. I could hardly look ahead as we dodged pedestrians, motorcycles, and cars jamming the streets and roundabouts. We were on our way to a Brazilian disco for a meet and greet. Our interpreter Adriana had another client for the night and would not be joining us. Andre and his friends stepped in to translate.

The club was enormous and as Greg said, "Full of sweaty bodies." Normally a body pumping paradise, there were now tables set up for record and book signings. Somehow I had pictured a more serene setting for a book release, but it was all about loud music, so why not here?

Paul and I sat down at a conference table facing the dance floor. Fans bearing merchandise began appearing to line up in front of us. At one point I looked up to see a T-shirt being handed down to me. "Please sign!"

I heard the words, but didn't register that they were directed to me, personally.

"Oh . . . no, I can't," I started to say. I was embarrassed for this person. "I'm not in the band." They were unfazed.

"But we know you are Paul's wife! You are famous."

Okay. First time for everything, I thought. I signed the shirt as a few more items were brought up and placed in front of me.

We were busy for over an hour, when I felt the jet lag I had convinced myself wouldn't be a bother for me and my unusually hardy pregnant self. Paul's official duties were winding down. Everyone else wanted to move on and get rested for our drive to the beach the next day.

As we gathered together outside the club, another hired car pulled up and our interpreter Adriana got out followed by the actor Jeremy Irons. He was her client for the day. We chatted with Adriana for a few minutes as Irons looked over our obviously non-Brazilian group and smiled. She later told us he said we looked so interesting, he wished he could cancel his obligatory appearance and hang out with "those American musicians."

The next day we all rendezvoused in the lobby for the car to pick us up. I guess this is what it feels like when bands actually go on tour, I thought, but what did I know. I could only hope there wouldn't be any drama. Our car for the day turned out to be a passenger van ready to haul us and our beach gear to the resort chosen for our stay. Greg had some issues finally worked out with "Gelatina." Greg decided the name "Jello" needed a little Latin flair now that we were in South America.

We managed to leave the city behind and head to the Brazilian coast. I let my mind wander over the language on storefronts and signs and still felt slightly as if we'd landed in a completely foreign civilization. Here in Brazil so few people spoke English and also didn't know Spanish. It was mildly comforting that we were in a big international city, but as we drove into the countryside, and the roads lost their city paved smoothness, I realized I didn't know anything about the place where we were headed. Was the beach resort seriously remote, as in no hospital for hundreds of miles? The van was hitting bumpy spots, and I looked over at Maria Ferrero. Andre's publisher surely had worked out any contingencies for the pregnant lady, right?

The terrain outside of our windows grew more rugged. Hills, bad roads, and more hills. The countryside stretched on revealing small (if any) primitively built houses and shacks. A dilapidated gas station appeared ahead. This may be the last opportunity for me to relieve myself, I thought, other than pulling over for a ditch on the side of the road. The gas station restroom contained a cement platform with a hole in the center functioning as the seat. "I am so pampered," I said, in my dreamiest pregnant lady-in-waiting voice.

Back on the road, we hit yet another jarring bump, and I felt a National Geographic moment coming on as I thought, "Great. I'm in the Brazilian outback, very pregnant, riding in a rickety caravan with Jello Biafra, who may or may not be a difficult travel companion himself (depending upon whether Greg was exaggerating this time or not), and I have to keep my cool. Or I'll lose the baby. Or have an emergency delivery. Maybe Biafra would have to assist."

I looked over at Paul, who as usual was lost in his own thoughts. It was up to me to white knuckle it alone. After what seemed like hours playing bumper cars, we arrived at Maresias Beach and the resort and discovered we had the place to ourselves.

Andre had really outdone himself. Our resort was a lovely string of single-story rooms all facing the ocean. The beach was empty. A few feet away from our back terrace, large, round dining tables were anchored in the sand, and staff appeared and disappeared quietly setting up dinner service for the guests—us. It was the first time I'd experienced such personal, exclusive service. Paul and I briefly checked into our room and headed to the water.

Jello, Greg, and Maria were already there. I waded in with my walking shorts and T-shirt to feel the water move around my legs and give my senses and nerves a jolt of cold relief. The unforgiving, underdeveloped route to this place was a distant image replaced now by the wild beauty of the Brazilian coast. A large body of water would always still any anxious or convoluted thoughts I might have. This was luxury. This is what it felt like to be pampered.

Paul dove right in, being the master swimmer he was, and Jello followed. I watched as they both came up for air. It was an odd pairing—Paul looking thoroughly in sync with the waves, Jello up to his waist in water, standing still, staring out at the ocean as if he were ready for a debate. Greg turned to me. "Gelatina's completely out of his element."

Despite the jaundiced hue of his skin a few days earlier, Biafra appeared pasty and undefined in the water next to Paul, who was tall and (being those several inches closer to the sun) tanned quickly. Jello lived in San Francisco. Maybe he didn't get outdoors much—and where was there a beach in San Francisco anyway? It wasn't southern California and LA with beaches stretching from Venice down to Manhattan and Hermosa Beach, if you were so inclined to drive.

After our swim, we all gathered at one of the tables on the beach and shared a lavish spread of fresh pineapple, melon, and freshly grilled meats. The scene reminded me of the photo spreads in my Bon Appétit and Food and Wine magazines at home: successful thirty-somethings sharing magical white privilege and cavorting beachside with their wine glasses artfully aloft mid-sentence. In those photos, everyone is smiling million-dollar-salary smiles. Our group looked less genteel, mostly in black, relaxed, and happy to help our friend Andre promote his book. Punk rock rules, was the common sentiment in the ocean air.

I was learning to accept the generosity of so many strangers who happened to be fans of my husband's music. I could relax. We deserved this break. Not once did I regret that Al and Patty had decided to stay back in Chicago. They didn't know what they were missing.

"Jello . . . How's the melon?"

***

Shortly after we arrived back in Chicago from our Brazilian trip, the Chicago Tribune Sunday edition ran a front page side banner with a picture of Paul and Al next to a blurb from Greg Kot, the Tribune's music critic. The hype for Lollapalooza number two was building, as was the press for Ministry's new album. Greg Kot was a fan and had interviewed them. For the article, Kot came to our apartment to talk to Paul on a day when I was at work. The article in the Tribune mentioned Paul and I lived on a quiet, tree-lined street in Logan Square, and we were expecting our first child.

After the Tribune article appeared, I suddenly started seeing small groups of club kids with serious expressions on their faces lingering near our apartment building in their washed-out, black jeans and dyed black hair. I tried not to let my imagination fill with images of these kids recklessly, impulsively lunging at me wanting something—anything—to be able to tell their friends they'd found where Paul from Ministry lived and they'd seen his wife. The nagging familiarity of panic followed. We had lived in the same apartment for three years already, and no one on our street looked like these kids. Our immediate neighbors were Mexican families and mostly young, white professionals with whom I rode the el in the morning.

I told Paul I had a feeling some of his fans were newly inspired to roam our pocket of Logan Square. He thought I was overreacting. I had to ask, did he not see Ministry was getting attention beyond the alternative press, that their level of fame was rising? His face was on the front page of the Sunday Chicago Tribune, a historically conservative national newspaper. Was he so wrapped up in tour preparations he hadn't yet digested the reality of what was happening around him, or was he just eating it up and not thinking about the personal consequences? Paul had the habit of being friendly and open to almost everyone interested in his music, unless they were a jerk or, in his words, "Trying to pimp me out to their friends." Plenty of visitors and friends of friends showed up at Chicago Trax to be somehow a part of the Ministry, Paul and Al magic going on at any given time. Did one of these acquaintances help Paul pick up or drop off a piece of gear from our apartment? I had enough drama at my job all day, interviewing and processing narratives of drug dealers and murderers, and in my pregnant state of mind and body, I didn't need any more vulnerability. Period.

The practical reality of becoming a parent was brought to my attention on a daily basis by my parents. They were beside themselves planning for their first grandchild. It was sweet, knowing they would ultimately be caretakers for our child when I went back to work. I had not seen the two of them this nervous and happy since my law school graduation, when I stood up with the rest of the graduates to take our collective oath in the service of the law. My father jumped from his seat at the Auditorium Theater and began shaking my hand like I'd just won a million dollar settlement for him. My mother hugged me and looked like she would burst into tears.

I indulged my parents and dragged them to every imaginable, all inclusive

"Cribs 'R' Us" type store to find a bed that was a simple, functional haven for a newborn's first year, and one that wouldn't tax my patience with its "cuteness." Not too simple to be cage-like, and not handcrafted from oak or maple wood to last as some sort of hopeful family heirloom. My parents were picking up the bill, and we finally settled on a crib-to-youth convertible bed in white with pale, primary colors on dresser drawers attached to the side. It was the sturdiest piece of furniture Paul and I owned that wasn't a vintage piece and over twenty-five years old. The crib passed muster with Mr. Barker, who I knew, appreciated my parents as if they were his own. Our child needed something to sleep in, and this bed was perfectly acceptable. Parenthood was knocking and telling us to "keep it down in there" with our usual obsessions over design and "feng shui." We could stomach a white crib with a few primary colors added to distract the eye.

Seven and a half months into my pregnancy, I went for a scheduled ultrasound with Paul. Everything appeared to be going smoothly. Did we want a picture of the results? I looked at the image and started laughing—not a typical parental response, I guessed, judging from the technician's expression. I handed the picture to Paul.

"Oh my god that's hilarious," he said, and I could see the mental gears preparing him to share this "progress" with his bandmates. The black-and-white image we brought home as a keepsake, a visual reminder of fantastic healthy prospects for the new life coming, showed a small head in profile and a bent arm extended upward with a tiny fist high in the air, as if in protest. It was our baby's power fist—a Freddie Mercury moment. We had an activist in the womb. I was of course delighted.

Final agreements for Lollapalooza were in place. To Crazed Management's credit (and Paul and Al's insistence), Ministry's position on the nightly show schedule was bumped up to where they would only be performing after dark. They weren't a jam band to watch lolling around in the sun with your partner on a picnic blanket. Practically speaking, this meant they were the second to last band before the headliners, the Red Hot Chili Peppers. I thought it was quite a coup for them. Ministry's set was dark, a nightmarish rush of anger and adrenaline. No ballads.

On July 14th, Warner Bros. Records released Ministry's Psalm 69 album to coincide with summer touring. The Lollapalooza tour was scheduled to run from the middle of July through the middle of September. Our baby was due in the middle of tour, in August.

The band's management, tour manager, and the record label were all aware that Paul needed to fly home when I had the baby. Casey Orr from the band Rigor Mortis would pick up Paul's bass parts for some of the shows. I was going to be alone at the apartment in Logan Square in the August heat. My boss Mitchell suggested Paul get a SkyPager for Lollapalooza. Mitchell had the service for when he occasionally flew to Texas on one of our drug cases, or when he took a vacation out of state with his family and had to keep in touch with our office. Before Paul left for tour, we bought the pager. I felt assured it was the best, immediate way to reach him and not have to go through all the channels at the festival.

My old friend Rick Buscher called from St. Louis to see if we could get him on the guestlist for the Chicago show. He really wanted to see the Jesus and Mary Chain perform. I offered to let Rick stay at our place, and he and I could catch up on his move back to St. Louis after living in LA for six years. Paul would be back home for a day between the Michigan and New York dates. Rick could drive with Paul to the Chicago date in Tinley Park.

Before Paul left to start the Lollapalooza tour, Leila Eminson offered to stay with me for the two weeks in August prior to my due date. Even though we hadn't spent much time meeting up in the months leading into summer, I was so grateful when she stepped in at the last minute to make sure I wasn't home alone. Leila was one of my angels. Her presence in my late stage of pregnancy was one less thing for Paul to worry about, and Leila and I had a chance to talk about life while she wasn't out on the road with any bands. She could do her necessary Invisible Records label business and go back and forth between hers and her husband Martin Atkins's place and ours.

Lollapalooza kicked off with more press and new fans of Ministry in a growing frenzy for each show. Paul carried his SkyPager around the festival grounds showing it off to his touring comrades from the other bands. Miki and

Emma from the band Lush asked him every day, "Any word?"

Rick Buscher arrived in Chicago during the week prior to the August 2nd Tinley Park show. "HOW YA DOIN'?" he clumsily asked in his best cornhusker's twang, trying not to dwell on my lopsided, decidedly unglamourous new body profile. On the day of the Chicago show, he drove with Paul in our van to the festival grounds in Tinley Park. They were later than expected in arriving for Jesus and Mary Chain's set, and Rick was only able to catch one song from the encore. The Ministry show that night would cement Ministry's reputation as the unstoppable standout at the festival. The weather was wet and damp, and the crowd rowdier and more impatient as the afternoon wore on prior to the band's performance. At the fairgrounds, giant clumps of mud became weaponized as Ministry walked onstage to perform. Al halted the show at one point, yelled at the audience, and gave them a choice: quit with the projectiles or the band quits playing and leaves. The crowd miraculously settled down.

Leila kept me company as Paul's placeholder (with no internet available yet to while away the hours), while my body continued its mysterious biological miracle without any fanfare or drama. I thought my friends must by now be bored or distracted with the lack of obvious milestone moments—no birthing classes, yoga tapes, mommy psych groups, or daily dietary measurements to monitor. No water breaking, no drama at all. The drama was elsewhere far away in Lollapalooza country: on August 11th, the tour's Jones Beach, New York show was a sodden mess and was rained out. MTV and every other news outlet spotlighted Ministry and seemed to pay less and less attention to the headliners, the Red Hot Chili Peppers.

The final Lollapalooza drama (from my perspective) could have ended tragically, but didn't. I was fortunate to have missed a daytime spectacle on the fairgrounds that had nothing to do with Ministry's stage show: no one in Ministry's management and none of our friends on the road with the band felt it urgent to call and tell me Paul had scheduled a bungee jump at the festival one day where the device was made available for the talent and audience during downtime. A bungee jump. Paul survived, and I caught a glimpse of a photo later in one of the music rags showing Paul's flight down what looked like the equivalent of a ten-story building with his mouth wide open, probably hoping he wouldn't piss his pants. Maybe he had a latent suicide wish or had second thoughts about becoming a father. Or maybe he just wanted a thrill.

I was near my due date, and our house phone rang every day with a reminder to call "Dr. Vijay" immediately if my water broke or if I felt I was going into labor. She also had a pager. Each day I was consumed with anticipation, boredom, self-doubt, and self-examination. ("Leila, I'm not a mother type, am I?" Leila: "Shut. Up. Who is?") I worried Paul wouldn't get the page or get to the hospital in time. My parents insisted they would drive me to Illinois Masonic Hospital when I was ready. I didn't feel I would ever be ready. I was done with waiting. The extra twenty-five pounds I had cultivated below my neck seemed already not a part of me anymore. I wanted my self back.

On August 25th, ten days beyond my due date, Dr. Vijay called and ordered me to the hospital for inducement. She was very matter of fact: "This baby is taking too long." My parents went into immigrant rush mode and were at my door in ten minutes, instead of the usual twenty it took to drive from the lakefront to our apartment. As much as I had always resented my father's drill sergeant manner of keeping his kids in line, this time I gladly did the idiot check around the apartment and headed downstairs to the car.

I have some time to kill before the doctor gets here, I thought to myself, walking calmly through the automatic doors at Illinois Masonic. "I'm almost eleven days overdue. My doctor called me here to be induced," I told the nurse at the desk. I adjusted my wedding band absentmindedly, wondering if I'd have to remove it. Less than a minute later, there were two attendants strapping monitors to my arms and my torso. The head nurse was at my side. "Baby, you in labor right now," she said, not taking her eyes off of the monitors. I had run out of time to worry.

This can't be right. Where was my husband? Here I was, in a wheelchair, counting room numbers, and memorizing faces in the hallway, while being transported from the lobby to a semi-private room. I may need a favor from one of these people later, I nonsensically thought to myself. Like what? A cigarette? A compact to check my lipstick? I was unaware Paul had already boarded a plane, having left the tour early in case something happened to me or the baby at this late date.

Labor was slow. I paced the corridor outside of my room, IV-stand by my side like a surrogate labor coach for my partner, a distraction from the boredom of waiting. I was told this walking might speed things up and nudge the baby to move down. Nurses came and went. When they left, I became anxious. I had creeping doubts about everything: Why isn't Paul here yet? What if the baby is sick, a boy, a girl? Physically, I felt fine wanting to lie on the bed and have everyone else do the work of delivery. I wished my parents hadn't just left me there thinking Paul would take over. I wanted to calm down, and my mind kept going to obsessive thoughts. Did his plane crash? Did I bring the right shoes to wear when I—we—leave the hospital? What am I doing here?

A few hours after my check in, Paul came into the room. "Hi, beautiful." His voice seemed to be coming from an otherwise silent audience, and I was the one onstage, in character, stripped of my lipstick and street clothes, instead holding up a pale cloth cinched behind my neck like a smock tossed on at a hair salon. I didn't feel very "beautiful." Not now.

I was in labor for twenty-six hours. When the baby was finally ready to leave its confines for a roomful of waiting hospital staff and one Paul Barker, I was ready to float out of there on an invisible wave of exhaustion. When the baby's head emerged, Paul turned away for a second, looked back with a nervous laugh, and the most authentic look of love in his eyes as he stared in the direction of my feet. We had a girl.

"Ursula Jeanne Barker—born August 26, 1992 at 8:42 p.m."

The electronic festival signs at Lollapalooza flashed our private news to thousands of people sweating in a different way from what Paul and I were experiencing. Back in the hospital room we waited for Ursula to be bathed, tagged, and made official. Physically, I was spent. Mentally, I didn't feel any differently. I didn't feel like a mom. The nurses helped me position Ursula for breastfeeding, and I hoped I was doing it the right way.

Paul and I were both starving. Michael Short rode over on his Laverda with Ellie. They smuggled in dinner for us from the Star Top: southern fried chicken, guacamole, and a shaker full of martinis. I could finally exit the stage and exhale. We asked Michael to be Ursula's godfather. He cried and nodded yes.

When she was handed to him that first time in the hospital, Paul held the baby like a museum curator holding a priceless work of art. He appeared afraid of how delicate her newborn body felt and moved. All of the months of waiting, speculating, and hoping for an intangible perfect outcome to a seemingly chaotic arrival were over.

Before visiting us in recovery, my parents stopped by the maternity ward nursery to have a look through the glass and see if they could recognize which newborn was their grandchild.

"Did you find Ursula?" Paul asked my mother, as he made room for my parents to sit down.

"I recognized that Serba face right away—are you kidding?!" I could see in my mother's expression she was having fun transitioning into her new role as elder matriarch of our clan. She could not have had a bigger smile on her face.

Paul and I seemed to be speaking in fragments to one another in the hospital and later at home, wondering what if anything we were doing was right.

"The street noise . . . awake . . . my flight".

Back in our own kitchen, in the August heat, the two of us went barefoot on the cold red-and-black tiled floor. Paul stood naked from the waist up, holding Ursula in a sling against his chest. I latched my arms around his thin waist.

"This is it," he said, and I knew exactly what he meant. This was right now. The beginning of something new, foreign, and frightening, but it was us. Paul studied my face with a nervous smile.

"So . . . what do we do now?"

20

The first two days at home I labored through breastfeeding. Our baby wasn't staying awake enough to make the effort. She cried when asleep and cried intermittently when awake. I wasn't sleeping much at all. My parents drove us to their place in Wisconsin to try and get some rest in the fresh air. We came back to Chicago after a day. The baby kept crying herself to sleep. We went in to see the doctor and discovered our new baby was losing weight. I thought the worst. She has some newborn illness they haven't found a cure for yet—that must be it.

The doctor spent a few moments checking her vitals, when she looked up at me and said with a smile, "This baby needs food! She cries because she's hungry!" Dr. Arekapudi delivered this diagnosis with what I could only assure myself was not an indictment against me. In the doctor's view, the baby either was not getting enough breast milk from me, or she was allergic to my milk. Fantastic. In addition to having an "incompetent" cervix to hold a child, I could now add "inadequate or unacceptable milk" to my medical chart. Poster child for "Mommy . . . NOT."

At least I could make light of our curious situation. Having so recently given birth I hardly had time to think about what I was feeling at all. I should have felt ecstatic, yet all I could muster were conflicting emotions. The baby was healthy and beautiful, but I couldn't breastfeed. I was relieved to be guilt free about what I was eating or drinking anymore. But how would I get back in shape when I wasn't getting any decent sleep? I did my best to appear positive to the outside world. Privately, I felt a nagging depression or complete panic and uncertainty whether I was ready for what lay ahead.

We switched Ursula to soy formula, and she immediately had more energy and color. Bottle feeding seemed to attract a new round of conversation starters for strangers—and some people we knew—about the benefits of breast milk: "Breast is best," and it's guilt-inducing cousin, "Are you sure bottle-feeding is the way to go?" Yes. I was very sure. I was as sure about that as I was that the person asking should "go" far away from me and examine their own high-mindedness. I'd give bonus points to the critics who inherently knew the matter was simply none of their business. In some cases, with newborns like ours, breast milk wasn't an option—unless my kid should start dieting at an early age. I wanted to yell, "Silencio!" to the critics. I was done with other people's helpful views. The entire experience was mine and Paul's alone. We were adults. And oddly, in this case too, we were not like other people.

Paul briefly rejoined his bandmates, and I could bond with the person behind this new familiar face. I could see my mother's eyes and mouth, Paul's long torso and legs, and my own small nose coming into focus.

The Lollapalooza tour ended September 13th, with the last show in Irvine, California. Two days before, on September 11th, Hurricane Iniki hit the Hawaiian island of Kauai. Paul's father Gordon still lived there in his house and still tended to Kay Barker's Bed and Breakfast, the family business. Paul was very worried about his dad.

Homes on Kauai were swept up seemingly at random in 140 mile-an-hour winds, leaving nothing but foundations like gravestones in their wake. Gordon Barker's 1940s army barracks style house was spared for the most part. The B&B had roof damage. Gordon was lucky. My mother liked to say, "God takes special care of babies and drunks." Gordon was a heavy drinker and had decided to stay on the island and take cover in his house. Paul wanted to see his dad.

Just three weeks after leaving the hospital with Ursula, Paul and I and our newborn baby were on a plane bound for Hawaii to give moral support (if nothing else) while my father-in-law waited for FEMA to do it's clean up and restore power to the island. For the duration of the long flight, Ursula slept, woke up, and wailed from the cabin pressure. Paul carried her up and down the aisles of the plane.

When we arrived at the airport on Kauai, my father-in-law stood there waiting expressionless, dressed as always like a local Hawaiian in wrinkled, ancient shorts and battered flip flops. He was silent as he held Ursula against his sweat-soaked, faded vintage Hawaiian shirt. Gordon had always groused when the weather was even mildly cool; he'd "have to put some pants on today." A true beach bum—in temperament, anyway. The weather was hot and humid. He complained very little with the baby close against him.

Gordon looked honestly relieved that we had come. Sterilizing formula bottles was a pain with no power in the house and a backup generator outside. It was a minor inconvenience to me, compared to the life changes forming from this backdrop of muddy, flattened landscape outside. Gordon was inconsolable over the annihilation of every other neighbor's house along Lokelani Road, here at the base of Nounou Mountain. We all knew the mountain by its colloquial name: The Sleeping Giant. We stayed with Gordon for a week. Paul needed to get back to Chicago to begin rehearsing for the upcoming European tour dates promoting Psalm 69. And I was still getting to know Ursula. In my mind, she was already a fully formed intelligence, whose eyes followed my movements occasionally when she searched for focus.

Our photographer friend Paul Elledge called to ask if we had time to sit for a family portrait—the three of us—at his studio. He had open studio time and had just become a father himself to a beautiful daughter, Lucia. We were so honored to be asked. The black-and-white portraits hanging in Paul Elledge's studio were as beautiful as Renaissance paintings. He photographed celebrities and increasingly, rock bands, including Ministry. Our family portrait turned out to be so stunning, we asked for a few copies to share with family. After the shoot, I was pleasantly surprised when Paul Elledge took me aside to ask if I would sit for an individual portrait when he had some free time coming up between clients. In my twenties, I had fantasized about being an artist's model, a subject to explore with a camera. Of course, I said yes.

Baby gifts began arriving at our apartment. Warner Bros. express mailed a "Steiff" bear. Growing up, in my family home we had Steiff toys, and they were highly prized in Germany and around the world. We had a couple of the bears, a mountain goat, and a giraffe. The trademarked "Knopf Im Ohr" (Bronze button pin in the ear) was there in all of them. The stuffed animals were rigid but thoughtfully rendered representations of animals in the wild. They were made to last, German craftsmanship at its finest, keepsakes.

I was touched by the connection to my own childhood and Ursula's new teddy bear. Bill Rieflin's girlfriend Frankie Sundsten stitched a quilt for us to put in the baby's crib. The quilt's mosaic of colors and delicate patterns reflected the close attention to background and odd forms in Frankie's own paintings. An original, handmade gift.

The Psalm 69 tour was starting at the end of October. Paul's brother Roland came to stay with us in Chicago. He was going out on the road with the band. A lot of friends were calling with congratulations on our new baby and good luck wishes for the upcoming tour. Lollapalooza and the attendant press hype had sold Ministry to thousands of new fans. The press accolades kept apace. The real gossip from the tour was far more interesting to me and everyone else we knew. It was now a confirmed fact that the fans at Lollapalooza were often so spent after Ministry finished their set that by the time the headliners, the Red Hot Chili Peppers, came onstage to close the night, many people had already left. I hung onto these bits of tour news knowing Paul often would "forget" to tell me what it was like being on the road. Ministry's insistence upon playing only after dark (stipulated to in their Lollapalooza contract) had paid off.

I sat in our newly outfitted baby room with Ursula, sorting through my thoughts on Paul leaving again. I was lucky to have my parents and good friends available if I needed a break. Leila had already stayed with me briefly. I wasn't planning to go back to work immediately, but the job now of learning to be a parent, and specifically a mother, was more consuming than any job I'd ever taken on.

Friends kept calling. Paul was on the phone with yet another old friend, an ex-girlfriend from Seattle. I had never met her. Paul told me some things about her, how she had broken up with him years earlier. And now she was calling and congratulating him on his success. She was an artist of some variety herself. She wished us well with our new baby. As their conversation continued, it became clear there was another reason for the phone call. The ex-girlfriend was in a financial bind. She asked Paul for money to help her pay for her own young daughter's move to Europe to live with her and the baby's father. Paul came into Ursula's room and, with his hand over the phone, relayed to me what was being asked of him.

Really. Europe. "You've got to be kidding," I said. "No. We have our own child to think about."

Paul was smiling. He knew that was coming. He told his friend he was sorry, but we couldn't help her. She then pleaded with him, curiously adding, "You know, you're FAMOUS now." As if that step up the musical food chain came with an attendant responsibility to share the wealth with anyone, anywhere, who had been his friend who now needed charity. Unbelievably egoistic. Paul thanked her again for calling, and after a while the call was over.

Before Ministry headed overseas, Paul and Roland drove with me and our new baby to have her passport photo taken. I insisted. I was planning ahead, anticipating more travel for all of us. Now that we had a baby, that wasn't going to prevent me from going to see Paul in other places. I wanted the experience as much as he did, and not having to go to my job made it essentially a moot point.

We visited a photographer's studio in the old German neighborhood along Lincoln Avenue. It was close to Café Selmarie, one of our favorite bakeries. It was fitting somehow that our baby was already getting her introduction to the immigrant communities around us. Ursula's cheekbones and blue eyes mirrored those of the Omas and Opas buying homeopathic remedies in Merz's Apothecary nearby.

Roland held Ursula steady, face forward in front of the camera for the photographer. In her pink one-piece cover-up, her expression was one of mild annoyance, rather than contentment with now being immortalized as an official citizen of the world. Such purpose in that expression!

Our baby's passport was issued on October 29th. Two weeks later, she and I arrived at Heathrow in London. From there, we traveled to Manchester, where Ursula met Paul's mother Jeanne for the first time. Jeanne lived in Manchester. She seemed self-conscious about being identified as the new "Grandmère"; although, it was she who'd suggested it. She was half French. Jeanne was slight and fit, in her black jeans and pale lavender T-shirt, with layers of bracelets adorning her arms; an outfit befitting someone much younger, but she looked great. She was full of energy.

"Beautiful jewels," I said, complimenting her bangles.

"Well, I don't understand why women of my age feel it necessary to wear such dowdy things," she replied. Jeanne carried herself gracefully, without a hint of anything grandmotherly, whatever that was supposed to look like. She was an artist who had her own business for much of her adult life. In Manchester, she designed and produced handknit sweaters with her helpers, to sell to ski resorts in Aspen and elsewhere in the world.

Ministry was scheduled to play next in Nottingham. With our new baby, and all of her required gear, I left Manchester, tagging along on the coach with Paul and crew. In Nottingham, we stayed overnight in a small provincial hotel where the maids looked to be barely sixteen years old. Their timid smiles, rosy cheeks, and prim uniforms suggested a future confined to a life of virginity, while they cleared the beds of strangers who stayed, had sex, and went on their way.

Our young maids were excited to have a baby in their midst. The crib they wheeled into our room appeared to have been fashioned in a much earlier century: a frail looking silver frame with slim immobile bars all the way around. It looked as though it hadn't been requested in decades. A tiny jail cell, more than a baby's crib. Nothing comforting about this sleeping apparatus supposedly designed for vulnerable infants. Paul and I looked at one another ready to burst as we waited for the maids to clear out. At that point I looked at the metal crib again. "I feel like I should be interviewing a client in there."

The next day, we were back on the band's coach and on through to the Scottish countryside to Glasgow. We stopped roadside at a small town with a few vendors selling locally crafted woolens. Everything was handmade. I bought a magenta, blue, and black tartan mohair lap blanket for my parents. "Isn't this the sort of thing your grandmother would have lying around her place?" I asked Paul. What did I know? I barely knew my own grandmothers, having grown up with an ocean between us. They lived in two different countries with two distinct languages.

Glasgow was the last of the Europe dates, and afterwards, band and crew flew home. When we arrived back in Chicago, Paul and I discovered a package had been delivered to the house. The return address showed it was from Paul's ex-girlfriend who'd asked him for money to move to Europe. Inside the box were all sorts of old baby clothes, a baby tambourine—a lot of what I considered hippy gear. Her old stuff. I told Paul I didn't want any of it and frankly hadn't asked for anything. It seemed to carry too much "bad juju." He told me to do what I had to with it. I packed up the box and dropped it at the Salvation Army.

The next day's mail brought a more hopeful gift for our new baby: a brand new, wooden pull-toy for a child just learning to walk. It was a Keith Haring Barking Dog on wheels. The sender was my good friend Steve Miglio in New York. He'd bought it at MOMA.

Ministry was back in the US finishing the Psalm 69 tour. They were booked for the Paramount Theater at Madison Square Garden on December 3rd, and I didn't want to miss the performance in one of my favorite cities. I hadn't yet seen a single show of the new tour. The extent of my presence on this tour had been sitting backstage in London while nursing Ursula. But I wasn't ready to leave her alone with someone else for a few days. She was too young, too susceptible to traumas I hadn't yet even contemplated. We decided Ursula would go with me to New York. She was part of our family now. It would be cold in New York, so I packed a suit for myself for backstage—black wool pants and a black Flora Kung short bolero jacket with a cut-out neckline and nothing else underneath. I looked fabulous and finally felt comfortable in my own skin again.

I also wanted to reconnect with my old friend Steve Miglio. He was the first artist I knew in Chicago after getting my first apartment and beginning to venture out to see bands play. We had waited tables together, and he took me to La Mere to experience my first punk rock club. I called Steve to invite him to the Ministry rock show and meet Ursula before heading over to the venue. Steve was excited to have a rock show penciled onto his calendar. Steve after all was a solidly committed rock fan, who had once swiped Lou Reed's cigarette butts from a suburban Chicago stage. In the intervening years after moving to New York, Steve did artwork for the label Tommy Boy Records, home to Queen Latifah, Afrika Bambaataa, and De La Soul. Steve still painted every day. He was always someone I felt really comfortable to be around, someone whose presence I had missed.

On the day of the New York show, my old friend Steve was excited to travel in a limo with me and Ursula. As the car descended into the underground parking, we discussed what her first limo ride might feel like to such a princess. Ursula was three months old and already on the go. She had already been on two plane trips, one overseas. She had her own passport and now was riding in style to see her "rock star" dad play one of New York City's most beloved venues. A fairy-tale princess. Did that mean I was a queen?

Backstage was packed. The big party was underway with people smoking, drinking, yelling, probably doing coke, and staring at their makeup in the performers' mirrors running the length of the dressing room. There were big names out in the venue. Chris Connelly was doing some of the vocals on this tour. He walked up to us, his cheeks thoroughly flushed. He was speechless. Chris was not a speechless guy. He had spotted Neil Young side-stage. I had never seen Chris looking so scattered and nervous before going on. He looked as though he had just run into a secret crush.

More people were attempting to squeeze into the dressing room to see the band. The show was sold out. As passwords to get into the room were being exhausted at the door, Lee Popa, Ministry's front of house sound maestro, yelled into the room," GERDA! Where is she? . . . GERDA! Some designer, 'Sprouts' something. He's outside. Says he knows the band, wants to design some clothes for them and shit. GERDA!! Sprouts?" Lee was another one of those friends from

Taylor Street in Chicago who knew a hustle and a con when he saw one and was not impressed by much. There were so many bodies between where I was in the room and where Lee's voice was coming from.

"Sprouts." Steven Sprouse. Someone already out of vogue or hanging onto (ahem) a thread. I paid attention to fashion, even the stuff I didn't like, having grown up with my mother, the tailor. Sprouse was wrong with execution and lazy with style, loud graffiti style, already done better before he came on the scene. I told the person next to me, "Pass it on. No Sprouts . . ." And the word went up the human chain, one shoulder after another, back to Lee: "No Sprouts!"

Ursula was visibly agitated as the volume of voices grew and the density of cigarette smoke in the dressing room was getting to be too much for her and for me. She was frowning and crying. I gestured an "ixnay on the arty pay" to Steve to follow me into a side corridor and out of this noise. We landed in a much brighter lit hallway that was empty, except for two other people probably doing what we were—escaping. Steve gripped my arm. "It's the most beautiful woman in the world . . ." he said, gasping as though he'd witnessed a miracle. He stepped away and to the side, gathering his composure.

As I looked over, there was Paulina Porizkova tentatively heading toward us in her perfect jeans and boyish hips. She looked prepubescent next to her husband, Ric Ocasek, with his long face and wrinkled neck.

"She's even beautiful when she cries!" said the supermodel, introducing herself and eyeballing the baby in my arms.

What a cliché thing to say, I thought. But I could live with that, coming from such a stunning beauty herself. Ocasek curiously began chit chatting with me as if we were familiar. He was eager to say how enthusiastic he was about getting "him" (my husband) and "his guys" to work on the new Cars record. Paul and I had already discussed the possibility. I knew that he and Al had no interest in going into the studio for that project. They were busy building their own fan base and didn't need to lend new street credibility to anyone else at this point. It was kind of a joke. I just nodded along to what Mr. Cars was relaying to me.

Paulina asked if she could hold Ursula. She looked to me like a kind person. I handed off my baby, and the supermodel seemed genuinely touched to be holding the dramatically unhappy one. Maybe there was recognition in the high cheekbones gently forming in their own way on Ursula's face. Some hint of Slavic sisterhood had registered with Paulina. She was entertaining my daughter, keeping her engaged with baby talk while occupied in her arms.

After several minutes of empty chitchat and pacing, I felt visiting hours were over. I was tired of playing polite. I looked over at Steve and said I thought it was probably time to get back to the dressing room. It took more than one ask to have my daughter returned to my arms. Paulina wasn't ready to let her go. She looked lovingly at Ursula when she finally released her. We headed for the door, and Paulina waved "Bye-bye" to my baby girl. It was awkward having something a celebrity seemed to want and didn't yet have—a child.

"We're in Madison Square Garden, Steve!" I was beaming for a change as we walked back into the dressing room. "Meanwhile, backstage at Madison Square Garden . . ." My mind was obsessing again about language and story, about mythmaking, and how this evening's events would color my daughter's own personal narrative. It occurred to me that I should bump up the timetable to the present for one little legend to get going. Thus, in an instant (in my own head), Paulina Porizkova became "The Supermodel Who Tried to Steal My Baby."

There was still a crowd backstage, but most had headed into the venue to see Ministry perform. Steve joined them for a bit, coming back to check on me nursing Ursula. "Wow. They really are a rock band. So wonderful," he said. I somehow needed to hear my old friend's approval of Paul's music and the live show. But I knew all along he would find it as exciting and visceral as everyone else.

When Paul was offstage and back in the dressing room sitting with me, a photographer from one of the metal rags asked if he could take our picture. I said sure. A few weeks later, snarky friends were calling Paul to alert him that the photograph of us taken backstage was in a magazine. The caption under it read, "Paul Barker and his Polish wife." Apparently, in one of the interviews he'd done on tour someone asked him about me, and he told them I was Polish and from Chicago.

Well, it was true. "STO LAT!" to that.

Ministry was on their way to other east coast shows. I flew home with Ursula. Christmas was a few weeks away. I needed to get back to my day job. A good night's sleep and a quick call to my parents, and the weekend was winding down.

I put Ursula to bed in her crib, went to our bedroom in the middle of the apartment and lay there taking my time falling asleep. The silence was a relief. After several minutes, I thought I could hear music coming from the front of the apartment. I fumbled for my glasses and hurried out into the dining room, tip-toeing my way to Ursula's room. As I approached the door, the sound I heard grew louder. It was a sustained humming. I poked my head into the room, and the humming stopped. Ursula, our little world traveler, was lying flat on her back with her mouth open and widening into a smile with all the wonder and recognition in her eyes that said, "I make sounds."

***

Christmas mail was piling up. Cards came from all over the country and from friends overseas. We had over 150 Christmas cards, mostly from friends in the music business and a few from family. It was our first Christmas as new parents, and the public outpouring of affectionate largesse was new as well. As a child, I was excited to open a few cards and hang them in my family's apartment to change the mood of the place into one of a more nostalgic, traditional picture-perfect holiday. It was a childhood custom—hang cards on the archways separating the dining room from the kitchen and living room. Now in adulthood, the scotch tape came out and I busied myself with framing out my own dining room with glittery notes. When there was no more space, I draped the cards to the floor and strung them together, snaking across the hardwood and into the next room. It was festive. It felt like home, even though it was only me and our new daughter for now.

***

It was the end of a very busy, action-packed year. The 1992 Grammy nominations had been making their rounds in the mail. In the past, Paul would receive official Grammy ballots, fill them in, vote for our friends, and hope for the best. This time, having survived the preliminary ballots,

the final tallies were in, and Ministry was nominated for their first Grammy award for Best Metal Performance for the track "N.W.O.". In the same category, they were up against our friends Nine Inch Nails and three other bands.

"N.W.O." was such a great track, great video, and there was much hope in the air that they might actually win. But the hype around Nine Inch Nails was bigger, and Al had the habit of pissing off industry people, mocking them behind their backs. In the Grammy world, politics played big. To Al, Howie Klein at the label became "Howie The Clown." And despite being finalists for an award, Al and Patty were adamantly opposed to Ministry making an appearance at the ceremonies. Their reasoning: the Grammy award for Best Metal Performance wouldn't be televised anyway. The band didn't need to be there.

Most categories weren't televised because of time constraints. Only the major awards like Record of the Year, Best Female Vocal, New Artist, and such made it to the screen. There was a separate smaller ceremony earlier in the day for artists competing for less popular or niche categories. I suspected Al wasn't interested in going because of the real possibility he'd be shown up by Trent Reznor, who by this time was probably on Al's hit list for becoming more popular in the industrial genre that Ministry was credited with creating.

Paul and I were a little deflated that we weren't going to LA; although, he told everyone he didn't really care. Right. The guy who had journaled many times his big desire was to be a pop star. Really, why not go to LA? The overriding, unspoken reason: Al had his habits to tend to and didn't want to be part of the industry that fueled his own career. He and Paul declined the Grammy committee's invitation to fly out for the event.

In February, when the Grammy Awards were scheduled to air, I took the train home from work and waited for Paul to get back from the studio. I answered calls from Cynthia Plaster Caster and my parents. Even my bosses at work were rooting for Paul. Everyone felt that hopefulness in the air, as if by association they were winners too. I was thrilled that Paul and Al's work was being recognized for one of the music industry's highest honors. That was enough for me. My mom wanted to know what I thought of Ministry's chances. I anticipated the question was coming. I knew the exact words she'd say. I'd heard something similar from my parents when I applied to law schools seven years earlier.

"Do you think they can MAKE IT?" my immigrant mother asked.

"Yeah, Ma. I think they can."

The Grammy festivities were about to begin. Not waiting for Paul to come home, I turned on the television, keeping an eye on the bottom of the screen where results for other categories were starting to scroll across. It was nerve racking. More waiting. Then, finally the news: "Best Metal Performance: Nine Inch Nails."

Hallelujah. That wait was over. I was disappointed, but I was happy one of our friends had won. What did it all mean now for Ministry and Paul anyway? Their professional momentum wasn't letting up. We were all mentally preparing ourselves to move away from Chicago, something we'd discussed much more seriously as of late. Plenty of things to think about, so many contingencies. The music world with all its bells and whistles, would still be standing. The band could go anywhere it wanted at this point. Paul's reaction to the Grammy news: "That's great for Trent. Whatever. Doesn't really matter."

I was adjusting to the reality of having a new baby, who took precedence in every aspect of my day. I had gone back to work. My parents came by daily to pick up the baby early and drop her back at the apartment later in the afternoon. The partners at my law firm encouraged me to get a whole life insurance policy now that Paul and I had a child. I knew how Paul felt about life insurance—it was a big scam. I told Paul the policy was mainly an investment to borrow against later in an emergency if we needed it. With a new child, we might need it. Paul couldn't argue with that. I had the agent schedule a time for a technician to come to our apartment and draw blood for the usual tests. I saw my doctor just before the blood draw, to satisfy myself I was healthy enough to be accepted for life insurance. My doctor had surprising news.

Less than six months after delivering our beautiful baby girl, she told me

I was pregnant again. Paul was floored. I didn't have time to process the news, taking it in stride. What was there to think about? He and Al had talked about moving out of Chicago, building a studio somewhere else, somewhere cheaper, so what was another change thrown into the mix?

"Fertile bastard," our friend Dan Field said, upon hearing the news. Dan and his brother Alex owned Sessions Skate shop around the corner from Wax Trax. Paul was busy telling everyone I was expecting—again. The Field brothers were good friends, moonlighting as road crew for Paul and Al previously and would again in the upcoming months. I was back to being hyper-aware of what I ate, where I went, and the nagging internal question, "What was I giving up?" And then, "What am I gaining? Is it worth it?"

I had no doubt in my mind that we could afford to raise another child. The momentum for Ministry kept going, and I was comfortable with the realization that Paul, my husband, was now, you know, famous. With the last three Ministry albums and all the side projects, he and Al established themselves as innovators. They were breaking the mold. Every record was a revelation to the fans and the press. They didn't adhere to formulas or write the ever-anticipated ballad to satisfy the label heads. Their work to me was part noise, samples, and parts woven together with unlikely time signatures to jar the attention into different thought patterns. It was loud. Some called it industrial—radical. I struggled with the idea that their technique was radical. What was so new about throwing bits and samples and repeated sounds together. Poets did it all the time. I did however love their results.

Despite being signed to a label, Paul and Al had a reputation for not allowing other people to dictate what they could or couldn't do artistically. The merchandising, videos, and album art had to be approved by the two of them. They were at Chicago Trax finishing Linger Ficken' Good, the third Revolting Cocks record coming out on Warners, and the label needed artwork. Our friend Rick Buscher was tasked with the assignment. We knew he was a fantastic artist with a killer sense of humor guaranteed to interpret and continue the hillbilly train wreck aesthetic of the Cocks. Rick was entrenched in St. Louis again after six years of slogging around LA. Warners was satisfied with the results, and the record went into production. This record, like all of the other Ministry records and side projects, would sell itself, with little marketing help from the label. Paul and Al didn't care so much, as long as the band had artistic freedom to do whatever it wanted.

The environment in Chicago was choking with talent, and it was a comfortable time for us to move somewhere else in the country. Paul and Al as an official team, "Luxa Pan Productions," could get away from the familiarity and distractions of Chicago Trax, make something new (and "ugly," as Paul liked to say), and have their own studio to muck around in. In that future, I would be busy with our two very small kids—wherever we landed. I had my profession. I could take a break.

We'd considered moving to New Orleans. For me, that would be professionally difficult because of the Louisiana legal system. The laws there were based on French codes dating back to the 1800s. Racism was a big problem, too. The west coast was out of the question for Al, who convinced himself that if he moved there, Los Angeles would slide into the ocean. Paul, Al, and Patty had all lived in Boston, and New York was out. They had friends in Austin, Texas. Ministry's guitarist Mike Scaccia was from Dallas. Texas fans were good to Ministry and the Revolting Cocks. Did we want to live somewhere warm? Is this even an issue, I thought. Paul and I can live anywhere. I had that survivor's blood in me. Austin was becoming the best alternative by process of elimination.

At night, Paul and I paged through real estate guides for listed properties in Austin. We were fortunate to have money coming in from publishing and recording advances. A lot of money. The Jourgensens and the Barkers were even more delighted to learn the real estate market in and around Austin had tanked in the late 1980s, coinciding with the savings and loan scandals across the country. Translation: property was dirt cheap in Austin, compared to Chicago. We saw one mind blowing photo after another of mansions for sale with maids' quarters, all for a price comparable to buying a two-bedroom condo on Chicago's north side. The place in Chicago would not even be close to the lake.

We fantasy house-hunted in our free time, and the rest of the week I took the el to my office, being as useful as my body would allow me. I did a few real estate closings for clients, did simple court calls, and did writing from home. My firm bought a Mac LCII for me to use at the apartment. It was the first computer I had exclusive access to regularly. There was no online service to use yet, unless we were willing to pay LexisNexis for the pricey privilege, as the big law firms and law schools were doing.

Paul Elledge called me at home to see when I'd be available for an individual portrait at his studio. In all the Grammy excitement, I had forgotten about his invitation. When the date was firmed up, he asked that I bring a few favorite articles of dark clothing for the photo session. Scarves were okay, too. My Paul was happy to distract himself away from Ministry and Al concerns for one minute and dig in our closet at home for wardrobe possibilities. The activity brought out the inner stylist in Paul, something else we had so terribly much in common. That, and a mutual obsession with shoes and footwear in general. I wondered if my face would be different now that I was pregnant again. If it mattered at all, Paul Elledge kept it to himself.

I wasn't fond of having my picture taken. Call it fear or aversion to the obvious. But in front of Paul's camera, I felt confident my expression would be simply and genuinely captured for what it was at that second in time. I wandered into the dressing area and studied my face before the makeup person added bits of powder here and there under the lights. I looked at the portrait of Gillian Anderson hanging to the side of the vanity mirrors. Paul shot her portrait at a time when she was working in Chicago at a restaurant he frequented. In her portrait, Anderson looks as though she could rule an island nation. I had so much admiration for Paul Elledge's work, and so much hope for all of our futures. I sat down on the stool provided, stared into the camera, sitting and moving any which way Paul and his stylist asked me to move.

Our own family was growing, our extended "family" was loosely planning a geographical move, and a member of the Ministry/Cocks collective announced he was getting married in the late spring—our friend Chris Connelly. A week before Paul and I were booked to fly to Austin to tour properties for sale, we packed up a rental car and headed for Kansas City to attend the wedding of Mr. Christopher Connelly and Ms. Cyan Meeks. The bride and groom met during Ministry's

Land of Rape and Honey tour, and at the time I thought Cyan was Ogre Nivek's girlfriend. Ogre was on that tour taking a break from Skinny Puppy. Now, five years later, we were all in the Rose Garden at Kansas City's Loose Park. It was May 8th, 1993. Kansas City, MO. Paul and I and nine-month-old Ursula briefly held court with Martin Atkins at the reception. I could still get a laugh talking to Martin, even though by now I was aware he had openly cheated on his wife, my friend Leila. Leila was also at the wedding, newly divorced from Martin. She looked happier than she had been the year before when she stayed with me, waiting for Ursula to come into the world.

Our friend Mr. Connelly wore a kilt for the ceremony.

"Congratulations! "I said. "And by the way, you're not the first guy I know to look good in a skirt."

(That would be Lou D'Angelo at Wax Trax, who liked to show off his hairy Italian legs peeking out from a pleated tartan skirt and combat boots, while serving gossip with a smile from the back counter of the store.)

After Chris' wedding, Paul and I flew to Austin with Ursula to look for a house. We met with Janet Gilles, a real estate agent Paul's friend Adam Grossman recommended. Adam was the singer in the Austin band Skrew.

Janet Gilles occupied her own niche in the local market, finding homes for buyers looking for unconventional properties. After finding our place she helped Al and Patty find theirs. Janet was known in Austin as the "Parrot Lady," a reputation she earned after releasing monk parrots into the downtown Austin community years before—colorful little creatures, which now thrived in nests along Town Lake. You wouldn't know they were even there except when in flight, squawking and fleeing from red-tailed hawks on a snack run. Janet's parrots thrived in the background along the lake, close to where the original Whole Foods "health food" store was housed in a dinky little building on Lamar Avenue. The original Whole Foods had the appearance of a small feed store, with bulk bins on the floor. Janet, the Parrot Lady, insisted we go there for a taste of what real Austinites cared about.

Janet Gilles was the ideal tour guide for two newly flush rock stars with a small fortune of cash available, now speculating on homes to buy. Al's words that we were all going to be fleetingly rich didn't matter when it came to our personal tastes, even with so many options available in Austin neighborhoods "close in" and out on the fringes. Paul and I ignored giant builder's models designed to match a half dozen others on the same streets. We only wanted something with character and enough space for us. Perhaps even a prefab. Floor-to-ceiling windows were ideal, a place to collapse on a few essential pieces of vintage Italian designed furniture. Al wanted bigger.

My life living in interiors was built on apartment memories. There wasn't a family house. My parents owned the apartment building we lived in growing up, but it was still apartment living, with a few strange, usually older characters staying put in their own spaces in the building, occupying their time staring at their own memories in photographs, or watching their own television sets to see the nightly news and the soaps playing during the day. As a child, I felt sorry for the other people living in "our" building. I resented having to mop the hallway stairs every other week or so, in the so-called common areas.

Three decades of apartment living, along with childhood car rides with my parents through the ritziest north shore suburbs, created an unconscious mental checklist of desires for a future dream house of my own. Something modern. The house Paul and I found on McConnell Drive was built in 1968 and designed by Leon Chandler, a famed local architect. Chandler commonly used Texas field stone on the exterior and interior framework of his residential designs. Our house was a ranch style, 3,500 square-foot hangar compared to the apartments we had called home. The exterior wood siding was painted an unfortunate tan color and may have been why the house sat on the market ignored for over a year. It had a sunken living room, five bedrooms, an office, a swinging '60s orange wet bar in the kitchen, and red shag carpeting in the big guest room. Little renovation since the 1970s, aside from a built-in hi-fi system and hideous wall unit of bookcases and cabinets in the living room, installed no doubt to update the room, but in reality made it darker and dingier. Later, after settling into the house, Paul and my sister's husband used axes to hack the shelving units straight out of the plastered wall—punk rock renovation at its best.

Going out of the back door to the house, there were steps up to a covered carport, connected to a mother-in-law back house fit for a home studio. The carport, along with our front and side driveways were spacious enough for ten cars to park. It was a party house—one designed for entertaining, with a front patio hung with benches running half the length of the house. We could step out from the dining room through the sliding doors to sit and have coffee on the deck.

The original owner was a local newscaster who in 1966 gained fame covering the Charles Whitman massacre on campus at the University of Texas in Austin. Whitman shot and killed fourteen people and injured dozens more from a perch inside of the University Tower. Walking off of our patio steps onto the front lawn, we had a view of the Tower and most of downtown Austin's skyline, being high enough on a hill in Westlake to look down. Charles Whitman was recognized as one of America's first documented mass murderers. Our house came with a history. Our house was perfect for us.

Paul and I returned to Chicago with Ursula, and I realized I needed to check on hospitals in Austin that would accept our insurance when our second child arrived. I soon discovered that Blue Cross in Illinois wasn't interested in having a patient deliver a baby in Texas or any other state. "You will be able to purchase a Blue Cross policy in Texas," I was told. Would it cover my pregnancy? "You'll have to check with that carrier."

I called the insurance company in Texas and was told we certainly could start a family policy in our new state of residence, and they would cover $275 of my pregnancy expenses. The remaining hospital, doctor, pre- and post-natal charges would not be covered. My current pregnancy was unhappily, insultingly considered a "preexisting condition." I told Paul we would have to go back to Chicago to have the baby. I called my parents and told them. They offered to let us stay with them when the time came, five months from now. I felt a strange irony in the universe telling us Chicago had to be the birthplace of both of our kids. I wondered how much more cabin pressure my pregnant body could take.

We were tying up loose ends in Chicago and preparing to move. Paul was working on material for a Pigface record in the studio, while I was packing and saying my goodbyes as best I could. Many of our friends we would see in Austin anyway, with summer tours coming up, and Ministry studio personnel making plans to work with Paul and Al in Austin. Other friends were going on the road with Lollapalooza. Leila Eminson was tour managing the band Babes in Toyland for the main stage at Lollapalooza number three. Sean Joyce was hired as the Babes' stage manager and drum tech for the shows. Paul planned to check in with our friends on the tour, and I wanted to see Leila one last time before we moved to Austin and geography would throw another variable into our lives already in a state of never-ending flux.

Lollapalooza was scheduled for early July at the Tinley Park Fairgrounds. Paul and I drove to Tinley Park, leaving our daughter with her grandparents for the day. We went early in the afternoon, when it would be easier to see friends and not too crowded to pose security issues at the gates or long wait times when I might feel uncomfortably overheated. I didn't have to keep reminding anyone I was five months pregnant. We did the rounds, saying hello to some of the roadies and sound guys who Paul knew from other tours and the previous year's Lollapalooza festival when Ministry performed.

It was getting later in the afternoon. We saw Leila, but Sean was running late having gone out carousing with Lane, the singer from Alice in Chains, for the better part of the previous night. The backstage outdoor areas were not crowded, but a few fans and people wearing lanyards were milling around waiting for bands to go on. A small group of men in their early twenties approached Paul. One lanky member of the group stood out, almost shaking with his dull, dyed black hair falling over his face. He walked straight up to Paul and said, "You're the great Paul Barker—what are YOU doing here?"

Something about his tone of voice gave the impression he was annoyed by Paul's presence and not looking for an autograph. He was standing a few feet away from me. I reached for Paul's arm and kept my hand there. Something about this kid's body language told me it would be better for us to be polite and move along.

"I'm Paul—that's right. What's your name?" Paul extended his hand.

This young man, a stranger to us and not a member of anyone's crew, looked momentarily disoriented as if he were not expecting anything cordial from "the great Paul Barker." He shook Paul's hand. Paul had a way of disarming fans and journalists, a finesse I appreciated so much. There was no reason to be a jerk when dealing with the public at a show, unless someone disrespected you as a performer or threatened you in some way. That's when the bouncers would step in and do their jobs anyway.

I was still a little bit rattled by the guy's abrupt manner and close proximity. I leaned over to Paul and told him, "I have to leave now."

Paul knew my history and knew not to question my anxiety if I felt my personal safety was in jeopardy. Being pregnant, there was no doubt my concerns were amplified. We left the fairgrounds shortly after that encounter. There was no argument, we had a household to pack up for the big move.

Back in Austin, our realtor friend Janet had found a place for Al, which had been a corporate retreat complete with themed bedrooms, outdoor pool with guesthouses and a slide, and a deserted airstrip once used for executives flying in on company private planes with their mistresses, concubines, or otherwise paid escorts. In a way, it was perfect for Al. He needed the extra rooms for friends coming in to work or just socialize with one of the "godfathers" of industrial music. Al's new place was an ideal hideout for him. A place where he could nurture his music ideas, his addictions, and his positioning as a proverbial "big fish in a little pond." Paul and I regularly joked about Al's big fish complex, but we weren't alone. Al didn't like competition. He had to be the ringleader of the show or there was no show. He was out in the middle of nowhere, a place where you had to go to see him and not the other way around. I didn't wonder why he and Paul got along so well. Paul was the straight man to Al's high wire act. The one goading Al into "making shit happen" and sitting next to the safety net when things got out of control. The dynamic between them worked, where Al hadn't achieved his current level of success with previous collaborators. I was backstage after one of the Ministry shows in Chicago, when Al was asked about Paul's bass work on a particular song. Al closed his eyes as if in some strange reverie and said, "Ah yes, Ion." He and Paul were locked in for the long haul.

Al's new "compound" was a relic from an era that had worshiped different kinds of excess—oil, booze, and hookers—but it had chief executive officer written all over the layout. The themed bedrooms paid a cheesy homage to Hugh

Hefner and his Playboy Mansion days and the notion that whatever happened there, stayed there. The few occasions I visited Al's place after we'd all moved, I returned to my car wanting to take a shower. It was a long fifty-mile drive back to Austin.

21

We closed on the house in Austin and were ready to move in July of 1993. I was six months pregnant. It seemed like in a day's time, huge moving trucks were parked in the alley behind our apartment in Logan Square, with enormous roadies appearing at our doorstep as though they were ready to break down gear at an arena show for Jam Productions. They were there to haul our belongings onto the trucks and drive to Texas. All of our tables, vintage furniture and lamps, music gear, baby's crib, books, and more books went. Memories of Chicago were bottled up—safely stored in my emotionally overstressed brain. I took polaroids of my pregnant belly and sent one to my brother in New York. I took one last look at the layout of this apartment in this typical stone two-flat in the city, took Ursula's hand, and headed for my parents' place by the lake. Ursula and I would be flying to Austin. Paul, crew, and drivers were taking the trucks.

My parents drove me with Ursula to O'Hare, and I had hardly any feelings except tremendous relief. This was our new life we were heading into and Chicago would be a place we now visited. In a few weeks, Ursula would celebrate her first birthday in a new house—our house—in Austin, Texas. My parents would fly in for that. I sat in the window seat on the plane and held

Ursula tightly, showing her the city lights racing past as the plane picked up speed on the runway. I stared out the window and without warning was suddenly consumed by a wave of emotion. I thought, "This is how you leave home?"

I felt a profound longing for some bigger fanfare, an easily remembered parting snapshot of friends waving goodbye, confetti, streamers, or something draping our airline seats. I looked out at the night's blackness getting darker as we pulled away from the city and climbed higher into the air. Pregnancy blues or new homesick blues, it didn't matter. The feeling was real and wouldn't go away. I was leaving with Ursula and our new baby, heading into a new environment where I had no friends or acquaintances, no expectations at all. I knew the real estate agent. I had been too busy to consider what came next. I stopped working full time in June, to pack for our move halfway across the country, packing and simultaneously trying to hold onto life possessions I couldn't part with and ditching the stuff that didn't matter anymore. I felt safe with Paul and the reality of finally living in our own house. What I didn't feel was any clear idea of what I was stepping into so far away from Chicago.

There was a time before marriage and babies when I had moved every year for what seemed like ten years. That was routine. This was different, like moving to a different country. I felt like the immigrant I had never been. The parallels to my own mother's life didn't occur to me at the time, but they were there—my mother flying from Germany to America in 1956 with Uli, who was three, and Raimund, newly born. She knew no one where she was going either. And, like me, she didn't speak their language.

Paul and the trucks arrived in Austin ahead of us. He met our flight at the airport. We collected our bags, and I stepped out of the sliding doors at Austin Municipal Airport and had to catch my breath. Going into the July heat and humidity outside, I felt heavier than my own body weight. Inertia, from the heat.

The rest of the day was a blur of people moving boxes into rooms and asking where did this go? Our house had five bedrooms and three baths, and plenty of opportunity to get lost and hide from the constant chatter of other people trying to get their jobs done. Part of me wanted to help. The combination of jet lag, stifling heat outside followed by instant cold air indoors, along with the added twenty pounds I was carrying on my frame said "no." I didn't know where everything was supposed to go once it came into the house. We didn't have a lot of furniture, so the bigger pieces were easy to sort. The rest would come later. I didn't care if our sleeping arrangements for the night would be some mats and sheets on the floor. I only wanted to feel at home.

I looked over the architectural drawings of the house, left for us by the original owner. I felt safe knowing Paul and I and our children would be happy here. We knew in the back of our minds we wouldn't live in this house forever, as beautiful and peaceful as it was. We were still in Texas, a far cry from the glitz of the big cities we knew so well. For the time being, this was home. I fell asleep barely cognizant of my normal body rhythms and thankful that at the very least, we were still in the same time zone as Chicago.

Waking up that first morning in our new house, I lay there adjusting to the dawn's light. I slowly moved from our bedroom at the south end of the house, down the long hallway, silently shuffling behind the stone fireplace facing into the sunken living room, moving past the kitchen, and finally into the family room and ending at the back house door. The tile and linoleum floors felt good on my bare feet. I needed some air. Outside air. The house was cooled enough for the one hundred degree July heat, but I needed to step outside into this new Texas landscape. I wanted to feel the air, what it was really like to live and breathe here.

Unlocking the door, leaving it half open, I stepped barefoot onto the walkway. It was hot, already ninety degrees at 6:00 a.m. As I stepped out further, I heard heavy footfalls to my left as if a crowd had suddenly begun running away from the house. I turned my head to see a herd of deer, one by one, jumping the fence from our backyard to the front. I was side-stage witnessing a nature ballet, as each performer flung its legs high into the air, coming down to a perfect landing. This was new. Then, outside was quiet again. No city noises, no car doors slamming, no voices at all. The rush of moving was over.

Later in the afternoon, when our furniture was put in place and the dining room was filling up with familiar faces—Al and a handful of road crew—there was a knock on the sliding door looking out onto the front deck. Everyone stopped talking. In all the deliberate concentration of unloading and unpacking,

I hadn't expected other visitors. For a second, I had a funny thought or even an expectation that the local authorities were coming by to tell us, "There's been some terrible mistake. YOU can't stay here. This is our neighborhood." I opened the door and was greeted by a cheery southern drawl.

"Well, hi there. Thought I'd stop by and welcome y'all to the neighborhood!"

I stepped aside, and in stepped our new next-door neighbor, Katherine Houston. She was cradling a homemade chocolate pecan pie. I was speechless, hoping I wasn't staring at the pie. I was also relieved there weren't any goons behind her.

We came to discover our neighbor was a teacher. She was wearing a bright "teacher's outfit," suitable for greeting her special-needs students at Eanes Elementary down the street. It was summer, but she'd been to some teacher function. Everyone else in the room quietly stared at her petite blonde form and big smile. Katherine didn't blink an eye. This roomful of night-crawling, former juvenile delinquents was no match for the antics she sometimes dealt with on a daily basis at her job.

We were unaware Katherine Houston and her husband Sam (a descendant of the Sam Houston, one of the founders of the fair state of Texas) had done some research on their new neighbors, and the neighbors' band called Ministry. To satisfy his curiosity, Sam made a pilgrimage to a local Christian bookstore, which also sold music. He asked one of the clerks, "Y'all have any Ministry records?" The staff was not amused. "We don't sell that kind of music here. That's not Christian," they told Sam. And with that stinging rebuke, Sam Houston, having never heard a single note of a Ministry song, became an instant fan.

The small group of male roadie types standing in our dining room, seemed to relax a bit at the sight of Katherine's homemade pie. Paul and I were briefed on the bios of our immediate neighbors to the north, south, and west. We thanked Katherine for stopping by and introducing herself and thanked her for the pie. She disappeared back through the sliding door saying, "Let us know if y'all need anything."

The second or third day in our new home, I woke up with a dry throat from the constant air conditioning in the house. Outside, even in the early morning, it was hot. What was I expecting? This was the south. I walked the length of the house to the kitchen and felt around in the semi-dark for a glass to fill with tap water. Our kitchen was standard issue 1960s: avocado green, small yet functional, with a breakfast bar overlooking the family room. The kitchen was poorly lit even with all the lights on, including the recessed lighting over the burnt-orange wet bar on one end. Our house truly was designed as a mid-century monument to entertaining. I moved over to the sink, still waking up, and reached in to move the scrubber. As I pulled my hand away, I felt an intense burning.

I looked down into the sink for a knife, thinking I had cut myself. It was a confusing sensation, like being stung by a bee for the first time. As I looked closer to the drain, I could see a scorpion in all of its two inches of armor. I screamed for Paul. My finger was swelling up. The burning sensation was relentless, as if I'd thrust my finger directly into an open flame and held it there.

The scorpion pierced the skin on my knuckle where there wasn't much flesh to bury its stinger. Paul and I waited to see if the swelling would get any worse, but after ten excruciating minutes, even the burning stopped. I was lucky. We were both a little panicked. I was pregnant and didn't need anything toxic like venom coursing through my bloodstream. Another odd "welcome" to Texas.

Having lived in Chicago my entire life, I locked doors behind me. Our neighbor Katherine walked over one morning across the driveway and tried the back door.

"Oh honey, you don't need to lock your door around here. Everybody knows everybody else."

That idea took a while to get used to. I called a local alarm company to update the alarm system in the house, nonetheless. We were planning on traveling a lot—at least Paul was—and I would otherwise be often alone at home with the kids. The alarm crew arrived with a salesman who walked me through the house, ominously noting "points of entry" and highlighting the amazingly quick response of local law enforcement if the alarm were tripped. By the time we made our way to the master bedroom with its walk-in closet and floor safe, this chummy alarm pro had tallied up the chances against an intruder getting his hands on me or my stuff with our house fully wired. I was convinced by his presentation, despite thinking all salesmen lacked self-esteem and that's why they chose those jobs. He paused briefly, staring at the safe in the closet. With a cheery note of finality, he assured me that in the rare event of a compromised alarm, "You just grab yer gun, and shoot 'em dead. Alright y'all! Welcome to Texas."

I must admit after forgetting the alarm code a few times and not getting to the follow up call from the alarm company quickly enough, I was impressed at how swiftly the West Lake Hills police showed up with weapons drawn. There were plenty of rich folks around us, but nothing ever really happened in Westlake, except the occasional toilet paper bombing of a high schooler's home or the occasional traffic ticket.

I once took my 1971 Alfa GTV sports car for a drive around the neighborhood to get the car washed and ready for tag renewal, when I was stopped going up the hill to our house. The car was silver and had black interior, no air conditioning, and currently no parking brake. But it was pretty. I pulled over, keeping my foot on the floor brake and waited for the officer to tell me the inevitable: my tags were expired. Instead, he emerged from his car, walked around the back of mine, and casually noted, "This an antique, innit?"

I said yes. "I only drive it a couple of months in the year. It has no air conditioning and black interior, and by the way, I was just on my way to get the renewal. Sir."

"NO AIR . . . no air." The officer circled the car a bit more. "Well . . . not a problem. You jes roll them windas down and drive like HELL."

The local police force, it seemed, made their money writing speeding tickets. I continued to hold my foot on the brake lest my illegal, sweaty antique begin sliding backwards down the hill.

"Thank you so much," I said, forcing a smile. I waited, but he just stood there musing over my car.

"Not a problem . . . now go get that thang legal." The officer was back in his patrol car and off he went.

I was finally beginning to accept the idea that our house was a safe place in a safe neighborhood. I was letting my guard down. A few weeks had passed since moving in. I could start setting up my office. I could call for newspaper delivery, put some books away. I could relax. It was early morning. I opened the back door to go outside and get something from my car, when I saw a figure moving in the bushes between our driveway and the Houstons' property, someone in camouflage gear crouched down, lurking.

I backed up. Christ. Please tell me this isn't some crazed Ministry fan who found us out, I silently implored the universe. Or the dreaded rare intruder who figured out we were new to the neighborhood and newly hip to the no door lock thing? I hurried back inside, locked the door, put on the alarm and called Katherine. "There's someone outside," I whispered into the phone, as I barely hid myself and my pregnant belly behind the laundry room door.

"Oh, that's just Samuel. He likes to play army. Don't mind him," she said.

Samuel (or Sam Jr.) was her eldest son, still in middle school, but tall, preparing to live up to the family legacy of combat with "the other side." Unlike the Mexican nationals of historic Houston conquests, Samuel only had some new neighbors from the gangster stronghold of the north—Chicago—to parry with. And one of them was pregnant. Not exactly an equal opponent in a southern gentlemanly exchange of fire.

"Okay," I said, and hung up the phone, still shaking.

***

My first impression of Austin: Everyone has a tattoo. Moving to Austin as a Chicago native, I soon came face to face with what seemed like an overabundance of body art. There seemed to be tattoo parlors (and strip clubs) everywhere in the city, except where we lived. In Chicago, if someone had a tattoo, chances were you didn't see it. Tattoos were covered by layers of protective clothing and long sleeves. In Austin, in the heat, everything was on display. There were more tattoos per capita, I felt, than there were rational people getting them.

Some things in Austin just didn't make sense. The overabundance of tattoos made about as much sense to me as trying to square the actual numbers of

Hispanic families in Austin (especially on the east side) with the difficulty we had trying to find a decent pinata to hang in the house—our show of solidarity with the natives.

I didn't have tattoos. Paul had one small inking on his upper arm. Four dots. An ellipsis. The first time I saw it I asked him why he chose that design. He seemed embarrassed and changed the subject. Was it his love of the number pattern one, two, three, four? It was his favorite time of day. What was the magic behind this sequential ordering, this rhythm? Was it the time of day when he would consciously pause to call a former girlfriend, to be somehow romantically, cosmically linked to her? That must have been it—he was such a romantic and a student of alchemy. One . . . two . . . three . . . four. Dance with me.

Our first days in Austin, I was growing more anxious to get out of the house, and away from the decisions of where exactly in this big house we should store all of our art objects, photographs, and mementos spilling out of boxes everywhere. A full week of one hundred degree days, unpacking bedding and kitchen gear for the long term, had left me exhausted and intensely focused on my mental health and the seven-month-old life inside of me. I needed to get out of the house. I needed a walk. My habit of walking everywhere in Chicago didn't translate well to being in the south. There were no sidewalks where we lived in Westlake. Outdoor exercise was impossible after 10:00 a.m. I was suddenly driving everywhere.

"Everyone says we should see the bats at night on the bridge when they come out for their feeding." I told Paul. It was a ritual at dusk for tourists and locals, to stand on or near the Congress Avenue bridge downtown where a colony of hungry, Mexican free-tailed bats would emerge a million strong and fly the length of the lake looking for food. Going to the bat bridge was a local attraction and something everyone had to do at least once. We strapped Ursula into her car seat, pitched the stroller into the back seat, and drove to Town Lake to stake out a good viewing spot near the hotels.

Paul parked the car, and as we stepped onto the walking path, a couple slowly road by us on bicycles. The two of them were smoking cigarettes. The woman steered her bike with one hand and balanced a beer in the other. It was my introduction to the slacker mentality in Austin. This was, after all, a college town.

There was a certain hush falling over voices in the crowd waiting for the nightly show. They seemed to already know when the cloud of bats would slowly fall from their hidden nests in the bridge's underpinnings. The light had to be exactly right. The sun was disappearing off in the distance. The crowd waited. The humidity at the lake was making me drowsy.

We watched as the heat and the stillness around us was suddenly disrupted by tiny pinpoints, connecting in utter silence just below the bridge. There were no individual flight paths. A giant swarm was getting into formation, falling down and forward in massive waves, as it moved away from the bridge and headed downstream. Black, odorless, silent in their ritual. They kept coming. Ursula, Paul, and I were transfixed, as if watching an animated horror film, a black veil floating by in the wind. Voices began speaking again, pointing to the mass emerging and flowing downward and away.

"This is supercool," Paul said. Yes. Maybe Austin, Texas wasn't just about beer, music, tattoos, and cheap real estate. Maybe there was a soul to this place after all. I stared out at Town Lake. The walking path around it stretched on for a few miles up to the downtown hotels and looped back to Austin High School and shaded public parking. "Thank god there's a body of water here to walk around. Otherwise, I'd lose my mind," I told Paul.

We drove away from the lake, looking at the Austin skyline, at the haphazard nature of the downtown buildings. The Lyndon Baines Johnson presidential library building sat like an anvil on the campus at UT. It was one of two interesting buildings in Austin, as far as I could tell. The other was the Erwin Center, a giant hat box fashioned from concrete where arena bands played.

I left Chicago for this, I thought.

Austin in essence really is a college town—just that. Get over it, I told myself. You'll be busy enough with two kids to forget where you are or aren't living on any given day.

***

The year 1993 was morphing into a year punctuated by emotional events seemingly one after another. In July, we moved to Austin. In August, Ursula celebrated her first birthday with her grandparents (my parents) coming to visit from Chicago and staying with us at the house. In my pregnant state, I felt sleepy, often. My body wasn't adjusting to the heat. It probably wasn't meant to. Paul was out with Al and otherwise unavailable.

"Buncha gypsies," my mother had said often enough, when Paul and I had finally broached the topic of moving away from Chicago. It was easier to frame the argument for moving in terms of money. We couldn't afford a house and a studio in Chicago. And naturally, we wanted to live somewhere where our kids could go to the neighborhood public school and grow up in a peaceful, loving environment—despite the potentially chaotic life of having a dad who was now a "famous" rock musician.

My parents were shocked when we decided to move out of state. But they themselves had left for the United States when they were our age. I told them the distance between Austin and Chicago was only as far as you felt it was. Airfare was cheap. They were retired. Texas became for them this imagined universe of tall people, deserts, dust, and peculiar accents. For all I knew, my mother imagined us now living the fictional life of her favorite country singers—Marti Robbins, Charlie Pride, and Patsy Cline. "Streets of El Paso" and "Crazy" could have resonated with her when she waved to me and to Ursula as we handed the ticket agent our boarding passes and disappeared down the jetway and onto our plane leaving Chicago for Austin on that last day.

Toward the end of August, my parents flew down from Chicago for Ursula's birthday. Arriving in a cab from the airport, they both looked as though they couldn't believe they'd come to the right address. My mother was shocked at the enormous amount of space in our house, the five bedrooms, and a mother-in-law house in the back. The backyard was big enough for an in-ground pool if we were in the market for one. So much space to move around in.

My mother pondered who would clean the place. "We'll hire someone," I told her. Our neighbors had a maid come in once a week. We could afford that. My mother looked anxious nonetheless, as if wanting to do something for me, something which made sense to her as my mother, to relieve my uncertainties living here so far away from "home," and relieve her own anxiety that we would be so far away. She had an expression on her face as though she herself would never have thought to hire a maid. She went into the laundry room and emerged with a broom, a bucket, and a mop. I was horrified. She smiled and insisted upon cleaning only the front doorway and stoop outside, neither of which were particularly grimy. It had to be done right away. She insisted and disappeared into the outdoors, reappearing a few minutes later, drenched in sweat and satisfied. "Now your house will always be clean." She was superstitious like that. Your house is dirty at New Year's? It will be dirty all year. We joked about her short career as a "Polish cleaning lady" in downtown Chicago when my parents first arrived as immigrants to the US.

I decided it was time to take my parents out for real Texas barbeque. The very first restaurant Paul and I went to with our realtor was the Salt Lick in Driftwood. The Salt Lick was one of those legendary barbeque oases surviving on its own in the brush-filled edge of the Texas hill country. At the time of our move to Austin, there was nothing else around it for miles but a few small ranch properties.

Driftwood was twenty miles away. Paul was out helping Al with his own move. The only vehicle we had at home to ferry my parents around was a Volkswagen Fox we'd bought used in Chicago. I couldn't fathom why Paul bought that car, other than the necessity to have a passenger vehicle to transport a child in a car seat. The Fox had no air conditioning. It was the height of summer in Austin. It was an unforgivably steamy drive out to Driftwood, even with the windows down, but I loved hearing my parents chattering with "Urszulka" about what a big girl she was to be turning one.

My mother must have sensed I was going to be alone with my children for long periods of time when Paul was working in the studio and touring. "I will help you, Gerda. We'll come back. Don't worry!" she said, more than once. I knew she meant it. We used up an entire roll of film taking photographs with my little Olympus camera—my parents with Ursula on our front deck; my mother holding hands with Ursula, walking in the dusty parking lot at the Salt Lick.

My parents stayed with us for a few days. During those nights and without my knowledge, my mother wandered through the house, unable to sleep with the air on. She came into my bedroom to look in on the baby, asleep in her travel playpen next to me, and to see if I was sleeping comfortably without Paul there.

During the day, my parents were happy to play with Ursula and take her shopping or go for short walks on our street. They had a chance to see a small part of Texas. "Everything is bigger in Texas," they felt compelled to say out loud at every opportunity. The Texas Tourism Board was obviously doing a great promotional campaign for my parents' benefit. I couldn't help but feel something was ending now with this visit. I had their seal of approval somehow, as my father inspected the air conditioning system in the house and declared he would be back later to give it an update for "efficiency." Always an engineer, my dad.

I stood with my daughter and my parents on the front deck of our house admiring the view downtown. We were waiting for their cab back to the airport. "Well kid, time to go," my father said, giving me a hug. He never could look at me or my siblings as adults with our own journeys in life. We were still just "kids."

"I will help you," my mother insisted again, looking around one last time. We both teared up when the taxi arrived in front of the house and I realized they were really going away. It had been a long delay for me emotionally getting to this letting go. Ursula waved at the cab, inching away down the driveway. "Bye Oma. Bye 'Ganpa!'"

"I will help you," repeated in my thoughts a while longer as I pulled open the sliding glass door and stepped back inside to the cool air with my Ursula, my mother's namesake.

I will help you. How would she help me from so far away? My mother had already helped me in more ways than I was even aware of at the time. From her, I learned to keep thinking of "bessere Zeiten" (better times) if I were inclined to be anxious about anything.

Up until my late teens I was prone to chronic bronchitis and throat infections in the winter and sometimes in the summer. My tonsils would become infected, spotted with white dots in the back of my throat, swelling up and making it difficult for me to breathe. One summer, my mother and my brother Raimund had to carry me to an upstairs bedroom at the house in Wisconsin and bend me over the balcony from the waist to open my lungs as my throat closed. We were ten miles from the nearest hospital. She didn't want me to die.

My mother had guided me through my silent third year of life, as I followed her around the house, and she would ask why I was so "in Gedanken" (deep in thought). I became her "ghost." I was not diagnosed with trauma at the time, but my inability to say even one word while I wore a blank expression was concerning enough for her to encourage me to smile. Throughout my childhood, she and my father would say, "Smile, sadface," if we were visiting other people at their homes. I listened and shook my head.

From my mother, I learned to study garment construction and to distinguish polyester from natural fabrics by feel. She taught me that having good manners and a meager bank account were better than being a dolt with a fat wallet. She also said you could learn a lot about a person by looking at their shoes.

My mother taught all of her kids that every person was worthy of respect, no matter where they came from. From her I learned if a man beats a woman, he has a problem, and she should run far away from it immediately and not look back. My mother was at first skeptical of my husband because he was a musician, and in her eyes musicians were prone to cheating. When she knew Paul better and his fully enveloping hugs whenever he'd see her, she would smile and tell me my husband was "sehr lieb" (very dear).

It was my mother who helped me through college-level German, reciting questions from the textbook and listening patiently for grammatical errors when I responded. She had been an excellent student before the war, before she lost her teenage years entirely. She had written poetry and won a contest for her writing while still in grade school.

My mother joined a "paddle club" of kayakers after the war. She'd met new friends after taking a kitchen job on the American Army base in Germany, where she would meet her future husband. On base, the soldiers often forgot her name—Ursula—and called her "Wanda" instead. She made a point to tell me she had happy times before and after the war.

My mother was so impressed when I was learning Chaucer for a seminar in Middle English, she insisted upon coaching me as I memorized the first ten lines of The Canterbury Tales. She would listen as I recited the lines to her, and she read along. Middle English was easy for her to decipher. She was good with written languages. She wanted to help me, and she did.

I wasn't sure how this help would work now with geography interrupting her ability to read my body language and see how I was really getting along with a second child coming so close after the first. But my mother always believed I would "make it" in the world on my own, no matter what I was doing. She had convinced me I was very much like my Grandpa Max, her intellectual father. To my mother, there was no such thing as low expectations.

A week after returning home to Chicago, my mother woke up in the morning, looked at my father and said, "Henyu ich muss sterben."—"Henry, I'm dying." My mother's heart was failing, and she had trouble breathing. She knew. Maybe she had known in Austin that time was running short.

I don't know how long my father tried to revive her, if he tried at all, if he tried to call 911, tear the covers off the bed, sit with her in the ambulance, or what was running through his mind. Hours later my father called me, sounding as though he had somehow been robbed. He was never very eloquent in expressing feelings other than anger. He said simply and loudly, "MA DIED."

Now eight months pregnant, I was back on a plane to Chicago along with Paul and Ursula. We would be there for a week doing what needed to be done and helping with funeral arrangements. I stared out the plane's window and felt nothing. Paul held my hand during the flight and balanced Ursula on his lap.

My father could not bring himself to the funeral home to choose a casket for my mother's body. He wasn't ready for that. My sister had also flown back to Chicago. It was up to the two of us to look at each other, shrug our shoulders, and silently make decisions on everything down to the flowers, based on how much our father wanted to spend. I couldn't make up my mind. It all looked so kitschy—the casket, the flowers. In the end, I paid for the flowers not wanting to start an argument with my father about money.

The ceremony was at the chapel at Maryhill Cemetery. When I was a child, my sister Uli joked a few times about how if she were caught in the crossfire at her high school during the 1969 riots, we could just "bury her at Maryhill." Was this place famous or did she just like the name? My sister had been dead for fifteen years. I couldn't recall ever visiting her grave. The irony in seeing my mother's gravesite next to hers wasn't lost on me. Why hadn't I visited? Why did they have to go? I could almost understand why my father was downing shots of whiskey with some strangers I didn't know at the Polish banquet later on. Still, I felt nothing. My thoughts were on the baby I was carrying, soon to be born into this year of traveling chaos.

Ruth Mainey, my friend since PRAXIS and Wax Trax days, came to my mother's wake. Ruth had her two young kids with her. I was grateful to feel the presence of a longtime friend who grew up as a practicing Catholic. I was not religious at all, but there was an aura of grace and silence and respect for the dead that for me was tangible coming from someone with faith. It was obvious Ruth had a lot on her own mind with her kids getting restless in the parking lot outside waiting to go home. Ruth had lost her own mother and knew what that meant to lose a parent just as you were becoming one yourself.

At the banquet after the funeral, I overheard my father tell a tableful of old acquaintances that my mother had had rheumatic fever twice during the war in Germany. One episode damages the heart. My mother had survived nine pregnancies and given birth to five children. Her doctor said she was lucky to have lived to sixty-five with a heart as complicated by history as hers.

A few days later, Paul and I were back on a plane with Ursula, heading home to Austin. In our house again, it was even more awkward negotiating the collection of boxes and scattered mismatched furniture pieces. I wanted to feel "settled." My sister Georgette and her husband had helped us move down to Austin and unpack. I wasn't comfortable with letting other people make sense of my life surroundings. That was the feeling I had had in Chicago when we finally buried my mother's body. I could decide on flower arrangements, but I didn't really have a choice. Predetermined ceremonies. Rituals. Observances. I was living it all at once, it seemed. I needed to slow down, take a deep breath. I needed to be mindful not to exert myself too much so late in my pregnancy. What choices did I have?

I needed a distraction from directing the slow process of moving into a new place. Paul and I hadn't finished preparing ourselves for a fourth member of the house. We needed odd pieces of bedroom furniture for ourselves and for the children, to make the bedrooms livable, functioning, and childproof. Paul's friend Adam Grossman suggested IKEA, which had just opened outside of Houston. We had a van. We needed someone else to go with us to load up. Adam was not available but knew someone who was.

Adam's bandmate, Danny Lohner, offered to help us. A couple of years later, Danny would call Paul to ask him to put in a good word for him when he auditioned for Nine Inch Nails, a job he would get. Off we went—me, less than eight weeks away from giving birth, driving in a utility van across the flat, even landscape of Texas Highway 10, with my life partner, and a chatty new friend and tour guide.

"I'm surprised that little gas station's still there." Danny took pains to point out living monuments of Texas country life still surviving roadside against the invasion of places like IKEA. I appreciated the small talk. It felt real and had zero to do with funerals or rock music.

The Houston store was on the outskirts of town, and thankfully we could avoid the bland modernity of the Houston skyline. Houston was home to a lot of Texas Ministry fans, but bedroom furniture was our focus for the day as we visited the "Malms" on display. I couldn't help but lie down a couple of times on a model bed and deliberate over colors with Paul. We were both very particular about modern design. No extraneous objects entered our living space, no matter how small the space or—as now—3,500 square feet of it. When we were first married, our ongoing search for an acceptable sofa was narrowed down to a) an oxblood-red leather Chesterfield (for some reason, an obsession for both of us, but too damaging to our newlywed budget) or b) something vintage and cool. In Chicago we had found neither, opting to hang onto our overstuffed black, vintage Italian Saporiti chair with its matching ottoman. The two of us could sit in it together. Our Chicago apartment in Logan Square had a built-in bench covering the heater in the living room, and that suited our guests just fine when we had someone over. Now with our 1960s stone ranch house to decorate, brand new furniture was becoming more and more of a remote option. IKEA bookshelves were about as sparsely design-pure as we could stand in our re-imagining of what a sunken living room needed. We bought those, a new bed, and headed back.

I needed to go along for this ride to have a final say on what worked or didn't in our new house. I would be the one spending the most time there. It was vital to be involved, to give myself some peace of mind, some sanity as I processed my mother's death, our move, our new city, the new baby coming. It was as if I were starting my whole life over again. Yes, I was relieved of the pressure of having to go to work for what seemed like the first time in my adult life. But I was completely in the dark as to what life would be like without phone calls to my mother to ask how she did it with five kids.

With all the heartache of this month, I nearly overlooked an invitation to a much happier event. Bill Rieflin, Paul's bandmate and dear friend, was marrying his partner of many years, Frankie Sundsten. The wedding was scheduled to take place in Seattle on the autumnal solstice. I could not travel one more time before having to head back to Chicago to have the baby. Paul flew alone to Seattle. While he was gone, a gift package arrived from St. Louis from our friend Rick Buscher. Rick had recently finished artwork for the Revolting Cocks' Linger Ficken' Good LP and was apparently enamored with the font he'd created for the project, a type of "wooden log" lettering. What he sent us was a Barker family coat of arms he'd designed, a house warming gift. Our new coat of arms consisted of the letter B superimposed in log font resting in the curve of an iron horseshoe, mounted on a wooden plaque carved like a shield. There was a hole drilled in the back for convenient hanging. I mounted the thing over the back door of the house. Our new home didn't need an alarm system after all! We were blessed with the inscription on the back of Rick's gift: "To The Barkers Good Luck 9/28/93."

In October, Paul, Ursula, and I flew back to our former hometown to stay with my father and wait for the new baby to be born. Both kids would be native

Chicagoans. Our Blue Cross insurance wouldn't pay for the delivery otherwise. While we waited in Chicago for the baby's arrival, Ministry's guitarist Mike Scaccia moved into our Austin house with his girlfriend Stephanie and their cats, while they waited for a more permanent place to stay, out at Al's.

Paul and I planned to stay in my parents' apartment by the lake for a couple of weeks. I couldn't help feeling as though we were imposing, looking over the apartment now occupied only by my father. I wanted to argue with my father over why he was so anxious to dispose of my mother's things in the apartment. Her dresses, shoes, pillows, plates she'd bought overseas, everything had to go. I couldn't ask why. I quietly changed out the hand towels in the bathroom left hanging since our last visit, now gray with dust.

Our son arrived eight weeks after my mother passed away. Claude Gordon Barker was born on November 6th at Illinois Masonic Hospital, the same place where his sister was born. Unlike his sister, "Gordon" took a few days to settle into a normal facial expression. His beautiful face was slightly compressed, and he had a larger than usual head size. He was twenty-one inches long, like his sister, and on his way to possibly being as tall as Paul. In the hospital, Paul surprised me with a new necklace bearing a single thin, silver disk hanging from it to celebrate this new life. I was excited to have a son. We didn't know the sex of our children ahead of time. After the delivery, my very sweet and direct Dr. Arekapudi noted, "You now have a girl and a boy. Would you like your tubes tied? It is easier to do now before you go home." If there were any magic lingering in the moment, that faded quickly. I had the operation.

A few days of rest, and the newly configured four Barkers were together on a plane heading back to Austin. In the preceding three months, Paul and I had celebrated our daughter's first birthday, mourned my mother's death at sixty-five, welcomed the birth of our son, endured that dizzying flight plan of back and forth to Chicago, and it was time to move on with our new life.

The sense of relief was short-lived. In December, we received further bad news. Our chef friend, Ursula's godfather, Paul's riding buddy—Michael Short—died. He was our age. Officially, it was a heart attack after a visit to New Orleans. Unofficially, we knew Michael liked to indulge old substance habits on rare occasions when the mood struck him. The news was crushing. With his passing, Michael held the distinction of being the only close friend whose friendship Paul and I had experienced together from beginning to end.

I thought of Michael, and how he honored his role as Ursula's godfather. Not only dressing in a formal suit for the baptism in Chicago, but dropping everything in the kitchen at Star Top to step into the dining room and take Ursula in his arms and hold her as though she were the most precious, beautiful creation he'd ever seen. After she was born, Michael had a hairdresser friend shave the letters "URSULA" onto the back of his head, wrapping around to the front. Black-and-white photos of his head were framed into a triptych for Ursula, with a hand-inscribed message from Michael on how he hoped she would one day forgive him his transgressions in this life. Not long after Michael's passing, we received a gift in the mail from Marlene Short, Michael's mother. It was a silver pendant in a teardrop shape on a necklace for Ursula to wear. On the face of the pendant was a child's stick figure rendering of the figure of St. Michael. The image was lifted from an early drawing Michael had made of his patron saint crowned with a halo. Sigh.

Our emotionally charged year wasn't quite over yet. At ninety-five years of age, "Grandpère" Roland Du Luart's eccentric life came to a quiet close. He calmly fell forward while shaving and was discovered by his maid in the master bath of his house in Cuernavaca. I had always hoped to return to that place and bring Ursula to see Grandpère. It was the place where she was conceived. Grandpère Roland's death was the final red light in our lives in 1993.

***

Paul's mother Jeanne called from Manchester, England. She was flying to Cuernavaca to settle her father's estate. She said she would be in Mexico for a brief period and then would very much like to visit us in Austin and see her two grandchildren. My father was spending the Christmas holiday with us as well, learning to live with the fact that my mother was absent from our lives now. Our first Christmas in Austin was thankfully developing into an unscripted, impromptu family get together. I suggested to Paul his mother's visit was an auspicious new beginning for us—a chance for her to get acquainted with her grandchildren and reestablish closer ties with her own son. Paul appeared doubtful, but said, "You're the wise one in the family."

The death of her father gave Jeanne a decent excuse for returning to the United States, a place she rarely visited since her divorce from Paul's father decades before. I looked forward to hearing whatever family stories she would share. Family was important. Paul wandered through the house looking as shell shocked as I felt to be a parent of two now, but happy we were all safe and healthy. What luck—our children would have two grandparents to distract them, while Paul and I would have some time to ourselves. I wondered how long Jeanne would be with us.

Paul's mother arrived in Austin with suitcases stuffed with old family silverware she'd picked up at her father's place. She told us she couldn't really take the stuff back to England right now: "Too costly." Could she store this stuff here? We had a big place. She apologized to Paul that Grandpère had left no inheritance for his grandsons. She then took baby Gordon into her arms briefly, and settled into conversation with my father about where he had been held during the war. She made a point to say she would really like to treat her daughter-in-law to dinner away from the kids. I was grateful and surprised someone else was looking out for my emotional well-being having been through so much transition these past six or seven months.

I thanked Jeanne for thinking of me and opened my arms to offer a polite hug or something like it. She simply handed the baby back to me, turned to Paul and asked, "Pawwwwwl, what's become of your friend, oh what was her name . . . Lisa. Dark hair. I quite liked her!" It seemed the conversation had suddenly shifted away from kids and current affairs and over to the details of Paul's past love life.

I didn't know what to say. Was she kidding, dredging up ancient history about Paul's ex? She must be exhausted from all this traveling, I thought. She must still be grieving herself. I knew he and his mother rarely kept in touch, but this wasn't exactly the time or place for Paul to fill in the blanks of his personal life. She wanted details about someone Paul was involved with before we ever met.

I changed my clothes for dinner. Paul and my father stayed home with the kids. Jeanne and I left for Castle Hill, a quiet slightly pricey place with a knowledgeable sommelier. Our next door neighbor had recommended it. I thought Jeanne would appreciate the atmosphere and food, being her father's daughter and all French as she was. I was missing my own mother. The desire to connect with Paul's mother left me hopeful for the evening ahead.

No sooner were we seated and studying the menu, when Jeanne leaned in and asked me, "How is your relationship with Paul? Does he treat you well? Are you having orgasms? It's important for women to have orgasms, don't you agree?"

Where was this coming from? Before seeing her now, the only conversations I had had with Jeanne were two brief hellos in England at Ministry shows shortly after Paul and I were married and once with Ursula, a few months after she was born. As we sat across from each other in this public restaurant, I couldn't decide if she was trying too hard to assert her own relevance or simply was so uncouth as to have no sense of boundaries or decorum. Paul's mother came from an aristocratic family. She'd grown up in a palace in France before the Nazis took it over. She was too old to be hallucinating from menopause, wasn't she?

I finally said, "Mm . . . we're doing just fine." I wanted to say my sex life with my husband was none of her business, but that would also be rude. There was something just wrong with the questions. It was as if she were talking about a stranger and not Paul, her son. She told me she worried that Paul and his brother Roland might have grown up to hate women because their mother had left them at such an early age. She adopted this third person narrative to examine her own behavior. Her earlier question to Paul about his ex now made slightly more sense. Did he treat women well?

Paul was not quite three when his mother turned him over to relatives to raise, if I remembered correctly. I hadn't agreed to dinner with her to hear a mother's confession of guilt for abandoning her own kids to become an artist. I thought she wanted to know me better. But it became clear my relief in being able to get away from parental duties for an evening came at a price. I could see where narcissism had left scars on Paul's psyche at an early age. Do what you want to do, all the time, at whatever cost to those around you, seemed to be a guiding principle in his mother's life. And when you did feel a twinge of guilt, seek therapy much later—if at all. And not with a real therapist. Your daughter-in-law will do. Her seemingly feminist position on orgasm was radical for someone of her age (sixty?) and generation. But it was overshadowed by what I perceived to be her religious-like devotion to herself. I resolved to smile and get along with Paul's mother. She was our children's only grandmother now. She could be charming and sweet to them when she felt inspired to do so. But I could have discussions about my sex life with women friends of my own age, thank you, if I ever felt the need.

22

After the new year, and with Al now settled into his new compound in Marble Falls outside of Austin, I was adapting to a new routine. I came to miss slipping on a silk shirt every day for work and wondered if being able to dress in luxurious fabrics hadn't been part of the allure in being a lawyer in the first place. (It wasn't. Not much, anyway.) Of necessity now, T-shirts and black walking shorts became my daily uniform in Austin. I hadn't pictured myself dressing like a recovering record store clerk, but it was unrealistic to think I could avoid soiling every shirt I had with baby formula, baby spittle, my own sweat, and sunscreen. I packed up my professional wardrobe and "Chicago" clothes and brought everything to Austin thinking at some point I would venture out again and find part-time legal work, but there was no financial need for that at the moment. My professional life was indefinitely on hold. In the grocery store of our West Lake Hills neighborhood, I could sense I was being scrutinized for not wearing bright blue running shorts or a tennis skirt or whatever uniform look was prescribed for mothers doing their own shopping. I didn't care.

At first, to go somewhere out of our neighborhood, I would drive to Wheatsville Co-op near the UT campus to buy organic baby food in jars, something our Westlake grocery didn't carry. When Central Market opened down the street from Wheatsville, I went there for organic produce and eventually made my own baby food. We didn't eat much processed foods as adults, why should our kids? I stopped at Central Market on the way back from the bank or sometimes just to venture out for European butter, soy milk, and always fresh flowers. The store had a vast assortment of exotic and in season wild flowers stacked in buckets to pick your own. I scanned colors first, then textures, and finally mixed them all up. The resulting bouquets were composed of something wild, something small, something weird, and always a flower or two tossed in for color to shake up any complacent tones there. The end result was like a collection of personalities on a subway train—a disruptive village in a vase. The weekly flower arrangements were my way of creating an evolving gallery of color in our house, always changing with seasonal stems. My favorites were the cocks crowns. Fully matured, they resembled rich red coral or human brains. Paul called them my "brain flowers." It was an amusing natural attraction.

I was strolling through Central Market with my cart and kids one morning, having adapted my wardrobe that day to cooler temperatures: black walking shorts and a black, thermal long-sleeve shirt with a discreet small, gold Revolting Cocks logo embroidered in the top center of the shirt. It was more of an insignia, like a Fred Perry crest or Prince's symbol for himself. The Cocks' logo on its own wouldn't mean much to the average person. I wandered down the soy milk aisle, coming upon the dairy section across from it.

"Whoa! Where did you get that Cocks' shirt?" A young, college-aged clerk drew back from stocking the European butters and stared at me.

"My husband's in the band," I answered flatly, not really trying to draw attention to myself.

"Who's your husband!?"

I told him, and the clerk immediately asked if he could shake my hand. "Please tell him it's such an honor to meet you, I mean to meet his wife! Uh . . . I don't know what I'm saying." He would not stop smiling. I slid past the clerk, plucked some Gerber daisies from the flower buckets, threw in some lavender thistles, and handed them to the girl at the cutting table.

"Mommy, who was that?" Ursula asked.

"Someone who knows Papa," I said, ducking out of Central Market before any more interrogators crossed our path.

"I got bagged at Central Market today," I told Paul when I saw him later at home. I pointed to the incriminating logo on my chest.

"Better you than me," he laughed, kissing me before I could register a protest.

***

As I set up my office and our files at home, I regularly took calls from Ministry's accountant at Crazed Management in New Jersey, and from our personal accountant in Chicago. While I stayed close to home, it made sense for me to keep track of quarterly tax payments, expenses, union dues, professional fees, and the dreary business detritus associated with the self-employed. Upon the advice of our accountant, I opened IRA accounts for myself and for Paul, funding those when the accountant suggested it was better this way than paying more of his income out in taxes. Ministry was bringing in that much money for us.

I continued paying my own licensing fees and kept my subscription to Entertainment Law & Finance. I signed up for Continuing Legal Education (CLE) courses to keep current on the law. Illinois soon required all attorneys to take CLE classes annually to maintain their licenses. I welcomed the hours away from home to sit and chat with other lawyers about music contracts and copyright issues. At one of my conferences I met a staff attorney with Sound Exchange, who encouraged me to get Paul signed up with them. Sound Exchange was beginning to collect royalties that often fell through the cracks when dealing with small labels. They also helped artists who were simply unorganized with tracking their royalties. I thought we should take advantage of every possibility to exploit Paul's music, even if the result was a few hundred dollars annually. Years later we learned that Al tried to claim he had 100 percent ownership in Ministry songwriting royalties collected through Sound Exchange. We filed a dispute with

Sound Exchange when I discovered the discrepancy.

When preliminary Grammy ballots came in the mail from NARAS, I saw them before Paul did. The final ballots came closer to the end of the year, and with Paul often out of town, I opened those too. I wondered how many other Academy members had someone else fill in their votes. I routinely checked off our friends' names or bands we liked. The Grammys were so steeped in the machinations of ageing white men and politics, who was hot at the moment, or whose name was at least recognizable to a majority of the members. Paul and Al didn't seem to care all that much about what was popular anyway, but NARAS membership was good for business, so we were told.

***

The Houstons turned out to be fantastic neighbors. They were more open minded in the uniquely church-obsessed environment we found ourselves in. They discovered we were on the same wavelength when Thanksgiving rolled up three weeks after our son was born. Paul and I had just finished prepping the turkey and placing the tray in the oven, when Katherine called. "Gerda, I have an emergency situation."

"What happened?" I asked.

"My oven died, and Sam's family is coming for dinner—fifteen of them. Do you have room for another bird in your oven?"

We had just installed a new, custom-sized oven to fit in our '60s style, double-wide oven nook, and yes we had plenty of party-perfect oven space. For a neighbor. Who needed it right now. After several hours of cooking time had elapsed, turkeys for both households were done. While Paul and I assembled the rest of our table, there was a knock at the back door. I peeked outside, and there appeared to be a conga line forming.

"Well, hello neighbor! Thank you for saving our dinner." In single file, in came what seemed to be the entire guest list from next door. We met Sam Houston, the elder and father of Katherine's husband, Sam. He broke into an a capella version of some holiday classic and stood with his arms out welcoming us. He was famous for his singing voice, we were told. It was a habit and a treat on holidays for his family. Now, we were family too.

*   *   *

I stayed home in Austin to raise our kids and to register some semblance of normalcy into our otherwise unorthodox lifestyle. I quickly discovered that I was not making any friends in Austin. The people I was meeting struck me as either opportunistic hangers on, fans of Ministry and the Revolting Cocks, or the other extreme, staunch church goers. Many of my friends in Chicago were somehow connected to the music business in the past or present, but they were my friends. They didn't want to only talk about my husband or his projects or his band mates. It was difficult timewise to meet anyone new who didn't have an agenda.

The music people in Austin didn't annoy me as much as the religious neighborly types, who upon meeting would get the important social strata cleared up for me right away. Within a minute's time, one question was inevitable. "What church y'all belong to?" I found it offensive and none of their business. Was I always so touchy about private issues? Or was being a parent and having to think of two other young lives a responsibility I took very seriously, to the point of obsession? Did I need to relax and settle into local social mores? Did I even care? I suppose in the back of my mind I contemplated future encounters with these same people at the schools and grocery stores, at least. I always politely responded to the big question with, "We haven't found the right one yet." It was absolutely true. We hadn't.

There were no upcoming tour dates, and Paul was driving the fifty miles to Al's compound to try and "get shit happening." In other words, songwriting, laying tracks, editing, or simply trying to get Al to wake up. I didn't like the word "compound," nor did I understand the utility in using it for a spread of property that was more open to whomever showed up than would be tolerated at a real compound. There was no gate to buzz you in. "Curly," Ministry's eventual tour manager for their Australia shows became Al's house assistant, taking care of the day to day. There were no regular staff otherwise to secure the property. On a given day you were more likely to see strangers' cars pulling up to drop off essentials for Al. Or Patty would make the essentials run. As it was in Chicago, here in Austin Paul and I didn't socialize much with Patty and Al. A few visits to Rosie's Café for tex-mex or Jovita's to see Don Walser the Hillbilly Yodeler, and that was about it. Patty or Al or both might stop by our house when they needed money—which often they did—or if they needed some other favor.

**

I wondered if after the rigors of touring and moving across the country with our new family, if we didn't long for a simpler social calendar. Austin wasn't exactly a cultural hotbed of innovation and art. When we first arrived in our new hometown, I was scandalized to discover the official Austin art museum was housed in a nondescript office building downtown and was largely irrelevant. A smallish population of full-time residents meant lesser need to inject much new life into what was already there. Being a college town, Austin had bars and little clubs—lots of them, clustered on or near 6th Street downtown. Tourists could count on a dozen popular bars to drink and dance, depending upon their musical tastes. Bands played a handful of live music venues, Liberty Lunch, Antone's, Austin Music Hall, Stubb's, and the Erwin Center, again depending upon your tastes. Living in Austin became an exercise in stoicism. Paul and I went out if someone we knew was playing or on tour, as we had done back in Chicago. But we rarely ventured out to see performances otherwise.

I hardly had the opportunity to consider that we were no longer late-night restaurant and bar hopping. We had done that sort of thing with friends in Chicago. In our new hometown, we didn't really know many people. Once or twice Al wanted everyone to meet at Rosie's a few miles outside of Austin and on the road out to his place in Marble Falls. Otherwise, not much to do in the off-studio hours. The pace of life in Austin, along with the heat made me sluggish and uninspired to do much exploring anyway, unless it was to a swimming hole or pool. But the frenetic pace of minding two small children hardly meant I was sitting around doing yoga poses and "manifesting" my happiness. Sometimes,

I needed the quiet, just quiet. As a law student, if I needed that peace, I listened to tapes of Gregorian chants—a lament for peace or piety. It was a form of meditation and focus on a discrete event. Minding two active little personalities for the better part of most days, I longed for any chance to briefly reach a meditative state of some sort.

What were mine and Paul's options for going out for an evening? We both preferred true live performances. We were in Texas now and within shouting distance of Mexico. I longed to see Mariachi bands or hear an honest to god great country singer, if such a thing existed in the new country world of women wearing jeans and boots just like the men. What I heard of new country was slicked up and didn't have any pain behind it. It didn't carry an interesting story, sound, or soulful narrative as the songs of the 1950s and 1960s had, the songs my mother listened to every day on the radio when we were kids. New country singers didn't have the hairdos either, so why bother. Sass without the soul.

We were thrilled when our realtor friend Janet told us the Jose Greco Dance Company was coming to Austin for a series of dates at the Capitol City Playhouse. Paul took a night off, and we ventured out to the venue. It was an intimate space in an old building downtown with low ceilings, highly buffed hardwood floors, and little physical distance between the performers and the audience. Neither of us had ever seen flamenco before. I knew almost nothing about it except the melodramatic stomping and staring going on in photographs I'd seen somewhere, sometime.

For the performance there were two guitarists, a handful of male and female dancers and singers, castanets, heels charging and pummeling the wooden floorboards in time with hand claps and call outs. So much odd syncopation and loud strikes to the floor. The audience was completely still, and you could hear the skid marks as the dancers lunged forward and back in their high heels. This was a live performance in a gypsy tradition of rhythms, call and response, bodies on the verge of touching and not quite. The whole theater of flamenco was in the story—equal partners face off, establish their ground. What a modern concept. Paul and I shouted, "Bravo!" at the end, satisfied by the action and the outfits, thrilled to hear and see world class performers who had nothing to do with our world of rock music.

After the new year arrived, Paul and I flew to Chicago with our children. It was close to Paul's birthday, February 8th. While we were gone, the house was empty, but the Houstons next door kept an eye on things. In the late afternoon on a school day, our neighbor Katherine took an urgent call from her son Samuel, who had come home from middle school for the day. He was alarmed to see a truck with a "bunch of guys on the Barkers' driveway" and they were moving something heavy around, from what he could tell from his bedroom window. Katherine left her teaching post at the school, drove her car up our street, turned at our side driveway, and went straight up, boxing in the unfamiliar truck. Katherine was unflappable. She stepped out of her car. "Can I ask what y'all are doing?" She directed the question to the guy who seemed to be in charge. As she moved in a little closer and he removed his hat, she recognized Al.

While we were out of town, Al had decided he would surprise Paul with a massively entertaining gift for his birthday, and he'd deliver it himself to the house. Al and the crew with him were attempting to unload a pinball machine onto the carport. Our carport was the only level spot in the back of the house when you reached the top of the drive. While unloading the pinball machine and negotiating the driveway, they dropped it. Paul's gift was now broken and upside down in the back of the truck. Al and his buddies were in the process of securing it in place before leaving again. Katherine, satisfied we weren't being robbed, retreated to her house and called me in Chicago. She thought she recognized the graphics on the machine. It might have been a Chicago sports team, but it was hard to tell. Chalk one up for "Uncle Al."

Al occasionally had such impulses to do something nice for Paul, but it was always surprising when it happened. More often it was his routine to take advantage of Paul's good guy nature, knowing Paul wasn't about to walk away from a project because Al was uninspired on a particular day or adamant about his percentages of songwriting credit on the records, even when this sometimes didn't match the reality of the work created. The pinball machine would have been a really generous gift had it panned out. But, for whatever reason, it was not meant to be.

Back home in Austin after our trip, Paul began what would be the equivalent of ten months on the road—the road between Al's compound in Horseshoe Bay and our house in West Lake Hills. One hundred miles round trip. At night, the drive was in near total darkness on the ranch roads. The first night Paul came home late from Al's he told me, "It's like Wild Kingdom out there," a reference to the old TV nature show that was a fixture of our childhoods. Deer, road runners, armadillos, raccoons, opossums, and the occasional mountain lion would haunt the roads back from Al's. There were rattle snakes all over Al's spread as it was.

Bill Rieflin flew in from Seattle to collaborate on songs for the new Ministry record and to lay drum tracks. I didn't see him at all. I was preoccupied with our new baby, while Bill stayed out at Al's place. This was the last time Bill would work with Al, the last time he would be a member of Ministry. Bill was only around for two weeks or so, long enough to work on the song "Reload" and two additional songs at the time untitled.

In preparation for his visit to Austin, Bill set his mind to asking Al for money from the advances coming in. Bill thought he was "late to the party" in realizing he should be getting paid for his studio time, apart from touring salary, and everything else. When the hoopla over all of us moving to Texas and buying property had died down, Bill felt left out of the loop. I never understood his financial arrangement with Al and Paul, assuming it was probably what he wanted. It made sense to me he might desire the autonomy and freedom to do other projects with other people because he was a world class drummer. I assumed he didn't want to be more involved in Ministry business. I was wrong. After arriving in Marble Falls, seeing Al a total of two times, and discovering Paul was running the show, Bill asked Al for $20,000 for a month in the studio.

Bill later told me he was appalled to see "guns and drugs" seemingly everywhere at Al's. I didn't know. Paul told me next to nothing about the working conditions, only that Al didn't want to do anything, and he (Paul) had to "make shit happen." Really? He could have left—we could have left Austin and done something else, couldn't we? Could we not? Did Paul ever even consider that an option? Ever since the massive success of Psalm 69, the Lollapalooza tour, and their own full-blown tour for the record, our finances were considerably better than either of us had ever imagined. But what price was worth daily aggravation? Al was wildly talented, unpredictable, and funny, but a control freak, from his marriage to Patty down to the work ethic at the studio. Now in Texas, making himself unavailable, hiding at home with everyone having to come to him, he was the one controlling the show, not Paul.

On paper, Bill wasn't technically a member of Ministry, only Al and Paul were. But he was half the rhythm section, a reliable font of new ideas for songs. He was a regular contributing songwriter for Ministry, the Revolting Cocks, and the other side projects, all of which had generated fans, fame, and world travels. Aside from the materialistic spoils, Bill was also Paul's oldest friend in the band. What was all that worth? Bill was adamant about being paid more for his time, but Al wouldn't budge. Bill told me Paul took it upon himself to negotiate on Bill's behalf with Al. Al still said no. Bill booked a flight back to Seattle, was paid for his two weeks studio time, and received credit for the songs he worked on when the album was finished. Al was surprised Bill gave him an ultimatum and that Bill in fact stuck to his word and quit the band. Al went around afterward telling everyone Bill was a "pussy" for leaving.

Bill told me he brought his cat with him from Seattle for what he assumed would be an extended period of time in the studio. During his relatively short stay out at Al's, his cat died. It was another red flag indicating it was time to leave. For his last official act as a member of Ministry, Bill refused to play on a cover version of Bob Dylan's "Lay Lady Lay." Bill told me he thought the song an "abomination" and he wouldn't be able to live with himself if he went through with it. Al was obsessed with the song. Paul hated it. I couldn't stand any version of it, and I had the horrible realization that this song represented everything Paul said Ministry would never do. This song was Ministry's BALLAD. Without Bill, the band went ahead and covered the song.

I wasn't privy to any of this at the time. I later told Bill I was sorry Paul kept me in the dark about so many Al matters. I was sad to see Bill go. He was a member of our extended family. He had spent many days at our apartment in

Chicago for rehearsals, recording, composing, and just visiting. And then—no more.

Although I wasn't privy to all of Ministry's internal politics at the time, I was watching the money. I kept track of Paul's travel itineraries and personal expenses for our accountant in Chicago. She was forever on the lookout for tax breaks, happy I had the patience to listen to the finer points of retirement accounts we were eligible for, and willing to discuss how much of our self-employment income should be sent to the government quarterly. Besides, I went to law school. I would be derelict in my duty as an officer of the court to ignore the tax laws, wouldn't I? Lawyers are required to take tax law in school. Theoretically, you learn the basics of the tax code so that you and your clients are keenly aware of legal ways to save money, and as a bonus, stay out of jail.

I filled in our accountant as best I could, physically standing in Paul's way at times to ask him for his current receipts. I liked to think of these accounting body checks as the real value of having a law degree I was technically no longer using. It was something I could focus on when I wasn't focusing on diapers, solo car trips with two small kids, and the constant oppressive heat.

Paul drove to Al's four days a week. He stayed overnight at least one of those days if they were in the middle of something or he was too exhausted to drive home. Often, they accomplished very little. "Al doesn't want to do anything," was a common complaint. "I'm just trying to make shit happen," was another. "I'm spinning my wheels with that guy." I had heard it all before, and frankly felt confident that between the two of them they would eventually come up with some brilliant new song ideas. I hoped.

When things were going well with Al, Paul's updates echoed back to his Pacific Northwest roots, his childhood growing up in Seattle, oddly resorting to seafaring imagery to describe what happened in the studio:

"I had to reel in Al today." Really. Must've been a monumental catch. Did you have to throw it back?

"I can barely get coffee down my gullet—in the middle of something right now." Aye, aye, and bye, matey.

I was becoming more familiar with our other neighbors who lived close by. The Cokers were the elderly couple to the immediate south of us. Mal Coker was retired military and his wife Mallie, a few years younger and still selling real estate for a living in Austin. She was tall, lean, and walked with her friend Helen every morning around the neighborhood. I immediately took to Mallie's quiet unimposing presence.

"Ever thought about joinin' a garden club?" she asked one morning, pausing her walk to come on our front driveway and be sociable. Mallie looked over the wild bushes and random aloe and cactus fanning out over the front greenspace that crudely hid most of our house from public view. I liked the mimosa tree the best, especially now when it hung heavy with delicate pink fans, blossoms peculiar to the species. I had my suspicions that our neighbors (aside from the Houstons) didn't quite know what to make of us and were politely fishing around for any indication of stability to present itself. No, I'd never thought about joining a garden club. (Did I look that old to her?) The idea of a garden club seemed such a relic of the past—a snip here, a snip there. Until you got on your knees in the early morning hours to pursue the weeds before the temperature outside would force you back into the cultivated interior of your suburban party house. Although technically speaking, we didn't live in the suburbs when I could see the UT Tower from my front deck and the walking path at Town Lake was a ten-minute drive from the house.

"No, I've never been a member of any clubs. I prefer things a little less manicured," I said.

Mallie Coker seemed satisfied with that and made a point of telling me the mountain laurel between our properties would be blooming shortly. I assured her I would make a mental note of this horticultural event. A month later, I stepped out onto the front driveway to pick up the newspaper, catching a distinct whiff of something which smelled like grape bubble gum. Walking further down toward the street, I could see patches of lavender colored blossoms emerging from the mountain laurel tree Mallie Coker had so deliberately directed my attention to. I was learning.

Mallie would offer to babysit at times when I needed to run a last minute errand. She enjoyed playing surrogate grandma to the kids. Mallie had no children of her own. She knew I was homebound with my two and was kind enough one day to phone me to say she came upon a pregnant armadillo in the shady ground cover along the fence between our yards. She thought the kids might be excited to have a look. They were. From our side, we studied the creature lumbering along, pacing and scraping the ground with her whiplike tail. The armadillo ignored us.

From Mallie I would learn which trees on the property were "trash trees" (Southern-speak for invasive and highly undesirable). Mallie was a religious woman who was quick to note that despite some in Westlake behaving as though they breathed rarified air up in these hills overlooking downtown Austin, our section of Westlake was in fact settled by "cedar choppers" clear cutting some trash trees to build up their homesteads. Mallie winked and smiled when she shared this neighborhood secret with me.

***

During spring planting season, streets in our neighborhood filled with dusty pickups hauling curious gardening implements and Spanish speaking landscaping crews. I drove to Home Depot with one infant carrier and one child booster seat securing my own constant companions. It was a field trip to buy flowers for the carport bed: silver leaf, coleus, marigolds. Marigolds were deer resistant. Deer didn't like the scent. The deer would eat just about anything else. My preference was for something more red or blue or both: wandering Jew. It was also deer resistant, having purple stems with pale pink buds crowning the tips looking everything like edible florets on a birthday cake.

Springtime was also a time for agricultural fires in Mexico. The residue clouded the surface of our sky with a faint copper hue. Not every year, but often enough to be reminded it was March or April or May. I told Paul I couldn't square in my head how this was still common practice in Mexico. It seemed so reckless.

"It's Mexico," he said, with all the understanding of someone who'd lived there briefly in the first years of his life and had a sense memory about the place.

***

In late February we heard from our old waiter friends from Chicago, Manuel and Guillermo, who at this time were living back in Ciudad Victoria in Mexico. It had been a year or so since Paul had seen either one of them. One of the last times he saw them in Chicago, they were in the studio at Chicago Trax having been pulled in on a whim to record background vocals for LARD, Paul and Al's side project with Jello Biafra. Paul and Al wanted some extra cheerleading behind Jello's vocals on the song "Pineapple Face." Manuel and Guillermo happened to be in the neighborhood. They were superfans and always up for a party at the studio. They couldn't say no.

Manuel and Guillermo were so generous and such genuinely nice people that when they called and asked if we wanted to visit them in Mexico, of course we couldn't refuse the invitation. Paul needed a studio break. He knew and I knew, if left unchecked, he and Al could spend weeks in the studio, scrap everything they'd done during that time, and do it all over again anyway. I still had no social network in Austin aside from Ministry personnel. Seeing some familiar faces from Chicago seemed like a good idea for both of us. So much of 1993 had been so loud with emotion, Mexico in comparison sounded serene. We made plans to drive from Austin with Ursula, who was now over a year old and walking. My sister stayed for a week at the house with Gordon, who was almost four months old.

Paul, Ursula, and I packed up the car (now a used 1985 Landcruiser with air conditioning) drove to the border at Brownsville, Texas and headed into the beautiful Mexican countryside on our way to Victoria. Ciudad Victoria sits at the foot of the Sierra Madre Oriental, a mountain range in northeastern Mexico. It was a ten-hour drive.

When we arrived at Manuel's place we were immediately greeted by various family members, with Ministry-fan friends stopping by later. The sparse, colorful, modest furnishings of the house had a familiar warmth. We ate fried eggs and tortillas Manuel cooked for us and eventually fell asleep completely spent from the drive.

After the nap, we headed into town, walking the cobblestoned side streets of Victoria with Manuel and Guillermo. It was all so new: the two-story, hundred-year-old stone buildings holding their own, jammed between newer, lighter steel constructs housing a government office, a café, a flower shop; hearing Spanish drifting in and out of range as we let Manuel steer us through the street vendors in a happy rhythm of familiarity with his hometown. Music drifted out from shopfronts, melodies we'd heard on Mexican radio and in restaurants in Chicago and now in Austin.

"Some of the music, the vocals sound so angry," I said to Manuel. "What's that all about?"

"It's a corrido. There are pretty much two kinds. Fighting songs and love songs," Manuel said laughing. "Same thing, huh?"

Ursula was excited to be somewhere new. She ran ahead of us and tripped, her tiny feet coming out from under her. Landing face down on the stones with a scraped chin, she deftly recovered her balance and kept going. Our daughter seemed determined to navigate on her own through these new old streets and fresh smells. There was a different history to this place. Perhaps she'll recall this time fondly, I told Paul. Perhaps she'll remember when she saw (for the first time) aging Spanish colonial style storefronts next to two-story ramshackle buildings painted in pastel shades, dogs running freely, and candy-colored dessert treats hand-painted on mobile carts going by. Along our route, older women we passed reached down to touch Ursula's fine golden curls. The women mouthed some sort of blessing as we continued on. They're so kind, I thought to myself.

Manuel and Guillermo of course wanted all the updates on Al and Ministry news. They regarded Ursula like uncles, empathizing with her over her scraped chin. We all laughed when I reminded them of the time I drove with them to Merrillville, Indiana in a snowstorm to see Ministry. Life is good here, they told us.

Guillermo suggested we take a drive out of town to visit the farmhouse of another friend, Miguel, who lived with his wife, an artist and writer. Their house and small farm lay at the end of a short climb into the foothills of the mountains nearby. We didn't need any convincing.

Miguel's house had no electricity. Miguel's wife Ariana appeared in the doorway greeting us as if we were old friends. She wore a long white cotton sheath, embroidered on the front bodice with shades of blue and purple stitching—colors of the night sky in this place. The stitches wove a lovely pedestal of color, bringing attention upward to her black hair and warm dark eyes. I complimented her on her dress. She wrote poetry. Paul and I adored the quiet natural environment and accepted our host's invitation to stay overnight to rest up for the remainder of our trip. Miguel strummed an acoustic guitar for us all and sang quietly. We discussed colors in the environment. And spirits. And ghosts. When it became too dark to see, we retreated indoors to candlelight and the coolness of the night.

I was fully humbled by the hospitality and strangeness of our hosts. It was a sharp contrast to the veneer of civility and entitlement I sensed in some of the people I interacted with on a daily basis in Austin. Everything on this hillside was so still, even the chickens outside were barely audible. As we were leaving and saying our goodbyes the next morning, Ariana went into the house, returning with a small folded bundle. It was the dress she had been wearing when we arrived. "Keep this as a reminder of where you've been," she told me, and handed me her gift.

The beautiful, mountainous landscape of Ciudad Victoria was a stunning contrast to apartment life in Chicago where I had last seen our two old friends. I could no longer picture Manuel and Guillermo being anywhere else but here. When we were newly married Manuel had given us a large abstract canvas he painted, awash with dark shades of maroon. I thought of that painting as we stood with our friends looking at the nighttime hills overlooking their city. Chicago had turned out to be too fast for them. Now, it seemed, it had become that way for us too.

***

On the drive back from Victoria, I told Paul I hoped I could feel at home in Austin as much as Manuel and Guillermo felt at home where they were now. Where was home? What did we need to be happy where we were?

Coming back into Austin, we passed Zilker Park, winding our way along Bee Cave Road, and the familiar St. John Neuman church where our son was baptized weeks before. As we drove up to the house, Paul and I were once again discussing what to do—if anything—with the front landscaping. It was now a mishmash of cactus paddles drying in the sun, aging aloe spires, Spanish daggers, rocky ground, rough tangles of invasive vines and groundcover, all left to wither untended for the most part during the long year of neglect once the previous owners moved away.

"Pampas grass would look fantastic right there," Paul said. It was his usual associative daydream to have a curtain of pampas grass in place to distract the eye. It was a wonderful idea. I knew it would be up to me to see it got planted sometime by someone. It was a big job, not something I could do on my own. I wondered if Paul made these brilliant suggestions to humor me, as if he really cared how the yard looked, as if he could contextualize how it felt to be in my shoes. He was consumed with what went on at Al's, leaving little time to indulge me or my landscaping projects and ideas. Pampas grass was exotic. It was something to keep me entertained and hoping for the future. I wondered if Paul was planting a seed with the hope that I wouldn't develop a serious desire to run away from home.

Lured by the novelty of our relocation to Texas, Jim Nash and Dannie Flesher flew into Austin for a visit. It was a welcome surprise. Wax Trax had filed for bankruptcy the year before, and I didn't expect the two of them to come to town for the SXSW music festival for any reason. As far as I could tell, they were in for a quick visit to see Al's place and ours.

Jim was diagnosed with AIDS the year before. I knew he was managing his health with the latest drug cocktails and undergoing some other treatments; although, what exactly was a little vague to me. He and Dannie both looked the same as they had the last time I'd seen them in Chicago before we moved. But as they walked through the front sliding doors on our deck, I could sense something was different about Jim. He carried himself in an almost self-conscious way. The Jim I knew had never appeared so stiff.

"I've got this thing under my shirt," he said, gesturing at his chest. I didn't want a peek, guessing he was wearing some kind of monitoring device to regulate his medications.

The two of them stood next to each other in the dining room as if waiting for their personal tour of the house to begin, and I leaned against our built-in credenza. It was the one design flaw in the house. The credenza was stained an antiqued cream color. The two-inch-thick balusters anchored to the back reached up to the ceiling and formed a semi-transparent wall between the dining room and the kitchen. The balusters were carved in what could only be called a "Western" motif. I could see Jim and Dannie's mental gears race past my shoulder to take in the full breadth of this one room and its contents.

"Gerda, isn't it time to take an ax to those saloon poles you're hiding?" Jim asked.

Nope. Not even a life-threatening illness could dampen that wit. Thank GOD. "Welcome to Texas, Jim."

From that moment, I knew he and Dannie were already immersed in redesigning the entire 3,500 square feet of our house and imagining the parties we could have with "That sunken living room!" maybe even turn it into a pool— for a day. I reached my arms out to both of them and wanted to squeeze them tighter than humanly possible.

"Going out to see Al's divine digs?" I asked (I was hoping the place was sanitized).

I wanted to assure them that yes, we would have to find an eight- or nine-foot-long sofa to balance the open space of "that sunken living room." Anything smaller would look like an abandoned settee lost in a lush forest of green wall-to-wall carpeting that flowed evenly over the steps going down.

Jim either mentioned it or I was hearing the words in my head now— "Princess Tinymeat." It must have been in my head, just another memory of just another band name he and I would say out loud for the sheer obliteration of rational thoughts invading an otherwise wildly entertaining day at Wax Trax. For the present moment, I wasn't even listening anymore, just watching these two fall back into place in my internal home movie.

I grabbed the Polaroid camera already put aside for their visit. I asked them each to pose for our "Wall of Shame" gallery—for the future. Paul and I decided when we moved in we would document every single person entering our house for the first time. It didn't matter if it was the UPS man or Sean Yseult from White Zombie. We asked, and usually got a shot in front of the white fieldstone wall in the living room. Our Wall of Shame.

It didn't cross my mind even once in the short hour or two Jim and Dannie sat at our dining room table or wandered the length of the house with their running commentary, that this would be the very last time I would see either one of them in person. They were always going to be my older gay brothers no matter how far away. Together. They were family.

"Smile, Dannie!"

And . . . SNAP.

Seeing the faces of friends up close, friends who visited for SXSW, was more vital to my emotional health than actually going to any staged events at the indoor and outdoor venues. It was even more fun when friends came to visit for no particular reason at all. After Jim and Dannie left, I didn't have the sense that this was somehow a farewell tour for Jim; although shortly after their visit his health deteriorated at a breathtaking pace.

***

In my legal world back in Chicago, it was easy to ignore annual large-scale events like Lollapalooza (at the time, staged in the suburbs) unless we knew someone performing or working the shows. In Austin, the annual SXSW music festival was one of the city's biggest draws for tourist bodies and tourist dollars. Streets downtown would jam with more traffic, endless taxis, rental cars, and music industry types on foot, all looking for the authentic "Live Music Capital of the World" experience, whatever that was. For the locals, now including us, it was mostly an annoying invasion.

A few miles from downtown, our favorite cheap taco dive, The Tamale House, would have a longer line out the door of the un-air-conditioned storefront next to a meat market along a strip of Airport Boulevard. It was one of our favorite places to stop for bean-and-cheese tacos before or after visiting Fiesta, the big Mexican grocery that claimed to be international in its selection of goods, but beyond a few shelves devoted to Dundee's Orange Marmalade and German pudding mixes, there was no mistaking the focus was on love for all things Mexican. There were the occasional Mariachi band in-store serenades, beneath an overhead jungle vine of strung pinatas and red, white, and green flags, and the house tortilla machine ejecting fresh tortillas into the hands of waiting bakers ready to stack and bag the piles with calm, consistent love for all things masa and for what they were doing. Fiesta was the place to go if you needed an authentic hand-painted ceramic piggy bank or devotional theme candles contemplating a spectrum of human wants and needs, ranging from the Virgin of Guadalupe, to more control over your man, or my personal favorite, "Law Stay Away" candle, depicting a beat cop menacing the holder with billy club in hand. Paul and I would see SXSW attendees —the ones in the know—wandering the aisles of Fiesta with their badges and bracelets (and eventually, phones) munching hot corn tortillas and house-made ceviche from the portable cart strategically positioned in front as you walked into the store. Paul would indulge himself with a ceviche cup brimming with chunks of fresh avocado and a lime wedge. Sublime. This was the authentic Austin experience for us, away from the bars on Sixth Street and the tourists filing through the State Capitol building or "Baby Acapulco" or any other number of margarita havens along Barton Springs Road.

One touristy place we did visit annually for a few years was Chuy's on that same strip of Barton Springs Road. We would surrender to the Tex Mex gods on my birthday, January 8th, the day that is also celebrated annually by fans of David Bowie and the King himself, Elvis. Every year Chuy's held an Elvis birthday celebration with Elvis impersonators serenading diners at their tables. And if you dressed up as Elvis or Priscilla, his wife, dinner was on the house. I once asked why my enchiladas weren't free just for sharing the same birthday with his Highness and all, but got a shrug and an extra bowl of chips for my trouble. We did dress Gordon once as the blue jean hillbilly Elvis sporting a slicked pompadour and eyebrow penciled-in sideburns. He was seven. His dinner was free.

Leila Eminson was in town for the SXSW festival this year, in her new role as an A&R rep for Warner Bros. Leila had split from her husband Martin Atkins since the last time I saw her in Chicago at the previous year's Lollapalooza fest. Leila was scouting bands in Austin, and Warners booked her a room at the Four Seasons downtown by the lake. Finally, I had a chance to see one of my old girlfriends. I told Ursula, she, Gordon, and I were going to pick up a friend who was in town working, and we were going out for lunch. I reminded Ursula that Leila stayed with me in Chicago right before Ursula was born.

I strapped the kids into their car seats and drove our Land Cruiser to the hotel. We pulled into the turnaround at the valet station, and one of the valets rushed over to my door.

"Just picking up," I told him. Behind him was Leila, ready to go.

Ursula stretched herself up and almost out of her car seat as she eyed the hotel guests milling around with their lanyards and bracelets, exotic indicators setting them apart from the valets and limo drivers waiting.

"Does Leila live here?" she asked, astonished by all the activity on the sidewalk and the fancy cars lining up.

"She does for now," I said, thinking this was simple enough information to impart upon the curious intellect of my almost two-year-old child.

"Wow!" Ursula was impressed.

Lunch with Leila was my opportunity to catch up with what was happening in the real world outside of Austin and Leila's recent past world of marital infidelity—her husband's. Leila was my personal reference library of encyclopedic facts on everyone and everything we cared about in the current pop music scene and some things we didn't care about at all. Leila made friends and connections quicker than anyone else I knew. She retained vast amounts of useful and useless gossip at the same time. Leila was a perfect fit for the requirements of A&R: a lot of chatter to keep the artists busy and tangentially aware that publicity and being seen was a big part of the business of music. Leila was a pro, having managed her and her husband's label, Invisible Records, and his music projects and career. She was a talker.

After our lunch and in the coming weeks and months, each time I'd have the kids with me on the way to Fiesta on the east side of town, we would drive along Town Lake past the anchoring hotel on the strip, the Four Seasons. "There's Leila's hotel, Mama," Ursula would proudly announce, pointing to the building. Another SXSW the following March, another visit from Leila and another stay at "Leila's Hotel," and Ursula was convinced Leila now, in fact, owned the place.

I thought about Leila, and our other friends in the music business who were married. I didn't think often of Patty and Al's marriage, although almost immediately after we'd all moved to Austin, I began hearing rumors that Al and Patty were getting divorced. Separating and getting back together seemed a hobby of theirs by now, and I didn't believe anything could have changed so dramatically between the two of them to warrant splitting up for good. Al depended on Patty for everything. Unless he had someone else to take care of him, the rumors could stay where they were.

As the months went on, I learned that the rumors were true. What may have prompted Al's decision to go ahead with a divorce was the fact that the state of Texas was the only state in the country that did not allow for alimony (or spousal support) in divorce cases. Whatever property and assets a couple had, that was split up at the end. Child support was mandatory, just like anywhere else. But unbelievably, spousal maintenance was not.

I later learned from Patty that as the divorce case continued, the court directed Al to settle his and Patty's debts. According to Patty, Al never did. Patty thought Al's filing for divorce was "a bunch of bullshit," and she didn't bother contesting it. The divorce was final in April of 1994. Three months passed, and to no one's surprise, they were back together—again. This codependency cycle of breaking up and reuniting as partners would spin their lives around for the next ten years. I found it a little disconcerting that Al's marriage was over less than a year after our arrival in Texas. What next?

Somehow I had found time for freelance work in between packing to move and actually settling into our new house. The German band KMFDM hired me to handle some legal business for them. KMFDM were on the Wax Trax label. They toured with Ministry in 1989, and we were friends, and I had fun conversations with their singer Sascha in my spaghetti German. I was woefully out of practice, not having any regular conversations with anyone. My mother and I had always spoken in our own patois of English, German, and Polish. Paul and I would mutter a phrase in German to each other just for fun: "Mach kein Quatsch" (don't do anything stupid). On rare occasions, I would think an expression was German, when it was really a common phrase in Polish and vice versa.

En Esch, the drummer in KMFDM, was in Austin in the summer of 1994, either on tour or visiting from his nearby home in New Orleans. Al was having a pool party to celebrate the new studio at his place, and En Esch was going but needed a place to stay. Paul and I invited him to spend the night at our house in Austin before heading out to Al's. En Esch was traveling with a woman named Isis, and they were grateful to take over an unused kids' bedroom for a night. When we had musician friends stay with us in Austin (as in Chicago) I did my best to be a gracious host, whether I personally knew them or not prior to their stay.

I rolled out of bed in the morning and headed down the long hallway to the other side of the house to make coffee for myself and anyone else interested. My thoughts wandered, thinking of slipping into the kitchen, and seeing again the new Elvis clock someone had given us as a gift hanging there on the side of the wet bar. Projecting out from the clock's face was the figure of Elvis in a rockabilly suit. His legs swung back and forth like a metronome—tick . . . tock. Elvis kept time in my daily life as I tried to ease into the sense of these Tex-Mex days in this Texas town called Austin. When you rounded the corner into the kitchen, Elvis' legs would swing back and forth and salute you with their jaunty "good morning" dance.

As I turned the corner into the cave-like ambience of our vintage kitchen, I heard a deep voice call out, "HA-LOWWW." I looked over to see a tall, bare chested, thin figure bent over the breakfast bar smoking a cigarette between his thumb and forefinger—Eurostyle. He was barefoot, wearing nothing but a tiny, olive-colored miniskirt. His skirt matched the kitchen cabinets.

"Guten Morgen, En Esch," I responded. He was just another morning coffee companion in the revolving cast of curiosity seekers passing through the Barker depot on their road travels through Austin. I complimented En Esch on his breakfast attire. I was beginning to look forward to going out to Al's for once without an ill feeling of dread. I was looking forward to hearing Don Walser, the Hillbilly Yodeler, and his band who were hired to play for the pool party.

I got the kids dressed and ready for the hour-long car ride to Al's. When we arrived, Paul seemed ready to relax for a day, swim in the pool, and play in the water with Ursula for a change from his daily routine in the studio. I watched from the pool's edge, holding Gordon in my arm, and from under the brim of my straw sunhat, viewed the stream of guests arriving. There was Adam Grossman from Skrew, with his wife Leslie (someone I adored). Mike Scaccia and his girlfriend Stephanie sat poolside. They finally had rooms to stay in at Al's place. For the life of me I couldn't figure out what Stephanie actually did for a living, but she made Mikey happy. Patty and daughter Adrienne made brief appearances and disappeared into the main house.

Don Walser played his brand of Texas swing, all the while sitting on a folding chair with his band surrounding him off to the side of the pool. He had the contented portly posture of a man accustomed to playing Big Daddy to a group of his grandkids. He was twice anyone else's age judging from the audience gathered around. His singing style reminded me of scratchy recordings I'd heard on the radio as a child in Chicago. My mother would be in the kitchen stirring something and listening to WJJD, trying to sing along with the English words in the country songs. I wasn't sure she even knew what the lyrics meant.

I thought of Al off somewhere in the main house, giving a tour to a guest to show off the "tastefully" themed bedrooms there, trophies symbolic of the previous owners' peculiar fetishes. I felt inclined to accept a cold Tecate beer from someone wearing a bikini and kindly offering me one as they walked by at the pool. Maybe the homey country vibe brought out a feeling of being part of one big family out here, for one day, with live music underscoring the sweltering heat. Yes, maybe it was Don Walser's voice. He was exceptional and would later become the opening act for the Butthole Surfers when they toured again.

Back at our place, and before En Esch and Isis left for wherever their cab was taking them, I had him pose for a picture against the fieldstone wall in our living room. En Esch obliged, appropriately adopting an S&M inspired gesture with his mouth open, a metal ball-bearing the size of a quarter balancing on his tongue. Gorgeous. Another score for the Wall of Shame.

23

While Paul and Al and the rest of the current Ministry lineup were in the throes of hammering out a new record, Crazed Management was approached with a request for Ministry to perform at Neil Young's annual Bridge School Benefit. The Bridge School Benefit was an acoustic, weekend long event in October, organized on behalf of its namesake, a school for children with severe speech and physical impairments. Neil Young's son was born with physical challenges and was the inspiration for the annual benefit show. Neil Young handpicked each year's lineup. Ministry's live show at the Paramount in Madison Square Garden in December of 1992 had apparently left a fond impression upon Mr. Young. I was thrilled for Paul and for Al. Thank god you have good management to nail down these things, I told Paul. The band needed this, especially at a time when they had nothing current to sell and no tours scheduled. It was good PR.

There was no question I was coming along for the trip. It was sure to be a weekend of freestyle performing and backslapping, and I was ready to leave my sister with the task of mothering our one- and two-year-old for a few days. I hardly had any time for myself. If I could shave my legs in peace, it was a holiday. Paul and I rarely had time alone together. Our family schedule was no schedule at all. Paul's rehearsing, recording, Al's seemingly daily crises, all kept Paul preoccupied and away from home for increasingly longer stretches of time. A once in a career opportunity to hang out with Neil Young for a good cause and have some personal private time was a blessing. There was much gratitude—in our house, anyway.

For the October 1994 lineup, Ministry would share the bill with Neil Young and Crazy Horse, Pearl Jam, Mazzy Star, Indigo Girls, Pete Droge, and Tom Petty. I was excited to go, to be able to wear some other clothes in public, besides my Austin standard—black walking shorts and T-shirts. The newly divorced Patty Jourgensen was coming in with Al, to no one's surprise.

After we settled into our hotel in Mountain View, California, we were picked up by limos and taken to the Shoreline Amphitheater. I was wearing a silver-gray pleated mini skirt, dark olive-green cropped short-sleeved top and olive-green lace up boots I'd bought on one of our trips back to Chicago. Jon and Marsha Zazula, Ministry's managers, were backstage when we arrived.

"What happened?! I've never seen you dressed in a hot outfit before," Marsha said with a big smile. I liked those two. They knew their business. Having shepherded Metallica's rise, the Zazulas were bulldogs about what they liked and didn't like. I was glad to see some familiar faces.

"Expect a crowd in Ministry's dressing room. People want to follow the freakshow . . . they're bored with their own friends," I heard a voice saying behind me. Our good friend Greg Werkman from Alternative Tentacles was in for the show and as always knew the right thing to say while Ministry's trailer was filling up with members of the other bands on the bill.

I sat there taking in the backstage scene, when Eddie Vedder from Pearl Jam walked up and introduced himself. He was with another band member and in unison they both said, "Ursula Barker, born 8:32 p.m., August 26, 1992, 7 lbs. 13 oz." I dropped my straw and stood there with my mouth open, surprised that anyone knew those statistics. Eddie reminded me that at 1992's Lollapalooza festival the news of our daughter's arrival was flashed onto electronic signs all over the festival grounds. I thought to myself, wow—these guys are alright. I wasn't a fan of Pearl Jam's music. Neither was Paul. In the interviews Paul had done for Lollapalooza, whenever a question came up about Pearl Jam, he would respond saying, "They're really nice guys." He wasn't lying, but it was a clever way to avoid offering an opinion about their musical output.

"Yeah, Paul thinks we're 'really nice guys,'" Eddie said, as if reading my thoughts. I almost spit out my drink. He had seen right through Paul's artful deflection and appeared to brush it away. It was telling, revealing a self-awareness that I found admirable. It was still surprising that Eddie remembered such nuances from touring. Lollapalooza must have left an abiding impression upon everyone there (and like me, not there).

"Do you have any pictures of your kids?" Eddie asked. I had a few recent photos in my bag.

"Hey, this looks like a fort my mom made when I was that age," he said, holding up a picture of Ursula doing a limbo run through an A-line tunnel she and I built with upholstered window-seat cushions. I bought the vintage rose-patterned cushions at an estate sale upstairs at Marshall Fields in Chicago. The State Street store had part of an upper floor designated for what I assumed were custom returns from wealthy patrons. Those cushions saved my sanity during many nerve-racking afternoons at home.

Eddie looked around the room, spotted Al, leaned over and asked, "What is up with that guy?" He asked me if Al was still using. He asked me about Patty, and if she was using too. I didn't know what to say. I knew to avoid saying too much to anyone about Al in the gossipy world of pop music. But everyone knew anyway. Al blabbed about his drug use in interview after interview. So, I let go and said, "Yeah, Patty parties with him. I don't know what they're up to. Who knows?" I was tired of explaining Al's daredevil exploits but felt comfortable divulging that bit of the obvious.

Paul walked over, and he and Eddie had a moment. While they were talking, I saw Eddie was holding a piece of notebook paper. He was carrying around the lyrics to "Lay Lady Lay," the Bob Dylan song. It was one of the covers Ministry was performing for the benefit. It was also the song Eddie agreed to do vocals on for Ministry's set.

I asked Eddie if I could take a photo of him with Paul, and he seemed happy to break for a candid shot. I tried a few angles, going in and going wide, but the framing was off. Eddie was about my height, five foot four. Paul, six four. Paul grabbed a catering box for Eddie to stand on, and I snapped a few photos.

I wondered how Al was dealing with Neil Young and some of the other stars in for the event. I wondered if he was being his usual showboating self. Often backstage I'd see him flapping his hands and dancing on his tip toes doing a kind of nelly gay routine, which I found mildly amusing—in an I Love Lucy kind of way. Maybe he was more Cuban than I thought.

I don't know exactly at what point Al started doing impersonations of handicapped kids backstage in the band's trailer. Maybe he thought he was being funny. It wasn't funny to me. Al—always having to be the center of attention. Christ. We were guests at this fundraiser. Al just didn't seem to care who he insulted anymore. Fortunately, none of the benefit's organizers caught his act. It seemed yet another event we were invited to where Al seemed too full of himself to want to connect with anyone else there. I guessed he felt threatened by the withering, slanted smiles staring up at him from wheelchairs at the side of the stage. "Stupid ass" was all I could think watching him.

Ministry was put up at a small hotel near the venue, miles away from Neil Young's place. We were invited to Neil and Pegi Young's house in the hills for a big barbecue one night of our stay. Cars were lined up outside our little hotel, ready to pick up and deliver the performing musicians and crew, up through the winding roads into the hills. Al didn't seem ready to go anywhere. He stayed in his room, doing whatever Al "thing" was on for the day. It was the whole day. The rest of us—me, Paul, Greg Werkman, and other Ministry friends and band members were left to wait. And wait. Finally, I couldn't take all the waiting around for Al. I didn't care anymore if Al wanted to be a primadonna, make an entrance late, or "whatever the fuck" was his problem. I told Paul, "Let's go. The driver's been out there for hours. It's really rude for us not to show up." Mike Scaccia liked my plan better than hanging out at the hotel another hour. We piled into one of the waiting limos and headed for those hills. It was a beautiful, long drive up to Neil Young's house, up an endlessly curving road that was wooded, narrow, and lush. We passed a little hippy grocery store, the only business on the road.

I had forgotten the feeling of being in a limousine, gliding along on your own private airstream almost, on a separate track from the rest of traffic. The sensation was similar to riding on a train, with the forward thrust into the hills, propelling ahead silently. I stared out the window, wondering what would be next for us. Meet some more legends. What could be more glamorous than that? If you cared about celebrity—which I didn't—this was glorious. But that wasn't what I was feeling at all. I was feeling displacement. Why were we here? It was for a good cause. We might never see any of these people again. Enjoy it while it lasts. What was Al thinking not wanting to celebrate with everyone?

"What is up with that guy?" Eddie Vedder had asked. I didn't know. It wasn't my decision to stay back at the hotel. I was happy to be away from there, exploring the view along the route from there to where the party was going on—to be in the moment in some way, since I was never going to be in the moment on a stage performing with my husband. This trip into the hills was so much better than lingering backstage in a dressing room before and after a show. It was personal, like what Jim and Dannie at Wax Trax managed to pull off with their pre-show parties for artists they invited to Chicago. It was intimate, a place where everyone could be themselves, not "on" for the press or an audience. I suppose Al needed that constant audience and didn't really want anyone to know him on a different level. Or, he just wanted to get loaded and watch TV in a hotel room. That was an option, too.

We were nearing the top of our ascent on this hilly road, and another limo came around a turn going in the opposite direction. As it descended, the driver in the other car slowed to pass us. A car window rolled down. It was the guys in Pearl Jam. "Go on up. It's all cool. Have some drinks. Hang out, man!" They were on their way into town to do something else. They told us they were staying up at Neil Young's house. It was an awkward revelation.

It was one of those rare moments when I actually wanted Al's company, to leave it up to him to crash the party. Our car climbed a little bit higher and stopped at some gates. We could see what appeared to be a twenty-foot-high tepee planted firmly on the acres and acres of "lawn" in front of the main house on the property. Maybe the tepee was a present to Neil Young's kid. Maybe it was a place to meditate. Maybe, just maybe, we should have come earlier. Muted lights were turning on inside the residence, and whoever was left outside for this soirée appeared to be heading in. I felt like a tourist gawking at that tepee.

It was dark and late in the evening. Mike Scaccia looked at us. "I don't know if it's right to go in now, man." The consensus in the car was, it wasn't. Our driver asked again if we were ready to go through the gates. Paul looked at me, then motioned to the driver to turn around and go back.

"All hail Ministry—or something." Mikey. A true gentleman from Texas, under all that hair and hangover after partying with Al all day. Sometimes, you just have to do what feels right. Do the right thing for your own peace of mind. I thought of that time we had all gone out to the suburbs to meet Metallica. The music was off that night, or so it seemed, and we left shortly after we'd arrived. We left then, and we were retreating now for different reasons. Save your dignity.

It was a lovely, quiet drive back to the hotel. I couldn't imagine what the others were thinking, but there was some satisfaction in having gone out at all and having at least seen Neil Young's spread and taken a beautiful drive up into the hills. We could all get a decent night's sleep.

The performances for the benefit were set during daylight hours. Neil Young looked to be having a great time nodding his head up and down to the music during Ministry's set. It was the first time I'd seen him smile, standing there side-stage and glancing over at the audience once or twice. For someone possessing his talent and catalogue, with a lengthy career to rival anyone's, he still had genuine enthusiasm for newer acts.

Before Ministry went on, there wasn't the usual sanctity of the dressing room at pre-show warm up—"Everybody out except the band." The atmosphere was much looser and friendlier, considering the short set times and little time to rehearse. I spoke with Pegi Young about getting some Bridge School swag for my kids. I met Tom Petty and silently wondered how many more famous musicians were my height or shorter. Paul seemed an anomaly with only Gibby Haynes from the Butthole Surfers, among his peers, anywhere near his height. While Ministry played, I caught up with Greg Werkman on what Jello Biafra was doing these days. Always the same response, "Biafra's a freak . . . and what else is new?"

When it was all over, I returned to Ministry's trailer only to find Al telling everyone he needed to head back to Austin right away. I asked Paul if anyone had said goodbye to Neil and his wife. No one had. I left the band's trailer and headed for our host's dressing room. I knocked and was greeted by Pegi. "I just wanted to say goodbye and thank you for inviting us this time," I said, and shook hands with her and with her husband. "Ministry's getting ready to head out."

I walked back to Paul and everyone else. Neil and Pegi came by the Ministry trailer a few minutes later. Neil shook hands with Al and Paul and thanked them for their service to the cause.

We were off again. I didn't want to steal away from this event without graciously acknowledging our host. I wondered if Al just felt intimidated or really didn't care at all about the whole scene.

***

My sister and I were getting out more with the kids, but oftentimes I would be alone with them. We went to Deep Eddy, an outdoor spring-fed concrete wading pool with a large shallow section perfect for parents with very small kids. Deep Eddy was built in the 1920s as a public pool. In the '20s the slides were higher, the bathing suits covered more skin, but the egalitarian approach of the place remained. We packed homemade snacks and ample water and staked out our spot on the concrete stadium benches near the deep end reserved for lap swimming. We could watch octogenarian lap swimmers peacefully go through their strokes as if time itself were standing still and waiting for them to finish. Paul would tag along occasionally, when he wasn't busy working at Al's or chasing down the solution to one of the band's daily dramas—typically, Al's dramas. The problems often involved money (borrowing ours) or talking to a label or promotions person because no one could talk to Al.

After our first visit to Deep Eddy, Paul thought we should try Thundercloud Subs across the street just to go somewhere new, but when we got there, there was no parking. We drove instead to its sister establishment a couple of miles away in somewhat tonier Westlake, where we lived. Thundercloud was a local chain in Austin, and we were all for supporting local businesses.

We walked in as a group—me, my sister, the kids, and Paul. No sooner had one of the sandwich makers recognized Paul, then a flurry of a half dozen tattooed arms went up behind the counter as if it were some sort of trading floor on the stock exchange. In this case, the traders were flashing a collective "metal" salute. No head banging involved. They all looked so serious and respectful. I thought it was charming.

Paul looked away, I suppose embarrassed and flattered. We sat down and waited for our sandwiches. From that day onward, I caught the knowing eye of the store's manager, a stocky Hispanic man heavily tattooed like the rest of Austin's under-thirty population. He'd give a nod and a cool smile when I came in with my kids. It was funny to speculate, "How do these guys know who Paul is?" We could thank Lollapalooza and MTV a little bit, for bringing Beavis and Butthead (with direct references to Ministry) into the living rooms of thousands of fans around the world.

Paul was usually busy out at Al's place, an hour's drive away. My sister would come by and help me with the kids as I was beginning a routine of walking in the mornings before the day heated up. I rediscovered the four-mile hike and bike trail that looped around Town Lake and Barton Springs near downtown Austin. I walked alone on the trail some mornings. On other days, my sister and I put both kids in a double stroller and headed to the lake. Janet Gilles, the real estate agent who'd sold us our house, would sometimes join me on the path. She was a longtime resident of Austin, having stayed in town after college at UT in her hippy protest days. Janet was from Odessa in west Texas, an entirely different cowboy mentality from the liberal urban vibe of Austin. Janet was a walking bundle of contradictions, but never confused about being a hardcore Democrat. I could listen to Janet's stories about local politics for hours. She told me once she'd spent an entire Saturday at a Democratic fundraiser, and in a lull sat down to read a biography of George W. Bush. She suddenly heard a familiar voice and looked up to see the enormously coiffed Governor Ann Richards smiling down at her, who then asked, "Why on EARTH are you readin' about that MO-RON?"

Walking around the path at Town Lake became my salvation on days when nothing seemed to get done managing two toddlers, a new house, and the day to day business and career decisions of my husband. I needed the walk. No more city sights to dissect into discrete snapshots as I walked by. I could focus instead on the water at the lake, like a Japanese gardener overseeing a koi pond. Occasionally, hundreds of cormorants filled the trees at the shoreline, looking out onto the water like decoys in rows waiting for a signal from their leader to drop down and get on with the day. I kept an eye out for the rare black swans who appeared some years on the lake, mere silhouettes, cutouts, shadows floating near the downtown hotels, appealing in their novelty. The black swans, close to extinction of their kind, paddled quietly beneath the water, hovering close to their silver-gray babies. Three signets nestled atop their mother's back, then two, then only one. The black swans were exotic, so much so, people and natural predators kidnapped them and the babies. Our realtor Janet could name all of the birds and knew all of their stories, too.

I walked often enough to sometimes surprise the shy nutria building small dams at the stream heads feeding into the lake. It was peaceful on the path. Once Paul and I were walking together when we came eye level with a bull snake. A low hanging branch, thinner than its own body, had sagged under the beast's weight. "They're harmless," our friend Janet said, when I told her about it later. I didn't believe something the size of a commercial fire hose could be considered harmless, but I took her word for it. With other Texas snakes, their markings told you whether you would live or die upon confrontation. We learned the common rhyme: "Red and black, friend of Jack. Red and yellow kills a fellow."

When he was home and awake, Paul joined me on my early morning walks. We'd park under the bridge at Austin High School and begin on the shadier side of the lake. A short distance in, we passed the rowing dock with groups of two and three rowers in orange life vests, holding their oars rigidly upright on the shore next to them. In the hotter months, we would sometimes round a curve and the path ahead was transformed into a sandy brown swath as groups of runners kicked up dust passing us by.

To amuse myself, I kept a watchful eye out for celebrities and celebrity lookalikes running or walking the path at the same time I took my walks. With Paul, the two of us had our first encounter with "The Poet" and "Anthony Perkins." The Poet earned his title through trial and error and brilliant styling on his part.

"Check it out, somebody's wearing green-apple oil," I nudged Paul and there was no mistaking the source of fruity essence permeating the air when this young man approached.

"You're right. He must've cleaned out the new/old '60s stock from some UT headshop."

The pervasive apple orchard effect would grow more intense the closer he came. It was fake, like a Jolly Rancher hard candy. We could only wonder what was behind The Poet's quizzical smile as he locked eyes with us and walked by, swinging his arms slowly, rhythmically. The Poet was a petite man, my height. His arms swung in a way and hung in a way it was easy for anyone paying attention to notice the arms were slightly longer than normal body proportions would allow. They were the arms of a sasquatch—not the classically large beast, but a stunted version. Perhaps his stature fueled his creativity.

"What do you suppose he's working on?" Paul asked me.

"New collection. 'Meditation Upon Medieval Fruits.'"

Further down the path "Anthony Perkins" or "Tony" was a near DNA match to the actor, only taller, ganglier, a gray-haired version of his "Psycho" persona. He often ran with two or three women—always women—who we were convinced were his proteges. He may have had some kind of stroke prior to his fiftieth birthday, which left him permanently listing to the left at a seventy-five degree angle as he ran. He didn't appear to be enjoying the run. Ever. Running looked like work for him. We wondered if when he stopped he was able to stand upright or had that lean curved his spine into a permanent eavesdropping stance: "Whaddya' say?"

Not to be outdone in our personal Parade of Horribles (and limping for added effect) came The Professor. His face was bifurcated, one half seemingly disfigured in a chemistry lab explosion at the university. His "normal" half appeared as a stern-faced middle-aged man with cropped, dark curly hair sculpted by professionals to accentuate his stony gaze and deeply set Mediterranean eyes that looked ahead—always ahead, as a precaution. His out of kilter half bore a vertical wine stain beginning at the hairline and spilling down over his eyebrow and lid, covering the cheek and over the bone, ending at his chin in a half veil. The Professor wore old athletic shorts made for a much younger body and tennis shoes that looked as though they had seen action on a tennis court. The shoes were not equipped with a cushioned sole or raised platform arch for running or even walking. His gait was awkward, a propulsion forward in a series of fitful half steps as if to avoid invisible lines on the path. He looked to us as a gentle monster. At the end of the day, the characters on the morning walk were not really horrible. They were more Pee Wee's Playhouse than anything else. I was introducing Pee Wee and company to our kids around this time, when they were also becoming enamored with Wishbone, the theatrical Jack Russell terrier who had his own show on PBS.

It was during the summer, on a day when Paul was taking a break from driving out to Al's. He and I had walked on the path and were home cooling off. Someone had sent Paul a copy of Nine Inch Nails' new record Closer—perhaps Trent himself or Danny Lohner, newly hired to play guitar on tour with the band. Paul was lying on our bed with headphones on and his eyes closed. I was trying to relax in these few minutes of silence with the kids out of the room. Paul sat straight up and pulled the headphones away from his ears.

"GOD . . . DAMN . . . he did it." He was smiling, looking almost envious. "What a great song. Good for him." The great song Paul was gushing about was the title track with its infamous lyrics of longing for bestial-like sex with a partner. I had heard the track weeks before. I agreed. It was a great song. In light of all the tedious hours in the studio with Al, Paul had the grace to acknowledge someone else had achieved something he himself longed for intimately. It was one of those moments when I loved Paul so much for being who he was—human and capable of humility.

The stream of Chicago people flowing into Austin to visit or to work with Paul and Al seemed endless. Sean Joyce had just come off of working tours with

Pegboy and another band and came to Austin for the month of December. He was
in to help with Ministry preproduction for the Big Day Out festival in Australia
at the start of the new year. Ministry was also scheduled for a one-off show in
Austin at Liberty Lunch two weeks before Christmas, and Sean was helping with
that show, too.

Sean planned to stay out at Al's in Marble Falls for the month. Unknown
to me during those first weeks, Sean was seeing an acceleration in Al's erratic
moods and in his drug use. Sean finally decided this would be the last time
he was willing to work with Al in any capacity after searching for Al one day
throughout the compound and eventually coming upon him sitting in his room
staring at a big screen TV. Al watched a lot of TV, even in Chicago. That was
normal Al behavior. But this time, Al was sitting there holding a guitar, playing
harmonica, and smoking a crack pipe, while watching a video of Bob Dylan
performing "Lay Lady Lay." Sean had been on the last few Ministry tours, with
Lollapalooza and the Psalm 69 tour, and he'd seen plenty. A crack smoking Al
was more than he was willing to deal with. Sean asked Paul if he could spend
Christmas at our house.

The holiday was coming up. I finished our gift shopping. Paul was close
to home, either running errands in town for the upcoming Australian shows, or
to take a break, when Al and Patty showed up at the house with their daughter
Adrienne. Adrienne was in middle school at the Austin Waldorf School. She
looked like a happy normal ten-year-old, with her shoulder-length reddish hair
and freckles and she smiled at me. Patty asked if they could leave Adrienne at
our house for a couple of hours. She and Al were going shopping for a bicycle for
Christmas and didn't have a sitter. "Of course," I said. I was happy to do it.

I was happy Patty and Al were getting along so well and appearing to the
world like caring, loving, responsible parents, despite their substance abuse
issues and the divorce. Although they were no longer married, it seemed they
were still trying to give their daughter a normal Christmas. I could keep Adrienne
occupied, having my own kids at home already.

Although the weather in Austin was rarely cold until January, this December
day was chilly enough for a heavier jacket. I hadn't noticed until Al and Patty left

that they had dropped off Adrienne without a sweater or a coat. I mined through my closet of old sweaters and found a black-and-white alpaca-wool pullover for Adrienne to borrow. Then I took her picture, in front of our "Wall of Shame" in the living room, in keeping with the family tradition of photographing everyone in our house for the first time. We would eventually amass photos of the usual suspects—Chris Connelly, William Tucker, Bill Rieflin, Patty Jourgensen, along with surprise visitors Jim Nash and Dannie Flesher, Paul Elledge and Leasha Overturf, Sunny Chapman (my jewelry designer friend from Wax Trax days), and Franke and Marston from Thrill Kill Kult. Some in this rowdy club were photographed holding a baby or toddler (ours). Adrienne appeared like a normal, freckled kid wearing an oversized sweater having a school picture taken.

The day wore on, with Adrienne helping me keep Ursula and Gordon busy. More hours passed. There was no word from Patty or Al. Cell phones hadn't come to be appendages yet. It didn't matter. I was slowly losing patience that no one bothered to call the house and give some indication when Adrienne might be picked up. I entertained the idea that she would have to spend the night with us. Al and Patty finally showed up very late at night and beyond any reasonable amount of time required to search out and buy a kid's bike. It was just another routine day of Paul and I doing favors for Al. I was angry that Al had no regard for us and our own kids and whatever personal time Paul and I had to spend together. It was getting old, having to constantly pick up the slack for the Jourgensen household.

Paul would sometimes drive out to Adrienne's school, pick her up, and take her home. The school was half the distance between our house and Al's. "Driver Paul" was on the responsible adult contact/pick up list at the school, in the event Adrienne's parents just couldn't make it over there. Now that they were back together again, her parents had even less of an excuse to forget when the school day ended. That is, unless they were actively forgetting.

I was grateful Paul wasn't losing his marbles out in the aptly named Marble Falls. I wasn't that sure about Al, but I had no idea what went on out there except through anecdotes and the usual studio talk. I was very familiar with the way things worked when they were at Chicago Trax: live chickens, Santeria rituals.

Normal stuff. Trax was a quick car ride from our Chicago home, and I could drop in whenever I felt the need. Living in Austin, I wasn't afforded that luxury. In Austin, I didn't know the details of Al's current drug use unless someone in the band or crew told me about it, and this, long after the fact. In Paul's case, I had myself partially to blame for his silence because of my early admonitions to him about Al's using in public. I couldn't be around that and hope to keep my law license.

Ministry was booked as a headliner for Australia's Big Day Out festival at the beginning of the new year. As many bands who had been to the continent before them, their management booked appearances in Japan to tag onto the end. If they were already on that side of the world, it made economic sense to do both countries. It was very expensive to travel that far with gear, crew, management, and the band, and hope to get decent advances to make money by the time it was all over. Festivals made money.

In conversation before the tour, Al seemed consumed by the idea that water drains backwards in the sinks Down Under. I accepted that as a given on a lawless continent supposedly inhabited by the descendants of criminals. I told Paul, "I would love to go to Japan and Australia. God knows if I'll ever get the chance again." I wanted to travel as much as possible and take the kids along so that they—and I—could spend time with Paul and experience new parts of the world. I was going to Australia and Japan, no matter what the tickets cost, and no matter that I'd have to launder and pack clothes for two seasons for myself and our two kids. It was summer in Australia and winter in Japan. Let's Go.

I arranged for my own flights with the kids to coordinate with the tour schedule. I asked my sister Georgette to come along. She was already getting paid to be our nanny for Ursula, who was now two and Gordon, who had just turned one. The four of us would fly into the Gold Coast, stay for a couple of days, then ride on the coach with the band to Adelaide.

My patience with being a single parent at times had run out. I was developing a penchant for drinking beer at home. Everyone in Texas drank beer, it seemed to me. Tecate with a slice of lime? Yes ma'am. It even looked refreshing. It cooled me off and left me feeling relaxed in the heat, instead of uncomfortable and tired. It was only beer, I convinced myself. But I would buy Tecate by the case at Costco. I was physically uncomfortable with four months of ninety to one hundred degree heat every day. That seemed unnatural. My body was slowing down. This was not my pace for living. If I had to stay inert for great stretches of time—not having a job to go to, not having blocks of time to explore anything that wasn't "kid friendly," and having little energy to write anything beyond a grocery list—then put me somewhere else. A different mood.

Perhaps I would have felt differently if we still lived in Chicago. I would still have friends and contacts there to be able to do adult things with other adults and not sweat getting a babysitter. I would know someone in Chicago who would know someone else. Here in Austin? I didn't know anyone I wanted to spend time with, other than my family. "Every day is an exploration," I would tell myself. You could do things with your children you could never afford to do yourself as a child. Wasn't that enough? Oftentimes I didn't bother Paul with my complaints about being alone so much. It was his profession that helped buy the house we were in, allowed us to fly to Chicago to visit friends, and it was his profession that allowed me to stay home and raise our two impressionable little darlings. But I was living in a strange kind of limbo. I was outside of his world out at Al's—I wanted no part of that scene. And yet, I felt uncomfortable in my own house, too. I was an insider. I was an outsider.

I had always told my friends in Chicago, if I ever got married, I would prefer the arrangement Georgia O'Keeffe and Alfred Steiglitz had, where they saw each other six months out of the year. That would be enough for me. Now living in Austin, Texas married to Paul, who was either in the studio recording or rehearsing or getting ready to tour or on the road performing, I was reminded again that I got what I had wished for. I was just in the wrong city to actually enjoy myself when my husband was away. And I was too preoccupied with keeping my children's needs above my own. That was a mistake.

But kids need a safe place. Kids need guidance and books read to them, and they needed healthy food in their stomachs. I cooked every day and taught them how. They needed baths. They needed sleep. They needed pediatric visits for checkups and vaccinations. I took trips with them to the co-op grocery store, where they could push their own kid-sized carts and pile random handfuls of snacks high, only later to be distracted from their hauls long enough to wander back out into the heat and the air-conditioned car.

Someone had to set up the backyard kiddie pool and make sure no one fell in or hurt themselves. My sister was a huge help, but how many times could we take them to the Austin Zoo to see the wild animals and ride the kiddie train? It was fun the first few times driving over to the tiny Austin children's museum to play with plastic foods in a micro kitchen or watch the penny drop and circle the well like a cyclist in a velodrome. But after that? I always thought only boring people got bored, but in reality I was bored all the time from the ongoing, necessary "event" planning.

Frantically looking for ways to keep myself and our kids happy and occupied, I established backup plans. I would strap them into the double stroller and hope they wouldn't get restless while I got in my four-and-a-half-mile walk around Town Lake before 10:00 a.m. and before the real Texas heat agitated everything and everyone. It was a time familiar to the locals, when the air stops moving and the heat stops your blood and you feel like you've pushed your head down towards an oven door and opened it, to be caught off guard AGAIN by the sting of a hot mask hitting your cheeks and chin.

I was Paul's sanctuary, too. Behind the bags of groceries, the multi-tasking machine I'd become as a mother of two kids a little over a year apart, somehow, I was home for him. Home was where the sanity lived. Our home did not resemble anything close to the "rock 'n' roll lifestyle"—whatever that was—or the chaos an outsider might see out at Al's place. I think fans expected everyone associated with Al was a drug addict or lived a life of excesses. Al was partly responsible for creating that image in the press, lumping the whole band in as his merry substance consuming mates just playing along with Pied Piper Al. That notion was as alien to me as it was to Paul.

I rarely talked to Paul about what I wanted that might stray from what we were living at the moment. I didn't have the time or energy to think about it. He and Al fed off of each other's talents and that symbiotic relationship worked to create epic records. It also left little time for Paul to think of anything else. That momentum was the guiding force in all our lives, for better or worse. I thought about staying and leaving that life often. Not seriously playing it out . . . just imagining. How would life be different if we lived somewhere else? What if things didn't work out with Al and his addiction dramas? How much longer could I watch and wait and still be sane, living in an enormous house of our dreams, before I would tell Paul "no" to working with Al anymore?

When we'd moved to Austin, Paul's income was ten times my salary as an attorney. I was happy to stay at home with our children and give my time and my life to my family as long as it worked. But it became an often lonely place when he was gone. I needed that constant dialogue with another adult, after sixteen hours of childcare. I needed my voice to be heard above the din of "Ministry" this and "Ministry" that. How do you become a fist, when you're always in shadow?

I decided it would be in my best interest if I left alcohol out of the picture for myself. I'd never had a problem drinking before moving to Texas. I could quit. I told Paul I thought I should quit drinking. He agreed. He didn't see why I needed to drink so much, anyway. I dumped the remaining beer we had in the house, and for the next week I stayed sober.

The "Australia/Asia" tour would get underway in mid-January, with all the crew ceremoniously shaving their heads before hitting the road. There was a family feel amongst the crew, many who'd been in the studio or out with the Cocks or Ministry on previous tours: Lee Popa, Paul Manno, Sean Joyce, Dan Field, and his brother Alex. I would be leaving for Australia with my sister and the kids about a week later. Oh Boy.

Paul began packing for the tour. I watched him as he lifted a pile of neatly folded T-shirts from his dresser and dropped them into an open duffel bag. A stack of underwear came next, all compact and folded. His army training was evident in the precise positioning of his clothes, notebooks, reading books, and tapes. He was going off to a battle of sorts, I told myself. At the onset of every tour, I would stand in front of Paul hours before leaving home for the airport and tell him, "You're gone already." He'd stop what he was doing and wrap his arms around me for a moment, as a way to somehow reassure me he would be coming back. He knew that I knew his head was already someplace else. He was distracted. He was barely there.

Tour personnel assembled at our house before heading out to catch their flight. After Paul and the others left, I walked around to the guest bedrooms, the living room, the wet bar in the kitchen, checking if anything had been left behind. "The Idiot Check," Paul and I called it. Make sure you have everything you need to travel. Once satisfied I had the house to myself again with the kids, I looked for some paper and a pen. I thought I should probably come up with a menu for the week and see what I needed to put on the shopping list. I came back into the kitchen and opened the refrigerator door.

There, sitting on the top shelf, "center stage" so to speak, was a single bottle of Beck's Bier. Someone in the crew forgot to drink it or didn't think it would be a problem to leave it there.

I had a little over a week of sobriety. I had personally swept the house clear of all alcohol ten days before. I gave up drinking, wanting to spare my family and my health. I stared at the bottle, lifted it off the shelf, set it on the kitchen counter, and waited. What was I waiting for? I had no idea. Was I waiting for guidance? Giving up alcohol was the easy part. But it didn't erase the reality that I was still exhausted with full-time motherhood, both physically and emotionally. And now, my partner was gone again for a tour, and I would not see him for almost two weeks. What's wrong with having one lousy beer anyway?

Normal people can have one beer to cool off and the day continues. But I wasn't one of those normal people. One beer was enough to focus my day and justify buying a twelve pack the next day and visiting the liquor shelves at Costco the day after that. It was senseless and so typical of someone with an alcohol problem. I was drinking again, and I didn't know why.

***

My sister and I were safely on board our flight to Australia with the kids, and I asked the Qantas Air people if Ursula and Gordon could meet the pilot. This was before 9/11. The pilot came through the cabin and awarded my kids their own "wings" to pin onto their backpacks. The flight attendants supplied us with baby Qantas backpacks filled with coloring books, crayons, and stuffed mini airplanes. It was challenging enough keeping a one- and two-year-old engaged on the ground. I was stepping into the throes of insomnia once we were in the air. Gordon's ears ached and into his mouth went the pacifier to relieve the pressure. Ursula always had to be moving. She wanted to explore the plane. In her two-year-old world it made little sense that we were going to be flying for a full day in someone else's "house"—the flight attendants'.

Paul and a guide picked us up at the airport when we landed, and we checked in at the hotel. Paul and I had one room, the kids were in an adjoining room with their aunt. We were all exhausted. Me, from the flights over, Paul from doing interviews and shows for a week already and from doing his "Paul" thing: keeping everyone else in the band out of trouble and all on the same page. He was usually the guy people went to when Ministry's tour manager, merchandise people, production people, and journalists wanted an answer they couldn't seem to pry out of Al. Or Al was simply too "busy" to sort out. Paul was that guy. The two of us settled into bed for the night, relieved to be together for a couple of weeks.

Sometime after we'd fallen asleep, the phone rang. It was on my side of the bed and woke me out of my jet-lagged slumber. I was disoriented and mumbled, "Hello."

"Oh. So sorry to bother you. I was looking for Paul. " It was a woman calling. Her voice had a casual tone. I was sure no fans here would know Paul's room number to call. "Hang on," I told her and handed the phone to Paul. He looked confused and said "Hellooo . . . It's late, my family's here," and yes, he was busy. When he hung up, he told me it was Courtney Love calling. Hole was on this tour. She was in the lobby. "Courtney said she was sorry she called so late. She wanted to meet for drinks. She extended her apologies and said to have a good night." I looked at him. Really.

I had already heard Al's slapstick, graphic descriptions of Ms. Love's "unkempt" nether regions ("Yeah! Like a coonskin cap . . .") and how supposedly liberal she was with her affections. It didn't surprise me at all she would hit on my husband.

"Oh, no, she's really just fun to talk to," and really smart, Paul assured me. I couldn't believe he would be so stupid as to cheat on me ever again, so I let it go. His one night stand on tour in Denver barely a year into our marriage seemed comfortably remote. I reminded myself that Paul more than once made a point to tell me he valued the insights of his women friends. There had been a lot of them in the different cities he'd lived in. I never felt any jealousy over his friends and girlfriends of the past. I never knew them, so how could I be jealous? In this case however, I felt an inexplicable urge to punch Ms. Thing in the face. It was 2:00 a.m., and what sane reason did she have for calling a married man?

I was too tired to care about the widow hitting on my husband or being an exhilarating conversationalist. I didn't want to hear any more road stories involving other women. Yeah. Good night. End of day one in Australia.

***

I'm not a beach person. Part of me wanted to hang out at the hotel bar and meet The Cult or some of Paul's touring friends from the other bands. But Paul wasn't interested. He wanted to step away from all of that and go to the beach with the kids.

My fair skin and poor eyesight necessitated an extra layer of industrial strength sunblock and prescription goggles if I wanted to do any serious snorkeling or wave hopping out in the ocean. Done. I was ready. But with two small kids always within my visual radius, swimming with them didn't sound like much fun at all. My sister and Paul played with the kids while I stayed close to the shore in my sunhat and bright orange "PTP" T-shirt.

On our second day in Gold Coast I stayed back at the hotel for a bit while the others went ahead to the beach. The time-change and jetlag screamed at me to rest. I casually eyed the minibar bottles of vodka in our room and mixed myself a drink. It was evening in Austin, wasn't it? I wondered as I mentally tried to justify this early cocktailing. Thirty minutes later, I wandered downstairs to the lobby where I met our guide from the previous day. I saw Lee Popa, who seemed a little pissed off about something show related.

I loved Lee. He was Ministry's sound master for the live shows, and he would whip up creative inducements for the local crews and promoters to let the band play as loudly as "artistically" possible. The guy who turned it up to "eleven"—Lee was the guy. He had that "Taylor Street in Chicago" Italian thing going on. I could never figure out if Lee was really hot about something or it was his nature to be brusque, then polite, a little more direct, then wham—"This is the way it's gonna go . . . and don't be a jagoff." No nonsense when getting his job done, and he was the best of the best. Lee understood Ministry's live show could only be better the louder it played in the venue. If that meant a few dollars changed hands, so be it.

I walked out of the hotel and down to the beach. Our guide cautioned us about getting UV-protective shirts for everyone. The destruction of the ozone layer was a tradeoff for living in close proximity to one of the wonders of the world, the Great Barrier Reef. I was feeling that heat, as I imagined I must by now look like a white seagull in flip flops with all the sunscreen I had on. I sat down on a towel, and before long the kids followed my lead. I stood up to go to the water's edge—there was Gordon right behind me. Ursula was busy with her shovel and bucket of sand. It was nice to be by the ocean. Growing up near Lake Michigan, I felt naturally drawn to large bodies of water to clear my head and feel that uncontrollable life force near my toes on the sand. The band's crew were off for an ocean boat ride with a guide. Our little family eventually headed back to the hotel lobby where industrious Gordon discovered a coin operated airplane ride. We watched him dip and come up in his tiny craft. I was glad to be on stable ground and not in the air at the moment. My kid's already nostalgic about flying, I thought. I knew it wasn't true. He was just being a kid.

With a few hours to spare before more Big Day Out commitments, Paul, my sister, and I took the kids and were off to a kangaroo nature park our guide had arranged for us. I instantly trusted this man, who wasn't very big physically, but he carried himself as though he'd killed a few people in his life—possibly in prison—everyone here had a prison story didn't they, somewhere in the family? He spoke of his love of beer and his disdain for lying wankers in the music industry who were cheap when it was time to pay tabs.

"They're in one of earth's paradises—fahkin' Gold Coast, mate—for fahk's sake, pay up!" I could imagine him waiting outside a bar, calmly smoking, well-oiled in the Australian sun—such intense rays, so close to the equator— just waiting for his man to appear and give him his money. Our guide had the professional demeanor of someone you could entrust your kids' lives with, as you drove along the coastline of this rough beautiful place. He had the backstory of the only guy left standing after a brawl. "Serves ya right, ya prick!" He referred to everyone else as a prick.

We did not hear again from Ms. Courtney Love. Perhaps Hole had already left the country. More beach visits, and a few days later all of us piled onto the coach and headed for Adelaide. I thought of "The Adventures of Priscilla, Queen of the Desert," the film about drag queens crossing the Australian outback in a bus, while we raced over vast plains and desert, miles of it, on our way to the old city. Al looked half-dressed and half "styled" in his socks and chopped-off fatigues, smoking and staring out the window of the coach. The outline of Adelaide coming into view reminded me of driving into Las Vegas—nothing for miles, and then you're suddenly on top of it.

Gold Coast had been heavily populated with white tourists. Here in Adelaide, we saw far fewer tourists, and the faces of ordinary office workers in the old town were mixed. I was mesmerized by the men's faces—there was nothing delicate in their facial bones. Their eyes seemed to be permanently receding into darkness. Aboriginal, I guessed, looking as though they'd been stuffed into their white shirt collars without regard to how the brightness bounced off of their skin in this Australian sun and made their complexions appear even darker. I wandered off the bus, stopping near a courthouse-type building, and studied faces as they passed by. A face like this should be on a bas-relief gazing down on this collection of white intruders disembarking from their bus, I thought. Ursula and Gordon, with their tiny bodies balancing big, blonde, curly hairdos appeared like their own little circus in this scene of grownups and gear. I wondered what this country would look like were it more densely populated than what we were seeing—faces in relief.

The show after Adelaide would be Perth. While the rest of the band took their day off, Paul and I went with our little family to the Aquarium of Western Australia. By now, Ursula and Gordon were seasoned travelers, jumping up to get a seat in this cab or that shuttle to inevitably see something fantastically peculiar to the place we were in. The idea of following some sort of curated "family trip" to anywhere was a wretched one, in mine and Paul's views. Kids will discover their own treasure in a big empty box just as soon as a tricked out theme park. At the aquarium, an underwater tunnel enveloped us with all the flying wonder of manta rays and little sharks. This was better than Disneyland or Universal Studios—and thankfully, much quieter. I was so happy to be with Paul and doing something so ordinary in such an extraordinary setting. We could go back to our hotel room, leave the kids to fall asleep with my sister, and spend the rest of the night talking or just feeling the warm familiarity of being safe and loved more than anything.

Al had the pleasure of witnessing first-hand the wonders of Australian water flowing backwards into hotel drains. I didn't regret not seeing much of the actual Big Day Out festivities but was thrilled to have personally waded into the waters near the Great Barrier Reef. I couldn't stand huge crowds, anyway.

I was ready to leave the scorching heat of the Australian continent behind. I took in enough heat at home. Onward, to Japan.

***

"Everything here tastes fishy." That was the word of caution from someone in the crew. Terrific. Having never-ending thoughts about who just had a nap and who needed one, our party arrived in Tokyo, and it was incumbent upon me now to find "child-friendly" snacks for our five days in Japan.

We arrived at the Century Hyatt in Tokyo, and a well curated welcoming committee from Warners Japan was there to greet the band. They bowed and offered Paul and Al small gifts. My sister and I took the kids to our rooms.

"Oh look! We're in the Barbie Suite," Georgette said, as we entered our rooms and our eyes fell upon pink chairs, tables, and writing desks so diminished in size as to make my one- and two-year-olds look right at home in this landscape of what looked like oversized doll furniture. "Is everyone in this country tiny? LOOK at this!" Only the beds appeared adult sized.

Granted, my sister was five foot nine. My siblings managed to harvest the tall genes from the family pool, unlike me in my five foot four radiance. The hotel room furniture was scaled down a good twenty percent from what we were accustomed to. We left our bags in the rooms and went to explore the neighborhood around the hotel. There was a temple nearby, presumably there for Japanese businessmen and travelers to meditate and pause during their otherwise carefully scripted days. I was imagining a narrative for myself on what people did here for fun and leisure, considering I didn't know any Japanese and couldn't converse with the locals.

If I'd felt we were living in a Ministry bubble before this visit, the stares from complete strangers on the street when they saw our kids added a sort of carnival sideshow element to our party. Ursula and Gordon with their large, round eyes, short curly blonde hair, full mouths, and pale white skin could have resembled anime characters to the average person in Tokyo. Elderly women approached us to ask if they could touch Ursula's hair—it was the same odd request we'd received from older women in Mexico. We hadn't been outside the hotel for ten minutes. Like Paul, the kids were extraordinary just in their physical presence here.

At dinner that night, it became apparent that the crew were right about one thing—everything DID taste fishy. A vague fish essence or seaweed aftertaste. It seemed to permeate everything. When I was ten, I spent the summer with my family in a small unincorporated town on a lake in Wisconsin. There was nothing to do but swim or go fishing. I had a bamboo fishing pole that stood twice my height in length, and I lugged it with some bait to the shoreline on most days. As we sat in the restaurant in Tokyo that first night, I was reminded of the distinct odor in the air when removing a hook from a fish's gills. Our Tokyo dinner carried a fish essence that was subtle but there in the broth, the udon noodles, the vegetables on my plate, leaving a hint of the sea on my palate.

The following day, I went off on my own in search of high quality leather goods made in Japan. I needed a new bag. I couldn't ignore this unique opportunity to see leather craftsmanship in this place where attention to the tiniest of details was an artform in itself—we were in the land of origami. One of our interpreters recommended a large department store within walking distance. Time for myself—what a luxury.

It was disconcerting stepping off the elevator in the store and immediately being greeted by a sales "professional." No browsing necessary. They were poised to bring forth every imaginable leather bag in the department, having already sized up my age, coloring, and casually studied taste in clothes and shoes the moment the elevator doors closed behind me. Finesse. They all had it. Not a stray hair or "fringe" out of line. Centered. I felt as if I'd be scolded for touching anything on my own. Thankfully, I wasn't an ugly American. I was my parents' child. My European reared parents habitually ridiculed every sweatpants wearing schlub they'd see out in public. "Big American. There he is . . ." my father would say. My parents were of the mind to dress up for travel, not down.

I finally decided on a square, black, boot-leather grade bag with a short strap, just large enough to hold a paperback book. A true handbag befitting a proper traveling mother of two out for lunch and tea, of course. I offered my credit card to the clerk who looked down, lifted a small tray, and tapped on it, indicating this is where that goes. I could visit Japan a few more times and not get the hang of this custom, I thought.

I was back in the street and found a food hall and a bakery where I gathered up treats to bring back for the kids at the hotel. At the checkout, with my arms full of roast duck and bread rolls, I offered a few bills to the clerk who did not look at me at all as she tapped on the tray next to the register. Christ. This place is so obsessed with cleanliness and the prescribed way of handling money. It was an oddly incongruous backdrop to the older woman I passed as her little boy stood to the side of the walkway to pee in the grass—in public view. The parked cars I saw all had sample packets of cigarettes tucked beneath the front windshield wipers, driver's side. Why the cars? Where do they throw the butts? I returned to the hotel. Ursula and Gordon bit into the rolls I brought back and they chewed slowly. I took a bite and was grateful they didn't taste like fish.

Aside from official Ministry business, I was happy to visit toy stores and let Paul have photography duty as he snapped away at the array of colorful taxis parked on the street and ready for hire. An artist's palette of colors, and each bedecked inside with lace-covered headrests, furthering the national narrative of "cleanliness." I took some photos of Paul holding Ursula up high against a screaming wall of neon messaging racing across high-rise buildings as dusk fell over Tokyo nightlife. I quite like it here, I tell Paul. I adore the engineered solitude of the urban temples scattered near our hotel where people in business suits enter and stay to meditate. I am just as amused as everyone else by the ubiquitous vending machines offering cups of ramen, sake, condoms, and neckties. And underwear. I make a mental note about Japanese groupies: "Bodies are linear and flat."

Al is overjoyed to discover the Cadillac of toilet seats at our Japanese hotel. We all admit this is the first time we have been warmed, washed, and massaged by the pot. By the end of our Tokyo stay, Al has thoroughly expounded upon the heroic strengths and virtues of these things, that I half expect to hear someone tell me he's finally had sex with and married one of them. On to Osaka.

Less than a month before Ministry's scheduled arrival in Japan, the Great Hanshin Earthquake jolted the southern region of the country where Osaka and Kobe are situated. There was no visible structural damage we could see upon arriving in Osaka. A similar bowing and gift offering heralded the band's first hours wandering around our new hotel's lobby. The furniture in the rooms bore the same exact dollhouse-like proportions as the last place, but we were thankful to also see spaghetti (again!) on the room service menu. It was the only noodle dish our kids would eat without making faces.

Paul and Al were scheduled for much of the day. My sister and I wanted a walk with the kids to do some window shopping, not really knowing what to look for except perhaps some new Astro Boy gear. Later in the afternoon Paul met us at the Osaka Aquarium. Another aquarium. It occurred to me Paul and I had moved on from art galleries and revolving cocktail lounges to now visiting penned-in aquatic life for local color. Was this a step up? It was something to do to entertain our kids. We started taking photos outside of this very modern structure of mainly glass and wondered how it too had survived the earthquake. I knew so little about retro-fitting buildings or creating brand new ones to confidently withstand the inevitable tectonic shifting going on beneath this relatively small patch of earth. I simply admired the building's look and feel inside. There was a large, central tank in the interior core. The quake had left minor damage, and we gathered around with other tourists already there to watch fully outfitted divers steadily repairing small sections of the tank. The divers were oblivious to us tourists who found their repair job as fascinating as the giant spider crabs silently gliding past their rubber suited bodies. Welcome to Osaka. Even though it was winter in Japan, I was able to buy kid-sized beach towels with Hello Kitty motifs and simple, colorful line drawings of octopuses and crabs from the gift shop. We made our way outside, past more grandmotherly types staring at Ursula and Gordon's hair reflecting so brightly in the outdoor sunlight.

Later, Paul and I went to a club with some label people to hear a local DJ spin records, including, of course, Ministry records. I didn't have any preconceived notions about Japan's club scene. The club was small, dark and had a lovely relaxed vibe. Al and the tour manager, Curly, had painted a much more sinister picture, one of local Yakuza—gangsters—running the clubs. To my mind, that was not so much different from big cities anywhere else in the world. Cash businesses attract money launderers of all stripes. I had face to face encounters with many of them as a practicing defense lawyer. Big deal. I didn't like Curly, and I took his opinions into account sparingly. He'd once told me his mother was an alcoholic and worked in a chicken factory to support the family and her wretched habit. It was one of the oldest tropes around, but he was such an arrogant Scotsman or Irishman or whatever he claimed, full of his own self-importance having worked briefly with Echo & The Bunnymen. He probably thought my stupid American self wouldn't recognize the cliché. I learned not to say too much around people like him—opportunists with no soul.

Two weeks away from Austin was the panacea I needed to restore myself spiritually and emotionally. This kind of brief travel to exotic places to spend time with Paul was good enough at the moment. We couldn't really explore much outside of the interests of two preschool-age travel companions, but I vowed to come back to Japan someday and really immerse myself in the country's "otherness," it's regimented social expectations, alongside it's panty-dispensing vending machines. Yes, there was a history to that, too.

On our flight out from Osaka, heading back home to Texas, Paul and I sat with our kids in the center rows of the plane, getting up to take Ursula to the restroom or simply to change the view now and then for the long flight. Shortly into the flight, I stood up with the kids to explore the rest of the plane. We hadn't noticed them at check-in, but a group of a dozen or more Japanese middle-school-age children had boarded our plane and were on a tour together heading for the United States. Each student wore a lanyard with their name and carried a camera strapped around their neck. Several girls jumped up from their seats as Ursula, Gordon, and I moved down the aisle toward them. "Is okay! We take their picture!" one said to me. It was meant to be a question, but was uttered with the breathless tone of someone just realizing they'd struck gold. I didn't know if photos of the adorable blonde duo in my care would soon be memorialized in someone's school project, but frankly I was flattered. I didn't care. The girls tried to suppress their giggles, pushing one another to go first. Ursula and Gordon thought it was funny getting all this attention from bigger kids on a plane. They were already used to the limelight surrounding their "Papa" and his "friends." Snap away . . . snap away.

I managed to swipe a handful of gratis airline postcards from the seat backs of empty seats on the plane. One standard image showed three women flight attendants giggling in their JAL uniforms and striped neckties. I penned a few cards and talked to Paul about the two of us getting away together. Upon my insistence, he agreed we should fly to New York for the upcoming Whitney Biennial. The Biennial was a big deal to artists chosen and to people like me, who would have the opportunity to see an international curated funhouse of newer artists. I'd only been to one of the shows. Paul had not been to any previously.

24

Returning home from Japan, I suddenly had a growing sense that Texas was a foreign country. I wished I could pick up the language of the locals, but each time someone called me "ma'am" I looked behind me to see whom they were addressing. I refused to say "y'all." Ever. Feeling at home was more than language, anyway. I amused myself with grown up adventures like slowly replacing the ancient drapes that came with our house. The family room with its floor-to-ceiling windows facing the front deck needed some color, in my view. I was homesick for the big city. I packed up the kids and went to the mall to JCPenney and discovered, to my delight, they had close to what I was looking for: deep-gold satiny drapes to offset the avocado-green paneling in our family room. It was a small victory for glamor.

Al came to the house for a rare visit and stepped into our back studio with Paul. When they returned to the house, I stood in front of the family room windows.

"I bought these gold, lame drapes just for you, Al. Perfect for showtime. Feel a drama coming on? Throw back the curtains!"

Al looked amused and played along. "I feel right at home." He asked me if I was starting to feel at home in Austin.

I lied. "I'm getting used to it."

My getting used to it meant I was tolerating Austin in part by having a few drinks every day. I didn't discuss my drinking, other than to tell Paul once again, I would quit. I had started drinking slowly, working my way up to four or five a day. I managed just fine doing all the things I needed to do. I watched the kids play in our backyard kiddie pool. A photo from that time period with my sister and Sean Joyce in the yard in the shade, sitting in our lounge chairs, holding beer cans and smoking cigarettes, captures that fine slice of suburbia, early 1995. I found myself drinking more, sometimes throughout the day. Paul noticed too when he was home. The more I drank, the more I felt isolated whenever someone visiting would leave in a cab for the airport to go home. I tried talking to Paul, desperately wondering if I might be experiencing depression. He looked helpless and offered no more than a hug before leaving the house again to go out to Al's.

Depression and alcohol. I'd had low blood sugar my whole life. Blood sugar, body and mind, biology—was it all related? I didn't know. Depression wasn't a theory all in my head—I knew that. It was as real as blushing.

My old friend Marnie Warren called regularly from where she was now living outside of Chicago. She was married, too and still painted in her own studio separated from her main house, much like Paul's home studio was here in Austin. We talked as always about painting and art and now my problems with alcohol. I called Marnie one afternoon in a panic. I had just finished a phone call with Paul, who was frustrated out at Al's and didn't want to listen to me crying on the phone about being overwhelmed and depressed. He'd told me, "Just don't be drunk when I get home." I had the distinct feeling that I was alone, and I was not allowed to screw up. I wasn't a bad person. I was a person who was struggling. I had an alcohol problem.

I had no clue what was happening with Paul and Al, and no clue what I was doing anymore. I didn't want to have to drink every day. I never pictured myself being taken care of by a man financially, and now this was exactly what I was doing. That was our choice, and I had agreed. Paul was solely supporting us, the man with "the biggest heart in America," who agreed with me to do whatever it took to simply live a comfortable life and sanely raise our kids in an environment where one of us would be there for them always, for milestones and discoveries they were making about themselves. The kids would know they were safe and loved. I stayed home. I allowed myself that luxury, and at the same time, let Paul come and go as he pleased, without any question. That was all part of Paul's job. He was taking care of Ministry business, Ministry dramas (Al's) every day, waiting for the revolving doors to spit out the next person or thing Al currently had an issue with. I was busy taking our kids to the lake for my walk with the stroller or reading with them or reading record-advance statements and royalty statements and divvying up Wax Trax royalties and paying writers on the side projects—Revolting Cocks, Acid Horse, Pailhead, and PTP. Or I went driving, driving everywhere: to the library to stay in cool air, to the bank, to Drug Emporium three blocks away for kid's cold medicine or coloring books, to the pediatrician's office for checkups, to the grocery store, to the mall, to a playdate, to the edge of the world. I went driving often out of necessity, but occasionally to center myself and feel relevant and needed.

Sometimes, I would stare in the mirror trying to convince myself what I did all day long was creative—raising and entertaining small children was creative, wasn't it? I had forgotten that through short periods of my life, I lived with low-grade depression, some trauma related, and that could explain why I kept staring at my face to see if anything was different now that we were making a life in Texas. Often what I saw in my reflection was two weary eyelids tugging downward like commas.

I felt gratified to mail royalty checks to songwriters, even if they were as small as sixty-two dollars to Steven Mallender and Richard Kirk from Cabaret Voltaire for Acid Horse's No Name, No Slogan. Everyone was paid. In a way, I was adhering to my mission to help artists get fair compensation for their work. I sometimes did statements by hand, until we finally bought a desktop computer for the house.

On one visit to the post office to mail checks to the songwriters, I had my son with me. He was just a year old and learning to walk about comfortably on his own, but he reached his arms up for me to hold him while we stood in line. The counters were busy, and I felt his weight on my arms. I set him down in front of me for a moment to check the stamps on the envelopes I was mailing. A woman my mother's age was standing in line directly in front of us. I flipped through the envelopes, thinking about what else I had to do that day. The woman in front of me turned her head around suddenly with a startled look, lowered her eyes toward the floor and smiled.

"Thank God, he's so handsome," she said. I looked down and there was my son, staring straight ahead and rubbing the woman's leg. Another one who "loves women," I thought, laughing as I scooped him up from the floor and away from more eyes staring.

The weather was warming, and I decided to plant a small garden in the backyard as a way to keep myself and the kids distracted and doing something different with our time. I remembered summer mornings picking tomatoes and thinning carrots in my mother's garden at their summer home in Wisconsin. My father had finished building the house with help from Polish immigrants he knew who were craftsmen. The transitions in that garden, the house itself growing upwards from a poured concrete foundation, had brought peaceful changes to my parents' summer days. Change was never something to fear. I knew that. I wanted a change. My day drinking had to stop.

A married couple Paul knew in Austin came to visit the house a few times after we were settled in. I liked them. They were both recovering addicts with several years of sobriety between them. They were younger than us, with an air of calm, focused attention to what they were doing. They had jobs in the local music scene but weren't club rats. On their next visit, I asked the woman of the couple if she would help me plant some flowers outside. After a few minutes, I told her, "I think I may be drinking too much."

"That's a start," she said.

I told her it never occurred to me I may have developed postpartum depression after giving birth to two babies fifteen months apart from each other. There was no time to get a mental health checkup after our son's birth, let alone therapy. Drinking alcohol seemed to elevate my mood, but it seemed all wrong and counterproductive. I'd feel full of energy and ideas for writing a children's story, and then those fantasies were forgotten for the day. I didn't know where to start to even think about getting help.

Our friend knew the local AA scene. "There's one place a lot of music people go to. I'll go with you, if you want to check it out."

I didn't want to disappoint Paul, who had enough substance abuse stories playing out every day working with Al and some of the other Ministry players. Paul didn't use drugs and wasn't an alcoholic, but he'd grown up with drinkers who later became committed teetotalers. He'd seen enough of that.

"Okay. I'll go," I told the woman. I disappeared into the house and brushed my teeth. I had been drinking that morning and didn't want anyone to smell alcohol on my breath.

My friend drove us to a meeting. I felt so guilty. Of what, I didn't know. Hiding my drinking? Okay. Was I just a sick human being now? Did that make me a bad mother? A bad wife? Getting out of the car, I asked her, "Do I look okay?"

"Except for the dried toothpaste—yeah." She reached over with a tissue and wiped away a spot on the side of my mouth. We went inside and took our seats.

I went to that meeting a few more times. It was possibly only in my head, but I felt everyone at the meeting was busy sizing up everyone else. It was distracting. I had a casual understanding of how recovery programs worked, from both my professional life and personal life experiences with friends. I looked around the room for the most ordinary looking person I could find to be my sponsor. It turned out to be a guy who brought a bottle of Yoohoo chocolate drink with him to every meeting. I took it as a sign he had a sense of humor and would appreciate the absurdity of my home life. His appreciation amounted to saying, "Ooooh, they're national," when I finally told him which band my husband played in. I became disenchanted with "the Program" as practiced by the people at that meeting. I didn't need to hear any more about rock hierarchies. I was further deflated when the Yoohoo Man informed me I should look for a woman sponsor instead.

A woman at one of these meetings brought her infant with her. I attempted small talk with the woman afterwards telling her, "I have two at home," pointing to her baby. It was meant as a lighthearted show of solidarity. But she stared at me, then moved away as if I'd said the most politically incorrect thing anyone could say to a new mother.

I was beginning to panic listening to other people share their stories about life on the road or their creative struggles. What I needed to hear were ordinary stories from ordinary people. I already knew one person extremely well who had his own creative struggles and self-esteem issues, and he was completely sober. I got that. It seemed clear the last thing I needed was to be around more "cool" music industry people. I found a different meeting.

At the new meeting, the man chairing it was a retired traveling salesman who'd been sober for decades. His name was Buddy. He would offer welcoming words to the group when the meeting began: "Damn it. I was headin' out to do some fishin' but here I am, stuck with y'all—a room fulla drunks. Lord help me." Half the room had been sent there by the courts. There were people on crutches hobbling in. There was no glamour, no agenda. These people were my people. I kept going back to those meetings. I stayed sober.

***

Back from Australia and Japan, there was this sense that Paul going back and forth to Al's compound would inevitably end with a finished record. Warners was interested in their progress. A group of journalists was assembled to interview Al at his place in Marble Falls to talk about the new record. Alternative Press came, who'd been such great supporters of all things Luxa/Pan Productions—aka Al and Paul—had to offer. I knew from Paul that the record was nowhere close to being finished. They still needed six songs. Bill Rieflin was gone. Progress was slow. Al didn't make himself available to the visiting national and international press, opting instead to sleep in and let Paul do the interviews. There wasn't much to talk about. Al's absence became the story.

In late spring, I was home alone with the kids. Paul was out at Al's. Our bedroom, on the south end of the house, had a large picture window facing the front driveway. The yard was heavily shaded in the front, with some sunny spots during the day. Off to the side of our bedroom window was a camellia bush. The camellia had dark, waxy, evergreen-colored leaves that matched the color of our house. The camellia bloomed into deep purplish-red flowers, offering a rare spot of color to the landscape normally camouflaging the house from direct view on the street. Next to our bedroom was my small office, and next to that was the formal entranceway to the house. We rarely opened the designated front door, except occasionally when a new UPS driver would ring the bell and the cathedral-like din of the echoing chimes would draw my attention to that door.

On one particularly bright spring day, the doorbell rang, I swung open the front door, stepped out to grab a package left on the stoop and walked a few steps out. I glanced over to the right and caught flashes of red on the camellia. I could see the bush heavily draped in blooms, so many, I felt I should bring the kids out to see. I could teach them the name of this singular plant growing so near to the house and so beautifully vibrant with color. Gordon was not quite two years old, and Ursula was almost three. I held Gordon's hand as we slowly walked down the front steps and out the door into the front yard, his small legs trying to race over to see "the flowers." We stood directly in front of the bush, and Gordon looked up at me. "Where, mama?" He tilted his head left and right in the exaggerated movement of a typical curious toddler, as he flicked the leaves on the plant.

"Right here," I said, holding up one of the blooms. I could see disappointment on his face.

"Right here! Don't you see? Can't you . . . ?"

Oh. Wait—no. NO. Is he colorblind? My father was severely colorblind. "Gordon, do you see these petals—they're red." He looked around. "Where red, mama?"

I felt helpless, consumed by the thought that our son would possibly grow up unable to distinguish colors—how many? I took his hand and told him, "You see different colors than I do, and that's okay," and we walked back inside.

This must happen to all parents of small kids, I told myself. You try to be ready for anything they don't comprehend. But they're not you, not little versions of you. They see what they see, no more, no less than their own view. I tried to mentally file away the notion of "impairment" and like many stay at home parents, fell right back into the rhythm of picking up cues for games to fill up the rest of the morning. I had the good fortune to stumble upon the Bob series of books at our neighborhood library, where we went later in the day to escape the heat and to read. The Bob Books were small paperbacks, the size of cocktail napkins, with simple line drawings and life vignettes. They were designed for small hands to manipulate and hold.

The world didn't end because our son was possibly colorblind to some degree. It was in fact a bittersweet challenge—like Ursula being left-handed, chatty, and always moving. Gordon was more introspective. Like a scientist, I told myself. Maybe he'd inherited my father's and Paul's talents for invention. Maybe he would see textures and outlines in a more pronounced way. Maybe, I should stop worrying. Maybe. Please let him be ok.

I was tired of wondering when Paul's schedule would open up. My questions were answered with random invites or announcements that Al was taking everyone to Rosie's, or Al wanted to meet at Jovita's. Or Al and his house manager Curly wanted everyone to meet at Ego's for cocktails and its cool bar. The atmosphere at Ego's was fun for its dark, smoky interior, but I didn't need to be visiting bars. And if I had to explore one more Tex-Mex menu to guarantee myself a night out with my partner, I would be on the verge of a relapse. Or maybe develop an urge to visit a shooting range to feel more "at home" in Texas. I didn't want that—any of it.

Motherhood was sometimes a performance. I couldn't have a fully engaged conversation with my kids. No parent can. Children wade through their levels of understanding upward. You are navigating toward them downward. They will refer to every adult woman, regardless of marital status or age as "that mom over there." I found it curious they would draw that conclusion. Was it because they saw mostly women in charge of the children we encountered in our daily life? They didn't seem to refer to every adult male as "that dad over there." I would correct their word choice with "you mean, that lady" or "that woman." I found myself drifting further away from intellectual pursuits of my own, not wanting to miss an opportunity to witness some understanding or "aha" moment in my kids. That required me to focus on them and their needs: food, shelter, nap times, play.

Where was the romance in my marriage? I hoped Paul and I would have some chance to go for dinner or an event in Austin or somewhere else that would require wearing something other than plain, black shorts and a plain T-shirt. When we first moved to Austin, Paul and Al were asked to give an award at the annual Austin Music Awards. Even for something as local as that, I had nothing new to wear. I looked around at the nominees: Don Walser, Ian Moore and his band, Junior Brown (who seemed to be perpetually up for an award). Junior Brown, whose light-gray, tailored suit with cowboy hat and boots was a shtick I preferred not to be photographed next to, but it was his own. The fashion dynamic in the room was about as interesting to watch as going to the rodeo or the state fair. The state fair was actually far more interesting for the show put on by the kid exhibitors standing with their prize pigs. At such a tender age, they were already such experts at animal husbandry.

The Music Awards weren't entirely provincial and self-congratulatory. The winners were talented and good at what they did. I just didn't care for the music—heavy on singer-songwriters and blues. I was spoiled by years of cutting-edge sounds and visuals. There was zero edge to what was happening locally, as far as I could see. Perhaps everyone was waiting for Ministry to shake up the local scene somehow. It would be a long wait for that to happen.

While Paul was busy trying to "make shit happen" fifty miles away from home, I amused myself with the idea that I needed new clothes for traveling or special events I was certain would pop up now that we were settling into Austin life and whatever social scene there was. The fashion world in Austin was virtually non-existent. Aside from really good thrift stores, one shop, "By George," carried interesting higher-priced boutique wear, and I occasionally snooped through the racks looking for shirts for Paul. Otherwise, Houston was a couple of hours drive from Austin.

I racked my brain for ways to get out and do things with Paul, to get him away from studio mode, as I had the habit of doing when we were still in Chicago. We had just spent a small fortune on music equipment to fill up Paul's home studio in the back. Why wasn't he using it? He could work on music at home if it wasn't worth his time to go out to Al's on a given day. His needs were met. What were my needs or desires? They weren't complicated at all at the moment in my full time role as a stay at home parent with a professional life indefinitely on hold. If I couldn't spend much time out socializing with my partner, at least I could make some headway in getting outfitted for an eventual date in the future when that would be possible. I told Paul I wanted some new clothes—just for me. I was regularly shopping for children's clothes and I hadn't bought a single new wardrobe piece for myself since buying a handbag in Tokyo. It was easy to fall into a fashion rut in Austin, and I was tired of it. I asked Paul to come with me to Houston, help drive, and help watch the kids. It was not a lot to ask.

Paul was at a point with Al where if Al kept forgetting what planet he was on—Ministry—Paul would have to quit making music with him. Or take a break, whatever that looked like. It was a scary thought. Here I was risking my professional life by staying home to raise our kids (in addition to having moved to another state where I wasn't licensed to practice law), and the foundation under us was no longer solid. What if I suddenly had to go back to work?

When we moved to Texas I was two months shy of practicing law full time for five years in Illinois. If I had the five years, I would automatically qualify for reciprocity with Texas. At the time, I thought it was a minor consideration, since Ministry was doing so well—I could take the Texas bar sometime later and be done with it. What if now was the time?

We had all worked so hard to get here, having faith we were doing the right thing. It was urgent to leave Chicago to set up in Austin because Paul and Al were on a schedule. I needed to remind myself that life was full of uncertainties. I was alive. I was a survivor and living my own version of the American dream. And I was confident that Paul and I could weather whatever came next—even if that meant Al would be out of the picture. I wasn't afraid of uncertainty, and I was not afraid of Al. What I feared was Paul losing his nerve.

I couldn't dwell on imagined future scenarios. I had told Paul countless times he had the talent and the drive to make his own music and work with a lot of other people we already knew, and some we didn't—take a deep breath and keep going. Paul agreed to take a break and drive to Houston for a day like a good suburban husband and humor me and my wardrobe dilemma.

The trip from Austin to Houston was a dull drive. We knew that from our IKEA trips. There was little to see along that road besides flat, undeveloped land for miles. It was so unlike our recent trip to San Antonio, the other major city within a day's drive of Austin. We had taken the kids to the San Antonio Zoo once. On the road heading out of town toward San Antonio, we could at least admire the Adams food company building standing alone along I-35, surrounded by acres of untouched pasture. Just beyond the stagnant sea of car dealerships and Costco, the Adams building rose up like a theater prop. It was designed by local architects in 1955, with neon letters pinned to its swanky exterior announcing the "Home of Adams Extracts." It was a reminder of a bygone era when artificial flavors were essential staples to satisfy a home baker's needs. In a town like Austin, with few architectural landmarks, the Adams building was a joyous reprieve with its modern, low-slung minimalist charm. The San Antonio drive had another curiously local attraction, the "Snake Farm." Front facing the highway it was a small outbuilding the size of a mobile home, wherein there was no farm, only a few gangly serpents in tanks built for the occasional spectators visiting who needed a teaser on the drive out to see the spectacular San Antonio Zoo. Our current drive to Houston was a bust by comparison.

Our precise destination in Houston was the Galleria. It had a deceptively charming name suggesting moneyed browsing at a leisurely pace, but in reality was just a mall where anyone could buy expensive resort wear. Dolce & Gabbana was our first stop. My three-year-old daughter was attracted by the glitz and animal prints hanging from racks in the shop and wanted to "help" me sort through it all. Paul wandered off with Gordon to explore the mall. It had been a few years since I'd seen quality fabrics and designer clothes, let alone touched them with my own fingertips. I tried on a black, boucle-wool winter coat with a black, fake-fur, super-wide shawl collar. The coat swung open, fanning out from its single, baseball-sized button. It was boxy and big, and I drew Ursula under the coat toward me while I stared in the mirror and played the glamourpuss. I felt like a pop star. I looked like Madonna.

The coat dwarfed my body, and its shape (or lack thereof) was oddly flattering. My credit card fell into the waiting hand of a very charming salesman named Anthony. He had an Italian surname and bore a slim resemblance to the actor Ray Liotta. He informed me he'd be moving over to Barney's soon. He also informed me he was a painter. I signed on to the store's client mailing list. Anthony swiped my card, and I walked out of the shop with a black garment bag holding the single most expensive article of clothing I had ever bought for myself. Even our custom leather Langlitz jackets were a third of that price each by comparison. I felt no regret. I told Anthony I would be back.

In the mail a few weeks later, I received some preview photo booklets with new collections for Jill Sander and Dolce & Gabbana. Not long after the first Houston trip, I coordinated an overnight trip back to Houston for myself, my sister, and the kids. One shopping trip was enough for Paul, who was more consumed by Ministry drama than I had ever really seen him before. He looked disgusted and exhausted from the back and forth to Al's, which rarely ended with any material he was happy with. "What is going on over there?" I finally asked him.

"I don't know. I can't seem to come up with anything Al likes."

"So take a break. Work on something else. What about Lead into Gold?" I told Paul I didn't think I needed to say it, but after this record he should seriously think about what he wanted to do. If that meant not working with Al for a while, who cared? We'd survive. It wasn't what I wanted to think about, but Paul's perpetual holding pattern waiting for Al could go on forever.

"I think there's still something there if I can get Al motivated. I have to see this through. We're not done."

At some point I suggested he should get Al checked into a rehab facility if that was the core problem. I waited for a few silent moments and we both started (sadly) laughing.

"Are you serious? That ain't ever gonna happen." Yes. I knew. Not a chance. I ventured out of my comfort zone once in asking Al personally if he wanted the phone number for my friend Tim in Chicago—Tim, my former driver at Kreiter & Gibbons. Tim had once asked me about Al and if there was anything he could do to help. I told Al about Tim growing up with the mob, using heroin for decades, finally getting and staying sober, and still having a fun life. Al told me thanks, but he wasn't ready for that. And that was that.

There was nothing else I could say or do to make Paul's life any easier, aside from taking the kids out of town for a night. My sister and I packed bathing suits for the hotel pool and drove back to Houston.

I thanked God for Georgette as she wandered out into the Galleria with my two very energetic children. She was their nanny anyway, and the three of them were heading to lunch at a new café and wherever else Georgette could keep her eyes on them and keep them entertained within a mall. My new salesman friend Anthony had brought in his portfolio to show me. He was thrilled my husband was in a famous band. He then brought over armfuls of fabulous clothes to try on.

I had so much fun with all of the attention and none of my usual concerns about everyone else's happiness. I picked out some classics: a black-and-gold pair of animal-print acetate Dolce & Gabbana pants, a spy coat in the same pattern, a giraffe-print cocktail dress, and a signature Dolce & Gabbana white purse, delicately adorned with cherries in the print. The bag was almost too faddish, but it was so beautiful and simple in design I knew I would wear it for some occasion. I was fitted for a thin, gray wool Jill Sander pantsuit with a long, single-breasted jacket to wear alone with nothing underneath, if that was the look I was going for. I was ecstatic that I couldn't think of a single reason to buy the suit, other than it looked fabulous on me. Someday, I could wear this to court, I convinced myself.

Anthony was by now handing me dresses he thought I should have in my closet. I liked an off-white Prada dress with matching coat for more formal occasions. (When exactly, would those be?) I indulged my new friend a little longer, until he handed over a chocolate-brown, tight-fitting, short-sleeved minidress that made me look as though I needed some white lipstick and an order pad. "I look like a diner waitress, "I told him. "Oh, come on!" He rolled his eyes and whisked the hanger away. No short-order camp for me, thank you. To no one's surprise, most of my haul needed tailoring. I walked out of Barney's with the receipts in my wallet. Georgette and I took the kids back to the hotel for a short swim and back to Austin in the morning. I had just spent what some would consider an obscene amount of money on myself. I'd at least be stylishly outfitted for those fantasy dinners and events away from my routine domestic duties.

I could have kissed the UPS man when the boxes with my tailored garments arrived later at the house. Georgette was over with her friend Aidis. Aidis was currently living in Austin too, but he and Georgette were old friends. Aidis, curiously enough, had briefly lived across the street from Wax Trax in Chicago. I didn't know him at the time; although, we might have bumped into each other on occasion in a club on a dance floor. He was very excited that he knew all of us now, including Paul. Aidis was a Revolting Cocks fan. Who wasn't?

My piles of new gorgeous fabrics seemed to engender a spirit of generosity in me as I lifted them from the boxes. Aidis was tall and thin enough to be a male model. I pinched the collar of my new spy coat and held it up in front of him. "Here. Try this on. You'll look fabulous."

He snatched the coat from my fingers, slid into it, and hugged himself tightly, closing off the front from any hurricane winds that might freakishly blow in from the Gulf of Mexico. "Oh—wait!" he said, as he collapsed and lay down on the deck outside, rolling back and forth in the coat. "It feels so expensive . . ."

Yes. Had the year been 2005 and not the current 1995, a reality-show appearance would have been imminent in my future. Here was my Housewives of Austin, Texas moment, perfectly executed—by a man. My charmed life. At the moment, I loved it.

Later in the evening, I waved the clothes in Paul's direction, but he couldn't be bothered with this frivolity. My salesman friend Anthony called the house, and Paul answered. "It's your boyfriend," he said, handing me the phone. He was practically sneering. "He's gay," I said, and took the phone away. What was that all about?

Paul didn't seem to understand I needed this small connection to beauty, to fashion, to something new that wasn't here in Austin, Texas. Even a conversation with a long-distance acquaintance (who happened to be an artist) was something to break the monotony of hot, dry, brown Tex-Mex days. Paul had ample opportunities to dress up, many more than I did. His wardrobe was much more extensive than mine. Our walk-in closet was stuffed with his vintage and new leather jackets, coats, boots, D. L. Cerney shirts we'd bought in New York, and the occasional sweet vintage Hawaiian shirt. It was my turn to dress up for the sheer joy of doing it. I could only wish for occasions to wear these things and hope those wishes became reality soon.

At times I felt as if he didn't want me to have fun on my own. What was he expecting me to do in this cultural void—write a book? Pursue a hobby in my nonexistent spare time? If I had a hobby at all, it was looking at art, and in Austin the possibilities were laughable. I sensed Paul's frustrations had more to do with Ministry and Al than they had to do with me. And in fact, they did.

Paul was at a breaking point with Al. He took a short hiatus from work. They were edging closer to finishing what would become Ministry's Filth Pig record, but the record was draining Paul's optimism to new lows. Crazed Management arranged for Paul and me to go to New York and take two days at the new Royalton Hotel. While in Japan, he and I had already discussed going to New York for the Whitney Biennial, so the timing was ideal. It was Mother's Day weekend. There was a little bit of official Warners business to take care of, but otherwise we were free to go to the Whitney or MOMA or do whatever city exploring occurred to us once our feet hit the pavement.

It was a gift to be out of Austin, alone with my favorite human being for three days without kids. We had the best time playing Spot the Celebrity in Tribeca. New York streets were always full of surprises, if you paid attention to the people walking by.

"There's the guy from Aliens," I said under my breath as we walked and debated where to have breakfast away from the hotel. The actor sprinted past us gripping a duffle bag, looking buff and determined to continue his routine after working out at the gym. Being in New York, away from everyone else's needs but our own, was our version of relaxing at a spa: two days at a Philippe Starck designed hotel, city walks, and a visit to the Whitney Museum to see the 1995 Biennial exhibition. Works from Jane Freilicher and Cindy Sherman were in the show at the Whitney, and we bought the catalogue as a keepsake to remind us it was possible to leave home and not worry about work.

When we returned to Austin, Paul had a lot on his mind. The short retreat away from Al helped him focus his attention and time on us, our family, and our marriage. He stayed at the house hours longer to make drawings with the kids and to play. Paul and I went thrift shopping and out for Vietnamese lunches. We had decided in New York to replace our unadorned wedding bands with something more personal—a custom design. What would that look like? Our original rings were simple platinum bands provided by a client at my firm in Chicago. Where the client found them, I didn't ask. We bought the rings in a rush after discovering "nobody" besides us wanted platinum bands in 1989. One cross country move, two kids, and six years later, Paul wanted something more unique to wear as a symbol of what our marriage meant and what held it together. When he could focus his attention away from Al and his dramas, Paul could be such a romantic.

We had a collection of Taschen architecture books at home and several Antonin Gaudi retrospectives. Paul flipped through the Gaudi photos of organic shapes and pillars on buildings Gaudi designed in Barcelona. Gaudi's nonlinear, twisted columns sometimes appeared like stressed bones, limbs stretched and split. Some had intentional bumps and imperfections on the surface. They were not smooth like normal columns, but textured. Gaudi's molded columns were the necessary inspiration for designing our new wedding bands. Some combination of the columns would work for each one of our new rings.

Our realtor friend Janet knew a jeweler who did custom design work and had a small studio in a historic building in downtown Austin, a block from the Capitol. Paul and I went to our appointment armed with an assortment of Gaudi books. We asked the jeweler to have fun with the images of columns and create something unique for each of us. The jeweler was amused by the unconventional request and accepted the challenge. We returned one time to approve some sketches. He had the right idea, and we let him run with it.

A few days before our sixth wedding anniversary, Paul and I picked up our rings and headed over to a tiny French restaurant we'd found not far from the jeweler's shop. Chez Nous was small, traditional, and served fantastic simple vegetable dishes and steak. The two-person staff was quietly wondering if we were even Americans. Sitting in the restaurant looking across the table at Paul, I felt a deep sense of being in love again, something that seemed to slip away with all of the travel interruptions and long hours in the studio. I finally had the sense that I was honestly beginning to feel at home in Austin.

Swapping out our wedding bands seemed to have a profound effect on Paul's work. It was as though he were reassessing the relationship he still had with Al and attempting to take more risks with the music to reflect the feeling of what was emotionally taking over in their creative collaboration. Al was an addict. There wasn't anything to celebrate there. Work with it. The music took on a much darker, sludgier, heavier sound, and it fit the current climate in the studio.

Not having a clear idea what we'd be doing with the kids for the summer, I signed them up for Gymboree classes at a storefront shop north of downtown. More driving, every day to classes that went from the end of May through the end of July. I waited inside and participated with my children, wondering, how did I ever get sucked into this prepackaged world of "fun for the entire family"? It was something to do. The kids were surrounded by cushioned slides, padded sawhorses, safety cones in primary colors, and a few kids their own ages. They rolled, clapped, and stretched for parents like me who were in between day care placement and preschool openings. It was something to do. It was inside. I could take a break and let the instructor guide them for an hour.

I met one mother who I cared to exchange numbers with, and we began visiting each other with our kids for playdates. She had a daughter and a son our own kids' ages. My first solid friendship in our new hometown didn't last. My new friend was also a new convert to her husband's church, and her social life was suddenly 100 percent devoted to her husband and church. Was there no happy medium between proselytizers and music industry stragglers in this town to socialize with?

Somewhere in this muddling around for connections and new friends, I was interrupted in my thoughts by a call from our old friend Sean Joyce. Sean may have been between band tours and was specifically calling the house to speak to me. I could think of very few reasons for Sean to call for me at this point in our lives; although, we'd remained friends since Wax Trax days. And of course, we had briefly dated before I met Paul.

"Dude, I'm at the Federal Building," he whispered into the phone.

"Wait, slow down. What are you doing there?" I asked. The federal courts were upstairs in the building, along with the US Attorney's offices and Immigration. I'd been to all of them.

"I have jury duty. I don't want to be here. There's a big mob case going on upstairs. You have to tell me how to get out of getting picked for this jury."

Sean, like most intelligent people, had perfectly rational fears of becoming a target for lowlifes engaged for the sole purpose of juror intimidation. Sean was hardly a body-builder type—more of a featherweight boxer type—quick on his feet as a drum tech and stage manager and accustomed to not taking criticism personally. This jury thing was a little too personal in nature.

"Tell the attorneys what you do for a living—working rock shows, traveling. I hope you're wearing your best punk rock T-shirt and Doc Martens. You should look like somebody waiting to stick it to the Man."

I knew Sean would take the advice to heart. He worked hard, was professional, and knew when to keep his mouth shut and maintain a cool head. Those skills made him immensely hirable in the clubby world of touring rock bands. For his court appearance, however, he could play the wildcard game and show up in a torn Effigies shirt with a shock of bleached spiked hair.

Sean was in luck. He was rejected by the prosecution in the first go around of "voir dire" in the mob case. He made a point to call me back and say thanks, and by the way did I need anything from Chicago? It was amusing to think I had actually helped a friend avoid responsibility, when I spent my days teaching responsible behaviors to my captive audience at home.

A short while after my call with Sean, I noticed our UPS driver pulling up the driveway and unloading a large box addressed to me personally. I rarely received packages from anyone, other than my father sending something for the kids or J. Crew, sending catalogue items I'd ordered over the phone. The return address on the box was the Jay's Potato Chip factory in Chicago. You couldn't find Jay's west of the Mississippi River, and certainly not in Austin, Texas. Jay's were like Chicago hot dogs and Italian beefs—often imitated, never replicated. I loved

Jay's. Sean knew that. I was now the happy beneficiary of a complimentary case of Jay's Potato Chips, thanks to my (now) best friend forever, Sean Joyce.

Thankful for the few friends I personally had left in the world, I returned to lamenting social options in Austin. As if my pleadings to the universe were finally heard, Paul and I met someone seemingly by chance at a motorcycle rally at Lake Austin on the other side of town. Paul was taking advantage of his break from Ministry work and decided looking at Italian bikes would inevitably put him in a positive frame of mind. We headed out to the rally as an excuse to get away from the house and Ministry drama and do something fun.

Our new friend's name was Joel. Joel was a few years younger than us and rode a Moto Guzzi. He came over to where we were having our own picnic in the grass, recognized Paul, and introduced himself. Joel knew Paul's music, but wasn't an obnoxious fan looking for two minutes of personal time with an idol. He wanted to talk bikes. Curiously, he bore a slight resemblance to Paul, not quite as tall but equally thin, with kind of a Stiv Bators look to him. His facial features were slightly exaggerated, like some line drawing caricature I'd seen somewhere depicting 1920s Berlin—almost grotesque in looks. Joel was not attractive in any traditional sense, yet I found him an appealing person to talk to, someone from Texas not embracing his hillbilly roots too much.

Paul and Joel discussed riding together, but Paul's schedule or interest in making new friends was just not there. I, on the other hand, was interested in knowing Joel better when he mentioned he worked for the University of Texas library system and lived near campus. I was starved for company with interesting people who kept up with music and didn't work in the music industry. I thought Joel could also be a useful resource if I needed help accessing the law library at UT for any reason later on.

Paul resolved his differences with Al and resumed going back and forth to his place. I called Joel on the off chance he was up for a visit to Deep Eddy Pool where I was heading with the kids. He met us there and as we sank shoulder-deep into the shallow end, we got to know one another a little better. I was still wary of people being friendly to me solely because my husband was in a band. Joel seemed genuinely disinterested in talking about Ministry life and more interested in talking about his own. That was a plus. He told me he had interned in Marfa at Donald Judd's studio. That was disappointing to hear. I wasn't enamored with Donald Judd's artistic output, what I'd seen of it. Judd's work lacked emotion, and that was the whole point of it. Machine-made objects laid on a floor so as to lose any relation to other objects or the artist himself—Boo! But considering there wasn't much interesting art in Austin as a whole, I gave Joel credit for looking outside the college campus and finding something worthy in Marfa. Judd put that tiny town on the map. Good for Donald Judd. Good for my new friend.

Joel and I met a few more times on campus, at the law library, at Les Amis, a divey café popular with students and slackers in Austin. We talked about Austin university life, and how it was easy to get swallowed up by trends in intellectual circles. No different really from art and music circles, and they usually overlapped anyway. Joel's best friend had just moved to Seattle, and he was thinking of going for a visit. Austin was beginning to get too comfortable for him.

"Not much changes here. Austin's a college town," I said. This was becoming my rote response to even myself at times when I didn't have an obvious reason for why I wasn't feeling at home in Austin. Like a lot of college towns, people came and left. I wasn't leaving for now, just trying to find my level of comfort living with the native population.

Where was my friendship with this guy going, anyway. Did it matter? Most of my friends in the past were men. I'd convinced myself that living in Texas was in fact an aesthetic experience, the value of which I would record in due time. I just needed more time, more experiences. Was this friendship part of that? Did I feel drawn to this kid because he looked like a younger, rougher version of my spouse when he was dressed in full leathers? Was I setting myself up for an affair? I would never do that to Paul. I loved him too much. Despite my loneliness and drinking, had I really been drinking too much? Did this kid notice anything? I didn't want to give off the impression I was available. Maybe, I was.

I didn't hear from Joel for several weeks. I was beginning to feel he was backing away from our chats, wary it would lead to something else wholly disallowed. Months passed before I saw or heard anything from him again. I missed our coffees.

Summer was dragging on. Paul seemed hopeful the Ministry record would get done. All that waiting for things to coalesce now had some momentum. At home, Paul shared a few details about the small country restaurant and businesses he'd been to in and around Marble Falls. Sometimes he'd pick up Adrienne from school. Paul was spending more time at home—our home. There were always projects to do on the house or errands to run. I showed him an article in the newspaper on how to construct a DIY bat house. For the first time in a long time, he was genuinely interested in having a teaching moment with the kids. He enlisted their help in constructing the bat house and choosing a spot in the trees for it in the backyard. They would find the perfect spot to keep an eye out for bats from their bedroom windows.

I nearly forgot about Al and had faith that eventually this Ministry record would fulfill another contractual commitment with Warner Bros., and life would roll along as it seemed to always magically do with Paul and Al. I trusted history would repeat itself. From our safe haven fifty miles away, I could never have guessed Al's celebrity or charm wouldn't be enough to distract his neighbors from comparing notes on the parties at his place or the characters hanging around who probably looked nothing like themselves: retired, rich, Republican.

We all accepted as a given the notion that Al had nine lives. His prodigious consumption of whiskey, wine, and illegal substances was a point of pride for him. The badass, hyperinflated persona, this Burroughs acolyte, always seemed to have guardian angels looking after him. No matter the excess, he got away with it. But excesses attract attention, and nothing lasts forever.

In August, Al's compound was visited by the local police and the feds. The all-night party at Al's came to an abrupt end, with figurative house lights coming on exposing the scorpions and human vermin scrambling for cover inside. Al, Paul's creative and business partner, was arrested for possession of heroin. We got a jail call at home. Crazed Management called too wanting to know if I knew any criminal defense lawyers in town.

How would they ever finish the Ministry record now, a beastly slog already having consumed two and a half years of Paul's patience, commuting for hours to Al's and prodding his partner to "make shit happen"? I wanted to scream at Paul, at Al, at myself for being so naïve. After bailing him out of jail, his lawyer informed Al he should lay low until his physical presence was required for the court hearing in September. Following the hearing and spooked by the possibility of future confinement, Al headed for Chicago. He was going back to Chicago Trax to finish mixing the record there. So much for our big plans to have a functioning studio in Austin.

Before there was time to fully grasp what was happening, Paul too was heading back to Chicago to stay with our friend William Tucker and finish production on the record. And I was again back to single parenting with a distant partner who was grappling with his own demons while trying to keep his livelihood alive. Ministry was his life and currently mine, too, but there was so much more to life than weathering the next Al flare up. Wasn't there?

I wasn't the perfect mother nor trying to be, but my heart and my intellect once again pivoted back to our children. I was responsible for them, despite any resentments bubbling up about my husband deserting me to tamp down someone else's drama. At times I wondered if he cared more about Al and being famous than he cared about me and his family. In a desperate moment I phoned lawyer friends in Chicago. My old boss Tom, former "prosecutor for the state," Tom Gibbons, was less than sanguine about all the back and forth to Chicago: "Quit clownin' around. When you comin' back?" I had to remind myself he asked me that question whenever I called to see how things were going at the old "oficina."

Ministry was embedded again in their dorm-like second home, Chicago Trax. Al's arrest and hasty retreat there were shocking news to some, but confirmation of the inevitable to everyone else. Ministry had hardcore supporters in Chicago and cart blanche privileges at Chicago Trax.

Just when our collective nerves accepted the new reality of crunch time in the studio, Al's personal saga lost some of its luster with other tragic events taking the spotlight. A week and a few days into October, we were all sidelined by news that Jim Nash suffered a major stroke and died at Northwestern Hospital in the city. He was forty-seven years old. The Chicago skyline of my twenties was getting smaller, and with it went an architect of my aesthetic. Chicago—the city where I was born, where I met Paul, where our children were born, home to the Wax Trax label and store where all of us had become bigger human beings by our devotion and love for Jim Nash and his partner Dannie—that Chicago hung heavy in my thoughts.

After two years of trying to settle into a normal rhythm of life in Austin, our lives were upended once again. How hard would it be to pack up the house, get out of Austin, and go back to Chicago or head somewhere else? I didn't know. Paul was not thinking along those lines at all. Austin was a stable home for him and for our family. In that mix, I was the center of it, his beacon of stability. At least I was supposed to be. And whatever Al did was Al's problem.

I was running out of ideas for constructive things to do while Paul was away. To avoid obsessing over Ministry's future, I thought I would spend time teaching the kids some practical skills. After all, there was more to life than just being able to play with your friends—"Papa" Paul did that for a living and was recognized around the world for his talent. Talent was invaluable, a gift, something to nurture wholeheartedly. It took discipline and time to develop that talent. Being good at anything took time, whether playing music or learning to be a motorcycle mechanic. I also believed there were few human skills more valuable, more essential for the soul, than learning how to cook for yourself. Knowing the basics was enough. It was something I was good at and enjoyed, something I could teach our kids.

We had amassed a good-sized collection of cookbooks and old copies of Bon Appétit and Food & Wine left over from my single days. With that wealth of reference material on hand, on a rare rainy afternoon I posed the question to my kids, "What should we cook today?" Their response: "Soup."

I had just bought the latest edition of The Joy of Cooking and started paging through recipes for something easy to make that didn't require a lot of finesse, just chopping and tossing into a pot. On page 100, I found the perfect creative vehicle for novice chefs: minestrone soup. It seemed whatever mess of chopped Italian plant life and herbs you had on hand would do. And orzo. Because any noodles made lunchtime better—even ones the size of rice grains.

Our knife block held a standard set of large and small chef's knives, paring knives, and one for bread. I had Ursula stand on the kitchen step stool to my side, while Gordon sat on the countertop to watch the two of us. I dropped a handful of kale onto a cutting board, placed one of the larger knives in Ursula's hand as I held it with her, and we moved the knife up and down in a zigzag pattern. What was left was a mosaic of green ribbons. I let her pick up the shards and toss them into the waiting oversized silver bowl. It was a game. It was Gordon's turn to play with a handful of basil leaves. We used a small knife and made "stripes" across the leaves from left to right, then picked up the basil and tore it with our fingers. The dissected green herbs were scooped up and tossed on the pile in the bowl. This impromptu cooking lesson was as entertaining for them as digging in the flower bed outside or holding a spoon to eat mashed potatoes. There was enough resistance on the surface of the object to make it interesting. Cooking became for me a metaphor for my own desire to tear apart and examine the essential tenets of homebound parenting. The soup, when it was finished, was delicious.

Afterwards, a pang of doubt set in and I wondered if I was being too liberal with my kids and sharp objects in the kitchen. I took them next door to see what Katherine Houston thought. "Start 'em young," was her quick assessment. The special-ed teacher in her was always there as a vote of confidence in my corner. I told Katherine I was grateful for her advice. "Gerda," she said, "be grateful your children will never need my help."

We headed back to our house. It was still raining outside. "Let's do something else fun," I said to the kids while I collected the house boombox, headed down the hall to their rooms, and plugged the box into the wall in Ursula's room. The music came up, the kids watched me and moved their shoulders up and down mimicking my moves as we spent the next fourteen minutes and forty-five seconds creeping around in a circle to The Sugar Hill Gang. "Rapper's Delight" was the ideal dance teacher. And learning how to conjure rhythm and rhyme was the ultimate practical life skill: " . . . the macaroni's soggy the peas are mushed and the chicken tastes like wood . . ."

***

After a few weeks, mixing was finished on the Ministry record. Paul was overwhelmed with Al issues and rethinking what he wanted to do about them. He flew home to Austin. We decided to take the kids to Dallas for the state fair. Yeehaw.

Perpetually dissatisfied with the recreational opportunities Austin had to offer a big-city vagrant like myself, the fair actually turned out to be the cultural lift I needed. As was my habit, I studied people's faces looking for clues as to what they actually did all day or simply to admire the symmetry of a face. Someone once told me Elizabeth Taylor was considered one of the most beautiful women in the world because her facial symmetry was as close to perfect as one could get. The left mirrored the right. I was more interested in looking at imperfections. They created more interest, like following a bump on a nose to see if it was possible the person owning it was a fighter and the nose had been broken in a fight or a fall from a horse, perhaps at a rodeo.

At the Dallas State Fair, there were faces representing all heritages and social standings. The state fair was an annual event to close a busy summer schedule before school began again, or a way to spend hard earned savings just this one time and make some memories.

Paul held up the kids in both arms to show them what it was like being six four, and I snapped a picture of the three of them in front of Big Tex, the official state fair mascot, standing fifty-five feet high in blue jeans, embroidered cowboy shirt, and hat. Getting lost again in the crowds, we regained our bearings by following processions led by gigantic hairdos that clearly indicated who the bosses were on those homesteads. Our two little blonde wonders posed for pictures clutching Mexican churros. And everywhere, mothers, aunts, girlfriends, and grandmas stopped what they were doing to point at our kids and utter a newly minted bit of southern hospitality:

"Wouldya look at that HAYER!"

Welcome to Dallas.

25

It was the end of autumn, 1995. With a little bit of time before Ministry would do the inevitable world tour for this new record, Paul and I flew to Seattle with our kids to visit his family and to see his brother Roland. Roland was doing sound design for Zombie, a gaming company. His office was in the Pioneer Square area of downtown. We met Roland in the square and headed to the ferries. I loved hopping on the ferries in Seattle. It seemed such a European solution to getting around and such a modern idea.

We drove to the docks, and the kids stared in disbelief as Paul steered our rental car straight onto the ship, bound for another shore. We parked behind some other cars, walked upstairs to the deck, and waited for the boat to begin its journey across. Nothing was better than this—our family, the four of us and Roland, in various degrees of distraction, staring out over the rails of the ferry, watching the shoreline receding on the stern end and stealing closer on the bow, as we rushed from the starboard side of the ship to the port. Paul knew all the nautical terms. He was in his element, standing tall with feet apart, holding steady on the deck, and staring at Puget Sound, so familiar to him. On our first trip together to Seattle, after getting married in Las Vegas, the two of us had loitered our way along the pier near the ferries, and Paul was in such a rush to exploit scintillating facts about his former hometown. Among them: the Aurora Bridge was a popular suicide bridge. Here was one of the westernmost landmarks in Seattle, a spot where the advice to "Go west, young man" would be taken literally by anyone ready to make the leap toward one final "success." Seattle was not Paul's favorite place to visit, but it had been a familiar home for much of his childhood and adolescence.

On the drive back to Uncle Charles's house, we stopped at the Ballard Locks. Paul was in a surprisingly paternal mood, excited to show our kids the fish ladder on the lower level and watch the hydraulics move the gates open and shut. We trained our eyes on the water levels rising and lowering to allow boats passage through the locks. On our way back to the car, I heard someone calling out behind us.

"Hey, great minds think alike."

Oh god, who could this be. People recognized Paul often in airports and on the street, but we were away from the greater public arena, anonymously wandering around his former hometown. I turned around to see a familiar couple with two small children heading our way. It was my law school friend Michelle and her family. We had not seen each other in a couple of years. Michelle was one of the handful of women I had studied with during those years of intellectual torching that allowed us to take charge of other people's lives—and in her case, other people's money. She was still at her corporate law job, and her husband was the stay at home parent with a software business. I felt a twinge of homesickness for Chicago, but also a deep gratitude for the power of marital equality and compatibility, and how it had propelled each of our families in a seemingly positive direction. And here we were in the same place at the same time. This accidental reunion bizarrely would happen again in another city in another year. But it was a classic moment of resuming a conversation with an old friend and picking up where you left off. I gave Michelle a big squeeze, and we said we'd keep in touch.

We returned to Aunt Alice and Uncle Charles's house. It was abuzz with cousins, their spouses, ex-spouses, and children, the youngest of which were ours. I could imagine what it must have been like growing up in this house with all the cousins. Miraculously, as adults now, everyone seemed if not warm to one another, then familiar as old friends are after a long absence. "How's life on the road?" someone finally asked Paul. The cousins all sat with their partners staring at us, as if they were all wondering the same thing—is this really Paul, and is he really famous? Here he was, sitting with his wife and two blonde toddlers with big eyes, who played with the house dog the same way their own kids did. It was as if everyone were adjusting their childhood expectations of what they imagined Paul would be like all grown up, to the reality of the man sitting at the table with them.

Cousin Andrew's ex-wife practiced family law in Seattle. Lyn and I traded courtroom dramas while her daughter played with Ursula and Gordon. I didn't miss for a second having to ferret out truth from fiction in family court.

Uncle Charles was now retired from teaching. He showed the kids how to feed peanuts to the crows outside on the back deck. Charles invited us to investigate the basement of the house for any remaining Paul memorabilia. As I walked down the stairs, I could see a large poster of the Ministry "stick men" figures hanging on a wall. It looked hand screened. It was Paul's design and was used for a Ministry T-shirt and for promos. His artwork was signed, "ill." Hilarious touch.

Uncle Charles laid out a huge dinner, as he always did for family gatherings. He was the chef of the clan. Roland made ratatouille with homegrown vegetables. I pictured all of them camping decades earlier, crammed together in Charles's camper truck somewhere in the Pacific Northwest. I loved that our kids were witnessing some of the men in their extended family assuming cooking duties. Paul seemed slightly distant with his aunt and uncle, and I thought the stress from this last Ministry record was evidently being borne by him, more so than his writing partner Al. There was such a glaring contrast between Al's life and ours. We were revisiting family ties and establishing new ones with our kids, doing what normal parents do on holiday—and that was a "cool" thing to do. I took for granted Paul was exactly where he wanted to be at this moment with his family. His professional dramas had to wait.

During our Seattle visit, Roland told us Bill Rieflin was in town. Bill and his wife Frankie had bought their first house together as a married couple. Bill invited us to come see the house and catch up with what the two of them were doing.

Bill no longer worked with Paul and Ministry, but he wasn't idle living in Seattle. He went on the road with Chris Connelly and William Tucker performing some of Chris's solo work. Together the three of them had visited us in Austin. When they arrived, Paul was either out at Al's or in Chicago, but I made sure to photograph Bill, Chris, and William in front of our Wall of Shame. During this Austin visit, Bill mentioned wanting to sign up for a guitar clinic Robert Fripp was putting together. I was surprised, not picturing Bill really as a guitarist. But Bill did admire Fripp's aesthetic and thought he could learn something new from him. Bill's drive for self-expression, even honing his skills with an instrument he wasn't necessarily famous for playing, kept him out there, being seen and getting involved with other extraordinary, talented artists. On the other hand, Bill also struck me as someone who wanted to stay grounded and to live where his painter wife Frankie wanted to live. That was in Seattle.

I valued Bill and Frankie's friendship. They were extraordinarily calm people, without any of the dramas associated with other artists we knew. Going to see them with our kids was safe. Paul and I occasionally had the nervous conversation about something our kids might see and be confused about while around some of the people he worked with: "Oh THAT'S something they'll talk about when they're eighteen and in therapy." We had no such concerns with Bill and Frankie.

Their house was a small cottage, with a lovely, manicured lawn in front and a lush, wild backyard where Frankie could indulge her horticultural talents. As a gardener, Frankie was a poet. Her painter's eye composed flowerbeds in back while she paused to smoke a cigarette. The garden was dense, a mixed bouquet of unusual, almost sorrowful blossoms. Frankie's garden had a delicate velvety tone to it, like her canvases. She possessed the visual and tactile dexterity of a painter, and it naturally wove its way into her physical surroundings—literally, the soil beneath her feet. She leaned over her outside work when we arrived, the lone human in that picture, surrounded by unearthly organisms growing every which way.

Bill seemed mildly amused with our clan, now four strong. Bill and Frankie didn't have kids, nor were they inclined to. Bill once told me he wouldn't want to pass on the "weird illnesses" in his family tree.

"Now children, keep your hands where the grownups can see them," Bill said to our two as we headed indoors. He was joking, of course. Our kids stayed close to Paul as we moved inside. The interior of the house was filled with light, and my attention was drawn to a small painting of Frankie's hanging in the living room. Ursula noticed it, too. Frankie had a few words with Ursula about the painting, while Paul and Bill did their usual, "What's new, what are you working on" routine.

We didn't have a lot of time to visit, having planned a trip to the monorail downtown. So far that day, we had had time for only a quick sub sandwich at a fast food place. The remnants of our lunch were squeezed into side pockets on the diaper bag.

When our visit was drawing to a close, we gathered our things, and Bill turned to the kids again. "Stay out of trouble, you two," he said with a smile. "What does he mean, Mama?" Ursula asked me.

We slowly walked back to the rental car, and my thoughts of where to go next seemed terribly ordinary, terribly pedestrian. Bill and Frankie were special people to us. I thought about how very special they were. Paul spent some of his starving artist years getting to know the two of them intimately when he and Bill first played together in the Blackouts in Seattle and then with Ministry and everything after. Bill and Paul had their own unique shared history, their own punk diary. When Bill stayed at our place in Chicago, he was a goof as often as a serious student of philosophy. Famished after working all day in the studio and returning to the apartment, he and Paul would trade lines from Hollywood Shuffle, Robert Townsend's hyper-real parody of life as a black actor in Hollywood:

"I ain't be gotten no weapons!" Paul delivered the line like a pro in a shakedown, grabbing a knife and fork for himself.

"Ho's gotta eat too," Bill would say when we were undecided about where to go for dinner in the neighborhood, or if we should jump in the car and go somewhere else.

I thought about these moments and further thought that our children should know firsthand just how special Bill's friendship was to us. I sifted through the remnants of our lunch in the side pockets of the diaper bag and found a few bites of sandwich wrapped in paper.

"When I say, 'NOW' pitch this to Bill," I said to Gordon.

Paul looked at me and started the car. We both looked over at Bill standing still on his new lawn and holding his hand up in a wave goodbye. Our car began to move, I turned to the kids and said, "NOW," and a half-eaten sandwich sailed out of the window dropping onto the grass at Bill's feet. Paul sped away laughing while I looked back at Bill and smiled. His hand was still in the air.

When we returned to Austin, I couldn't be bothered to think about the band having to tour on the new record. I dragged Paul to Costco now that he was finally home for a bit. We habitually went straight for the books section in the store after the diapers, cereals, and bottled water. There were always more children's books and the occasional biography to pick up. The biographies were for me and not confined to any particular genre: Liberace, Jimmy Carter, Poor Little Rich Girl, the story of the Woolworth heiress Barbara Hutton. My latest thrift store find was a biography of Wyndham Lewis, the painter. It didn't matter if the person was wildly famous or died in obscurity. Their histories fed my need for a good story.

We had already amassed quite a collection of cookbooks for me to flip through and every subcategory of nature field guide for the four of us. I asked Paul if we were ever going to have time to go camping and actually use these field guides.

"Well, I hope so," was all he could say. I hoped so, too. Otherwise, what was the purpose in buying The Audubon Society Field Guide to the Night Sky or the North American Birds, North American Wildflowers, North American Weather, North American Mammals, or the hideously inviting Field Guide to North American Insects and Spiders? What purpose then? Was I supposed to wing this one alone with the kids, too? When I discovered Paul had a vintage hard copy of Mushrooms of the Northwest stashed on our bookshelves, I had to find out if he'd ever used it.

"Maybe . . ."

Christ. Dreams and wishful thinking only get a person so far. From my perspective, I needed to be sure how to actually forage for poisonous mushrooms I was for sure willing to use on a certain colleague of his if the opportunity ever presented itself. Yes. I was sick of Al's shenanigans, too.

As autumn days grew shorter, sunsets in Austin seemed less colorful than other places I'd been, even Chicago. There appeared to be no color strata at all, unless I just wasn't seeing any for myself. I did my daily errands and looked through recent photos searching for one good shot of the four of us to use for a Christmas card. It would be the first in what became an annual tradition. I chose the photo and wrote a snappy caption, before handing the negative to the photo clerk at Costco for processing. When the cards were ready, Paul and I addressed the accompanying red envelopes and off they went to our fifty or so favorite people around the world. Afterwards, Paul got back on a plane and headed for Chicago, planning to return at Christmas. I kept one copy of our new Christmas card, posting it on the refrigerator where it would stay all year and every year after. The next year's edition was posted beneath the first and so on. Later on friends would tell us they kept our Barker family cards ordered in the same way on their own refrigerators, finding them too entertaining to remove.

I realized I was missing Chicago, missing Paul, and missing my friends there. I needed a break from Austin, too. It was a very disorienting time for me and undoubtedly everyone else. The idea of a home base seemed fluid again, precarious. I booked a weekend flight out to Chicago, a room at the Drake Hotel, and told everyone I was coming. The kids could stay with my sister. The Drake was within walking distance of Barney's, and I felt inspired to do a little handbag shopping for my birthday coming up. Surely the Barney's in Chicago could accommodate my extraordinarily good taste. Our old friend Ellie Fairey from Star Top found our wedding present at this Barney's: a French-made, porcelain teapot with matching café cups and saucers.

After checking in at the hotel, I walked over to Barney's, and a beautiful spray of sunlight illuminated one of the first display cases I came upon on the ground floor. My eyes fell on a red, sculpted evening bag in the shape of a little wedge-like canoe. The outer body of the shell was covered in red silk. Two thin, red, whiplike leather handles arched across the top like a "to go" box. Inside the bag there was room for a credit card, a compact, a lipstick, and nothing more. It was perfect. I bought two bags by the same Vietnamese designer. The other had a slightly larger wedged form in a different colored silk. I gave it to Ellie when I saw her later that weekend thinking, "What are girlfriends for?" Paul and I took advantage of my current close proximity to the Georg Jensen collection of silver jewels and art objects on display in their store anchoring The Drake Hotel. Oak Street Beach across the street may have been frozen on this December weekend, but we were together bracing ourselves against the harsh winds whipping down Michigan Avenue. Paul would later revisit Georg Jensen where he bought matching "Infinity" rings for the two of us, each silver ring curved and molded to resemble a Möbius strip. Love was infinite, wasn't it?

***

Toward the end of the year, we were notified that Ministry's Psalm 69 album had reached one million units sold. It was certified platinum. Shortly after, our UPS driver was the bearer of a half dozen or more framed gold and platinum records he delivered to our doorstep. The framed discs were sent to our house in Austin for safety and convenience. Some of the individual recipients, like Mike Scaccia and Al, would get theirs here, rather than at Al's place. In Chicago, Paul Elledge would get his platinum Psalm record at his Grand Avenue photography studio. Reid Hyams would get his at Chicago Trax. My husband Paul claimed again not to care about these things.

"It's cool. Whatever."

In a way, I understood that sentiment entirely. I didn't display my degrees or law licenses in the house, not even in my office. I knew I had them. I was nonetheless excited by all the fanfare in having a pile of heavy, slim gift boxes delivered from Warner Bros. It was another thank you. Not quite the same as when I'd see my own name listed in the acknowledgments on an album, but still humbling. I knew Paul wasn't about to disrupt the ambience of our swinging '60s house with a generic nod to sales figures. Ultimately, that is what gold and platinum records represented. The numbers varied country to country too, like Canada. Canada required less sales to hit gold. Each territory was different. Paul would prefer thrift store paintings of bullfights on our walls over some industry trophies. Bullfights celebrated the chase, not the prize. We had a handful of matador portraits waiting to be hung up and admired.

After Christmas, Roland Barker came to stay with us for the month of January. He was in town to make music but was not going out on the road this time with Ministry. Filling up time before tour, Paul and Roland huddled in the back studio of our house, recording new tracks Roland was putting together for a virtual game for Zombie.

At the end of Roland's stay, Paul and I discussed getting our kids into some social activities to be around children their own ages. Our neighbor Katherine was always helpful as a resource even though her sons were considerably older than our kids. She thought dance classes might be a healthy outlet for Ursula who, in Katherine's eyes, seemed full of endless energy always running between our two houses and the yards. I signed Ursula up for ballet classes at a studio in our neighborhood where a few of Katherine's elementary students were going. Our daughter finally had an outlet of her own.

I was diligently attending AA meetings, chairing meetings, and wrapping my brain around the concept that I couldn't drink anymore. I was okay with that. I had managed to fly alone to Chicago to see Paul for a couple of days and just be good to myself, and not once did I pick up a drink on that trip. That realization was a thrill in itself. Prior to moving to Texas, I hadn't had the desire to zone out, so why make it a habit now? I didn't want to obliterate myself with alcohol. Someone had once tried to obliterate me, and I survived for a reason. I had a mission, always. I needed a clear head to accomplish anything. Meeting with other sober people was a reminder that I needed to stay sober for myself first. Otherwise, I would be no good to anyone else.

Looking around me I was grateful to have healthy, happy kids and a marriage, which despite challenges felt stronger than ever. I could pat myself on the back for that. Physically, I felt better and both Paul and I were happier; although, Paul couldn't grasp the idea that I was never going to be "cured," that I simply could never drink again. He wasn't one for absolutes. His attitude about alcoholism surprised me, knowing he'd grown up with two boozy relatives in Seattle who later gave up drinking for good. There wasn't any shame in that, and no shame in recognizing I had a disease which had no cure. Paul didn't have a problem with alcohol and perhaps couldn't appreciate alcoholism was a progressive disease. I couldn't hope to have just one martini as we'd done in the past. One would never be enough, not ever again.

I wasn't doing anything more than going to meetings every day, talking to people afterwards, and reassuring myself and my husband that I was recovering. I didn't think it necessary for me to actually "do the twelve steps." My brief experience with asking someone to be my sponsor had been a huge disappointment. I could tough it out on my own—as I always had, with every other challenge in my life. I thought I was "good." We didn't keep alcohol in the house, aside from an unopened bottle of gold-flecked sake—a present from a Warner Brothers rep in Tokyo when we met at the hotel during our stay months before.

My sister Georgette insisted I go drop in to see Paul while he was on the road for the upcoming "Sphinctour" for Filth Pig. The US dates went from the end of March until the end of May. It would be good for my mental health as well as my sobriety, and she would stay with our kids. Ever the nanny and "Tante" to the kids, my sister tried, as Paul and I did, to normalize our home life considering Paul's unorthodox work life and schedule. Georgette had no children of her own yet as a comparison, but she was full of common sense lessons for her niece and nephew. How much do you explain to small children about what their parents do for work, anyway? She told the kids, "If any of your friends ask what your father does for a living, tell them, 'He plays with his friends. What does your dad do?'"

I was looking forward to getting out of town again on my own. I needed that time alone with Paul, however those "date nights" presented themselves. It would be healthy for our relationship to be in the same room together without anyone else begging for attention or yawning and saying, "I'm hungry." It would be a couple of months before the Tall One would come home from touring. New Orleans was on the band's itinerary at the end of April, so a perfect place and time for a change of scenery away from Austin.

Ursula began swim lessons with "Ms. Debby" in Tarrytown, the old money, old-growth-tree-lined neighborhood of Austin. I found Ms. Debby through the parenting grapevine—my next door neighbor Katherine and her school teacher pals. Debby Oatman herself was a retired schoolteacher popular with local parents, and she had her own pool. Once Gordon was out of diapers, he was going to see Ms. Debby, too. I was relieved our kids were getting foundational skills to survive in the world. I wondered if I should take lessons, and if I could find the time to properly learn to swim at my age. Then, the thought was gone as quickly as it came.

***

In the meantime, Cynthia Plaster Caster was thrilled I was living her dream—married to a famous musician. She adored Paul. She seemed to think he came from some elusive stock of talented souls she would never have access to, not as a partner or even a boyfriend. She could only cast them, immortalize their body parts and be friendly. Cynthia was very particular about whom she approached for a casting. Jimi Hendrix headed the list of her achievements, which stretched to the present day. Noel Redding, Jello Biafra of the Dead Kennedys, Chris Connelly of the Revolting Cocks, Jon Langford of the Mekons, and so on. She didn't take requests, either. Her only requirements? Extraordinary musicianship and someone whose music she really liked. A lot. It also helped to have a little swagger in the mix.

Cynthia felt now was the time to finally ask me if she had my blessing to approach Paul for a cast ("He's currently my favorite bass player!") and well, what was I to say to that? I didn't think Paul would have a problem with the idea of participating actively in someone else's art, especially someone who was such a good friend. Especially since I would be the "plater," the one to prep him for his cast. Without giving it a moment's thought, Paul said, "Are you kidding—of course!" It was as if he were expecting to be asked.

Cynthia had had Paul in her sights for some time. When the Revolting Cocks began releasing records, she was eager to cast almost all of them: Paul, Chris Connelly, Bill Rieflin, but curiously, not Al. Al Jourgensen had offered up himself for a cast around the time Cynthia immortalized our friend Jello Biafra. Cynthia called me and whined about Al, and how she felt uncomfortable when he approached her. "Ohhhhh, Gerda. I don't wanna cast HIM!"

She had her reasons, which she declined to divulge. I suspect Al didn't understand Cynthia didn't take requests. When the inclination and opportunity arose in Cynthia's mind, that's when it happened. She was an artist, after all.

I hadn't planned on returning to Chicago so soon, but with Ministry already on tour and Chicago dates approaching on the itinerary, Paul's "portrait" was on Cynthia's radar. Ministry was scheduled to play the Aragon Ballroom in early April. Paul and Cynthia could coordinate a reasonably uncomplicated time for both to meet up for the session. I booked a flight out, planning to rendezvous with the artist and model. Chicago was where many of our close friends still lived, and there would be press commitments and all the usual circus associated with our former hometown. Timing was everything.

I was flying again alone, grateful to have some adult time away from Austin, and thrilled to be interrupting Paul's endless schedule. I missed Chicago almost as much as I missed him.

My flight out had a layover in Atlanta. I took a seat and began rereading Nabokov's Lolita, my favorite travel book. It seemed appropriate somehow to absorb my thoughts in the adventures of Humbert Humbert and his sexually precocious step daughter, while en route to seeing Cynthia Plaster Caster. As more passengers crowded into the terminal, more frequent announcements began piping in over the din of the waiting area. The weather on the east coast was getting worse, and flights were being rerouted. More news. More cancellations.

I called Cynthia from one of the payphone cubicles set up at the gate. "Doll," she said, "just get here." Cynthia called all of her friends "doll." I appreciated the positive note in her voice reassuring me that yes, I would be collaborating on a Cynthia performance soon enough.

I took a seat at my gate, read some more Lolita and listened to the gate crew announce more delays. I let my mind wander. Paul had never been to Cynthia's apartment. Except for a handful of current friends she trusted, I couldn't imagine very many people had the privilege of seeing her place—unless they were coming for a casting. Like now. It needs to be now, damn it, I thought while looking up periodically for flight updates.

I looked at my watch—a simple black Tag Heuer—a Christmas present from Paul. He had a thing for watches. Paul bought watches for me that sometimes complemented his. In this case, a Tag Heuer with a bezel. He gave me watches as if we could sync our lives in this way, looking down at our wrists, as a reminder of who we were when we were apart. So romantic. When he wasn't busy looking for Georg Jensen jewelry for me on the road, he would find unusual compact mirrors and shoes he knew I would like. I hope this all works out smoothly and Cynthia gets what she wants right away, he'd said.

I did not want to return to Austin, having timed this adventure with all involved down to the minute, it seemed. With Paul gone so much, I spent a lot of time scheduling our personal lives out of necessity. Back to checking my watch. I stood up to stretch and began walking over to the airline counter, and there stood my fate.

Oh . . . NO. The universe must have a wicked sense of humor. As I approached the counter, I recognized the face on a tiny figure of a man standing in the center of a circle of five similarly dressed white men. Really pale white men in button-down shirts and cheap suit jackets: Ralph Reed was booked on my flight. Reed was the spokesman for the Christian Coalition. I was doomed. Reed was a born again Christian, vocally anti-abortion, vocally anti-liberalism on any issue involving personal rights, especially women's rights. Cynthia's pastime of making art objects from the likenesses of rockstar penises was about as hair-raisingly anti-Christian as you could get. This was a bad omen.

I looked at the screens above us for the next round of cancelled flights. I knew this trip was not going to happen. I sat down and waited, desperately visualizing where I was staying in Chicago, visualizing the interior of Mia Francesca, where Paul Elledge and crew liked to go with us when we were in town, and visualizing seeing my Paul, back in Chicago, with at least one night together alone.

Another fifteen minutes passed. Ralph Reed and his fan club were gone, having made alternative plans. I asked the gate agent if there was any chance I'd make it onto a flight to Chicago before the evening was over. They offered a hotel room until the morning or a flight back to Austin. Christ. I called my sister in Austin. There was no point in heading to Chicago a day later than we'd planned. Paul would be too busy to see Cynthia, and possibly too busy to see me as well. I called Cynthia again, but it was late. She didn't pick up the phone.

I returned to Austin with a feeling of having unfinished business to sort in my head. I was depressed and I had been doing so well. I felt utterly deflated, disappointed. And, as many other alcoholics before me, I didn't think there was anything wrong with stopping at the liquor store in the neighborhood and treating myself to a nice bottle of wine. Just this one time. I deserved it after all my hard work trying to keep everything together, didn't I? Unfortunately, the one time led to another, and I was back to my old crutch.

The Chicago trip aborted, there was still the upcoming Ministry show in New Orleans to look forward to. At the end of April, my sister stayed at the house to watch the kids again. My last trip to New Orleans was in 1991 when Paul and I made a second brief visit, saw Trent Reznor and his crew, and tried to decide if we too wanted to live there and raise a family, if we were destined to have one. We decided against it after hearing subtle and sometimes blatantly racist comments in conversations we had with some of the local shopkeepers. It also didn't help that we were spooked by a mangy gray cat staring in our windshield at a mom and pop gas station on the outskirts of the city. The tabby had one blue eye and one yellow. The image of the voodoo kitty convinced us New Orleans was not in the cards.

Before heading for New Orleans now, I called Dannie Flesher to see how he was faring. Jim Nash had passed away in October from AIDS. Maybe Dannie needed a break. I jokingly told Dannie we should get together in The Big Easy and hang out, go to the "tittie bars." He laughed, and said he was too tired and too busy to make the trip. I was on my own.

I arrived in New Orleans to an empty hotel room. The band was doing sound check at the State Theater. I was grateful for the quiet hotel room all to myself. With my drinking habit back in low gear, by the time I walked into that room in New Orleans, I was primed to investigate the room service menu for later to see what high octane New Orleans specific house specialties were available. The band was leaving after the show. The best reasonable option (in my mind) was to order a cheese and fruit platter once I was back at the hotel and to order some red wine with it. That seemed civilized. I was on break from my day job. No one would know. Paul finally appeared at the hotel, and we were able to catch up with our married selves and the usual Ministry stream of drama. Al was becoming more paranoid, that was the gist of it.

The New Orleans show crowd was raucous like most, and I wondered if our friends in Nine Inch Nails were coming to see the band now that New Orleans was home base for them. Someone told me Trent was already there at the venue. I wandered around, going into the audience, something I rarely did. Onstage, Al had a glaring contest going with drummer Rey Washam. I couldn't tell if it was an act or one more of Al's seemingly endless tantrums. Rey kept on playing and glaring back at Al.

I thought about the last time I'd been in town with Paul. We had come to see Nine Inch Nails perform. We'd gone backstage with everyone and right before they went on, we were instructed by the tour manager to get onstage and stand to the left, behind where Trent would be singing. This required walking across the stage to get there before the band walked on. The crowd was restless, anticipating the hometown show and was not happy when Paul and I suddenly appeared on the stage, breaching the sanctity of the Nine Inch Nails experience for them. There followed a chorus of loud boos. The pit committee, led by one faceless pack leader yelled, "GET YOUR ASS OFF THE STAGE!" Even the great Paul Barker had detractors, it seemed.

On that same trip to New Orleans, we went for drinks at a club with Trent and some of his show crew. Most striking of the bunch was a clean-cut, athletic guy who stood behind Trent at the bar while Paul and Trent yucked it up on their bar stools. The guy with the gym-grade body hovering next to Trent was his new bodyguard. I was not expecting that. I spent a few minutes chatting with Trent's wardrobe handler, a dark-haired beauty who was anxious to discuss our common dilemma: where to find affordable, feminine, underwire bras in size double D.

Now again, back at the State Theater, Ministry finished their set. I watched drummer Rey Washam storm offstage and head out of the club in the direction of the coach parked outside. Paul was at his heels doing the "Paul thing" of keeping the tour running as smoothly as possible. Rey later told me what set off Al. Al was glaring at him onstage because he felt Rey was either not keeping time or not playing loud enough—ridiculous assertions coming from a drug addict and simply not true, according to Rey.

I found myself blending in with the exiting crowd, trusting I would be rescued by the tour manager or a crew member or Paul himself and led back to the dressing room or the coach waiting outside. I was almost to the exit door of the theater when I felt an arm linking into mine, and there was Trent Reznor.

"Hi, Stranger," he said. I was so happy to see a familiar face offsetting those last few minutes of chaos. I wanted to congratulate him on his band's ever rising success. "So, what's up?" I asked. He leaned over. "Well, I have this budding drug problem . . ."

What the hell? There was some commotion at the doors, with the rest of the band coming out. Trent and I were separated. I looked around everywhere, but he was gone. Drug problem. I searched in vain for Paul, who'd apparently caught up with Rey and was begging him to calm down. Ministry had three more weeks of US dates before heading to Europe, and the last thing anyone needed or wanted was a defection in the band.

I found Paul finally and told him I was worried about Trent, like I should do something. Paul didn't want to hear it. He had his own troubles trying to keep peace on the bus, as usual. Rey later told me Paul's constant apologizing for Al was embarrassing if not also painful to listen to. Rey wanted Al to be accountable for Al. Paul or anyone else stepping in to mediate just aggravated the situation more. All those giant egos clashing seemed inevitable. I was surprised it didn't happen all the time. Thanks to Paul, it seemed, it didn't.

Our friend Paul Elledge was in New Orleans documenting the tour, shooting photographs inside and out, and as my Paul and I had very little time left before he had to leave again, "Photographer Paul" snapped away. Out of those attempts to capture what was going on between the two of us at the moment, there is one photo where I am standing with Paul outside the tour bus as the band is preparing to leave. It's dark, and Paul and I are in profile. He leans in toward me with his hands at my waist. I am against a wall with my arms folded in front of me. That photo essentially depicts the coming and going away again of our relationship. Paul always the one leaving to go somewhere—the studio, on tour—and I was not invited nor needed. That was HIS world. I didn't have such a retreat. I stayed back. I had to. I filled my days with making our kids' lives and Paul's business affairs my life.

In the photo, I am wearing a short-sleeved black turtleneck over my gold-and-black, animal print Dolce & Gabbana pants. I bought the pants just for myself—for me—at the Houston Barney's store, and they felt and looked fabulous. The pants stood out under that streetlight as a badge, a piece of armor holding me up, saving my identity. It was a rare moment of being equally present to the rest of the seeing world that yes, I mattered in this picture, too. I loved that photo. It was blown up and hung with other portraits in Paul Elledge's Chicago studio for a couple of years. He said it was one of his favorite shots from the tour. This knowing two Pauls of such notoriety was confusing at times when Leasha Overturf (Paul Elledge's wife at the time) and I were talking about one or the other "Paul." We'd fall into saying, "My Paul . . ." to make a point.

I made my way back to the hotel for the night. What would I want someone to do if I confided in them about a substance "problem?" There I was, with my own problem, trying to help someone else. It was too late to make any outside calls. I called down to room service for my wine and cheese midnight snack. I was further distressed to hear, "Kitchen's closed for the night, and we don't serve liquor after 10:00 p.m." Wonderful. Can't wait to go home. I slipped out of my Dolce & Gabbana's, turned off the bedside light, and fell asleep.

Back in Austin, I called Cynthia Plaster Caster and asked her to take some notes on my trip to New Orleans before I became too distracted with my kids. She liked the idea of preparing journal entries for someone else's journal (mine) and thought it very "GTOs" (Girls Together Outrageously). The GTOs were a collection of Cynthia's groupie friends in LA in the late '60s who came under the care of Frank Zappa. Cynthia also told me writing down my exploits would take her mind off of "daydreaming about the bass player in Brainiac." Cynthia and I had been friends now for almost fifteen years. We tried unsuccessfully once to compile her diary notes and memories into a book. Not giving up on my girlfriend, I had recently offered to help manage her career since we talked regularly, and each of us had a network of contacts. For me, it was a way to get back to working on something aside from Paul's business and orchestrating our kids' social calendars.

I hung up with Cynthia and called John Malm, Trent Reznor's manager. He seemed bothered that I was worried about Trent and seemed uninterested in passing on a message to have Trent call me. I called Danny Lohner to see if he could give me Trent's direct number. Danny was currently working with Nine Inch Nails. Danny gave me the number to Trent's new place in New Orleans, and I called a few times leaving messages with people there who were undoubtedly Trent's house handlers, considering his band's massive popularity. My final message for them was to tell Trent to call me to talk about Paul, revolving cocktail lounges, and Trent's current "problem." I went to bed.

I woke up to the house phone ringing at about 3:00 a.m. I sat up thinking it was Paul calling from the road. It was Trent. I said, "What the hell happened to you, leaving like that. I was worried." He told me he was unhappy. He had no real friends, no real life, just one populated by myriad acquaintances and parasites. He wanted to feel better about himself and what he was doing.

"Why won't Al let Paul work with me?" he asked. His voice was getting louder.

What was this all about? I couldn't believe there was some sort of prohibition in place preventing Paul from working with anyone he wanted to. That was silly. But maybe Trent knew Al better than I did.

"What are you talking about? He's on tour right now, you know that. Paul

loves you. He'd be thrilled to work with you—he already has. Are you kidding?"
I couldn't imagine Paul NOT working with Trent. Trent, bringing the anguished
sex-starved vocals, and Paul with his signature spine-numbing bass and
fascination with making "ugly music." How could that not work?

"Why don't you take a break and come to Austin. We have a big house to
hide in," I said.

I felt the mood lightening on his end. I told Trent I was managing Cynthia
Plaster Caster's career now. He laughed and offered his services "as her driver." I
told Trent Paul would call him, and we said goodnight. When Paul did eventually
call me from a diner in Tulsa, he thought it was "so fucking dumb" that Trent
thought there was some Al edict preventing Paul from working with other people.
There were "only so many hours in the day," and he told me he'd call Trent
when he had a chance. In Cynthia's transcription of my notes on my trip and
subsequent phone call from Trent offering his services to be her driver, she wrote,
"Baby, he can drive my car ANYTIME."

It would be almost ten years before I spoke to Trent again. In the intervening
life years, he got sober and worked on physically getting in shape to the point
where I was stunned to see the new Trent. He stood in front of me at Stubb's in
Austin on the outdoor patio in back, in bright sunshine before a Nine Inch Nails
soundcheck. Physically, his body mass looked like two of the old Trents in one.
He put his arms around me and gave me the biggest, longest bear hug I'd ever
had. The guy seemed to have acquired some new chiropractic skills, too. It felt
like a thank you.

Paul and I had brought our kids along for this reunion of sorts.

"And who are these people?" Trent asked, looking over at our kids. They
were ten and eleven by this time and fairly unimpressed with any of our friends.
Music friends came and went on their way, and this one would be like any
other—to them.

***

With Paul and the band on the road again, I was left with little adult conversation other than long distance phone calls. I was beginning to feel I'd worn out my welcome with some Chicago friends; although, no one hung up on me when I called out of the blue. My painter friend Marnie called regularly, as she had done when we were still living in Chicago. Marnie could go on and on about her current beau and technical difficulties with certain paint formulas changing, and I didn't mind at all. Marnie was a talker, but I needed the banter to sustain my sanity.

I reached out to Rey Washam's girlfriend Annette, in a raw attempt to nurture new contacts in Austin. I needed new rituals, new insights, something to take my mind off of drinking. Annette and I made plans to have dinner with Gibby Haynes's girlfriend at Mezzaluna, a northern Italian restaurant downtown. A girl's night out. It was something I had rarely looked forward to in Chicago for many reasons, usually time constraints. Currently, I would make the time and pay a sitter for the kids.

My dinner companions were professionals with evolving careers of their own. Rey's girlfriend Annette worked in advertising for the Austin newspaper. Gibby's friend did something in music and was possibly studying law at the time. It was fun being out with new people, but that feeling of being new in the neighborhood lingered. Where did I fit in? What was the art scene in Austin? Was there one, and I was simply missing it? I wanted to know. Or was the small music community all there was? My desire for the new didn't end with the ascendency of our nuclear family. What did other women talk about anymore? These were nagging questions I wanted the answers to.

Going out alone felt a bit awkward. Not because my dinner companions were single and I wasn't, but simply because Austin was still new to me. We had been settling in for a couple of years, but making new friends had not been easy, nor high on my list of priorities. A lot of grief, adjusting to life with a new son, and the confusion of traveling back and forth to Chicago, and settling into a new house had taken up a considerable amount of my time and thoughts. For this night out, I celebrated my freedom, donning a Lilly Pulitzer summer dress and bare, strappy sandals I'd bought at Marshall Fields in Chicago when I was still in law school. Tales of womanhood—that's what I longed for. I wanted to hear the stories these two women had to tell about their own lives.

I was happy to be having dinner with two funny opinionated women, away from diapering and elemental cooking lessons at home with my kids. As a single woman and living in Chicago, I could tick off the number of women friends who were getting married and having babies, and who'd fallen out of communique with those of us who were not. I was always happy for my friends and their choices. It didn't matter that they were unavailable much of the time. We were still friends. It didn't occur to me that anyone would consider me unavailable now that I was married, had two kids, and a rockstar husband. Was that supposed to be a social jinx? I hoped not.

I didn't know what to expect from the dinner conversation, but what I was gleaning from it was making me question my willingness to be open to new things at this point in my life. My dinner companions were nice, interesting people, but did I really want to discuss the benefits of a high colonic—over dinner? Colonics, or cleansing enemas, were currently all the rage. Sitting in dim lighting over drinks and dinner, happy to be away from tending to bodily functions of an as-of-yet not potty-trained son, my brain couldn't switch gears quickly enough to engage in the pros and cons of fancy enemas as means to self-care. After having a second child and a semi-absent partner, self-care had become a distant memory. I felt pampered when I had five minutes to brush my teeth.

Did I have common interests with these women or were our partners and music connections about all we had in common? It wasn't their fault I was trying to catch up to the adult world after a few years of ignoring subtle shifts in dieting or the latest self-improvement technique. I was not invited to go out with these women again, and I wasn't surprised. But Annette was planning to go to Amsterdam to see Ministry, and she and I would connect again there.

After the girls' night out, I thought more about how women take care of their bodies. Other women went to the gym. I wasn't interested in working out indoors. In law school, my study partners swore by Jane Fonda fitness tapes. I walked. Outside. Maybe I needed to adjust my thinking on all sorts of things. I wasn't giving up walking, no matter what. Walking was my meditation.

When the air outside was unhealthy at any hour, I tried walking indoors at our neighborhood mall before business hours. Other people did it. I went once or twice, wandering through a nearly empty mall, where a still-life of stagnation unfolded before my eyes. Security bars locked over storefront windows with lifeless, fully dressed mannequins caged in for the night; the fluorescent lighting and endless beige walls and corridors amplified the absurdity in searching for a relaxing meditative state in an enclosed man-made maze—one with bad lighting. Who actually enjoyed this regimen? I passed by another small group of long-retired grandmotherly types and headed for the exit. There has got to be a saner way to get in a long daily walk, I thought. Maybe a treadmill?

I talked myself into buying a standard issue, manually operated treadmill. Paul helped install it in our main guest bedroom when he returned home for a break in the tour. The treadmill lasted as long as it took for the kids to figure out how much fun hopping on and falling off the thing was when it was moving. The treadmill remained dormant for months. Maybe I needed to try some other indoor exercise. Yoga. Why not? That was safe.

I bought a yoga tape at Costco. The kids were together in the family room playing, and as soon as they heard the television on where I was, they bounded over and plopped down in front of the set. I positioned my back straight against the fieldstone wall framing the panorama of windows facing the front yard. I was seeking serenity in what was theoretically an ideal natural landscape. I tried my best to assume basic yoga positions and followed along with the instructor on the tape. Ursula and Gordon played along, aping the new postures I was desperately trying to hold on this "forest" of green carpeting in our sunken living room. The two of them fell over laughing. Yes, yoga. I tried manifesting my true desires with yoga. And here on the rug next to me were the fruits of some of my true desires looking up and giggling.

Yoga. So relaxing, as long as there are no children around or you can leave and go somewhere else for self-care sessions. I didn't feel I had that luxury. We had enough money to afford a full-time nanny, and my sister filled the role until she was able to find another job as a baker, something she was trained to do. When that happened, I felt uncomfortable with the idea of handing our kids off to a stranger while their dad was away. I never felt a desperate need to go off for a body scrub or have some other pruning work done. It smelled a little too "rock wife" in character. It was just not me. If we had the notion to hire another full-time nanny just so I could get away, I could easily go back to work. We didn't need the extra salary. And our kids were not going to be raised by strangers so I could be "professional" again. I would go back in due time when Paul was able to spend more time at home.

I was no longer a professional. That didn't bother me. What I was doing was more important at the moment. My friend Marnie would take breaks from painting in her Chicago studio and call me sometimes during the day. "This is the hardest job I've ever had," I told her. I divulged my thoughts to Marnie because I trusted her. She was one of my angels, someone who exemplified the creative life of a woman artist. The painstaking work she did making paintings and my struggles in my own ever-changing set of daily challenges were equally exasperating at times. How do you shower yourself without locking your kids in the room with you? There were a few occasions when I took baths with both of them and made a game of it. They were getting too old for that.

I found it difficult to keep our books straight and still find time to write in my journal. My kids became my project, my outlet for creativity. If we were staying in Austin, and I was to keep my own identity intact, I had to shelve my desires for the moment and accept the roles of teacher, art director, moral guide, cook, and driver to my kids. I didn't have a network of old friends to turn to in Texas. Only phone calls. As Ministry's reputation continued to grow, I became more protective of the kids and of my own safety, again. I called my Chicago friends for laughs.

Our director friend Doug Freel was out with the band for the current Ministry tour. He proposed tagging along, filming the band's performances around the world. Doug had directed Ministry's "Reload" video for the current album. In the video, Paul and Al are outfitted as John and Jackie Kennedy reliving the Dallas motorcade story line. For the current tour, Doug filmed backstage parties, the band warming up, and behind the scenes dustups at the live shows. As bonus footage, what Doug also captured was Al's ongoing paranoid narrative, fueled exponentially by how many substances he was consuming on a given day.

At some point on the road, Al was pleading with Jolly Roger, their current tour manager, insisting he needed a bullet proof vest or he wouldn't perform onstage. A mystery assassin was out to get him. While his penchant for storytelling and hyperbole raged onward with each tour stop, Al convinced himself he had seen someone in the audience pointing a laser at him. Really.

I'd spent enough time around the band members and on tour buses by now that I knew from experience they watched a lot of movies to kill time. Al and Paul were legendary in their sampling skills using among other things, soundtracks. Listening and relistening to sounds, over and over again. Repetition. I later asked Director Doug, "What would you say is a ballpark number for how many times Al's watched The Bodyguard? You know, Whitney Houston? Laser pointers?"

Doug was absolutely silent. Then he burst out laughing, running with the image. "Yeeeeeeah . . . those things will drive your dog crazy." Indeed.

Al got his vest.

I was hearing bits and pieces of stories from the road from Paul, who typically did not share many details about daily dramas. I was on my own filling in the fun stuff. In May, I took the kids to LA for a few days to spend time with their dad while Ministry was in town for two shows. We stayed at the Mondrian hotel on Sunset Boulevard. Doug had some directorial ideas to film us with Paul, while he was in full tour mode and on the road. The kids and I arrived early and waited at the hotel for the band to arrive.

I was trying to hide my drinking from Paul, but when he arrived, he found an opened half-pint of vodka while rummaging around in a bathroom drawer. I told him it must have been left by the maids. I imagined Paul was too busy dealing with the ongoing murder plot against Al to dispute anything I said.

In between press duties and soundcheck, Paul took a break for a drive to Venice Beach with us. Doug and his friend Jeffrey Kinnart arranged the trip and tagged along. In the finished documentary of the tour, there are shots of Paul pushing the kids on swings at the beach and walking alongside them in the sand. It was a poignant contrast to another scene (later cut) where all of us are backstage at one of the LA shows and Al is trying to cozy up to Ursula, to get her to pay attention to her "Uncle Al." In the scene, Ursula has her eyes on Al as he leans in towards her. When Al is too close for her comfort, savvy little Ursula flinches as if surprised by a jack-in-the-box and grabs onto me to save her. It was so odd. She had met Al many times before. She must have sensed some manic paranoid vibe in the room—what kids detect.

Back at our hotel, Doug urged us to take a short walk down Sunset and get some coffee at The Source. He had mentioned it a few times at the beach and was persistent now about getting over there.

"It's an institution . . . and we're guaranteed to run into Fabio." He'd mentioned Fabio at the beach several times, too.

Doug convinced Paul that the gym where Fabio worked out was around the corner from the restaurant, and yes, "He's always there." Somehow Doug also knew Fabio was a big music fan. Wouldn't it be great to catch some scenes of Paul meeting Fabio—the greatest living male model to grace the covers of romance novels worldwide? Women swooned in his presence. Some men lost their wits around him, too.

We'd heard enough, and wanting to humor Doug, the entire group of us walked over to The Source, found a couple of tables, and settled in. The restaurant served diner food and was one of those popular places frequented by neighborhood locals looking for gossip—the food almost seemed beside the point.

We were barely in our seats, when the kitchen's swinging doors parted with great authority, held open in place by a solid figure of a man exhaling as if he'd just finished a few laps. I could see why the "wimmins" were drawn time and again to novels with his likeness fulfilling the four corners of their covers.

Fabio.

I could swear Doug staged the whole thing. But he assured me he hadn't. Doug was already thinking of where this might fit in his movie, as he quickly charmed Mr. Fabio with small talk and introduced him to Paul. I couldn't look at him. "Hunky" men were not attractive to me in the least, and I was afraid I might utter some damningly off-topic opinion to this human incarnation of an SUV.

Fabio took a seat and began making small talk with Paul on one of his favorite subjects—music. Paul was from Seattle. Fabio LOVED musicians, he said. He especially LOVED all the "excellent music" coming out of Seattle. (Fabio also noted that he LOVED the restaurant's pancakes.)

Fabio continued his Seattle theme, naming a few Seattle native sons. He loved the Steve Miller Band. Who else, besides Steve Miller, could possibly cast some sunshine over the perpetual mist of a typical Seattle spring day?

Paul finally spoke. "Um . . . Jimi Hendrix?"

Sadly, this segment of their conversation was edited out in the final version of the film.

Following the band's second LA show, Ministry left for Sacramento. I flew back to Austin with the kids, happy we had seen Paul "at work." If the kids could weather running around in LA, they'd be comfortable navigating the canals and riding bicycles in Amsterdam. That was our next tour stop to see Paul on the road.

While Paul performed on stages across the country, our daughter was busy rehearsing with her ballet classmates as I prepared her for her first dance recital. The recital was ten days after our LA trip. It was at the high school auditorium with full costume changes and production values. I offered to help backstage with several other mothers, dressed in one of my Lily Pulitzer summer dresses and strappy sandals feminine enough to show allegiance with the aspiring ballerina. For many of the little girls, this was the first official test of their stage presence and poise. Many of them were on schedule to become properly educated young Texas ladies. At three and four years old, I couldn't take such ideas seriously as some other parents clearly were inclined to do. As would happen now with sometimes unhappy regularity, our male head of household could not attend this milestone event. While our ballerina bowed and curtseyed in time with her peers, Paul waited in the wings to go onstage at the Warfield Theatre in San Francisco.

As Paul continued touring the country with his bandmates, I toured local preschools searching for a place where our kids could explore their own creative impulses. Paul returned home for a few days before heading to Europe, and we toured schools together. Choosing a preschool was one designated family-related task he could manage. It was something to compartmentalize and didn't require accommodating someone else's drama—an easy paternal duty and a necessity in between ports of call.

Our neighbor Katherine recommended a few schools currently without waiting lists. Who knew there'd be a wait to consider? Not us. Paul was equally buyer beware as I, with all of the options. I knew very little about choosing a preschool other than what I read in parenting magazines or heard from friends in Chicago. Together we visited the closest preschool, located across the road from our neighborhood elementary school. The staff didn't appear enthusiastic about their jobs. The next school (where Katherine's boys had attended) did have a wait list but could possibly squeeze in our eldest in a couple of months. I didn't have the patience for that kind of uncertainty, already living according to the tentative nature of Paul's schedule.

The last school we visited was a favorite with the Austin music crowd and tail-end Baby Boomers. It was in an old house, which looked to be a hundred years old and dependent upon natural light and the charm of well-maintained wood floors inside. The place had a lot of character, detailing reminiscent of a craftsman house. There was a fenced, shaded front and backyard for the children to socialize and get their hands dirty. The lead teacher, a local musician who played guitar and sang to them, would introduce the kids to the music of a different composer each month. Dress up and play, lots of singing, and reading aloud. The kids already enrolled at this school seemed engaged and happy to interact with another peppy young teacher sporting colorful braids and leading them in an art activity. I was charmed by happy faces of children dressed in clothes they could get dirty in outside, who were free to do so if that made them happy. One little boy wore a football themed T-shirt paired with a pastel-colored tutu pulled on over beach shorts. Manufactured "cute," this place was definitely not. It was perfect for our kids. It was near our new favorite bakery, Sweetish Hill. I was sold.

Whatever lack of personal experience in this kind of structured play either one of us possessed didn't matter. It was a first step, pointing our kids into the unknown of their own education away from home. I agonized over whether we made the right call. For once, I was relieved to see Paul unfazed by this new drama, my anxiety, and trusting my ultimate decision on where the kids would go. I was no expert, but I did have twenty years of classroom politics behind me, and that was good enough. We were not religious people, but it seemed to me that choosing the right preschool was like choosing a Sunday school. At three and four years of age, our children were highly impressionable.

Their first few days there, my sister and I picked up the kids after school and treated them to gingerbread cookies and small cartons of chocolate milk at Sweetish Hill. It was a smooth transition and no big deal as far as the kids were concerned. They wanted to play along with the new scheme of things.

I was relinquishing parental reins to strangers, resetting my schedule of household maintenance and PR glad-handing with Ministry's management. I couldn't afford anything else new beyond adjusting to an empty house for a few hours five days a week. The psychological shift was huge. Paul was back on the road, and I had complete privacy for the first time in many months. I could take a bubble bath and shave my legs again.

A few dates into the European tour, I came home in the morning after running my usual errands and found an urgent message from our bank on the answering machine. A bank officer wished to speak "personally" with Mr. or Mrs. Barker regarding some recent transactions. Oh god, what now, I thought. It seemed we were constantly lending a sympathetic ear, along with money, to the Jourgensens. Was that it? Vexed by the tone of voice on the machine, I dialed the number. Did a tour advance not clear the bank? Were we victims of identity theft? Texas had the charming distinction of being the state with the highest incidence of ID theft in the country, a useful bit of information I picked up at an entertainment law seminar in Nashville earlier in the year.

No, the bank officer assured me, our personal information had not been compromised. The reason for their call: they wanted to know why I had just bounced twelve checks. I had no idea what they were talking about. I became suspicious that the person on the phone was an imposter posing as a bank employee to extract information from me about our accounts. After a few minutes back and forth, I realized this person on the line was legit.

I still had no idea why there would be an error on our account. I balanced the checkbook every month after writing a long series of checks. I separately wrote Spurburn Music checks to other songwriters when necessary. When I dropped off deposits in person, the first thing I did when I arrived home was balance the checkbook again and file away receipts or invoices connected to payments. I was meticulous in keeping records for tax purposes. I had to be. This accounting wrinkle was a mystery. I went ahead and authorized the bank to cover the checks with money from another account we had and told them I would look into the discrepancy.

By the end of the day, after researching our files to find where I'd made such a costly error and not coming up with an answer, I was getting anxious. I wished Paul were home to help piece together what had happened. The money at issue was around five thousand dollars.

When Paul finally called, my discombobulated panic over somehow misplacing thousands of dollars was now his problem too. I heard an audible sigh on the other end of the line.

"Oh Gorgeous, it's my fault. I left money on the dresser. It's in an envelope."

What money? When? I didn't know whether to be furious or breathe a sigh of relief. I hurried down the hall to our bedroom and pushed aside every object on Paul's dresser, searching for the mystery envelope. Under a heavy glass vintage ashtray, there it was. The maids who cleaned our house once a week secured the envelope for him. They had cleaned under it and around it three times by now. Thankfully, the entire amount was still intact. Paul then "came clean" about the money. When he was frantically running errands in the hours before leaving town for tour, he drove to the bank and withdrew several thousand dollars in cash. The money was to cover some crew per diems or someone's late bonus or some other exigency. At the last minute, before heading to the airport he received word that the funds weren't needed after all. Management had covered it. At the last minute, while performing the usual "idiot check" before leaving the house, he took the envelope full of one-hundred-dollar bills from his bag and placed it on top of his dresser. Then he left. The decision-making process behind withdrawing the money from our account, up until the act of leaving the money behind was unilateral. He neglected to tell me. He forgot. I could have screamed. But it was typical Paul Barker. Paul was, after all, Ministry's point man and fixer. I should have known.

Paul was frequently lending Al money and getting reimbursed by their management. That was routine. Three hundred dollars here, two-fifty there. If a Ministry record was close to delivery, Paul was the person the label went to for a straight answer and reassurance that the recording budget was being well spent in the studio. The label people could make sense of Paul's first class dining-car explication of the facts over Al's munition-filled, exploding bullet-train version. Ministry fans might find the bullet train flipbook version a sexier image—but so is dying young. The label wanted real live data.

At other times, Brockum, the company handling their merchandising, required artwork to begin churning out T-shirts, and they would call Paul for updates. Tour managers worked out tour kinks with Paul's specifications. Oh that Paul—what a guy. I delivered the envelope full of cash back to the bank.

At some point before the end of Ministry's Filth Pig tour, word reached me that someone with access to the band's dressing room had stolen a crew member's address book full of personal information on everyone in the band. Home addresses, phone numbers, all of it. Whether inspired by Al's paranoia or the real possibility there was a Ministry stalker following the band, I poked around for more information. There were details emerging about this stalker: a blonde, white male with a seemingly legitimate press pass, who had taken pictures (along with the address book) and was overheard bragging to someone that he would be "taking a little road trip." That was enough detail to set my maternal instincts into warrior mode. Paul, for whatever his reasons, didn't think I should worry.

I called Paul Elledge's studio in Chicago. They had gone out to shoot photos at many of the shows on the tour, and Paul Elledge knew exactly who the suspected thief was. He had taken a few shots of a scruffy blonde who seemed overly eager backstage, carrying on some fiction about being friends with the band. Paul and his wife Leasha actually were friends with everyone, and the guy seemed like a creep. I asked the Elledges if they could send me copies of some of their photos. "I want the kids' school to be aware of this nutcase," I said.

Leasha overnighted black-and-white, eight-by-ten prints that I then turned over to the kids' school. Phoenix School had kids of parents who were Austin celebrities, attorneys, and judges, so security beyond the norm was nothing new to them. I just didn't want someone stalking me or my kids.

There was a confounding duality motivating me. I was consciously trying to keep daily life as normal as possible for our children, and at the same time I was drawing attention to the fact that our family life was not normal at all. But I soon came to realize it was to my great advantage that my husband and his various music projects had supporters in all sorts of unlikely professions. One of the Phoenix School teachers worked part time at Liberty Lunch as a bouncer. Amanda Ferguson, a full-bodied Scottish girl, smiled when I handed her the photos. She looked at them, slapped her foot-long Maglite against her palm, and started laughing. "THIS guy? He's not getting past me." At her second job, Amanda corralled unruly rock stars and their fans with her imposing voice and physique, including a very intoxicated Courtney Love, whom she was tasked with driving to and from a gig one night. Amanda meant business. But the most disarming thing about her had nothing to do with brawn and commanding vocal cords. During her hours as a teacher, Amanda taught the children sign language.

Kim Longacre, the head teacher at Phoenix School pulled me aside one day. Here it comes, I thought. One of our kids is showing early signs of social isolation. A rebellion was imminent.

"I just wanted you to know your kids are really great, and Gordon is such a sweet boy," she told me. Kim went on to say she rarely encountered such compassion and kindness in a preschooler. He went out of his way to help kids smaller than himself. A budding empath. Great news, I thought. We must be doing something right.

As the Ministry tour rumbled on, no one encountered the mystery stalker again. There were no further sightings of this character anywhere. He'd vanished, and as far as I was concerned, no news was good news. I stashed the stalker photos in our big, black filing cabinet in my office. Another crisis averted.

With the kids going to school five days a week, I looked forward to introducing myself to new people I met at their school. It was a situational thing, of smiling at other parents, hoping for a grain of commonality between us to keep a conversation lively or at least moving beyond what developmental stages our kids were in.

My sister and I sometimes tag-teamed picking up and dropping off the kids. I would arrive at Phoenix School wearing the same clothes I wore every day to go about my errands and walks at the lake. There would be the obligatory hello to one of the other attorney moms arriving in her court clothes to drop off her newborn and a four-year-old. I couldn't justify leaving an infant with strangers, but that was her life. On one of the rare days I wore a sign of allegiance to the music business emblazoned across my chest, a tall figure sporting a T-shirt and shorts, a "dad" looking ready for a barbeque, approached me with a knowing look.

"Nice shirt. Don't usually see moms wearing those," he said, referring to my Throbbing Gristle T-shirt. It was the lightning bolt design with the TG logo. I was happy I still had the shirt. It was an import, a heavier cotton than most. I liked it almost as much as my Motorslug shirt. My absolute favorite band shirt for quizzical looks was Big Black's: "From Chicago's Finest Forges, Big Black Tools—Power Where You Need It.'"

"Thanks, and no, I'm not in a band," I said preempting the next question I was sure would be coming.

Jody Hunt introduced himself while two dark-haired urchins tugged on their sneakers behind him. One of the girls was our daughter's age, the other slightly older. Maya and Tessa Hunt became the first two real friends our kids made completely on their own. And Jody's wife Ellen became one of my closest friends.

In looks, Ellen Hunt didn't resemble any middle-class Texas breed I'd grown accustomed to seeing by now: salon hair or hippy hair; piles of jewelry or barely any. Ellen had tightly curled, shoulder-length dark hair framing a long face reminiscent of an Egyptian idol. She also didn't have any tattoos. Ellen was Jewish. Her husband Jody was not. She spent some of her formative years in El Paso growing up in a family of metalsmiths—jewelers—and traveling to jewelry trade shows with her mother. Ellen currently had a small business sewing hats for kids. It was something she did for fun.

Ellen kept her hands busy shaping, forming, pressing, cutting, and forging objects in a way which made sense to her, and not so much to me. Ellen Hunt, I soon discovered, was an architect by trade. She was on furlough, as I was, to raise her kids while her spouse worked as an executive in the Austin software world of newness that also made little sense to my novice brain. I admired Ellen's ingenuity, fluidly transitioning from architect to stay-at-home parent who made hats. She told me during her "punkette" days in college, she was a fan of Betsey Johnson's clothes. I had zero interest in the girlish splashes of tulle and corsets common in Johnson's line—they never fit someone with my figure. Ellen and I had different tastes in clothes, but we shared a similar art and design vocabulary. She would talk about a particular Le Corbusier building (or "Corbu" in her terms) with the same enthusiasm as when admiring a Polish amber pendant necklace I had or a 1920s silver tea set we saw in a thrift store on Congress Avenue. She loved our collection of thrift store bullfight paintings as much as we did. We gabbed endlessly about quality in all things we choose to surround ourselves with in our daily lives.

Her husband Jody had played in Austin bands when they met in college. Jody was friendly with the guys in Scratch Acid and The Jesus Lizard. Jody's music vocabulary was broad and familiar. He told me he had once rigged a tape loop of Skinny Puppy songs to play outside of his and Ellen's place on Halloween when trick or treaters came bounding up to the door. Jody was a fun guy. When our children met at Phoenix School, the Hunts were living in north Austin in a neighborhood of bland '70s and '80s single-family brick houses. In a few short years, the Hunts were feeling positively triumphant when they found a house to buy in Westlake near us, designed by the same architect who had built ours. The Hunts kissed their north Austin starter home "adios."

Jody didn't travel as much as Paul, but he was often out of town on business. As a consequence of those days of waiting for our spouses to come home, Ellen and I became simpatico on a level I didn't share with most other people. I finally had a woman friend to spend time with and someone who could talk intelligently about raising kids or just as intelligently about the art world and music.

I didn't feel so isolated anymore. The kids were having fun learning social skills at preschool, while I segued into preparing and packing lunch for them every day. I would occasionally hear a report from their teacher Amanda on how they were getting along. Amanda would also remind me I wasn't perfect. More than once she pulled me aside with a minor gripe about how I wrapped and packed homemade lasagna or mac and cheese for lunch. I habitually wrapped leftovers in foil for warming, a huge miscalculation on my part. We didn't have a microwave at home—for aesthetic and political reasons we chose not to buy one—but the preschool used theirs daily. I was happily ignorant of microwaving etiquette. "What can I say?" I sheepishly apologized to Amanda, not wanting to incur the wrath of the part-time club bouncer.

In July of 1996, I flew to Amsterdam with the kids to see Paul. The band had a short four day window of time to play two shows and sightsee in the Netherlands. It was getting easier traveling with small children, but it was a headache trying to arrange a babysitter at the hotel so that I could see the Ministry shows. The babysitting service was booked up leaving me no option but to stay back in our room with the kids. For their part, they weren't content with sitting in a hotel room while Paul was out, "playing with his friends." They refused to go to sleep by the time I was ready to wind down and watch a movie or write postcards from the road.

Before the band went on, Paul called and detected my frustration with a) not being able to find a sitter and b) having so much trouble getting the kids to calm down after an overseas, overnight flight. The two of them were giggling and chasing each other around the room. Paul was not happy I wasn't coming to the show.

"Can't you spank them or something—Jesus. What is the problem?"

No. I wasn't about to spank our kids. I wasn't about to repeat the sins of my father who physically and emotionally beat his five children. My siblings and I lived our twenties struggling to recover, peeling away layers of insult and bruising. Paul knew that, and Paul didn't believe in corporal punishment either. What was he thinking? He seemed intent on criticizing my inability to control the kids, when he himself couldn't possibly appreciate what it was like being with two small children twenty-four hours a day. Then it occurred to me he must be having his own issues again with (who else) Al.

"I'll deal with it. Have a good show," I told him.

I hated feeling resentful toward my spouse whom I missed terribly, but I didn't appreciate knee-jerk reactions from him. He could go back to warming up for his show, but what option did I have other than deep breathing and praying the kids would go to sleep. They didn't. At some point, I told them we were going for a walk. I mechanically snapped open the travel stroller for Gordon and walked out of the American Hotel into a pedestrian-filled street. Anxious for some relief, I swung the stroller into a late-night convenience store, bought a tourist size small bottle of some colored liqueur of indeterminate flavor, brought it back to the hotel, and just gave up being a parent for an hour, downing the alcohol and calming my nerves enough to not care that I didn't make it to a rock show. At least the three of us could entertain ourselves staring out the windows at the canals below. After that short bit of sightseeing in the city center, the kids fell asleep. I had to laugh thinking about where we were staying— the American Hotel—as if we fit in with some herd of tourists. But the American was a popular place for bands to stay when they played in town.

Rey's girlfriend Annette was in Amsterdam, and the following day she and I met for lunch while the band was busy with soundcheck and press. I ordered a glass of red wine to have with lunch. Annette asked me if I thought it was a good idea to be drinking during the day with the kids around.

"I'm so off from flying and this one glass should calm my nerves," I told her. So much for hiding the fact that I was drinking again. I could get back to going to meetings when I got home. Not now.

With the shows over for a few days, Paul was safely out of management mode. We had a window of time for ourselves, and decided to rent some bicycles. Everyone in Amsterdam rode them as if it were second nature—even the very old. I watched women twice my age carting groceries home with all the poise and grace of athletes out for an evening run. Paul put Ursula in front on his bicycle, and I rode with Gordon on mine. It felt liberating to be away from the hotel, feeling like we were all part of the same family and not some third, fourth, and fifth wheels on the Paul Barker touring company. Family mattered to Paul, but the band was his number one priority when he was on the road. They had to be. They had expectations to fulfill, the audiences and their own. Theirs was an extraordinarily tight show, tight schedule, and sometimes I couldn't help feeling as if my presence on the road was an interruption and completely unnecessary. On the other hand, when else would I see him, if not here?

We rode our bicycles over cobblestones with abandon. There was no time to overthink safety issues in this place where everyone rode bicycles and left room for human error. We traded the bikes in for a gondola ride on the canals. It was my first time in Amsterdam, but Paul had been before and cheerfully pointed out landmarks along the canals. There wasn't enough time to visit any of these places, but I hoped the next visit we could wander through the Rijksmuseum and say hello to the Vermeers or go see the Van Gogh museum. I could always hope.

After a couple of days, it was back to solo travel with the kids and negotiating their pace and mood. Checking in at the airport, I wondered how we'd make our connecting flight in another city in another country. Connecting time between gates was shorter than I anticipated. When the time came to switch planes, I told the kids we'd have to really hurry if we were going to make it onto the next flight. Gordon desperately needed to use the restroom. I told him to hold it. I felt awful having to say it as we ran through a tunnel clutching our carry ons and ignoring anything that might be dropped along the way, aside from our passports tucked inside my vintage Pucci train case. We made it to the gate on time, and I almost cried getting on the plane. Some reward for wanting to make myself and my kids feel like we were a part of their dad's life, no matter where his work took him. I was exhausted. Please let them go to sleep now, was all I could think about while I buckled the kids into their seats.

Somewhere in flight I had the idea to write a story with my kids' input into the character's life. They were fortunate to be surrounded by picture books and story books at home. When I was with them alone at night, I would often read one of their favorite's, Ten in the Bed, by the English author Penny Dale. In the story, a small child struggles to fall asleep with their collection of stuffed animals who come to life and want to play. I asked my kids what our character liked to do, what they liked to eat and drink.

"Chocolate milk, Mama," Gordon said with great authority.

"Cheese," Ursula chimed in.

Alright. I thought of the Swiss Miss brand of hot chocolate they liked. Alliteration was good. Repetition would work for a children's story.

"She eats swiss cheese and drinks chocolate milk," I said. "NO!!!" came the chorus, "Not together!" The list of character traits was slowing. My two storytellers were getting sleepy. I kept going.

"We'll call her Swiss Miss Miss Swiss Cheese Miss Moon. How's that?"

Good, was the answer, as two small faces dropped onto blankets touching their chins and draping over their bodies. I could soon close my eyes, too.

Ministry's Filth Pig tour went on through the middle of July. Paul came home, and we could think about where our lives were and where we were going next, now that Al was no longer anchored to Austin, but we were still there. Ministry was doing a show again in Chicago at the end of September. I wanted to be there with Paul for the show and booked flights for myself and the kids. We came in at the beginning of the month for two weeks. During our stay in the city, I spoke to Paul Elledge's ex-wife Judith to coordinate play times for their daughter Lucia and our own kids. Ursula and Lucia were born three-months apart, and we tried to get the kids together whenever we were in Chicago and all of us had time.

On one of our afternoons, Paul Elledge had Lucia for the day and my husband had time off, so the two dads and I took the three kids to a ceramics painting studio that had just opened and was run by someone Paul Elledge knew. "Paint your own" ceramics was becoming a new fad. Kids and adults could choose blank forms to paint any way they wished with materials on hand at the studio. The finished creations would then be fired, cured, and paid for to take home. Our three little artists painted their own salad-sized plates, and Gordon and Ursula together decorated a serving platter for our house in Austin. It was a rare peaceful few hours for our kids to do something creative with the dads. Paul Elledge was becoming better friends with all of us, but especially Paul, with whom he could talk about Italian motorcycles, and how he needed to have one and all other things Italian. We were thrilled to have another design fanatic as a friend, and that was a good thing. The fact that he also had a daughter who was growing up at the same pace as ours, and they were friends too, was an unintended bonus.

I returned to Austin with the kids, and Paul stayed back in Chicago. At night I would set the house alarm and put our kids to bed in their separate rooms. Inevitably, they would start whispering and together come running down the hallway to my end of the house. They were afraid when the house was so quiet without "Papa." I felt it, too. I made room in my own bed for them to lie down on either side of me, and together we would listen to Patsy Cline's Greatest Hits, a cassette Paul gave me before he left on tour. The two of them would pretend to groan when "Walking After Midnight" would begin with its sunny intro. It played upon their attentions like hypnosis, so that by the time the song was over my little squatters were lying perfectly still and asleep.

I had been home for a few days when I received the new Bon Appètit magazine in the mail. Flipping through the issue, my fingers stopped at an article on Mia Francesca's in Chicago. We had had dinner there with the Elledges when we were in town. Within the layout of the article were snatches of some lovely photographs taken by our friend Paul Elledge that were hanging in the restaurant dining room. Paul would return annually to the Italian countryside to document familiar and some new faces living the country life. Those images were now in a whole new forum. I called my Paul and asked him to congratulate Paul E. on the Bon Appètit spread.

Now home again in Austin, I reconnected with my friend Joel, who I hadn't been in touch with for months. I saw in the local newspaper that Beck was performing at the Austin Music Hall at the beginning of October. I wanted to see the show. Joel wanted to go, too, and we made plans to meet beforehand. Paul would still be in Chicago for a few days. I didn't want to go to a rock show alone.

Rey's friend Annette was also going out to see Beck. It seemed like it was THE show happening that night in Austin. On the night of the show, I met up with Annette and Joel at the Star Bar, a hip little dive close to the venue. We caravanned over to the Music Hall and took our seats up in the balcony. It felt good to be out at a live performance. The venue was sold out, and the floor was literally vibrating, similar in my mind to seeing a Revolting Cocks show with the whole audience up and dancing.

It was the first time in years that I could recall being at a show without Paul, to see someone perform whose music had nothing to do with us or our friends. There was a great freedom in not having to pay attention so much, since I wouldn't see the band later in the dressing room—although, I had a backstage pass, compliments of either Annette and her connections at the newspaper or through Ministry's own connections. I could take in Beck's show for what it was. I had a profound feeling of being myself, being an independent person again. It felt healthy and right. Motherhood for all of its joys also felt destructive at times, like giving up a part of myself, perhaps permanently. As I stood up in the balcony I thought for a moment about the previous months of traveling, enrolling our kids in swim classes, preschool, and dance classes for Ursula—things I had to do for my family. This Beck show, going out for a night with new friends, was just for me.

I looked over at Joel, who like any other Beck fan was absorbed in the singer's slacker lyrics about being a "loser," a sound appealing in its woozy vocals and simple dance rhythms. It wasn't revolutionary, cutting-edge anything. It was a fun show, and I enjoyed it tremendously as did the mostly college crowd. I left the venue thinking I needed to concentrate again on clearing my head and body and quit this alcohol thing for good. This time, I was doing it for myself, not Paul or the kids. On the car radio I heard my favorite new pop song by the band Primitive Radio Gods: "Standing Outside a Broken Phone Booth with Money in My Hands." It was an infectious lament and a college-radio hit. The song sampled part of a B. B. King vocal: "I've been downhearted babe, been downhearted . . . " I would vote for the band on the Grammy ballot, which arrived later in the mail for Paul, who never had time for these things. After the Beck show, I didn't attempt to contact Joel again. I imagined he took that trip to Seattle he said he'd been wanting to take to see his best friend. I went back to my AA meetings. I didn't miss our coffees and was glad to let that all fade away.

26

I often wondered while Paul was away in Chicago rehearsing before this 1996 tour, how it was that he didn't experience loneliness. He saw Al in the studio when he showed up. He saw William Tucker and Chris Connelly and our other friends. But he went to bed, as I did, alone. It would be well over a decade later, when I discovered a box of letters and cards he kept, with cards from past friends and girlfriends, that I learned my husband was not entirely solitary during his nights out of town preparing for tour. When I found the box, I was reluctant to read anything in it. My curiosity won out over my usual good judgment when I saw one greeting-card-sized envelope, hand inscribed: "Strictly Confidential." It might as well have said, "Nothing To See Here, Mrs. Barker." It had a summer 1996 date on it. I opened the envelope. It contained one piece in a string of correspondence my husband carried on with one of our female friends during the time he was in Chicago and rehearsing for the 1996 tour.

My discovery was a journey into a narrative I was unfamiliar with, conversations I was not a party to. Discovering a small stack of these envelopes from the same sender was jarring. This was someone I was still in touch with and considered a friend even though we lived in different cities. One card included a Polaroid photo of her wearing a black belly shirt, exposing her navel, and delivering a sideways glance to the camera. Come hither. It was a sign of vulnerability—no, availability, for late-night chats she was having with my husband, which she seemed to be enjoying immensely from what her messages revealed. At one point she even thanked him for the ring he gave her. It was a thank you gift, for what I didn't know. For listening to him? Giving someone a ring is a very intimate gesture. And to think the year before he had suspected me of having a boyfriend—a salesman from Barney's in Houston who called our house to see if my box of clothes had arrived safely. It had, and he was GAY. Not boyfriend material. He wore suits—not belly shirts. No flirty glances exchanged between us. He was just fun to talk with about fashion and art for crying out loud.

When I found myself reading one side of this two-way conversation, I could feel the anger rising and subsiding. Paul hadn't had time for an extended call to me, but he had time for this. I put the box away. I couldn't blame him or myself now for something I wasn't aware of when it—whatever it was—was happening. Maybe it was purely platonic. I didn't know about any of this in real time. So many years later, it seemed yet another thing Paul "forgot" to mention. I put the box away.

It was years after the fact when I discovered the notes. I never mentioned it to Paul. I had to let it go, or I would again jeopardize my sobriety and my sanity. It didn't matter any more. I had moved on.

At the end of September, Paul finished with Ministry's 1996 touring schedule and returned home to Austin. The end of the tour came at an opportune time to catch up as a family. I could focus my attention on working for my friend Cynthia Plaster Caster and helping her pursue a book deal. I spoke to an agent for William Morris agency in New York and sent out press kits to MTV and a few other interested parties. I was happy having Paul home and fully engaging as a partner and in his role as a father. With him home, I could spend time thinking about my own work outside of family matters.

It wasn't incumbent upon Paul to "make shit happen" at the moment. But we were never fully out of touch with the music scene that was so much a part of our lives. And soon enough, we received an invitation to an October wedding for one of Paul's earlier collaborators, Ogre Nivek. Ogre was the singer for the band Skinny Puppy. Ogre, Paul, and Al Jourgensen composed the PTP track "Show Me Your Spine" for the movie Robocop. Ogre also cowrote a few Ministry songs and had gone on tour with the band. I mailed him checks for nominal royalty payments, which occasionally rerouted to our house. For reasons unclear to me and Paul, Ogre was getting married in Texas. Although we were all on hiatus from flying in the short term, Paul and I now had a road trip to take with the kids. We were heading south to Glen Rose, Texas.

I liked Ogre. After he and I met the first time, I asked Ogre if I could call him "Herr Oh-gair." I thought the name Ogre had such a depressing sound to it on its own for such a sweet soul as himself. The German honorific "Herr" and my euphonious take on his name softened his persona in my eyes. Ogre had no objection and found my pet name for him charming.

He was one of a handful of Paul's musician friends who upon first meeting left you with the impression he was either painfully shy and soft-spoken or alternatively, flying high on drugs. We met on the Land of Rape and Honey tour on the coach, when he was in fact high, and wearing the informal uniform of the industrial music scene: sleeveless ripped T-shirt, painted on black jeans, engineer's boots, and matted black hair looking for a gust of wind to toss it further over his eyes. We'd had a few friendly conversations while he was on the road with the Revolting Cocks and Ministry in 1989–1990, moments of time to get acquainted in dressing rooms and on the bus. Despite the ominous connotations to his name, he didn't grandstand like some other singers we knew. He was in fact a lovely person. Ogre's solo music, and with Skinny Puppy, was connected to Paul's in a stylistic and historical sense, and I appreciated their friendship for all it was worth.

We were on our way to Ogre's wedding. Another wedding. People we knew were still getting married, some for the first time. What an awkward qualifier— the first. What did I think about marriage anymore? It was an evolving thing. For better, for worse, in sickness and in health, and watch out for what your spouse intentionally or unintentionally leaves out of the picture. Did I leave some things at the door, too? I wondered what Ogre's fiancé did for a living, as I reached behind my seat to offer snacks to our kids sitting patiently strapped in their car seats wondering what new adventure was at the end of this new drive. The road to Glen Rose was thankfully not all highways.

We stopped at a town halfway to stretch our legs and buy film for the camera. Paul pulled into one of the parking spaces next to what we guessed was a drugstore or a hardware store. It was probably one of the few small businesses in town family-owned for generations. What drew us into that lot was the name of the establishment screaming at us in raised black letters against a fieldstone wall facing the parking: "BARKERS" it said. Our old Landcruiser idled next to our family name, and Paul jumped out to snap a photo. A frame of a name, on the side of an old building. Paul once told me his grandmother Kay Barker was born in San Antonio. The Barkers, it seemed, had an established Texas identity before we ever moved there. It all somehow made sense.

The universe of retail leisure was all around us in the few square miles of this small town in Texas with its population constant enough to justify a hardware store. We bought our film for Ogre's wedding and were back on the road. When we eventually arrived at our destination there were rooms available at the Glen Rose Motor Inn, home to a half-dozen ground-level rooms untouched by any remodeling energy since its opening day in the 1960s. Motor Inn—Motor Out. We were staying for only one night.

The wedding couple's attire was a page torn from a Romantic-era novel. Ogre in a turn-of-the-century, black frock coat over a champagne-colored, satin sherwani-style tunic—something a groom might wear for an Indian wedding ceremony. Layers of white ruffles framed his neck and more ruffles spilled out at the jacket's cuffs. Ogre looked at peace with the world and happy to see us. His fiancé Jessika was serious and stunning in an eggshell-white long-sleeved, fitted gown. The Morning Star Chapel was open air, outdoors, and staging for the ceremony was a fieldstone half-wall propping up nothing else but prairie land behind it. Stained cherrywood pews for guests were arranged to face the wedding couple. It was a small crowd of people we didn't know. The bride and groom bowed their identical pitch-black chin-length hair and exchanged vows before an ordained minister. I noticed at least one guest in the front row in a white cowboy hat and polished brown cowboy boots. Perhaps the bride was from Texas. The event was otherwise informal.

After the ceremony, we wandered over the grounds where banquet tables were set for guests. A large state of Texas flag whipped the air at the edge of the field where we stood with our children. The kids discovered a black iron sculpture of a calf set up with a short lasso for smaller guests to practice their roping skills. Was the sculpture always there or was it dusted off for special receptions?

Ogre came by, hugged Paul and said hello to our kids. My camera always poised for family portraits, I asked Ogre to stand with Paul and the kids away from the other party goers. Ogre, in all his finery, leaned his ruffle enshrouded head against Paul's shoulder as if they were brothers. Paul, wearing his own weathered brown cowhide "country gentlemen's jacket," likewise tilted his head toward Ogre, and the kids held their father's hands while I snapped a few pictures for posterity. They all looked so happy.

It was a nice break for everyone's sanity. It was no surprise Al wasn't at the wedding. Ogre had had some kind of falling out with him a few years before. It was an earlier time, when drugs were the entertainment fueling that friendship. Ogre, from what I could now see, had grown beyond that stage of "creativity" and moved on. Congratulations.

***

Paul came home from the '96 Filth Pig "Sphinctour" only to go back to Chicago countless times over the next twelve months. As far as I knew, Al was once again living in Chicago for the time being. It wasn't easy on anyone in our family. The day after Christmas, Paul flew to Chicago to organize the studio to work on the next Ministry record. They had a budget from Warners, and if Al was staying in Chicago to avoid Austin then Paul would be going there to work. Rey Washam left Austin to join them a few days later. Paul and I once again began our daily ritual of long-distance phone calls. On January 8th, I received flowers ordered from a Polish flower shop in Chicago with the attached note written in

Polish. The flowers were from Paul. It was my 39th birthday.

While Paul was flying back and forth to Chicago, he was trying to settle on an apartment there as a home away from home for the duration of work on the new record. Of course, no one knew for sure how long the work might take or even hazard a rough estimate. Creative work didn't have a timetable. It took as much time as it needed. Ministry records took even longer. It seemed so naive that our move to Texas had been with a spirit of adventure—a new place for all of us to live and for Paul and Al to have their own studio. Now with Al firmly planted back at Chicago Trax and basically living at the studio as far as I could tell, what rationale was there for us to stay in Austin? At the end of February, I took the kids to Chicago for a week. Our kids were three and four now and too much for overnight visits at their grandpa's. We stayed at the Comfort Inn on Diversey near Clark Street. It was one of the two "rock 'n' roll hotels" where touring bands commonly stayed. The other was the Days Inn a block away, where I stayed with the kids on another visit later in the year.

During this end of February into early March 1997 trip back to my hometown, I again tried to make everything as normal for our kids and myself as possible under the circumstances. We spent time as a family with Paul Elledge and his daughter. All of us went together for the first time to the Chicago Children's Museum at Navy Pier, where the kids made paper airplanes fly from a second-story tower to the audience of us adults below. Our kids played "tag you're it" swinging from the railings bordering the walkway along the Chicago River downtown, across from the Marina Towers corncob buildings, and they smiled as a threesome for their parents' cameras. We took reams and reams of film pictures to remind us of where we all were together in the short amount of precious time left before "real" school would get underway for the girls. They were both starting kindergarten in the fall.

When I boarded the flight back to Austin with the kids, I was already missing Paul and Chicago. At least we could afford to have all of us traveling for these family visits, but the lack of continuity in seeing Paul was uncomfortable for me. I knew he would be back by the end of the month, but I couldn't think in concrete terms how I would keep myself busy with him away so much, other than to bury myself in parenting and making life seamless for our kids. But there was no way of escaping the physical reality of waking up and again my partner was somewhere else. This was our new normal. For how long, was an open question.

After I arrived back in Austin, our local elementary school sent notices out for their Kindergarten Round Up, a parent event to find out more about the upcoming school year. It was a first chance to meet teachers and other parents of children just starting their education. It was a morning assembly. Ursula would celebrate her fifth birthday a few days before September 1st, barely making the cutoff date for the academic year. She was absolutely ready to start kindergarten. She craved new friends and adventures. I heard about it every day. She had so many questions. Most urgent on her agenda was how many new friends she would have. I assured her she would make a lot of friends once school started, so many she'd forget all their names in the first week.

I would be attending the Kindergarten Round Up alone, while Paul took care of business in Chicago. Eanes Elementary was nearby, a short block away at the end of our street. Our next-door neighbor Katherine Houston taught there. Eanes was the oldest and the original elementary school in the district. I loved the low-slung interconnectedness of the 1960s era buildings, situated unassumingly into a grassy knoll along Bee Cave Road. From the street, the school campus seemed to disappear into the landscape. I would have walked over, but Bee Cave Road was a busy thoroughfare in Westlake with no pedestrian walkway or light where a person could cross safely. "People here just love their SUVs," I told Paul, as we lamented periodically the lack of walking paths near our house.

The weather was still cool outside. I slipped on a vintage, deep-brown suede car coat with a black leather collar I had saved for trips out of town. It was a necessary reminder that I still had my own style to indulge, even as a stay at home parent. I had cool weather jackets and boots I would never give up despite living in Texas, some things that took years of thrift store combing to collect. At times I stuck out like the northern city slicker I was. Tough luck to the detractors, if there were any.

Walking onto a school campus for the first time in years, I felt the same anxiousness I had felt about my own new school experiences as a child. The difference now was I was anxious in a positive way. I was curious to see who else was venturing out for this assembly. Paul and I were aware our district was home to some Austin film people and some otherwise wealthy entrepreneurs. John Mackey of Whole Foods lived three houses down from us. This was before Whole Foods became a monstrously successful household name, a place for people with too much money on their hands. I occasionally saw Paul DeJoria of Paul Mitchell hair product fame tooling around in his black Maserati or standing in line at the local Albertsons. I recognized his face from his company's magazine ads. Thank god there were rich and famous people who still amused themselves by ditching anonymity for a quick visit to the masters, otherwise known as grocery store chains. Perhaps these people also believed in public schools, as we did. Terrence Mallick, the filmmaker, had a house a short walking mile away from us in the neighborhood. Our little enclave was by no means posh, but it was discreet and safe enough for most needs. The super rich, like Michael Dell, were two miles further in, protected by a permanent staff of armed bodyguards and gates. In a town as small as Austin, it wasn't difficult to run into celebrities and the moneyed class if you knew where to look.

I walked into the assigned classroom at the school and took a seat. I looked over the other attendees already seated and locked eyes with a man across the room. He was sitting with an attractive dark-haired woman, who was doing most of the talking between them. He looked familiar with his slightly receding hairline. Although they sat far away from me, it finally registered in my brain that I was staring back at Mike Judge—Beavis and Butthead Mike Judge. I vaguely recalled someone telling me he had kids and lived in Westlake. I looked away to see who else among the local luminaries might be stopping in to make an appearance, roughing it as an engaged parent of a soon to be public school student. I glanced again at who I guessed were Mike Judge and his wife, and he was looking my way again, too.

I may have been off the open dating market for ten years now, but I wasn't blind. This guy was staring at me, checking me out. So what, I thought. Let those eyes roam where they will. As long as that's all it was, who cared? It was an odd setting for surreptitious cruising, though. I looked away.

A few days before Easter, I booked flights to New York for myself, for Paul, and for the kids. We were invited to the east coast for a special extended family celebration. Maria Ferrero, Ministry's publicist of several years and my dear friend, was getting married in April. I was looking forward to the trip. Maria and I became instant friends while I was pregnant with our first child, and we met up in Brazil for the book tour, where we shared a sometimes hair-raising ride through Brazilian backroads with Jello Biafra. Maria was someone I could call in a panic about what the hell was going on with my husband's fellow band members. She would often call me to talk about real life issues that had nothing to do with the insularity of the music world. I needed that. Me, on my end sipping a cocktail (going in and out of sobriety), and Maria smoking a joint on her end. Girl talk. Maria made me laugh.

Paul was back to work on Ministry songs. He and Ministry's management signed a one-year lease for an apartment on Leavitt Street in Ukrainian Village on the north side of Chicago. It was a typical Chicago apartment in an older three-flat, similar to the place we lived in for four years before moving to Texas. The apartment was Paul's new sanctuary away from home—a clean room to sleep in and a ten minute drive to Chicago Trax. It was a place where he hoped to have some peace away from the studio—a place to think and compose, away from other people's personal problems. I hoped sometime long before the lease ran out, we would discuss ideas he and Al had for the new album's cover art and who would do it. That would be a clear signal to me the record was almost finished. I could hope for that small favor.

In the months prior to our daughter's first day of kindergarten, I flew back and forth to Chicago with the kids six times. Some of those times we stayed at the apartment Paul rented, we stayed at the Elledges' place or stayed in hotels. Our kids now had their own American Airlines' frequent flyer accounts. I kept the cards in my wallet.

During the first week of April 1997 in Austin, there was an outbreak of chickenpox. Some of our kids' preschool friends had it. And, despite being inoculated against the virus with a new vaccine the year before, both of our kids were exposed and tested positive. Their symptoms were mild compared to typical chicken pox cases. But they were contagious, and no airline would allow them on a plane. We weren't flying to New York for Maria Ferrero's wedding. We weren't flying anywhere. I hated having to cancel our trip. I hated to miss my friend's wedding to the one guy she'd finally met who really made her happy.

We couldn't leave the house, let alone the state. On the day of Maria's wedding, I sat between my children on the linoleum floor of our family room with paper instructions and allen wrenches, and together we built a honey-dew-colored, nine-drawer cabinet from Ikea to while away the time. We took snack breaks to look out the patio doors at the deck and watch the occasional hummingbird fly by. And Paul, "Papa" Paul, was back in Chicago.

The kids recovered from their illness. Summer was beginning. Paul was in Chicago. We heard from our good friend Greg Werckman, who had recently parted ways with Jello Biafra and Alternative Tentacles after seven years. Greg was now doing A&R for Mercury Records, and he was getting married. He was calling to invite us to the wedding. It was our second wedding invitation for the year, but this one seemed entirely possible. The ceremony was scheduled to take place outdoors at a Sonoma, California vineyard. Greg and his fiancé needed a ring bearer for the service, and he asked if our son Gordon was available. Gordon was almost four, and I wondered if that was a little too young for such an official duty. Greg was confident that as long as we showed up and Gordon could walk down the aisle, everything would be fine. Greg had a way of assuring you everything was manageable. His years of working with Jello Biafra, and before that as a booking agent for Hunter S. Thompson, had cemented his resolve in getting through any potential crisis. Working with a four-year-old looked easy to him. I loved the idea of dressing up and getting out of town for a formal event. Greg was such a good guy and hilarious to be around, so there was no question we'd be available for his big day. It was another opportunity for Paul to take a break and be available for me and our kids as a family before Ursula started kindergarten and all the constraints on our travel plans that would go along with that. Paul was of course solidly behind any plans to attend Greg's wedding, so the event was on our calendar for August. In the meantime, I had hundreds of summer hours to fill with two preschoolers and I was open to suggestions.

The Houstons next door were planning a day trip to the San Marcos River to go tubing. Katherine invited me to come with the kids, and we didn't fight off the invite having not much else on our schedule. It was something new to do. Tubing on a river flowing at its own pace had a relaxing sound to it, as opposed to the tube runs at Schlitterbahn, the popular waterpark in New Braunfels, Texas where we had been once before. The Schlitterbahn tube runs were like amusement park rides. Some of them were carved into the natural landscape of the Comal River but were monitored by aides and ticket takers at the dramatic start and finish. By contrast, drifting along on the San Marcos River in an inner tube would be less focused and rushed. It was another way to cool off on a humid day, another foray into the nuanced world of Texas outdoor fun. Thankfully, the kids were tall enough now to avoid scrutiny at the tube rental stand by the river. I packed our lunches, and we were off.

Katherine advised me to bring water shoes in case I needed to find my footing on the river floor during the course of the float. I put on the only suitable footwear I had, an ancient pair of black Converse high tops I'd packed away after hiking on Kauai before the kids were born. My high tops still bore the patina of red clay around the soles and eyelets for the laces—they were good enough for tubing. I didn't feel the need for pro footgear on this outing. It wasn't as if we were heading out to shoot the rapids somewhere. I couldn't imagine those even existed in the region of Texas where we lived.

I had vivid memories of white water rafting with my brother Raimund the summer before high school at Wolf River in Wisconsin, a few hours' drive north from Chicago. We went as part of a youth group with Bethel Lutheran church, an old congregation at the opposite end of our block on Springfield Avenue. The church had a recreational activity building for youth behind it, next to the alley. It was somewhere to go after school during the week to stay out of trouble. Going to the rec building wasn't an organized affair. If someone was there, they let us in. No religion required. The building had a pool table where, if you were a kid in the neighborhood, it was available to use. My brother and his guy friends joined the after school youth group. I only cared about the pool table—it's where I learned to shoot pool. One day Raimund brought home forms for an upcoming rafting trip. I could go along if I wanted to. It was a day trip with chaperones and counselors who went several times every summer. My parents let us go to get us out of the city for a day.

I remembered the sense of terror in my whole body while being hurled against the frothing waves on Wolf River. The water was calm for brief stretches of time, then our raft picked up speed, racing past whirlpools, leaving little time for us to take in scenery along the river bank. Raimund and I were in a group in one raft. Two other rafts were ahead of ours, when we approached a fork in the river, and our raft began veering away from the rest. It took a sudden violent pitch into the air, and Raimund was bounced into the water at the edge of a whirlpool. "Cliff," one of the counselors, jumped in after him and single-handedly lifted my brother back into the raft and out of danger. It looked so effortless for Cliff. Luckily for Raimund, Cliff was a former Olympian.

That distant memory lingered as I followed our neighbors' car on the road to the San Marcos River. Another image much closer in time and oddly connected to my current family history crept to mind. It was from the film, River Wild. In that film from 1994, the narrative follows a family on a rafting trip. In one scene, their young son is wearing a Ministry cap for the ride and is listening to the song "Psalm 69" on his headphones. I recalled getting a request for the sync license for that film. Yes, we collected some royalties for the Ministry uses in River Wild. And yes, if he couldn't be here in body, at least in spirit Paul's presence was felt on the drive to the San Marcos River.

When we arrived in San Marcos, the kids and I settled on one tube for the three of us and lined up behind the Houstons and their friends, who'd brought their own beer for the float. I wasn't drinking anymore, but I didn't begrudge anyone else's desire to do so. Alcohol wasn't legal in the park but was fine on the water. Crazy, I thought. We'd only planned to be out for a couple of hours. Sam Houston briefed us on general guidelines for steering our tube, as much as there were techniques for steering a rubber ring as you would a small boat or canoe. I had no experience with canoeing or kayaking either. Paul did. He was on the crew team in high school and had upper body strength I didn't possess. Paul was also not with us for this trip, so I was on my own trusting my own faculties.

We launched our tubes into the water under a canopy of century-old trees. The shade provided cooler air and a painless introduction to this leisurely float. I reminded myself outdoor rites of passage like this were important in establishing a child's love for nature and having fun without having to spend a lot of money. I thought about conversations I'd had with Paul about success, money, and kids.

"How much does a person need? When is it enough money, when do you have enough stuff?" he would ask. We were conservationists, buying what we needed to be comfortable and happy—that was the idea. Although we'd bought a house, a few motorcycles, and two cars, none of them were new. But they reaffirmed our identity, philosophy of living, and sharing that way of life with our kids. Paul and I would sooner duck into the dollar store next to our favorite tortilleria (Fiesta) than spend time in a furniture showroom. The dollar store had cool junk: glitter stickers, thin cotton gloves, Halloween candy and drawing pads for the kids, and black cotton turbans for me to wear in the shower. We cruised in there together often enough that on one occasion when I walked in alone, the Pakistani counterman looked a little confused as I approached the counter with my usual pile of things and set it down. I lingered a moment looking into the front display case filled with mini Nivea tins, trays of cheap birthstone necklaces, small appliances, lighters, and incense packets. The counterman looked past me, then had to ask, "Veddiz *Him?*"

Yes, veddiz him, I mused as the San Marcos River carried us off slowly. Buoyed along by spring-fed waters below us, the kids were getting bored with the steady pace, and began toying with the idea of spinning the inner tube for fun. After half an hour or so of drifting, I could see ahead in our route where the river appeared to be branching off to the right.

Our tube slowed, as the others ahead of us passed the intersection in the river. I expected we would float by the break as everyone else had, but I could sense the tube slowly listing to the right. I tried spinning it back to the left to correct our course, and nothing happened. We were drifting away from the group. I dropped my feet into the water and felt for the bottom. It was deeper than I anticipated. I was standing on the tips of my toes feeling the gentle pull of the tube continue. My mind began racing, and I began shouting for the Houstons. What else could I do? I didn't know where this alternate branch of the river would take us, or if we would end up lost, deposited somewhere remote away from our car and unable to contact anyone.

My eyes looked over the shoreline and back over the water, and I could see Sam Houston swimming toward us. He grabbed the side of the tube that was empty next to the kids and pulled us away and back to the point where we'd veered off course. I was thankful I didn't panic, and that Sam was there to rescue us. The kids thought it was all part of the hazard in tubing down the San Marcos River, and they picked up their running commentary about how fast we could go in an inner tube and when would we stop for lunch?

"I'm hungry, Momma," Ursula said. It was precisely what I needed to hear.

In July, I took the kids on one final trip to Chicago before school began. Paul Elledge was inspired to do a new family portrait of the four Barkers while everyone was in town, and it would be one more excuse to drag my Paul out of the studio. Just like old times. I rented a car for ten days to get myself and the kids around with or without Paul. We could visit friends and see my father.

My Paul's Ukrainian Village apartment was very close to Paul Elledge's ex-wife Judith's place. Judith lived with their daughter Lucia. All the adults agreed while I was in town with our kids, we'd visit Judith and Lucia and do fun things as a group. Judith was also an artist and an endless resource for things to do geared toward kids but stimulating enough for everyone else. Yay for the moms.

Many of the friends Paul and I now had and spent time with in his off hours were primarily Paul's friends, connected to us through his work as a musician. I was Paul's wife, so by association, I was their friend, too. It didn't bother me as much as it forced me to reevaluate what I wanted from friendships. It occurred to me that spending time with other women who navigated through their work and personal lives while taking care of their kids' needs was something I needed in my own life now. Visiting with Judith could be a learning experience. It could also be the start of a friendship I could have if we for any reason found it necessary to move back to Chicago.

We arrived at Judith's place, a freestanding, small house built decades earlier at a time when immigrant families had migrated in and out of the neighborhood with each generation. Inside, one of the first things I noticed was the ballet barre stretching across the doorway to her daughter's room. Ballet was one more common interest our girls had to keep them busy and charmed with each other's company. There was a warmth to the house, full of cultural cues that said it was the home of an artist. Judith had extended family in Italy, in the region where her ex-husband Paul Elledge still visited once a year to take pictures that would eventually grace collectors' walls. Judith had a European air about her familiar to my own sense of my immigrant upbringing. Judith's connection to Italy was personal and deep.

"Do you want to see something amazing?" she asked, when I came into the kitchen. "Tell me if you already know this. It's a trick I learned from my family." She grasped the steel faucet over the sink with fingers from both hands extended. I didn't say anything.

"This is what you do to remove garlic smell from your hands when you're done chopping," she said. I had never heard of that. "It's like magic! It really works." The science behind this magic was well known to real chefs, and now I knew, too—molecules are transferred from one surface to another. Judith's enthusiasm for sharing this family secret put my mind at ease, at a time when I was constantly grappling with how to make sense of all the traveling I was doing with young kids and make peace with the reality that my husband was now semi-living away from our own house. I really appreciated Judith's company. We spent a few afternoons together taking the kids to the park and the neighborhood library—just letting kids be kids.

On this trip, Paul and I had the opportunity to introduce our progeny to the new Chicago Trax building and staff. The studio had moved and was now situated close to the old Cabrini Green housing projects along Division Street. Paul was excited to give us all a tour of where he was spending his days away from home.

Upon first impression, the new studio building seemed less inviting than the original studio on Halsted. Punching in a security code to open the metal gate, it occurred to me this place was a true compound as opposed to the imaginary, impenetrable safe haven Al thought he had in Texas. I was delighted to see Erica

Medinger, a familiar face from the old Chicago Trax, but the concrete starkness of the new building felt so corporate and cold. I trusted Paul was taking care of himself and getting out of this place enough to spend time with other friends in the city. I couldn't help but feel like an interloper going from room to room in the new studio, listening to Paul explain to our kids what went on there. At the old Trax, everyone on staff had a nickname. Here, they were mostly strangers and self-absorbed as we passed them in the halls.

The story of lives. Lives transposed. Lives running parallel and splitting apart. My life with Paul so far away allowed him the room to breathe and make music amidst the long-standing realities of working with Al. I didn't get it. I didn't have to. I got that he felt there were more records to make with Al, and I had to respect that. His close proximity now to Paul Elledge and to his own life as an artist and father could only help my husband put perspective upon a manageable idea of fatherhood at this point in his life. I wished we all lived in the same place, but we were not coming back to Chicago. Paul and I discussed it. We knew it would be too disruptive, too expensive, and ultimately unnecessary for our life and his career to grow. The last thing we wanted was to take our kids away from the stability of living in a house with their own rooms, their own friends, a good school, and a sense of continuity absent from their dad's schedule and thoughts.

Chaos was the reigning force in Paul's artistic life for now, it seemed. It had been that way for a decade already. We could all live with that, couldn't we? I was soon once again back on a plane to Austin with our kids. Paul joined us shortly after. We had Greg Werckman's wedding to attend on the west coast. Wardrobe decisions had to be made. Fun in the California sun—a capital idea.

Wondering what was appropriate for a late summer afternoon wedding at a vineyard in Sonoma, it didn't take long to decide I would wear the off-white Prada sleeveless dress I'd bought at Barney's two summers before. The fabric was slightly textured, almost quilted, and didn't rise to the level of formal wear (in my eyes anyway). Any hesitation I briefly had about wearing off-white to a wedding was dispelled by the reality that our son was an official member of the wedding party, and so what? Some guests would undoubtedly show up in black for this wedding—some of Greg's "freak" friends—and I had a policy against wearing black to weddings. I also didn't own anything colorful and appropriate to wear. A wedding was a celebration of something new, not a burial of the past. No black.

I took the kids to the mall to look for a proper white long-sleeved dress shirt for Gordon and some dark cotton pants. Ursula and Paul had closets full of partywear and were covered in any event.

Greg and his fiancé Candace were married on August 3rd, 1997. We arrived early for the ceremony, and as it turned out, the bridesmaids were clad in off-white formal dresses. My son and I blended right in. As expected, several guests showed up wearing black. Paul snapped photos of me with our children at an empty picnic table away from the reception area. With their blonde tousled curls, the kids and I came off brilliantly, looking like models for some Calvin Klein "mother with children" ad. And unbeknownst to their parents, all the flying back and forth over the summer had begun to take its toll on our children—or at least the youngest. When the ceremony finally was underway, Gordon was fast asleep in his chair. The bridal party managed without disturbing his slumber, and without his ring bearing expertise. Greg, as usual, thought it was "fine."

Afterwards, Paul and I were seated at a large, circular table under white canopied tents with the other guests of the groom. On the opposite side of the table were Jello Biafra, Mike Patton (the singer from Faith No More), and several other music industry friends of Greg's. Some we knew, most we didn't. Greg came over and said to me, "Well, the freaks are all here," and rolled his eyes. It was his signature gesture, acknowledging the reality that working and making a living in the music industry was like herding circus animals. Wasn't THAT the truth?

***

Ursula graduated from preschool sporting a pale blue cap and petite blue gown. In late August, her first day of kindergarten arrived. She insisted upon taking the school bus home. The bus ride was only a few minutes long, but she held onto that strand of independence as if her personal reputation were already on the line. She would celebrate her fifth birthday by the end of the month and was about to get busy with a new social life so alien to any in my own experience. Paul was in Chicago on our first child's first day of kindergarten—another milestone missed. I felt sorry for him.

I had spectacularly built up the first day of school for our daughter long before she ever entered a classroom. She was ready to make new friends and have a good time. I didn't realize the power of a mother's assurances made to her own child.

I had a rough idea of what time the school bus would begin its run and deposit kids near the house behind ours at the end of the school day. I imagined Ursula would be her usual energetic self and come bounding across the neighbor's property and onto our back driveway. I heard the bus and walked outside. I looked forward to this new routine of ours. I watched as she hurried down the few steps from the neighbor's property, her backpack expertly adjusted behind her, I thought, like angel's wings. She had a worried expression on her face.

"Mommy. YOU said I would have so many new friends when school started, and I don't have ANY new friends."

Hm, not what I expected. It was, however, an opportunity for a lesson in patience—my own. Christ. This would require a little more finesse than a simple, "Tell me all about your first day!" I silently wondered if Paul would ever feel such joyous first impressions as this one, delivered like an unfavorable employee review.

In the meantime, as real school got underway, I found myself doing a poor job of managing Cynthia Plaster Caster's career. Her life was so unconventional, her creative output so "untouchable" by most standards of taste, it wasn't surprising there was no playbook I could reference. She sold copies of her casts—her casts of rock stars' penises. Independent German television people seemed to be intermittently interested in interviewing Cynthia for their own projects. There were erotica festivals. Cynthia needed a book deal. She had legal issues with Frank Zappa's former manager in LA. I finally had to tell Cynthia the current state of my personal life was challenging enough, despite having the flexibility to fly back and forth to Chicago throughout the year. I had too much caretaking on my plate already and a marriage that was mobile to a ridiculous degree at the moment. I couldn't take on any more projects right now. Attending to a client's needs—even one client such as herself—wasn't realistic or fair to her.

Paul flew home for Thanksgiving and Christmas. He wouldn't dream of sending me off on my own to find a Christmas tree. He was so much better at wrapping gifts than I was. It was a ritual. It mattered. After the new year, he was gone again. We'd reached a compromise. If he came home for the holidays, he'd miss my birthday. My birthday celebration could wait. I was used to waiting.

It was sixty-three degrees and sunny in Austin on January 8, 1998. My birthday. We had a little party at our house, "we" being me, my kids, and our friends Ellen and Jody Hunt with their two girls. I ordered a huge spread of Szechuan food from Formosa Café, a Chinese place Paul and I had been to a couple of times. Their Szechuan eggplant was to die for and my favorite dish. I picked up the order, brought it home, and set it out on our finest Fiestaware. My sister Georgette baked a Barbie cake for the occasion. It was my fortieth birthday.

Prior to our last Chicago trip, the two Pauls entertained the idea of Paul Elledge bringing Leasha and Lucia to visit us for Easter. We hadn't yet had guests stay with us who also brought their own kids. I loved the idea. It would be another chance for the three of our kids to spend time together and the four adults to gossip, see the bats fly out from under the Congress Avenue bridge, and linger outside in spring-like weather.

The Easter holiday was coming up. Paul and I were looking forward to having the Elledges come out to Austin for a couple of days. I made a reservation at Fonda San Miguel for Easter brunch. Fonda San Miguel was an Austin institution. Their chef Miguel Ravago whipped up gorgeous, regional dishes from the interior of Mexico. No Tex-Mex to be had on that menu. Fonda San Miguel was our first choice for special occasions like Father's Day or Mother's Day.

Having the Elledges over for Easter added a new level to our friendship, to see them out of their element in the slower-paced life that was Austin. There would be no hustle to go anywhere, other than brunch at our favorite Mexican sit-down place. I routinely watched Paul and Leasha at work shooting photographs live in the pits at rock shows or at Paul's studio in Chicago. There was an urgency and level of professionalism to their work at the live shows that I hadn't seen with other photographers. I watched the two of them perform their magic with the precision of a Formula One race crew in front of the stage: Leasha juggling canisters, loading film, dropping the empties, switching out lenses, performing three tasks in the time it took Paul to lean the full force of his talent and eye into the camera, hunting for one seminal shot of the band. In a minute, it would start all over again. Fans would stage dive over their heads. Timing was everything, as they stood temporarily buffered by the ever-present massive bouncers in front of the stage. I didn't wonder at all if they were able to enjoy the shows. Our photographer friends were part of the show.

The Elledges arrived for the weekend, and on Easter Sunday, Paul's daughter Lucia and our two kids wore their Easter outfits out on the front deck for picture time. The Houstons next door were having their annual egg hunt for all the kid cousins and siblings, and the three kids at our house ran over to join the search party. Gordon discovered the Golden Egg hidden in one of the Houstons' trees and walked away with the twenty-dollar bill inside.

Many more pictures later, and I reflected on the fact that we had never had guests with kids staying with us before. This visit was . . . nice. I thought about that sense of continuity, of necessary stability in our lives. Being here together reaffirmed for all the kids that there were other families out there whose parents traveled often for their art, for their business, and it was a way of life. This was our life. And it was okay. It was okay, despite what I knew of it that wasn't okay twelve hundred miles away—the precarious life support system set up to keep Al going and working, allowing my Paul to continue doing what he did best with his talents. In my heart I knew the Al dramas wouldn't last forever, if much longer at all.

Paul and Leasha appeared to be enjoying the chance for all of us to ham it up in the confines of our swanky mid-century modern splendor of a house. Red-and-black flocked bathroom walls in the guest bath—a drag queen's dream—what was there not to love? They were on the road more often than my Paul was at times, and hotel living had its limited charms to go along with reliable wake up calls.

We drove down to Town Lake, ostensibly to see the bats, but kept driving, taking in the sparsely developed downtown entertainment district with its handful of clubs and bars and the state capitol building. "Less cluttered skyline in Austin," I said. What else was there to say? Almost country living? It felt almost disingenuous. I sometimes missed seeing Chicago's dense skyline looming on the horizon, staring back at you on the drive home from O'Hare.

After the weekend, the Elledges flew home. My Paul was on a plane following their lead not long after.

***

In May of 1998, Paul's lease was ending for the Leavitt Street apartment and he would be returning home to Austin. Ministry's new record was not quite finished. Paul needed a break. For me, summer meant bearing the one hundred degree days again while trying to fill those days with Paul finally coming back to be physically present in our lives. Now that we were locals in Austin, we sought relief from the heat by visiting Sculpture Falls, our local swimming hole, and Schlitterbahn, the sprawling water park in New Braunfels. It was a day trip for us. At other times, there was always the lure of the big city—any big city was fine with me—to get out of the cultural black hole of our current home. We drove to Fort Worth, Texas one day to spend time at the Kimbell Art Museum in all its modern glory.

A rare opportunity to leave Austin presented itself. A show had just opened at the Guggenheim Museum in New York: The Art of the Motorcycle, a somewhat controversial design exhibition running from the end of June until the end of September. The show was a retrospective look at 114 motorcycles chosen for their design and historical significance. The bikes were nestled within a mirrored, silver staging area designed by the architect Frank Gehry, in a pattern that flowed from level to level, down the interior spiral of the Guggenheim. It seemed like the perfect exhibition space for the show. Frank Lloyd Wright had conceived of the Guggenheim's beehive-shaped concrete exterior and its interior levels in that spiral that some critics compared to a parking garage. Motorcycles on display in an art museum was an idea a little too egalitarian—perhaps a little too blue collar—for some of the art world critics and the international bourgeoisie. But for us, it was on. We were going.

Paul Elledge was also cued into a possible fieldtrip, and we coordinated our schedules. The plan was to fly to New York with my Paul and the kids, stay with my brother in Brooklyn, and meet up with the Elledges when they arrived in town from Chicago. I wasn't aware if Paul and Leasha had a job to do in New York or if they were just coming for fun. I suspected work was in the mix somewhere, and sure enough, when we finally met at the museum, the rest of their Chicago team was with them.

Motorcycles, engines, and speed were thematic emblems in my husband's personal aesthetic and in his music. Ministry's "Jesus Built My Hotrod" video was the most visible and loud example. The cover art for Paul's solo Lead into Gold EP Chicks and Speed: Futurism was a nod to Paul's love of bikes and Duchamp's plaited imagery in his Nude Descending a Staircase.

When Paul was struggling to come up with a title for the Lead into Gold record, we were sitting at our old kitchen table in Chicago, Paul fidgeting with his knitted hat—his tuque—on the table in front of him. He suddenly pulled the hat over his head, stretching it as low down over his forehead as it would go. The exercise with the tuque was a superstition, a tic. Very lumberjack, in my mind.

"Are you trying to contain yourself? Your head won't explode. Give it some time," I told him.

"YES. I need to contain myself." He looked agitated.

Miraculously—well, not really—the title of the record fell together quite easily after that. Chicks and Speed. Judy Pokonosky from Wax Trax became the model "chick" on the cover. The motorcycle in the image was my 1972 Ducati 250 Mach III, the bike Paul bought for me a month after we were married.

Paul also wasted no time in sneaking his own bike into Ministry's "Stigmata" video and the video for the Revolting Cocks' "Stainless Steel Providers." As part of the storyline for Stigmata, the H-Gun crew filmed Paul on his Morini chasing his partner Al on foot down a smokey Chicago street lit up at night like a crime scene. It was art imitating life—an imagined snapshot of their very real working relationship.

Walking into the Guggenheim to see The Art of the Motorcycle was an affirmation of Paul's and my own appreciation of Italian design in everyday objects. As someone who'd ridden on the back of an Italian sport bike and had to lean into curves in the road, I could appreciate the symmetry in showing off these sculptural pieces in a curving, receding landscape of ramps going up and coming down. I thought it was brilliant planning on the part of the Guggenheim. The aerodynamics of riding at sixty-five miles an hour were breathtaking, and the bikes on view standing straight up staggered along the ramps mimicked how they would look in motion.

Our four-year-old son, always fascinated by the dynamics of how things moved, inched his way along the ramps smiling, doing his own 360 degree turns and looking up to the higher levels full of more motorcycles. Who cared what the critics were going on about when in reality there were smiles all around in our self-contained tour group. We snapped roll after roll of pictures next to throngs of tourists, many of whom loudly affirmed they were visiting a museum for the first time. The attendance records for The Art of the Motorcycle show were the highest in the museum's history. Our motorcycle mechanic from Chicago, Fred Cousins, was a late arrival to town and met up with us to see the show for himself. It was truly a "Chicago family" affair.

There was something magical about New York. The last time we'd visited with the kids, we spent time with my brother in the east Village, afterwards flagging a taxi to our next stop. When I stepped into the cab after my daughter, she grabbed my hand with an excited look on her face and whispered, "Mommy, our cab driver's a genie!" I took my seat, looking up to see a pale-peach-colored turban resting on the driver's head in front. Childhood wonder. I couldn't spoil the moment with a correction. She was barely four at the time. We instructed the driver to take us to the Plaza Hotel. The kids wanted to see where the boy in Home Alone held court like a prince.

After the Art of the Motorcycle show, I was happy to go down into the subway with Paul, the kids, Paul and Leasha, and their assistants and catch a train on our way to dinner. I was happy to be waiting for a train, happy for the city smells of the underground tunnels, the humidity, and even the occasional whiffs of garbage. I thought about how my Paul had started seriously riding motorcycles in his early twenties, Leasha in her teens, and Paul Elledge was just getting into the habit. I hadn't had the time to practice riding alone much but spent many hours on the back of Paul's bike. Despite the varying degrees of riding expertise between the four of us, we were all design addicts, pure and undeniable. And we had just seen some beautiful bikes. I was happiest of all that our two young children were able to experience firsthand the beauty of exquisite manmade objects in such a thoroughly modern setting. There was great satisfaction in that. Tada!

***

Paul was back in Chicago and I heard from Leila Eminson who was on tour doing artist relations for the Backstreet Boys. Backstreet were on their Comeback tour performing to sold out audiences filled with preteen and older girls. My own daughter's post-kindergarten crowd loved the Backstreet Boys. Leila asked me to come to the Austin show and bring the kids. The band was performing at the Erwin Center, the one venue in town suited for arena rock or a large event like Cirque du Soleil. I had seen the inside of the Erwin Center only once the year before after donating $200 to our local PBS station and in return getting tickets to see Sesame Street Live. From Big Bird to boy bands—progress, in my Austin social calendar.

Backstreet Boys' current show included a segment of audience participation: little girls from the audience onstage with their mothers being serenaded by the Boys. Leila thought it might be fun for my daughter to be a part of all that on the big stage in Austin, since she was already performing on her own with her dance class. Ursula agreed, I relented, and Gordon wanted to come along for the show. I thought both kids were equally ready to be exposed to art and performances and not be left out for any reason. It was a family credo. The kids went where I went to see Paul perform. We had on occasion even gone so far as to cut down adult earplugs to tuck inside their small ears—a grown up thing to do to make Papa's shows sound "better." Ursula found out a few of her schoolmates were also attending the Backstreet Boys show. Our friends the Hunts were bringing their girls out, too. Our tickets were free, we had VIP seats to a pop music event, and that was good enough for me.

The evening of the show, we arrived at the Erwin Center early to connect with Leila backstage. She was pressed for time, but managed to give us a short tour of the backstage area before escorting us out into the venue and into our reserved seats in the front. We passed Nick from the band, and Leila briefly introduced us as friends here to see the show. Leila and I walked into the arena moving past bodyguards and bouncers stepping aside to let us through and out to our seats. I looked up and noticed a small group headed by one of the moms from school and noticed her glaring at us while she sat with her daughter at her side. It was a karma moment. This particular mom was one of the mothers at the neighborhood pool who looked aghast the first time I appeared at the pool with my children and revealed to the world that I looked fabulous in a black bikini. Hi there! The woman never seemed to crack a smile. I wondered if her life was truly that miserable or if seeing us emerging from the backstage area burned a new ulcer into her gut.

The Backstreet Boys were true professionals onstage with their perfect harmonies and smiles, at one point being airlifted above the crowd to drop chocolate kisses to fans in their seats. My son fell asleep midway through the show as many a preoccupied little boy's temperament would have run out of patience after an hour of constant crooning. My daughter decided at the last minute she was "too shy, Momma" to get onstage with the other preselected girls, and I was perfectly cognizant of just how fragile and vulnerable kids' feelings could be. Kudos to the band for their sheer professionalism. The show was every bit what I imagined a live show in Las Vegas would be like. When Paul and I were married there we missed seeing Nudes on Ice by a few seasons. Those performers undoubtedly were no Backstreet Boys, but those girls would have been equally disarming to watch.

***

Spending much of my time with our kids and thinking about what they would recall later in their lives inevitably made me think of my own memories of growing up in Chicago. As a child, it was hard to ignore the politics of the Democratic Party that made that city function in an orderly way, especially for voters like my parents who owned their own homes. If the sidewalk outside needed resurfacing or the corner needed a stop sign, our precinct captain came by to assure my father these things would be done immediately, especially in an election year. How many times had I heard, "Henry, we can count on your vote in November, right?" Absolutely.

I had the sense raising kids in Austin was a little less transactional, a little less "neighborly." Texas was largely a Republican state, with Austin being the outlier of the political landscape. Of course, LBJ had been a Texan and a Democrat. He championed and signed the landmark Civil Rights Act into law in 1964. But things were different now in Texas, it seemed to me.

It was 1998, an election year for the state, and for us as registered voters. Paul and I always voted. As adults, there was no excuse not to. That was part of our personal aesthetic as much as what car was in our driveway. There was a gubernatorial race coming up. George W. Bush ran for re-election as governor and won in November. As I had all of my adult life, I paid attention to candidates and local elections as much as the national contests. In that spirit of keeping myself informed, I listened intently to the opinions of our neighbors and fellow parents of small children. I fully appreciated the fact that our little enclave in West Lake Hills could be considered privileged. With that street level outward appearance of money, some candidates for office felt compelled to venture into the neighborhood to knock on doors and shake hands with the locals.

One afternoon a candidate running for lieutenant governor appeared on our front deck. I recognized him immediately. He had on a loose button-down shirt and khakis, and behind him stood two or three staffers looking like second-string benchwarmers waiting for their big moment. I didn't much appreciate a lone stranger knocking on our glass sliding doors unless they were carrying a package for delivery. I was irked at the specter of this group of strange men seeking the "homeowner's" attention. I slid the glass to the side and ignored the outstretched hand hanging in the humid air between us.

"I know who you are, and I have never voted for a Republican in my life. I certainly won't be changing that practice any time soon," I said.

And with that, I slid the glass back to lock the door and stared out at an unsmiling Rick Perry looking as though he needed to collect his thoughts and smooth his hair for the next porch down. In a few years, the inimitable Texas journalist and humorist Molly Ivins would dub Rick Perry "Governor Good Hair," and that title clung to him better than a bejeweled tiara on a drag queen at a pride parade.

***

The new Ministry record was close enough to being completed. It was a record they could theoretically have finished in 1997, but songs were scrapped and replaced, and so it went. 1999 was off to a punchy start, as if the next twelve months were merely live rehearsals for the new century coming up. Life felt as though it were moving at half-speed. The year was progressing, and Paul was home from Chicago, not yet obsessed with the upcoming, inevitable tour for Dark Side of the Spoon. Paul Elledge was performing his magic for the album art. Things were falling into place.

The kids were both in school. At times like this, Paul and I could afford to spend a good portion of the day together running errands and going for Vietnamese food alone. Or we could skip out to the thrift stores, go grocery shopping at Fiesta, and eat warm, freshly made corn tortillas on the car ride home. These rare, quiet times gave us a chance to reflect upon what we wanted out of Austin and what we missed about Chicago. Simple things.

There were scores of Mexican taco trucks and tex mex everywhere around Austin, but we both craved chile rellenos (and chile rellenos tacos from La

Pasadita). Chile rellenos were labor and time intensive to make at home. Weren't they? We decided it might be fun to try making some ourselves. Cooking was my domain. In the matter of the rellenos, I was willing to ignore my general skittishness about deep frying with a veritable vat of cooking oil. Paul was willing to give it a go and help with prep. We drove to Half Price Books and bought a copy of Diana Kennedy's The Cuisines of Mexico with an authentic chile rellenos recipe inside. Yes, please.

After picking up a bag of Fiesta corn tortillas, hot from the grill that morning, we found Oaxacan cheese to stuff the chilies as they were done at La Pasadita, rather than use traditional "picadillo" (seasoned pork) suggested in Kennedy's book. Otherwise, I was happy to follow Kennedy's recipe and made pork-infused tomato broth for serving. Paul tied on an apron and began whipping some egg whites.

The two of us rarely cooked together; although, he would stand outside manning the grill when we barbecued. That was the extent of his kitchen duty. Paul appeared ungainly in an apron because of his height and thin frame—the Hawaiian aprons we used were suited for my much smaller body. In an apron, I thought he vaguely resembled a praying mantis wearing a French maid's outfit, but of course I didn't tell him that. He heard enough French jokes coming from my mouth to fill a stadium. We constantly made light of his French heritage, usually capping these quips with a final, "Oui, oui . . .Pee Wee."

I worked on the tomato broth. The chilis were stuffed, dipped in egg white foam, ready to be lowered into a deep pan filled with smoking hot oil. Seeing Paul standing over the pot of hot oil, brought to mind the mad scientist jibes perpetually floating around our house. In the past, these throw-away references were aimed strictly at Paul at work at the mixing console. These days, our son delivered his own edgy take on the theme. He was fond of sitting on his skateboard, positioning our guinea pig as a hood ornament of sorts in the front, and sailing across linoleum floors in the house at alternating speeds just to do it. We encouraged our kids to be adventurous, as long as they didn't hurt themselves (or the pig).

After a few minutes of watching our chilies surf the roiling waves of hot oil, they were oozing cheese lightly encrusted in their tawny shells. Paul plucked them out with tongs and onto paper towels to drain. They were beautiful. Plated with a ladleful of tomato broth, our lunchtime experiment was ready for tasting. The tomato sauce had a whiff of cinnamon and clove. Neither of us said anything as we took our first bites followed with a bite of corn tortilla. Paul closed his eyes.

"Oh . . . my . . . God. Gorgeous . . . this is SO fucking good."

Yes. The chili rellenos were miraculously good. Staring at one another with eyes wide and mouths full, it was one of those rare, intensely vulnerable moments we all have with someone who really knows us and our likes and dislikes.

"These are so good, I could cry," I said.

"I KNOW."

Maybe this wasn't domestic bliss for other people, but it worked for us. I was relieved to have Paul home. Discovering ridiculously delicious food was an experience to share, like looking at art or agreeing on what music to listen to at home.

***

One singer consuming our imaginations at the time was Scott Walker. His singing style made it difficult to ignore the lyrics in the songs. Pay attention children, it seemed to say. I had a funny thought one day when we were having coffee at home and Scott Walker was playing in the background.

"You know, the way he writes, it seems like the words were put together—literally, strung together—by someone who can write English words perfectly well, but doesn't actually speak the language, "I said. The song playing was "Plastic Palace People." Paul didn't say anything.

"Wouldn't it be hilarious to find out Scott Walker doesn't actually speak English? All that stuff about 'Billy . . . sailing over rooftops, a string tied to his underwear'—it's all nonsense, "I said.

Paul put down his Boy Scout Troop No. 54 coffee cup and smiled at me.

"Yeaaahh. That would explain a lot." Then a serious look came over his face, as if I'd just given him the secret to writing pop lyrics.

"I love you," he said, and laughed.

***

Paul and I were preparing ourselves mentally for another Ministry tour and the possibilities for me to come out either alone or with the kids to Chicago. Our regular UPS driver arrived at the house one morning, going to the back, and actually ringing the bell, something he never did. I walked out onto the carport.

"This delivery, I wanted to make sure someone could sign for it, "he said, while unloading one after another long, tall box bearing the Gibson Guitars logo on the side.

"Looks like guitars," I said, handing back the paperwork. The driver had a huge grin as he lined up a stack of eight boxes against the house.

I scanned the receipt. "Gibson EB 750" and so on. I wondered how many of these were for Paul and which ones were for Al and the other two guitarists going on the road with them.

"Must be nice," the driver looked over our haul as if it were Christmas morning.

Sure. We're the envy of the neighborhood, surrounded by tools of the trade. Were it only so straightforward and simple. These "gifts" were earned.

***

Comedy. Tragedy. Drama. Life with Ministry as the template for our routines. It was a life. Ours. In May, a few days after Mother's Day, the house phone rang, and I recognized Dannie Flesher's voice. We didn't typically hear from Dannie;although, I occasionally called him to say hello.

"Gerda, I need to talk to Paul." Dannie was in a hurry. He didn't seem eager to chit chat as he normally would.

Paul was in the studio in back. I dashed outside to tell him he had a call from

Dannie. Paul was in a lighthearted mood, preoccupied with going on the road again. He came into the house, and I handed him the phone. He listened for a moment nodding his head. His smile disappeared quickly.

"What?! WHAT THE FUCK." He looked terribly distressed. "Ok. I'll tell them. Dannie, I gotta go." He tossed the phone on the kitchen counter.

"What happened?" I expected the worst. Dannie was never short with me. And during all of my Wax Trax years with him and Jim Nash, I was privy to all sorts of novel iterations of crazy.

"Tucker. Tucker happened. He's dead . . . he killed himself. Dannie's over there," Paul looked at me, adjusting his voice to the news.

William Tucker was one of our friends in Chicago. This was bad. Tucker played guitar with Ministry on the Mind is a Terrible Thing to Taste tour. He had since moved to Chicago and had been living there for ten years, working on music projects with Chris Connelly and other friends. I had seen Tucker the last time I was in Chicago, and he looked ill.

Paul walked into the family room. The phone rang again. He picked it up.

"I know, I heard. What am I doing? Trying to cope and stay busy!"

I heard more clichés as Paul really had nothing concrete to say. It tore my heart out to hear him struggling for words. He and I both knew Tucker had been in physical pain for months and was trying to come to terms with a medical condition that apparently would interfere permanently with his ability to have sex—that was my understanding of his prognosis. What comforting wisdom could anyone have offered him?

Paul looked inconsolable. And then suddenly, he snapped out of it. He had a tour to focus on. As always, he had an uncanny ability to look away and ignore the worst situations. He'd looked away so many times with Al. He would come home after spending a full day at Al's and getting nothing done. "I'm spinning my wheels," he'd say. It was another cliché I heard so often it had no impact anymore. He'd become so good at ignoring Al's addiction fallout, his paranoia, and his nodding out. It was as if it didn't matter. Paul was on to the next task, forging ahead to "make shit happen." But this situation was different. Paul and Tucker had a genuine friendship and a professional rapport. Paul stayed at

Tucker's apartment on trips to Chicago. They were of the "mutual appreciation society." Tucker's death was a big blow. He was family.

When Ministry's Dark Side of the Spoon was released the following month, the record was dedicated to William Tucker. Paul had a hand in the final dedication; although, he thought it was a gratuitous gesture on Al's part. Paul told me Al hadn't appeared sympathetic to anyone else's grief over Tucker's death. It seemed Al commiserated in his own unique way.

The band was gearing up for rehearsals, and we took the kids to Chicago for a few days. Once there, Paul decided he needed a new look for this tour. Paul was no fashion novice; when he and I first met, his head was partly shaved, and he wore a beret. But in the ten years we'd been married, his deep-brown, wavy, long hair was a constant, changing only in length by negligible degrees.

"I want my hair to be the color of silverfish," he said, as we passed Powell's Books on Lincoln Avenue wandering around our old haunts. He had seen the color somewhere in a magazine. Gun metal or a similar shade. A photographer friend recommended a hip hair salon on Lincoln. Paul went for the appointment.

"That color is only available in England," the stylist told a much disappointed Paul when he explained what he wanted. "Those chemicals are illegal here. I'll try my best to get you close, but it may be more platinum than silver." When the stylist had finished, Paul's long, brown waves were gone and in their place a mass of platinum. Not the dirty, shiny silver-wavering-on-green he'd hoped for. His hair looked like a wig. And I liked it. Briefly. I thought it would fit right in with their scheduled video shoot for the song "Bad Blood." "Bad Blood" was one of my least favorite Ministry songs, but the video would sell it—another part of the package to keep the band's name out there.

Visually, the video narrative would again have Al excavating a junkie's world of body fluids: Paul, now crowned with a full head of hair gone white, balances Al against a mixing board, while a bloodthirsty nurse teases them with a transfusion apparatus nearby. I hated the video but thought Paul's hair was outstanding. It worked.

Moving into summer and out from the sadness of Tucker's passing, Ministry was on the road again. I took care of business at home and attended my regular recovery meetings, once even taking the kids to the meeting place to drop off coffee. As with all previous tours, our house phone was my lifeline to Paul while he was away for this long stretch of time. Another tour, another round of check-ins home from hotel lobby phones and production offices. Road gossip didn't matter. Our conversations felt like rehearsals for the eventual day he'd come home. I only needed to hear his voice as much as he wanted to hear mine.

The band member line up this time was different—they went out minus their guitarist Mike Scaccia. Mikey had done enough drugs with Al and was now committed to following a recovery program to stay sober. That meant no drugs, no alcohol. He had kids to think about.

On a blistering hot day in June, I answered the house phone and was surprised to hear an unfamiliar voice say my name. Musician friends called the house when they were in town and desperate for a local lunch date, and I recognized most of their voices. Sometimes, Paul and I would go to a soundcheck to see a friend just to say hello. When I realized Mikey was on the phone, I reminded him Paul wasn't home. "Do you want me to give him a message?"

"No . . . I was really callin' for you."

Me? This must be bad. I couldn't handle any more bad news after Tucker's death. What was on Mikey's mind? Mikey was thoughtful and funny when he was around me, but the extent of our conversations usually centered around food and our kids. The first time I met Mikey in Chicago in 1991, I arrived at a Paul Elledge photo shoot with a massive bowl of homemade guacamole and chips. Under his black leather jacket and Rigor Mortis T-shirt, the Texan in Mikey nudged a big smile to his face when he saw the guacamole. He came over and introduced himself. Mikey was also a fan of spaghetti sauce I made with mushrooms, a dinner I cooked for everyone in the house when he stayed with us for a couple of months after we moved to Austin.

"I was calling to apologize for some things," he said. "I wanted to apologize, and just say if I've ever done anything to hurt you, I'm really sorry."

The hesitation in his voice was so out of character, like someone recovering from amnesia who can't get their stories straight. I couldn't imagine how Mikey had ever hurt me. His cat had clawed our newly upholstered leather chair while he was house sitting years before. That was old news and not a big deal. After racking my brain for a minute, I finally understood what he was doing. Mikey was trying to make amends to me. He was following the process of step nine in the twelve-step program of AA. I knew it, because I'd been through it myself.

"Other than bringing your psycho cat into my house, we're good," I told him.

I was happy to hear him laugh. Mikey's laugh had a little whistle to it. His laugh reminded me of Muttley, the canine sidekick of the cartoon character Snidely Whiplash. Good old Mikey. I appreciated the gesture. He may have had a history of blackouts while drunk. I don't know. I was fairly certain he knew I had my own ups and downs with alcohol. He knew I would understand what he was trying to say.

***

In November of 1999, Ministry was nominated for a Grammy award for the song "Bad Blood." Their competition: Black Sabbath. For the second time, there was no real debate over whether we would attend the Grammys. Al (and seemingly Paul) couldn't be bothered with conventional sucking up for publicity purposes. He didn't care about awards.

In February 2000, on the night of the Grammy awards ceremony, Black Sabbath won "Best Metal Performance," and Ozzy Osbourne took home his trophy. A UPS package arrived at our door from the Grammy committee a little while later. Paul unpacked the box and inside was a small, felt jewelry pouch in light blue—Tiffany's trademark color. He opened the pouch and lifted out a brass-colored medallion about two-and-half-inches wide attached to an emerald-green satin ribbon for display. The inscription on the medallion read, "42nd Annual Grammy Nominee" on one side and "National Academy of Recording Arts & Sciences" on the reverse circling the raised image of the gramophone logo.

I laughed out loud. "Tiffany's couldn't be bothered with making our platinum wedding rings, but they were happy to make this bit of bling. You should tie that thing around your neck and wear it every day," I said. My husband was highly amused.

27

It was a couple of days after one of the kids' field trips to McKinney Falls State Park outside of Austin, and I found myself biding time in the shade on a walkway at the elementary school. Waiting to go inside and have lunch with my daughter. I was thinking about the field trip, the parents I'd carpooled with, exclusively women, and how all of us showed up for our kids when asked to chaperone these events. As I waited there, one of the women from the trip appeared on the walkway and joined me. Cesca Judge was doing what I was, waiting for a chance to see her girls. I talked to Cesca whenever our paths intersected at birthday parties and field trips or on the walking path at Town Lake. She liked to walk there in the mornings with a partner, too.

Cesca and I fell into ruminating about our former professional lives. She had an engineering background. We'd both put our careers on hold to stay home with our kids, while allowing our husbands to pursue their creative lives. Mike Judge was long finished with Beavis and Butthead but was working on King of the Hill now. Cesca asked me if I planned to practice law again. Eventually I probably will, I said. This response led to other bigger life questions.

"I don't know what I'd do if Mike ever left me," she said.

That seemed to come out of nowhere. To her, it seemed impossible to imagine, having to go back to the work she had left behind.

"I don't know what I'd do either," I told her.

The idea that Paul would ever leave me or I would leave him wasn't something occupying my mind at all. Mine and Paul's lives were so intertwined, our relationship evolving slowly and steadily. We had followed each other this far and had survived still able to laugh, love each other, navigate the world of parenting, and maintain respect for one another. The universe would lose a chunk of the natural order of things if anything drastic were to change. I couldn't imagine a scenario where it made sense to be permanently apart. We'd been temporarily apart for long stretches of time and that was part of our routine. Why leave, anyway.

Perhaps after the Ministry trials and dramas were finally over and the kids were on their own, we'd be free to travel to places we'd never seen before— together. Do the Grand Prix circuit in full, as Paul had hoped after our first experience with Formula One racing ten years earlier. I had those thoughts occasionally. In listening to Cesca, I was reminded of the old adage, "Men don't leave unless they have someone else." If Paul ever left me, it would be his fear of losing his pop star image that would be the thing pulling him away and onto someone else, something to lift his ego a notch, and ultimately that would have nothing to do with me anyway. It was too cliché. On the other hand, I was prepared for anything. I was, after all, a pragmatist.

"You and I will survive handsomely if anything ever happens," I assured Cesca, hoping to put a positive spin to the conversation.

It was reassuring in a way to know I wasn't the only one around whose spouse didn't have a normal schedule or normal civilian life. Our husbands were in the public eye, with contacts around the world, and the potential for all kinds of threats to our personal lives was real. Cesca and I were on the sidelines of fame, both living in those bubbles. I, for one, felt it was exactly where I was supposed to be. I imagined she felt the same. We were both intelligent, beautiful, caring women pressing ahead with seemingly mundane mommy duties that were in fact foundational in our kids' young lives. The mundane decisions matter. I knew Cesca didn't buy store bread with high-fructose corn syrup in it either. I knew, because we'd hit on that fun fact at some other event. Life went on.

How do you become a fist when you're always in shadow? That question still haunted me. On the surface I was adequately raising our kids and keeping an eye out for something new for me to do. On the other hand, I was living vicariously through my husband's professional ups and downs, and what if something happened to him? What would I do?

It had been seven years since my last day of practicing law full time in Chicago. During my time away, law practice changed dramatically. Everyone was using online research tools. Filing court pleadings in person was becoming a thing of the past. Solo attorneys drafted pleadings and briefs on their own computers, obviating the need for legal secretaries. Laws changed.

Paul and I mulled over the possibility of my going back to work. I decided to sit for the Texas bar exam as a first effort in scoping out options for myself in the local landscape. It was progress, momentum, some way to alter the course of my thoughts about doing something useful outside of the hermetic existence of the household I was managing and trying to feel good about. I needed a change. I was sober and going to meetings, and I needed a new focus in my life. Going back to criminal defense practice seemed like a painless reentry, and I considered what that would look like. Chicago had its gritty landscape of successive generations in gangs and crime. I couldn't envision a culture of such louche characters bent on committing felonies in Austin proper, let alone our neighborhood of West Lake Hills. When the temperature outside hit 102, where would they even hide a weapon? Was Austin a white-collar crime market?

Without rigorous preparation or studying, I sat for the February 2000 bar exam. The results two months later confirmed my suspicions about my grasp of oil and gas law, an area of practice peculiar to my current home state and a newly reinstated section of the essay portion of the Texas bar. I didn't pass. I signed on for a Bar/Bri review course and registered to retake the exam in July.

Ministry had new management. It was a new year. Crazed Management was long out of the Ministry picture. Walter O'Brien and Concrete Management were now in their place and somehow not living up to Al's standards. Al fired O'Brien just as Ministry was about to rehearse and go out with Ozzfest for the summer. Ozzfest was important. It was guaranteed to be a much needed promotional boost for the band after another years-long studio marathon session had ended with a finished album. The question now was, who would replace Walter O'Brien for the tour? Before any of us had time to fully digest our suppers, Paul abruptly received word that Ministry was bumped from Ozzfest. No need to worry about new management.

Everyone was thrown off by this sudden change of plans. I had to ask, "Didn't Ministry have a contract in place for this tour?" They couldn't legally be dropped, could they? Now that the band was without management, there was nowhere to turn for answers. Promotional people, booking personnel, and newly minted tour support began calling our house at all hours from different continents to find out what was happening. It had been several years since I'd actively practiced law, but as a lawyer you don't stop thinking like one when the clients dry up. You have an instinct, a gut reaction. My lawyer self fully entertained the possibility we would have to take some kind of legal action. I called around to the collection of lawyers we already knew, who had worked for the band on different projects. The attorneys triaged immediate possibilities to hire and in what city or jurisdiction they would have to be located. I finally spoke to some lawyers in New York who took up the case. The band filed a lawsuit. Our friends and immediate neighbors found out Paul wasn't going away for the summer after all.

(At the next SXSW festival, the Ozzfest documentary We Sold Our Souls For Rock 'n' Roll was shown as part of the music festival's film program. Sharon Osbourne was in town to take part in a panel discussion on the film. Our next-door neighbor's son, Patrick Houston, was home for spring break and had tickets to SXSW. He took a seat in the audience for Sharon Osbourne's Q&A on her film. When he had a chance to ask a question, Patrick turned to Sharon and asked, "Why wasn't Ministry doing Ozzfest?" Sharon looked surprised and told the audience she was unable to discuss an ongoing legal matter. Patrick followed up with, "Paul Barker is my next door neighbor." Sharon then said, "Tell him to be kind.")

The Ozzfest litigation went on for close to a year. The matter was resolved and the lawsuit dismissed. All parties involved agreed the settlement reached was to each side's full satisfaction. Life went on.

Without any tours or recording sessions, Paul was home for the summer. In July, I was practiced, rehearsed, and ready to retake the bar exam. For this second time around, Paul, Ursula, and Gordon comically sang "I Believe in Miracles" as they dropped me off at the Long Center by Town Lake, where I joined hundreds of other hopefuls ready for the two-day hell fest. The Long Center was an older, still modern beauty of an orchestra hall where Paul and I had once gone to hear the Austin Symphony perform.

At the end of the first day of testing, my husband and kids and I made a necessary pilgrimage to Sandy's Frozen Custard shack in walking distance of the venue. It was one of our favorite funky old places near the park, a place for corndogs or mixed cones when dinner at home wasn't possible, or the July heat made cooking a torture for the chef—usually, me. I felt more confident about retaking the bar this time, more prepared. It helped tremendously to have my own personal cheering section, my family's emotional support present and accounted for. It didn't matter what the test results were this time around. We would figure out where to go from there. In October, my answer came in the mail. I passed.

The idea of going back to practicing law was a good one in theory. Five years of solid experience in Chicago looked substantial enough on paper to meet the requirements of jobs open with the state of Texas and with small private firms. I picked up a letter of recommendation from one of Sam Houston's brothers, who'd been a prosecutor with the state. I sent out a dozen resumes and waited.

Before the summer and seemingly out of nowhere as far as we could tell, Al and Paul were contacted about the possibility of Ministry appearing in Steven Spielberg's upcoming film, A.I. A.I. was originally a Stanley Kubrick project based on a short story Kubrick had acquired the rights to. He and Spielberg spent several years discussing a film adaptation. Somewhere in those discussions, the name Ministry came up. They were Stanley Kubrick's favorite band.

After Kubrick passed away in March of 1999, his widow asked Spielberg to take over writing and directing the screen adaptation for A.I. Several scenes in the screenplay called for a live band to be playing at a "Flesh Fair." As an homage to Stanley Kubrick, Spielberg thought Ministry should be the band performing at the fair. Now someone had to broker the deal and get the band onboard. That someone was a music industry veteran named Michael Brokaw.

Michael Brokaw was introduced to Al and Paul through a mutual acquaintance. Brokaw had a history managing rock musicians. He had worked with Fleetwood Mac for ten years and with Lindsey Buckingham for thirteen. Brokaw also knew his way around Hollywood deals. Some of his current clients were lighting designers for big movies. Brokaw offered to negotiate the deal for Ministry, but wasn't looking to manage the band—at first. Another friend of Ministry's, Jeffrey Kinnart, got involved as a day-to-day liaison between the band and the production personnel. Paul had mixed feelings about the time frame for coming up with original music to sync with the band's scenes but realized they needed to work on song ideas immediately. Filming began in August, with most scenes shot at the Spruce Goose Dome in Long Beach, California. It was the hangar built for Howard Hughes's historic plane.

The musical partnership between Paul and Al Jourgensen was at the beginning of the end, from what I could tell: Paul made music, it went to Al, and sometimes they were in agreement. Work on this film's music had to start somewhere. Someone had to "make shit happen," as I'd heard so many times before. That someone again was Paul.

It seemed to me Paul was doing everything he could to generate ideas. They were going to be performing as a band in the film. They needed to start writing like a band. Paul and our friend Max Brody holed up in Paul's studio behind the house, and the two of them worked out some ideas for the scenes.

While Ministry's musical identity was on the line and required being camera ready, Paul convinced Al to see our dentist and take care of the nagging issues he was having with his teeth. In light of Al's drug history, there was a lot of work to be done. Al also needed to look good for the film.

Our dentist practiced a brand of holistic dentistry he'd learned in his native Norway—treat the whole body when treating the mouth. Dr. Tor Guten (or "Doc Tor" as renamed by the Luxa/Pan punsters) sussed out Al's medical history fairly quickly and began the process of making Al's mouth pretty again. Doc Tor determined Al was due for oral surgery and a soft diet for a few days. Al was again in between places to stay, and we agreed it would be beneficial for everyone's work schedules to have him stay at our place and recuperate after the surgery.

I wanted to share the A.I. movie news and was on the phone with Maria Ferrero, Ministry's former publicist, catching up on our latest. I heard someone knocking at the back door. Obviously, a stranger—neighbors didn't knock. I was annoyed to be interrupted on the call, especially with Maria. She was an old friend and member of my girlfriend squad.

It was Al at the door. He was with someone. I thought, of course he's got someone with him for his dental procedure. Probably a new girlfriend. Al always miraculously found women to take care of him, especially when he was at his most vulnerable.

The person with Al didn't look like one of Al's typical girlfriends. No red hair, for one thing. As I stood there eyeing this person standing at my back doorstep, I couldn't help but wonder, what gender is this? I thought she was a man. She swept in behind Al and didn't say much.

Paul and Max came into the house. After a few rather uncomfortable moments, they all retreated to our back studio. It seemed Paul and Max were surprised by the appearance of this new person called "Ty" Coon. Paul was further surprised Al was considering her as a contributor on the A.I. project. She was there to provide additional vocals.

Paul had the same look on his face that I'd seen back on the Mind tour in 1990, when we were all in New York waiting for the Ministry interview with MTV—the interview Paul was shut out of when Al enlisted Ogre from Skinny Puppy and Martin Atkins from PIL and Killing Joke to get on camera with him. Paul's opinion didn't really matter much then or now.

Eventually, Ty came back into the house alone. I thought it best to be welcoming. I gave her a tour of the house and showed her where she and Al would be sleeping. We started walking together down the long hallway to the other end of the house.

Paul Elledge had shot my portrait when I was five months pregnant with Gordon. That photo of me—alone—was hanging in the hallway gallery of our house. Ty walked up to it and asked, "Is this a Paul Elledge?" I answered yes. She walked away from the photo saying, "Wow. He can make anyone look good."

Yeah. He can.

This person of fluid gender (for the moment) was a guest in my house. I wanted to smack her, but I restrained myself. Paul could deal with these two on his own time.

Our company was with us for a couple of days. Having to supervise school-aged kids, I had my schedule. Paul and Al were busy in the back with Max Brody, and I suggested to Ty that we go with the kids to Rollingwood Pool. We had a membership at the neighborhood pool where middle school kids practiced for swim team and moms got a break.

I rarely engaged with any of these mothers but occasionally saw someone I knew at the pool. The first time I visited the pool alone with my kids had cured me of any desire to mingle with the regulars. At that time, I made the mistake of peeling off my T-shirt and standing there in my black bikini. One of the moms at the other end of the pool looked up at me and leaned in to whisper to her companions in the mommy set. I can confidently say, I'm pretty good at detecting when someone's talking about me. They all looked over and stared, until they realized I was staring back at them and not looking away. Most of the other moms wore one-piece bathing suits or "tankinis." Something more modest than a bikini. Maybe they were covering up scars or C-sections. I didn't know. I didn't have that problem. And I didn't care what they thought of me.

When Ty and I walked into the fenced in pool area, I waved at the pool manager Brian, a big guy who was a Ministry fan (oddly enough). We situated ourselves in deckchairs on the side of the pool. Ursula and Gordon saw some friends and went in the water.

Ty stared at my legs. I had removed my shorts and was sitting in my bathing suit bottom. "Oh, I hate when I get that cottage cheese flab on my skin," she said, pointing to a barely detectable ripple of uneven smoothness on my thigh. I just nodded.

I wondered what cave Al had pulled her from. I didn't say anything. She's Al's friend. They have work to finish. Ty lit a cigarette. The lifeguard mechanically left his seat and walked over. He stood in front of Ty. "No smoking at the pool y'all."

I knew that the moment she lit up. I watched her squirm when she had to put it out.

During that week, Al had his teeth worked on. The dentist told him to rest and let his mouth heal. I cooked almost every day as it was, and sympathetic to Al's plight, I baked some stuffed manicotti. Everyone in our house liked pasta, and it was mushy enough for Al to be able to eat dinner with us.

Al and Ty sat at their end of our dining room table. We were discussing the upcoming filming in Long Beach. From Al's end of the table came a quick, loud crack of someone passing gas. Al smirked and nudged Ty. "Excuse you," he said to her. Then he very casually announced to the room, "We were kind of busy last night. Heh, heh, heh."

I was so happy my kids weren't old enough to understand that fascinating, scatological "Al" bit of minutiae. I looked down at my plate.

"Good manicotti, Gerda!" Uh-huh. Thanks for the applause.

While Al recuperated, Paul received a call from his father in Kauai. Gordon Barker was turning seventy in August, and a crew of his loyal island friends were planning a party on the beach. Our whole family was invited. It was a good excuse to get away from Austin and clear the air before the A.I. shoot, and the kids could finally spend a little bit of time getting to know their other grandfather before school was back in session. I booked the flights and found a small hotel for us on the beach.

The Barkers four enjoyed a splendid week on Kauai, swimming and snorkeling in the ocean at Poipu, hiking up the Sleeping Giant, dipping toes into the Queen's Bath in Princeville, and getting acquainted with a beach bum crowd of rabble rousers gathered to show their allegiance to the great "Gordini" Barker on his seventieth. Gordon the Elder was charming as always, lifting his glass to his namesake, our own Claude Gordon.

Paul, the kids, and I made the necessary reconnaissance trips to a few thrift stores on the island. In one, we discovered a pile of vintage dark-blue "Honolulu PAL" (Police Activities League) T-shirts for our two boys and one girl. And, in what appeared to be the oldest charity shop in Kapaa, an estate donation drop off spot favored by the aging doyennes of Kauai's high society, I found something for myself. On a dressmaker's mannequin pushed into a corner near an exit door, I caught sight of patterns in earth-tone-colored zig zags spiraling down a V-neck knitted dress, cut to snugly embrace the slim vixen wearing it, circa 1970-something: an original Missoni. I asked if it was for sale. I didn't even bother to check the size. And we—the dress and I—headed back to the beach.

***

In September, Steven Spielberg and his production staff were ready to shoot Ministry's "Flesh Fair" scenes for A.I. For the stage line up, the "band members" going to LA were Max Brody, Adam Grossman, Duane Buford, Ty Coon, Paul, and Al. I told Paul I was coming to LA for this. I had enough of staying on the sidelines waiting for the opportunity to participate in person in my husband's amazing professional feats. You may never do this again, I told him. "I want to be there."

I paid a visit to the principal's office at the kids' school to get permission to take them out for a few days. The reason for the absence was a kind of family emergency: watch a movie being made with their dad in it. I called the kids' old preschool teacher Amanda to see if she could come with me as their nanny. My sister had a full-time job as a commercial baker and couldn't help with babysitting much anymore. Amanda was thrilled—except for the flying to LA part.

"I hate flying. I seem to attract the worst mid-air turbulence every time I'm on a plane!" she warned. Appealing to her Scottish sensibilities, I said, "Oh, did I mention we'll all be staying on the Queen Mary? It's docked right next to the soundstages."

"Well . . . I suppose I could take some anxiety pills or something."

"Amanda . . . we'll see Jude Law in drag."

"ALLLL RIIIIGHT!!!!! I'LL GO."

I decided a few months earlier I had enough of cutting my own hair with a hand mirror, a comb, and hair scissors that hadn't been sharpened ever. My friend Ellen had a hairdresser who had a chair at a shop on Lamar close to where the original Whole Foods store had been before it turned into a franchise monster. The old Whole Foods was now a used records shop with three parking spaces in front that never seemed to be occupied when I drove by. The hair salon was behind the record store.

I made an appointment with my new hairdresser, Danny "from North Carolina, honey," who assured me he would take care to make me look presentable to the Hollywood crowd. "Let's give you some nice LA hair," he said, while lifting a few strands and pondering the color. "And OF COURSE— we need to dye those eyebrows. I like things that match."

Soon enough, it was time for the band to leave for two weeks in LA. I stood on our deck and waved with Ursula and Gordon as we watched the Lincoln Town Car limo floating down the front driveway with Paul in the back. "Wow, dad's gonna be in a movie!" It must have finally registered in the kids' minds that not every dad got to do this. Their dad was certainly special to us, but no matter how much we traveled or had unusual guests coming by the house or working with Paul in the back, all of that seemed normal. Going away to be in a Spielberg movie was definitely not normal.

A week later, Amanda, the kids, and I were heading to the airport in another hired car. This one, I ordered. Why not? This was a special event for us, too.

Amanda, the kids, and I settled into our seats on the plane. As we began picking up speed on the runway, I looked over at Amanda on the other side of the aisle. She was positively gripping the armrests. I hoped she would be calm for most of the flight and get over her anxiety with flying. I looked over again. "Wait for it," she mouthed to me.

We were in the air, cruising along. The kids were quiet, sitting with Amanda. The seatbelt sign turned off. I clicked open my belt, leaned over to stretch and look for my journal, when the plane suddenly rose and fell, and I was bounced from my seat. It happened again. I heard someone gasp. I looked over at Amanda.

She was staring at me and nodding. "SEE."

The air turbulence finally settled down while I contemplated the next few days of Hollywood weirdness. Of course, for me the most exciting draw to this movie production was the possibility to see costume designs for the film. I wondered what the wardrobe magicians would cook up as a common theme for the band's look. I never could get excited by an over-the-top signature look like Al's, with his hacked at the knee army fatigues, combat boots, flip up binocular-like shades, dreads, or longer dreads—always some kind of headgear. Al's Chicago cop hat was a trophy I wore once when Al decided I needed that symbol of authority covering my legal brains, while we all drove in a packed van to see Metallica in the suburbs of Chicago. Al's early bandanas, à la Adam Ant, and even multiple crushed straw cowboy hats for the Revolting Cocks shows got a little stale after a while. They reminded me of Slash from Guns N' Roses. Too LA. It was positively freaky when Rob Zombie miraculously started dressing a lot like Al. Again, too LA. I admired Jello Biafra's "no look" to Al's urban combat-zone shtick.

Paul was waiting for us when we arrived at LAX. He had a rental car and we drove to Long Beach. We, like the band, were staying on the Queen Mary, a luxury liner turned hotel that had been docked since 1968. The ship had five hundred cabin rooms lining nightmarishly long corridors that would make those tricycle scenes in The Shining seem like pleasant daydreams. Stanley Kubrick would approve. The rooms had portals opening out to "the sea"—the ship was grounded in five feet of water. How many royal panties flew out those portals in its heyday? I wanted to know. I asked several staff. They seemed annoyed, and I let it go. I was having fun.

Jeffrey Kinnart, the band's liaison on the production, met with us aboard the ship. There were other musicians and crew wandering around the hotel who were working a "techno fest" all day next door to the Queen Mary on the pier. The rest of the five hundred rooms were completely sold out to tourists hoping to catch a whiff of the preserved refinement exclusive to this Queen's ship. The ship was also haunted—another big draw for the tourists.

Everyone seemed perfectly giddy to be part of a Hollywood production. I sensed an added glee in Paul's voice for those short weeks of filming, imagining him "moored" to a ship in the off hours from filming, a perfect harmony between his penchant for maritime lingo—"I need to reel Al in!"—and recovering his "sea legs," so to speak.

Jeffrey Kinnart collected us to go on set. We headed into a separate elevator on the ship and over to the hangar next door where the filming was happening. I looked around the stage set up for the band's scenes and was motioned over by Paul to meet Spielberg's co-producer, Kathleen Kennedy. She was friendly, smiling at the kids, making small talk while I looked around at the sparseness of the set compared to the number of crew people milling around. Amanda was calm, taking it all in for the time being, from what I could tell. In another instant her eyes were wide and unblinking as we espied Jude Law in full sci-fi drag. In a slick, long black coat, his costumed form was still beside Spielberg, waiting for his direction. Haley Joel Osment lingered on the sidelines, the only "human" square-looking piece of the entire scene. During the filming of the band's scenes, Paul discovered many of the crew were Ministry fans.

Paul escorted our visiting party through the hangar, stopping to say hello to the prop designer keeping watch over dumpster-sized bins of sculpted metallic creatures—spiders? The hangar's interior was dark like the finished scenes in the film. I didn't have the honor of meeting Spielberg himself. He was engaged with the actors. Amanda and I were able to watch the band "play" on the stage. Somehow she ended up standing next to Spielberg and almost lost it when the director accidentally stepped on her foot.

Paul and I later met with Michael Brokaw in Burbank. I thought I'd seen so much extraordinary craftsmanship and focus already, but Michael was taking us on a tour of where the real soul of the movie was massaged and fixed— wardrobe. I didn't say a word. I was in awe as Michael led us through a roomful of seamstresses, finishers, and patternmakers bent over their work, past color swatches and Polaroid shots stuck onto the side walls of the place. I didn't dare think of taking a picture. For me—in my world—this was sacred territory. The common language in the room was Russian. I could understand bits and pieces. I imagined seeing my mother (were she still alive) after this trip and describing the stages of garments in production—pieces being finally lifted up, flattened by hand, fitted, ironed, and fitted again to the actors' bodies—pure heaven.

At one point in the day, Amanda, the kids, and I wandered over to Ministry's trailer. Biding time and fully made up between scenes were Adam Grossman, Max Brody, Duane Buford, and Al. Al was in full skeleton-face makeup smoking a cigarette. He lunged at Gordon in a half-hearted goofy attempt to scare him, but the kid wasn't buying his vamp. "I know it's you, AL!!!" I snapped as many photos as I could get away with, and we headed back to the Queen Mary. We later rendezvoused with Amanda and Paul to the Griffith Observatory to have a good look at those hills made famous by James Dean in the movies. There was a limit to our ability to go on set while Paul and company were busy there, and that was fine with me. My old friend Leila was in town in between tours, and she was highly entertained by the thought of meeting me on the Queen Mary. Despite her world travels, she hadn't experienced an old luxury liner yet, either. Leila and I strolled the ship's massive corridors with the kids and took them shopping at the ship's gift store, where they tried on court jester's hats and flipped through coloring books detailing the Queen Mary's provenance and history. It felt so good to catch up with Leila and to brag a little in the shadow of the Spruce Goose, where behind the scenes myth making for the movie was going on, a movie coincidentally featuring my husband's band. It was another marker, another testament to Paul and Al's considerable, devoted talents. I wasn't one to brag about Paul's successes but this time was extraordinary for all of us. To have your music chosen for use in a film was fantastic in itself. To appear as a band in a film playing your own music was a collaborative effort on a whole other level. There wasn't much room to improvise.

The following June, Al and Paul were flown to New York for the east coast premiere of A.I. I stayed back in Austin. Their attendance at the premiere was necessary for promotional purposes. The two of them had refused to attend the Grammys twice when they were nominated, but the Grammys were competitive, and Al didn't like to lose. The A.I. movie premiere was a singular honor, nothing to share with peers in competition, a time to bask in the limelight. Outside the event at the Ziegfeld Theater, the MTV crew handed Paul and Al microphones to interview their fellow cast members arriving on the red carpet. Al in his newly dyed lime-green hair, wearing black coattails like a circus master of ceremonies, was loving every minute of the attention. Paul, sporting newly sculpted lambchop sideburns and moustache, wore a white tuxedo jacket and black bowtie, looking as oily as Eric Roberts in Star 80. Paul and Al hammed it up, themselves mugging for the paparazzi. I had the distinct impression Hollywood would be calling again in some format or other for these two.

Following the A.I. filming, Michael Brokaw became Ministry's new manager. Paul pestered and convinced him over six months of pleading to work with the band. Michael was someone I felt at home with. He was from the big city, the Bronx to be exact. We both took long walks for exercise. I was astounded he could read the paper while getting in his walk. We both were equally level-headed when it came to dealing with famous people.

At exactly dinnertime nearly every day, our house phone rang. "It's that Michael Brokaw guy, again!" the kids would yell from somewhere in their rooms or the kitchen or already seated at the dining room table.

"G!" I would hear, picking up the phone. Early in our acquaintance, Michael lost patience with reconciling the spelling of my name with the actual pronunciation. "Can I call you 'G'?"

Michael was the first and only one of Ministry's managers with whom I talked about everything relevant in our personal lives—our kids, our marriages. We talked about my on again, off again drinking, Paul's "ostrich syndrome" of looking the other way when Al was clearly out of touch with reality or just not getting work done. We also talked about industry gossip. Michael liked a good gossip. Michael also had a killer sense of humor and an excellent memory for detail. He once sent me his VIP pass to the annual Soul Train Music Awards because he knew I was a big Soul Train fan and I would feel honored to receive it.

Michael negotiated with Sanctuary Records on a deal for a Ministry live record. He was able to work out some lingering debt issues with Warner Bros. and for a while he was satisfied to be making money for Al and Paul and helping them rebuild their brand after several years of stagnation or just plain lack of inspiration. He was doing a spectacular job for Ministry.

Paul was back from his big screen acting debut. We talked about Gordon's upcoming birthday. He was turning seven. Gordon wanted a party at home. We threw some ideas around, and since our son seemed to like computer games with mazes, Paul had the notion to build a life-sized maze with tunnels on the carport using cardboard shipping boxes and tape. We had plenty of supplies lying around, and the Houston boys next door offered to help. It seemed a fitting bridge between the old school idea of giving a kid a simple box to play in and the newer games everyone wanted to play on their computers at home. As a family we preferred not to do things the conventional way as it was. With a seven-year-old and his mainly boy posse to entertain, Paul and I decided it was time for the Barker family to take a break from pizza parties followed by a round of laser tag at the usual indoor arenas. By now, I think all of us knew DIY was sometimes more fun and personal.

To follow the DIY spirit of the outdoor maze being built, we bought an industrial-sized scroll of butcher paper for our in-house artists to decorate. Using colored markers, Paul and the kids went to work composing a marine-themed mural on the endless paper reel. Seeing the three of them so cheerful while intently bent over their individual drawings, it occurred to me that we could tape the rest of the blank butcher paper onto the folding tables set up for guests in the family room. We could lay out markers and supplies for the kids (and adults), and they could make their own pictures.

With their sea creatures elaborately executed on paper, Paul and Gordon rolled up their scroll, carried it across the room, and unspooled the finished mural, wrapping the paper around the walls and wet bar leading out of the kitchen and into the family room and dining room. When guests arrived, they could look up and immerse themselves in the endless "aquarium" floating overhead. In his role as a father, Paul was happiest when he could make art with the kids. He spared as much time and effort as they needed to finish. Making visual art on paper was not my area of expertise.

I put together an hors d'oeuvres menu for the party and needed to order a cake. We knew a baker in town who had worked with my sister and had since opened his own shop up north near the Dell campus. The weather had cooled off a bit now that it was autumn, and I drove my car up to the shop. For whatever reason I always had trouble remembering the man's name, and I referred to our baker friend as "Chef Louie." He had the swarthy looks and demeanor exemplifying his Lebanese heritage, and he reminded me of my very Italian friend Lou D'Angelo from Wax Trax days. I pulled up in front of the bakeshop in my silver 1971 Alfa Romeo GTV sports car, and Chef Louie came out to see what I was driving. The distinct roar of the Italian engine had distracted him.

"I could drive this car," he said, lowering his head to look into the passenger side. This was the ultimate macho compliment and a way to endear him to us for any future favors. I just loved the Alfa's tiny side mirrors and the weight of the door when it slammed shut. And it was silver. Black interior. Molded wood steering wheel.

"I need to order two cakes. One for grownups and one for kids," I told him.

"Doesn't matter. Whatever you need, I do," he said, staring back at the car. Checkered flag for the hostess.

I thought it would be more fun for everyone in our house if we invited kids and their parents to Gordon's party, along with teachers and some of our musician friends who knew our kids. Cesca Judge came with her family. Her youngest daughter was Gordon's classmate. Mike Judge came along, and it was his first time in our house. For all I knew, it was also the first time he and Paul had ever officially met, despite being commercially linked together for ten years via Beavis and Butthead episodes featuring Ministry and other Paul projects, and having kids at the same school in the same classrooms for a few of those years.

I heard more than once from adult guests, "This is my favorite house in West Lake." Those visiting for the first time couldn't believe the direct view of the UT Tower from our front deck and the story behind the house, the tower, and Charles Whitman the shooter in the tower.

I laid out the hors d'oeuvres and "Sammy's Mom" (who was English and a painter) was pleasantly interrupted from her self-absorbed thoughts for a moment to try one of my creations. She was so taken by the endive spears I dotted with teaspoon size dollops of smoked turkey.

"I haven't had 'Ahn-deeve' forever!" she gushed.

You are welcome, I thought. It took trips to three markets to find any of the currently fashionable yet elusive greens for my new favorite recipe. Thank you, Bon Appétit. "Sammy's Mom" resumed staring at Marnie Warren's painting of "Laura" hanging in our dining room.

Ms. Ramsdell, who had been both Gordon and Ursula's first grade teacher, pulled me aside to say how much she loved our family and was happy we lived in the district. She confessed, out of curiosity, she had once asked the birthday boy Gordon if he'd ever been to one of his dad's concerts. His response was immediate.

"Yes. I have seen my Papa rock," he deadpanned.

Ms. Ramsdell would be forever entertained by this tidbit of "pop" history.

Amanda Ferguson sat drawing at a table in the family room with Max Brody and the music crowd in attendance. We had last seen Amanda when she accompanied the Barker clan to LA for the A.I. film shoot.

I looked around the room at Ms. Phillips, Ursula's third-grade teacher who was close friends with her college buddy Terrence Mallick, the Austin filmmaker, and who always told me Paul and I were doing exactly what we needed to be doing, raising two talented, genuinely nice human beings. I thought about how it was a pleasure to be in close proximity to such gifted individuals working in the arts in this small community of Austin film. There was Ursula's friend May's mom, who was the art director for the Spy Kids movies. And there again was Mike Judge pointing out particularly well-designed bits of our overhead homemade scroll to his own seven-year-old daughter.

And finally, I looked at my husband Paul, my supremely talented and funny Paul. I thanked my lucky stars every day for what I had right here, no matter what personal ups and downs came our way.

***

All of the years we lived in Austin, I looked for ways to connect with the kids' school and the community we lived in. Much of that community was committed to their church congregations. We weren't churchgoers; although, Paul and I were both technically Catholic, and our children were baptized in the Catholic church. Community service was still something I felt passionately about, and I became a Democratic Party clerk and then a judge for primary and general elections. I pursued my passion for justice, but it was my passion for the arts that drove me and gave me a sense of relevancy—a way to cope with the idea that we were stuck in Texas for now, until our kids finished school.

In 2002, our son went into the third grade. Some parents in earlier years initiated a "Gallery Greats" course for third graders. The program was put together by Cyndy Phillips, who'd been Ursula's third-grade teacher, who loved art and knew our family history. I volunteered to lead the class for the current year on their monthly exploration of individual American masters. Each monthly session was an hour long and interactive, with the kids sometimes emulating the artist's style on paper. I searched through the artist bios, the posters, and the previous years' programs to come up with my own presentations.

The first month, I showcased the work of Jackson Pollock. I brought in my own posters, paint bottles full of acrylics, and individual sheets for the students to lay on the walkway outside of their classroom. My attire for the day was all Pollock. I wore my old lace-up Knapp work boots, jeans, and a white T-shirt and stood beside a sheet of paper demonstrating how Pollock moved himself around the four corners of a canvas on the floor. The kids went wild, dripping paint, and moving like migrant workers seeding the fields around them.

Emboldened by my progress in teaching kids about art (and much to my surprise) I was shocked to discover there was only one woman artist featured in the existing Gallery Greats material—Mary Cassat. Cassat's work seemed such an easy palatable choice. She was an American master, but Cassat became famous after moving to France and hanging around the Impressionists. It seemed to me another woman artist embodied the American maverick spirit better than Cassat—Grandma Moses. I pieced together my own program on Grandma Moses as a pioneer of American folk art, underscoring her lack of any formal training. My students were far more interested in her life trajectory than the simplicity of her everyday landscapes. That was my goal—to have them develop a sense of history in looking at art.

As I came to the end of my volunteer stint, my final program choice was so obvious, I thought it a stroke of genius on my part. I understood the attention span of third graders was malleable. I also knew that young minds are open to visual learning from the time they're staring at their mothers' faces. Faces. Portraits. Photography. There wasn't a single photographer featured in the Gallery Greats. Having focused upon previous generations of artists for examples of American visual art, it seemed natural to wind up the program with a contemporary master, someone specializing in photography.

We had one personal friend who happened to be a world class photographer. I called Paul Elledge's studio in Chicago. "How do you feel about unleashing Paul's work on a roomful of impressionable eight- and nine-year-olds?" I inquired. Leasha laughed. "That sounds cool. Let me talk to Paul." I had a feeling my pitch would work, and it was a sly way to promote one of our friends. It was also yet another instance where I asked for and got what I wanted because no one told me, "You can't do that."

Within a week, UPS delivered my Paul Elledge props: a carousel of about fifty slides, some prints, and a bio. There was work in color and Paul's usual, gorgeous black-and-white portraits. Famous faces like Oprah Winfrey and Bill Clinton. Rock star images of my Paul and his bandmate Al Jourgensen. The Smashing Pumpkins. Black-and-white scenes of the Italian countryside. There were studio portraits and rock show action shots. For a study in the beauty of mundane everyday life, there were photographs of country folks and Italian artisans shot in Italy on some of Paul and Leasha's annual trips there.

I told the kids Paul Elledge was known around the world, and he worked all the time making his living shooting pictures. And—he was our friend.

"That's your Dad!" One of Gordon's classmates nudged him while I advanced the slides, clicking away, giving brief descriptions of what was going on within each frame. "That's Willie Nelson! These are COOL!" Hands went up with questions. I felt a thrill in being able to show these kids something dynamic and maybe more immediate to their senses than painted canvases. "Look at their eyes," I said. "How do you feel about the picture being black and white?"

As I packed up my supplies, I felt consumed by the constant need to feel relevant in not only my own kids' lives, but in a bigger world sense. I was tired of being at home, without a purpose other than coming up with a new recipe to try. I was not writing at all. I told Paul, "I need to write a book about our lives." "Great. Now you can support ME." Always good-natured, my Paul. Always forgetting that I had been supporting him on every level since the early days of our relationship.

I went back to the basics I had learned. Write about anything. I called our old acquaintance Jason Pettigrew at Alternative Press to see what was currently popular at AP, and we wrote emails back and forth. There never seemed to be a good time to write. A paragraph here. A sentence fragment over there. I busied myself with schedules, everyone else's. Paul on tour schedule. Paul in the studio schedule. Piano recitals, swim lessons, ballet, soccer, a birthday party at Mr. Gatti's Pizza, for the second time in a month. Another party at the "disco" bowling alley on the campus at UT. I was exhausted with the banality of being at home taking care of everything to keep us afloat. I would call my friend Ellen and ask, "What did you see?" on her new rounds as a docent at the Blanton Art museum on the UT campus.

I struggled to write. I struggled to make use of my time as an engaged parent, and I continuously ran out of options. I toyed with the idea of freelance writing my own restaurant reviews because I believed whoever was doing that job currently always got it wrong. But parenting duties were still squarely on me. Barring some emergency, Paul wasn't in any position to take over many parental obligations. He was too busy corralling Al and his own cast of players. It was getting monotonous. "Al doesn't want to do anything. He sits and watches videos. I have to keep trying to make shit happen."

***

2002 was shaping up to be a quiet year in the Barker household, another lull in between Ministry records. Paul as usual was trying to "make shit happen," and I was trying to keep our kids occupied with summer approaching and no travel plans while "Pops" worked.

The band were finishing their latest album, Animositisomina. I fondly recalled visiting the Sonic Ranch studio near El Paso where some of the album was recorded. I flew to El Paso with the kids on a school break to visit Paul. We were greeted at the airport by Paul and Tony Rancich, the studio's owner. Tony was a tall, charming, fair-haired soul who offered to take us into Juarez during my stay with the kids.

Tony's family had once lived on the 1,700 acre pecan plantation in Tornillo where his studio was based, a property bordering the Rio Grande River across from Mexico. We drove into Mexico through a small lesser known border checkpoint near his property. Tony took us to the open-air markets where I looked for Mexican blankets for the house. He spoke flawless Spanish and insisted upon haggling with the vendors on my behalf because he knew them all and that's how business was done. Tony had been sparring with merchants in Juarez his whole life. When we returned to his place in Tornillo, he offered to let the kids sit on the hood of his truck and drive through the plantation to look for muskrats. He told us about the real history of his family property, the constant back and forth with INS patrols driving through looking for illegal river crossers. Tony also told the kids a charming tale of how gangs of wild chihuahuas (sporting red bandanas) roamed the Chihuahuan desert nearby and to be on the lookout. I appreciated his humanity.

Ministry was in the mixing phase of what would be Paul's last record with Al. Al was now being stewarded in private by his new wife, who appeared to be pushing him in a positive direction for the first time in a long time. "She helped him get sober," Paul said. He seemed upbeat about Ministry's future.

The first time I met the Mrs. Jourgensen (or Number Two, as I liked to call her), she and Al drove across the country from New York with her and his belongings to settle into a new place in Texas. They pulled their good-sized moving truck all the way up our side driveway and hopped out to look around the outside of the house. They arrived with two other people who I also didn't know. I offered to let everyone stay at our place, but Number Two simply said they already had accommodations. We exchanged some small talk about good thrift stores in Austin, and I brought out my vintage Pucci train case as an example of what wonderful finds could be had. I adored the sound the metal latches on the case made when they clicked open like two switchblades. Wife number two ignored the fine craftsmanship of my favorite travel bag as she stood there surveying the family room and the open floor plan between the dining and living rooms. "You have such a nice, big place," she said with a distracted look coming over her face. Something in her tone of voice gave me a chill, and I flashed back to a time in my very first apartment—the moment before I was nearly strangled to death. I had the impression Number Two wasn't trying to be polite, nor was she happy for us.

"Yes, thanks. Paul and I worked hard for what we have," I told her. I was generally bored with meeting Al's girlfriends and groupies over the years. I didn't really care to delve deeper into getting to know yet another woman who would be taking care of his stuff, even if she helped him get sober. I wanted Paul and Al to finish their record, do a tour, and move on with it. Paul Elledge agreed to do the art and photography design again for the new record. It had been the longest hiatus between Ministry tours, and with Al getting back into shape, everyone was hopeful.

It was July, and as I had done in the past, I habitually ran errands and did grocery shopping before 10:00 a.m., before the punishing, pulsing one hundred degree heat began to settle in. No wonder everyone leaves town for the summer, I thought, as I wandered around the aisles at the Safeway. The grocery store was fairly deserted, no usual sports jerseys emblazoned with the middle school "Cougars" or "Westlake Chaps" or moms chatting about church choirs and the price of gas to fill up their Toyota SUVs. I was startled to hear someone calling out my name. I turned around and recognized one of the parents I saw regularly at soccer games and at the pool. I knew she was someone's mom but was at a loss to connect her face with a child I knew.

"Mrs. Barker, I'm so glad to run into you!" Oh no. Really. What did I do now—wear a sundress exposing my knees or something equally deplorable and unbecoming of a "Westlake mom?"

"Well, I know y'all's family are involved with the arts, with your husband being in a band and all. Did you know the school board wants to cut art and music for the elementary kids? They want to give them more gym classes. The board has it in their minds that the budget needs trimming and the kids need more exercise or something like that. Art teachers are expensive, I guess."

"How thoughtful of them!" I said. "So, what does that mean? And this is conveniently happening in the summer when a lot of families are out of town." Wow.

I pulled into the carport at home and left the groceries sitting in the car. I walked across the Houstons' yard next door to see my good friend Katherine. She was on break from teaching for the summer but tutoring students who needed to catch up.

"Yeeees. The school board is tryin' to shove this plan through before all the parents are back from vacation," she said in her Alabama drawl. "They want the kids to have art and music every other week. Kids don't learn skills on that kind of schedule. They need practice, Gerda, you know that. You oughta do somethin' about it. Go to the next school board meeting. Bring Ursula and Gordon."

I thought about it for a moment. Me, alone raising opposition to a group of stuffed shirts at a school board meeting. In the all-consuming world of Texas high school football mania the arts were a nice distraction not a necessity. But as a parent, I didn't trust what other people thought was good for my kids. I sensed the familiar nudge of activism in my brain saying, "Go ahead. Make their day."

"I could do a petition to get their attention. That might be fun—use my advocacy skills from a former life." Once again, I wasn't waiting for someone to tell me "no."

The pernicious cutting away of arts programs was all too familiar. It had been going on for decades around the country. As a high school sophomore in Chicago, I joined a campus-wide protest and walkout from Lane Tech to Chicago's City Hall downtown when major cuts to art and music were debated. As a technical school, two of the five disciplines taught at Lane were specifically geared to train future artists and professional musicians. A Lane walkout meant thousands of students leaving class for the day. Some walked the ten miles past Wrigley Field and south to the Loop. Some took their bikes or the el. We made the news.

In my mind, I could frame a petition on behalf of myself and other parents in our district with two simple arguments: First, many parents in the community made their living in the arts, in music, and films in Austin. Secondly, broad exposure to art and music benefitted students' critical thinking skills. I opened our home copy of the district-wide school directory with students and parents' addresses and phone numbers. There wasn't yet a comprehensive way to bomb email boxes, so I worked with what I had. I began calling people I already knew or was at least familiar with. Whether it was the summer heat or just general lethargy, apathy, I heard some surprising responses.

"What can we do? They already have their minds made up. This is a formality." One parent whose son played soccer with Gordon, told me, "My kids don't need all that art and music—they have their sports. Sorry, I just don't see your point." Most people I reached were receptive.

I called some well-known names in the directory. My friend Mary, whose husband Gary was co-founder of Keller Williams Realty. "This is so stupid! But look at the dinosaurs on the board," she said. I called Cesca Judge, Mike Judge's wife, who also did see my point. I spoke to Beth Black, a popular local singer whose daughter was one of Ursula's dance friends. I knew several photographers. My friend Corliss had been the staff photographer for the San Antonio newspaper. I walked with Corliss occasionally around Town Lake and was always impressed by her cop-like maneuvers getting her car into a parking spot facing head out, an old news photographer's trick for the quick getaway when covering the city beat.

Delving deeper into the community around the school, I went to see the head of the dance studio where Ursula had taken ballet, tap, and jazz classes for seven years, and where so many local parents dropped off their school-age girls. "Alisa" recognized a chance for good PR. "Hell, I'll ask my instructors to make a personal appearance as a troupe for that board." Alisa enjoyed an excellent reputation in the community. At one of Ursula's early-summer dance recitals, a small group of adults, including Michael Dell and his wife, were escorted into the studio flanked by bodyguards in suits who moved as coolly as members of the Mossad. It was just another sweltering day in Austin. I sat with my friend Ellen, studying the rich and famous across the room sitting on folding chairs just like everyone else and watching politely while little girls danced their numbers.

Katherine Houston warned me school board meetings sometimes dragged on for hours if enough people showed up to comment on agenda items and the board felt like listening, a tactic perhaps to discourage parents from attending at all. I informed my kids they would be escorting me to the board meeting with their sleeping bags in tow.

Over a hundred parents signed my petition to keep the arts program intact and find other more "creative" ways to trim the school district's budget. I was thrilled to see the healthy turnout of parents and neighbors who came to voice their concern over how their tax dollars and constant fundraising dollars were being spent. Other parents took the podium after I gave my speech. Alisa's dancers were there and would have pirouetted around the room, had there been any room to do it. Too many people. The regional paper, the Westlake Picayune, had a reporter and photographer routinely covering school board meetings. My kids and I appeared on the front page of the Picayune for the following issue. A local news crew was there filming the meeting. I drove home afterwards with the kids and thanked them for being so patient while their mom tried to make their world a better place.

Stepping in line at the grocery store the next day I saw my favorite checkout clerk, Marva. Marva was a few years older than the others. She was the only black checker at the Safeway, and she was a longtime Austin resident. She had worked at our neighborhood store for over a decade. Marva knew everyone in the neighborhood who shopped there. I always enjoyed talking to her and hearing what weekend plans she had with her husband. Often those plans were church-related, but she and I talked politics now and then.

When the person before me was finished checking out, Marva looked at me with a big smile. She was anxious to tell me she had seen me on the local news the night before.

"I was at my friend's, and I seen you on the TV. I said, 'Hold on . . . I know her. She's lookin' good!'" Marva thought my little speech was inspiring.

In the end, none of it mattered. The Eanes school board went ahead with their cuts. I let it go. I did my part. Their consolation of more PE classes was like the proverbial spitting in the eye and telling someone it's raining. The elementary school kids in our district collectively attended more after school soccer, football, baseball, basketball, lacrosse, cheerleading, swim team and yes, dance classes, than arguably any other school age kids in the state of Texas. What they didn't need was more physical education.

About a year later, following a steady barrage of surprised parents' complaints after returning from vacation and having their ears chewed off by their kids, who were missing art and music classes, the school board reversed its decision. By then, I was so over living in Texas. Paul and I again lamented how we loved our beautiful, modern, soulful house, with its view and its 1960s interior. If only it had been built *somewhere else*.

OUTRO

We complicate our own lives. "Keep it simple and keep moving" was a mantra I would go back to again and again. It didn't matter that my petition to save the arts program wasn't "successful" until later. I liked to recall the sense of satisfaction I felt after all the movie hoopla when A.I. was released in 2001, and I had no idea where we'd all be going next. It wasn't important, because I was happy to be alive, happy to be sober, and had faith I was exactly where I needed to be in my life. I was a fighter, a survivor, and always an optimist.

Toward the end of that year, Paul and Max Brody were booked to perform as Pink Anvil, a side project the two of them had been playing around with for a while. Two shows were planned: a Halloween show in Austin and a New Year's Eve show at the American Music Hall in San Francisco. Performing on the same bill in San Francisco were the Melvins, Mike Patton, and Jello Biafra doing his own unscripted floating between acts. I desperately wanted to spend New Year's with Paul but couldn't square how we'd pay for my travel with current Al and Ministry related finances perpetually up in the air. I happened to be on the phone with Paul Elledge and his wife Leasha and shared my New Year's Eve travel dilemma with the two of them.

"Oh, you can use our miles. We have tons of 'em," Paul E. told me. Their frequent flier accounts were phenomenally stacked with free flights, the happy result of constant domestic and international travels. I had forgotten what gracious and generous friends we had. It seemed such an impossibility to get out of Austin for New Year's, then suddenly I was booked and ready to go. The Elledges were also working the San Francisco show for their own pleasure, for fun.

Paul and Max flew to the west coast a couple of days ahead of time. When I arrived at the airport for my flight, I was floored to find out I was booked into first class. It seems our friends from Chicago decided I should be treated like a rock star myself. I boarded the plane, relinquished my coat to the flight attendant, and stepped into what I could only describe later as my own personal pod. There was no one else flying first class. The plane was a larger jet for international travel, and first class was its own island distinctly segregated from the rest of the passengers. It was as dimly lit as a cocktail lounge. I felt pampered by the reclining bed of a seat, the warm service, and a soft sleep mask. I could relax and linger over real china and endless attention to my individual "needs." "Everything alright, Mrs. Barker?" Yes. Everything was just swell.

Our hotel in San Francisco was the Commodore, an unassuming, brick structure, which might have been a rooming house in an earlier era in the city. It was fabulously fitting for our collective bohemian lives. Leasha and I ventured out to Saks in the afternoon to window shop and waltzed into an enormous winter coat sale. To think I hadn't bought a new winter coat in nine years since moving to Austin. A good coat was necessary for traveling, especially traveling back to Chicago. Leasha nabbed a car coat in a large houndstooth black-and-white check that looked fantastic with her near-white pixie hair. I was unconsciously pulled in the direction of a maroon Italian "baby llama" swing coat allowing me to channel my inner Audrey Hepburn. Life felt really good, for the moment.

We walked back to the hotel with our new coats and to reconnect with our spouses. When we arrived, as if in a relay, I grabbed Paul's arm and the two of us kept walking, and I sensed we were moving at a quicker pace. It always happened when we arrived in a big city. The walk was faster, an urgent calling to absorb as much detail as possible from our surroundings. We all had dinner in Chinatown in the evening with our old friend Greg Werckman whose Ipecac label was supporting Paul's Pink Anvil project and the New Year's show. Yes, life felt good again.

Ministry had one more tour to go before Paul finally said no more to Al and no more to Ministry life. Paul Elledge would art direct and execute the images for the record. In the meantime, Al had a new wife who everyone—management, touring band members, me, Paul—hoped would set Al straight and focusing on the music. I trusted this tour would change things for Paul. He would be unburdened from keeping an eye on Al and finally get back to work on his own solo projects. And me, I was still looking for what I wanted next.

We all want something.

ABOUT THE AUTHOR

Gerda Barker is an American writer, editor, former criminal defense lawyer and wife of an industrial rock music icon. A devout Chicagoan and follower of noone, she currently resides in Portland, Oregon where she walks for miles and miles every day. Her philosophy of life: "Mmm, I've done better."

www.ingramcontent.com/pod-product-compliance
Lightning Source LLC
Chambersburg PA
CBHW062320120626
46553CB00015B/12

9 798985 196405